The Chronological Guide TO THE BIBLE

100
200
300
400
500
600
700
800
900

The Chronological Guide
TO THE BIBLE

THOMAS NELSON
Since 1798

NASHVILLE DALLAS MEXICO CITY RIO DE JANEIRO
www.ThomasNelson.com

Adapted from *The Chronological Study Bible*, copyright © 2008 by Thomas Nelson, Inc.

Portions formerly published as *The Life and Times Historical Reference Bible,* copyright © 1997 by Thomas Nelson, Inc.

Contributing scholars: Timothy B. Cargal, Mark W. Chavalas, James R. Edwards, John O. Gooch, Lowell K. Handy, Craig S. Keener, David T. Landry, Robert Lintz, George Lyons, John S. Mason, David Merling, Gerald P. Morris, and John W. Wright.

Thomas Nelson, Inc. titles may be purchased in bulk for educational, business, fund-raising, or sales promotional use. For information, please e-mail SpecialMarkets@ThomasNelson.com.

Editorial Services, Design, and Typesetting
Koechel Peterson & Associates, Inc.,
Minneapolis, Minnesota 55406
www.koechelpeterson.com

ISBN: 978-1-418-54175-0

www.thomasnelson.com

Printed in the United States of America

24 25 26 /TRM/ 15 14 13

TABLE OF CONTENTS

Contributors . . . vi
Introduction . . . vii
Reading Theological History . . . vii
Rearranging the Bible's Canonical Order . . . viii

EPOCH 1 Before the Patriarchs (Creation–2000 B.C.) . . . 1
The Beginnings of Human Civilization . . . 2

EPOCH 2 The Patriarchs, Israel's Ancestors (2000–1500 B.C.) . . . 7
The Changing of the Empires . . . 8
Egypt in the Middle Bronze Age . . . 13

EPOCH 3 The Rise of a Unified People (1500–1200 B.C.) . . . 16
Egypt and the Exodus . . . 17
The Conquest of Canaan . . . 34

EPOCH 4 From Tribes to a Nation (1200–930 B.C.) . . . 39
A Tribal Confederation in Israel . . . 41
The United Monarchy in Israel . . . 47

EPOCH 5 The Fall of Two Nations (930–586 B.C.) . . . 66
The Divided Monarchy in Israel . . . 68
The Neo-Assyrian Empire . . . 76
The Neo-Babylonian Empire . . . 87

EPOCH 6 Exile and Return (586–332 B.C.) . . . 102
Exile in Babylon . . . 104
Wisdom in the Ancient Near East . . . 110
The Persian Empire . . . 115

EPOCH 7 Between the Two Testaments (332–37 B.C.) . . . 135
The Greek Empire . . . 137
The Roman Empire . . . 142

EPOCH 8 The Coming of the Messiah (37 B.C.–A.D. 30) . . . 143
Introductions to Jesus Christ . . . 145
Early Lives of John the Baptist and Jesus . . . 147
Beginning of Jesus' Ministry . . . 151
The Galilean Ministry . . . 154
From Galilee to Jerusalem . . . 163
Jesus' Final Journey . . . 164
Final Ministry in Judea . . . 166
Jesus' Final Week in Jerusalem . . . 168

EPOCH 9 The Church Age (A.D. 30–100) . . . 178
The Gospel to the Jews . . . 180
The Gospel to the Gentiles . . . 183
The Gospel to the Gentile World . . . 184
The Gospel from Jerusalem to Rome . . . 198
Apocalyptic Writings and the End Time . . . 213

Index . . . 218
Photo Credits . . . 225

CONTRIBUTORS

Timothy B. Cargal, Ph.D., served as University Lecturer in Philosophy and Religion at Western Kentucky University (Bowling Green, KY), and is pastor of Northwood Presbyterian Church (Silver Spring, MD). Dr. Cargal is author of *Restoring the Diaspora: Discursive Structure and Purpose in the Epistle of James.*

Mark W. Chavalas, Ph.D., is Associate Professor of History at the University of Wisconsin—LaCrosse (La Crosse, WI). Dr. Chavalas is editor of *New Horizons in the Study of Ancient Syria* and *Emar: The History, Religion, and Culture of a Bronze Age Town in Syria.* He has had nine seasons of archaeological field work in Syria.

James R. Edwards, Ph.D., served as chair of the Department of Religion at Jamestown College (Jamestown, ND) and is Professor of Religion at Whitworth College (Spokane, WA). A specialist in New Testament studies, Dr. Edwards contributed to *Nelson's New Illustrated Bible Dictionary* and is author of *Romans* in *The New International Biblical Commentary.*

John O. Gooch, Ph.D., served as curriculum editor for the United Methodist Church (Nashville, TN) and as Assistant Professor of Religion, Metropolitan College, St. Louis University. He is the only known youth minister with a doctorate in Patristics. Dr. Gooch is coauthor of *A Pocket Guide to the Bible.*

Lowell K. Handy, Ph.D., serves as Senior Lecturer in Scripture at Loyola University Chicago (Chicago, IL), and is Indexer/Analyst for the American Theological Library Association (Evanston, IL). Dr. Handy is author of *Among the Host of Heaven: The Syro-Palestinian Pantheon as Bureaucracy* and *The Educated Person's Thumbnail Introduction to the Bible.*

Craig S. Keener, Ph.D., is Visiting Professor of Biblical Studies at Eastern Baptist Theological Seminary (Wynnewood, PA). Dr. Keener focuses on New Testament background and is author of *The IVP Bible Background Commentary: New Testament,* as well as seven other books. He remains active in campus ministry.

David T. Landry, Ph.D., is Assistant Professor of Theology at the University of St. Thomas (St. Paul, MN). Dr. Landry is coauthor and coeditor of *The Christian Theological Tradition.*

Robert Lintz, Th.D., served as Bible editor for Thomas Nelson Publishers (Nashville, TN). Dr. Lintz is associate editor of *The Wesley Bible,* editor of *The Life and Times Historical Reference Bible,* and author of *Shepherd's Notes—Exodus, Ruth, Esther.*

George Lyons, Ph.D., served as Professor of Biblical Literature at Olivet Nazarene University (Kankakee, IL) and is Professor of Biblical Literature at Northwest Nazarene College (Nampa, ID). Dr. Lyons is author of *Pauline Autobiography* and *More Holiness in Everyday Life,* and is a specialist in the Gospels and Paul's letters.

John S. Mason, Th.M., served as Professor of Biblical Studies at Daystar University College, Nairobi, Kenya, and as a missionary in Eritrea. He is editor of the *Tigrinya Grammar,* and assistant editor of the *New Geneva Study Bible.*

David Merling, Ph.D., is Associate Professor of Archaeology and History of Antiquity and Associate Director of the Institute of Archaeology at Andrews University (Berrien Springs, MI). Dr. Merling has directed archaeological digs in Jordan, and is coeditor of *Hesban After 25 Years* and author of *The Book of Joshua: Its Theme and Role in Archaeological Discussions.*

Gerald P. Morris, Ph.D., served as adjunct Professor of Old Testament Interpretation at The Southern Baptist Theological Seminary (Louisville, KY) and as Assistant Professor of Biblical Studies at Ouachita Baptist University (Arkadelphia, AR). Dr. Morris is author of *Prophecy, Poetry and Hosea.*

John W. Wright, Ph.D., served as Visiting Assistant Professor at St. Mary's College (Notre Dame, IN) and the University of Notre Dame and as pastor of the Winamac (IN) Church of the Nazarene. Dr. Wright contributed to *The Anchor Bible Dictionary* as a specialist in Second Temple Judaism, and is Associate Professor of Religion at Point Loma Nazarene College (San Diego, CA).

Information current at time of writing

INTRODUCTION

The Bible is really a library of books in one. In fact, the 66 books of the Old and New Testaments were written by more than 40 people from all walks of life over a period of more than 1,000 years in three different languages; and their contents cover a variety of ancient peoples and cultures. Most of the books of the Old Testament were written for the Jewish people, the nation God chose to help Him bring His Son Jesus into the world. The books of the New Testament were written initially to the first-century followers of Jesus who were scattered in a variety of cultures throughout the Roman Empire.

If we are to understand and appropriate the Bible's life-giving message today, we need some sense of the historical and cultural context in which its diverse parts appeared. Unfortunately, the individual books of the Bible do not always provide that information. At the time that these books were written, readers would have been familiar immediately with the events and customs the writings describe. But thousands of years later, we read the same words under entirely different circumstances and risk misunderstanding or only dimly understanding them if we neglect their historical and cultural background.

The Chronological Guide to the Bible will provide you with a guide through the history and culture of the Bible. It will help you follow the flow of events in the Scriptures and see where sacred history and secular history converge into one story of salvation. You will learn how sacred history fits into the context of secular history—why an event happened, how events relate to each other—as well as the cultural, religious, political, and geographical background that influenced the events.

Reading a Chronological Text

This chronological guide's attempt to *rearrange the Bible text in the order of the events it narrates* may be a bit unsettling at first for some Bible readers, as though it is a violation of the integrity of the Bible. The goal of this chronological guide is not to replace the time-honored canonical arrangement, but instead *to honor time as the setting in which the biblical record appeared.* Readers who study the Bible via this guide will return to their traditional Bibles better equipped to read them. Acquiring a sense of the flow of the Bible's story will put flesh and blood on its message.

Rearranging the Bible is a fallible human effort. Even those who have earned advanced degrees in the various fields of biblical studies would disagree on any particular rearrangement. The editors of *The Chronological Study Bible* (upon which this guide is based) were forced at times to make hard decisions, to choose one location at the neglect of another that is equally plausible. In such instances, an honest effort has been made to acknowledge another possible arrangement and to present its case fairly.

In the case of debated issues this biblical guide avoids presenting a single, biased perspective. Rather, it treats evenhandedly the entire spectrum of credible opinion on disputed matters—both the views of traditional, conservative Bible students and those of modern, critical scholarship. No attempt is made to persuade readers that one particular view is correct; that determination is ultimately their prayerful and thoughtful responsibility.

READING THEOLOGICAL HISTORY

One goal of *The Chronological Guide to the Bible* is to help readers acquire a greater appreciation for the historical dimensions of the biblical message. The Bible is not a theology book arranged according to topics: God, man, sin, salvation, etc. Nor is it simply a chronicle of events from creation to the final consummation. Historical events are often the Bible's subject matter, but these events are always reported from the perspective of theological history. It is in the arena of history that God has chosen to make Himself known.

History and the Old Testament

The Old Testament is centered in history. It describes historical events and is addressed, at one level at least, to a specific historical audience: the Hebrew people. This makes the faith taught in the Bible very different from the beliefs of other ancient Near Eastern peoples.

The peoples surrounding the Hebrews built their religious beliefs on the rhythms of nature. The world had visible patterns, but to its inhabitants these rhythms were unexplainable, uncontrollable, and therefore attributed to the gods. There were gods to represent all the phenomena of nature: gods of the sun, moon, rain, storms, rivers, seas, and the earth itself. The typical religious expression of such religion was the myth, a story that explained these unexplainable features of nature. For instance, almost every people had a myth of a deity who was dead for part of the year and alive for the rest of the year—a story that explained the recurring cycle of the seasons.

The God of the Old Testament is very different. Most importantly, He is one God. All the phenomena that other peoples regarded as gods are simply the creations of the one God. In the other religions of the ancient Near East, nature was divine; in the Bible, God both created nature and was more than nature. The God of the Bible deals with His creation not in recurring, regular patterns, but in one-time, extraordinary moments of self-revelation, in recognizable locations on earth.

For this reason, the Old Testament's primary

mode of communication is not myth, but history. The writers wanted to tell how, at specific moments in history, God chose Abraham, blessed Jacob, and saved Abraham's and Jacob's descendants from slavery in Egypt. They wanted to tell how God established His chosen king over Israel, how God allowed that kingdom to be destroyed, and how once again God rescued His people from captivity. To tell their very different sort of faith, the Israelites used the art of history writing, and the Old Testament itself contains some of the very earliest examples of this art.

Of course, not all of the Old Testament consists of history writing. But even the parts of the Old Testament that are not history writing usually appear in some historical context. The oracles, speeches, and poetry of the prophets are not history, but they are addressed to real people in real historical situations. They recall God's mighty acts of the historical past; they promise that God can and will act in history again. The books of wisdom and philosophy, which do not speak of history at all, such as Proverbs and Ecclesiastes, are nevertheless identified with the historical context of King Solomon's court. Even the psalms, intended for regular repetition in public worship, often provide a historical background, such as Psalm 3, superscribed as "A Psalm of David when he fled from Absalom his son."

Israel understood God as a God who acts in history, and for this reason almost every religious utterance was read in light of the history of God's mighty acts. Therefore, unless the reader knows the history of Israel and the ancient Near East, the Bible will always be, to some extent, a closed book.

The New Testament and the Old

The Old Testament was the Bible of the New Testament writers. Old Testament images and concepts filled their minds. Allusions to the Old Testament appear on nearly every page of their writings. The teaching of the Old Testament was basic to their thought.

These New Testament writers also believed that Christ was God's final revelation, the One who brought the earlier revelation into proper focus (Heb. 1:1, 2). Indeed, the risen Christ Himself had explained to His disciples how He fulfilled the Scriptures (Luke 24:27). Thus New Testament writers understood Him to be the One who brought to completion God's plan of salvation recorded in the early chapters of Genesis.

History writing in the New Testament is a theological history. The authors believed that the purpose and meaning of history could be found in Christ. Therefore, the history of which they wrote was salvation history. God's earlier saving works looked forward to the Cross. God's bringing His people out of Egypt became a pattern for Christ's atoning work. At the Passover meal commemorating this deliverance from bondage, Christ made the bread and wine symbols of His death and of the new covenant (Luke 22:19, 20). History had reached its highest point in Him. So Paul, the most influential teacher of Christianity, described the risen Christ as the one "through whom are all things, and through whom we live" (1 Cor. 8:6).

The Message and the Historical Setting

While both the Old and New Testaments present their message on a historical frame, the message takes precedence to the historical setting. The writers of biblical history did not write in the same manner as a modern historian. Ancient history writers were not as interested in "when something happened" as they were in the meaning of the events they were recounting. Therefore the reader of biblical history must be aware that many of the concerns that dominate modern history writing (specific dates, discussions of natural causes) simply were not very important to most of the biblical writers.

REARRANGING THE BIBLE'S CANONICAL ORDER

The individual books included in the Old and New Testaments as authoritative are called "the canon." For some readers, the placement of these books in our English Bibles (called "canonical order") is slightly confusing, since it does not always follow chronological order. Rather, it follows the order of the Latin Vulgate translated by Jerome in the 4th century A.D.

A reader can follow the Old Testament chronology easily for the first dozen books (Genesis through 2 Kings), but after that the chronological order often disappears. The books of Chronicles through Esther backtrack and retell many of the events already described. Portions of the books of Psalms and Proverbs refer to times that are centuries apart, and the prophetic writings, speaking of widely different times, are not presented in straight chronological order.

The New Testament reader also faces some chronological uncertainty. The life of Jesus appears in four Gospels, and while all four Gospels report information about Jesus in general chronological order, none do so strictly. Certain sayings or events appear in differing sequences in the various Gospels. Each of the authors had a slightly different purpose and audience in mind and structured his materials in order to achieve the greatest effectiveness. Determining the events of Paul's life is not simple since the information from his letters does not always connect directly with the narrative of the Book of Acts.

Thus the canonical order presents a dilemma. To understand the Bible the reader must understand something of the history to which the Bible refers. At the same time, though, that historical background is not readily apparent from the order of the books in the Bible itself. *The Chronological Guide to the Bible* makes the Bible's historical background more accessible by *rearranging the Bible text according to nine epochs of time and providing a chronological Bible reading list within each of those epochs.*

Moving Whole Books: To begin with, whole books of the Bible are relocated according to the historical time period narrated in the books. This reordering disrupts the canonical order of the books, and though this might seem irreverent to some people, it actually continues an ancient practice. The order of books in the Septuagint (the Greek Old Testament) differs from that of the older Hebrew Bible, and some of the Septuagint reordering is reflected in our English Old Testaments.

The early Greek translators, thinking a chronological order would make more sense, moved such books as Ruth, Ezra, and Nehemiah from their positions in the Hebrew manuscripts. The Book of Ruth does not appear after the Book of Judges in the Hebrew Bible, but near the end of the Bible. The books of Ezra and Nehemiah come before the books of Chronicles, even though they narrate events occurring later in time than those narrated by Chronicles. When the Old Testament was translated into Greek during the Hellenistic era (336–37 B.C.), the confusing chronology of the Hebrew Bible was changed by relocating several of these books. The Book of Ruth, for instance, was inserted between the books of Judges and 1 Samuel, while Ezra and Nehemiah were placed after 2 Chronicles.

Moving Portions of Books: Chronological confusion is not restricted to the order of whole books, however. The contents of certain individual books are not in chronological order, making it difficult for a modern reader to comprehend the historical context. So in addition to reordering whole books, even the contents of individual books have been rearranged—quite extensively in books such as Isaiah and Jeremiah—to follow a chronological outline.

Combining Portions of Books: Moreover, various books have been woven together. For instance, the historical books of Kings and Chronicles are often interrupted by prophetic books or passages that pertain to the time described in the history. The four Gospels are combined into one presentation following the sequence of the Gospel of Mark. Certain of Paul's letters are inserted into the Book of Acts.

Principles of Rearrangement

Rearranging the biblical books chronologically is by no means easily accomplished, since Bible scholars differ on almost every important point of chronology. The rearrangement in *The Chronological Guide to the Bible* is based on two distinct chronological goals. First, it provides a *relative chronology*, placing related events together without fixed dates. For instance, the prophet Amos spoke in the northern kingdom of Israel during the reign of Jeroboam II, and so the history of Jeroboam II is read alongside the words of Amos that refer to Jeroboam's time. Second, this guide provides an *absolute chronology* tied to historical information and fixed dates (or at least tentative dates). An absolute chronology enables readers to place the biblical history in the larger context of world history.

There are imposing difficulties with any attempt to construct either relative or absolute chronologies. Many biblical passages offer no chronological specificity. Even among books and passages that provide some indication of a specific historical context, the intended context is not always clear. For instance, the oracle of Jeremiah 14 is dated to the time of "the droughts," and Jeremiah's original audience supposedly had no trouble identifying this time. Modern readers, however, are not so fortunate: Were these droughts during the reign of King Josiah or King Jehoiakim or King Zedekiah? Jeremiah's prophetic career spans the reigns of all three kings. In the Book of Joel another prophet responds to a locust plague that ravaged the land of Judah. But when was that plague? Different scholars place Joel in at least three different centuries. All one can do in selecting a time period for the Book of Joel is to look at clues within the prophecy itself and then, in all humility, guess.

Genesis Through Joshua

The books of the Bible that narrate the earliest events do not provide specific years or refer to specific events or names that can be dated by other means. Even such a central figure as Egypt's pharaoh during the Exodus is never referred to by name. Moreover, the years that are given are often suspiciously round numbers—such as 40 years, which may be simply a symbolic number representing one generation.

Due to this lack of specific chronological information, scholars disagree widely on exactly when to date many events of early Israelite history. The Hebrews' exodus from Egypt, for example, is dated by many scholars in the 15th century B.C., whereas other scholars place it 200 years later, during the 13th century. The choice of either of

Cyrus Cylinder. Terracotta, Babylonian, ca. 539-530 B.C.
From Babylon, southern Iraq
photo by Marco Prins and Jona Lendering

these dates does not affect the chronological sequence of the narrative. Thus both dates are given without stating any preference. The dates of the Exodus, wilderness wandering, and the conquest under Joshua are interrelated; consequently, the date a person favors for the Exodus determines the dating of the other two events.

The Exodus and Wilderness Wandering

When presenting relative chronology, the passages of the Bible are ordered according to the history that is narrated in the passage, not according to the time of the book's writing. For instance, the books of Exodus through Deuteronomy narrate the events of Israel's departure from Egypt and the subsequent wilderness wanderings. In *The Chronological Guide to the Bible*, these books appear in the historical context of the Exodus, although many scholars argue that parts of these books were written much later. Regardless of when these books were written, their narrative can be appreciated as marvelous literature telling a story set in the time of the Hebrew exodus from Egypt.

Samuel, Kings, and Chronicles

The books of 1 and 2 Kings represent historical accounts that were evidently put together in their current form during the Babylonian exile (597–539 B.C.). Yet, because they narrate events as far back in time as the death of King David (about 970 B.C.), the books of Kings are not located in *The Chronological Guide to the Bible* during their time of writing (the Exile), but rather are divided up and associated with the various historical eras which they narrate.

The history of the Israelite kingdoms is recounted in two full-length histories. The first is recorded in the books of Samuel and Kings, and the second appears in the books of Chronicles. The two histories are very similar; indeed, 1 and 2 Chronicles often quote directly from the earlier history of Samuel/Kings. Yet there are some marked differences in perspective. Whereas Samuel and Kings emphasize the religious leadership of prophets, Chronicles emphasizes the role of the priests. In order to present both historical accounts in their entirety, while staying as close as possible to chronological order, the two histories alternate. The account of a particular historical time appears first as told in Samuel or Kings, then the same history as told in Chronicles follows. This dual history begins at the reign of King Saul and continues until the destruction of Jerusalem, at which time a single chronological account resumes.

The Kings of the Divided Monarchy

Israel and Judah kept careful records of the lengths of reign of their rulers. The Bible's dates for the kings are relative dates, cross-referencing them to one another: for instance, Ahab became king of Israel in the 38th year of Asa king of Judah (1 Kin. 16:29). Since no definite year is given for the beginning of Asa's reign, however, this information alone is not enough to establish Ahab's dates.

An additional problem occurs when the years of reign are totaled. When the years given for the kings of Israel and Judah are added up, Israel's totals do not always correspond to Judah's. These apparent inconsistencies may appear for various reasons. When one king dies and another is crowned, is that year counted twice—as the last year of the deceased king and also as the first year of the new king? When a crown prince rules as regent while his royal father is still alive, as happens more than once, are the years of the coregency counted in the reigns of both kings? These questions make it difficult to utilize the years of reign in calculating an overall chronology. To provide a consistent presentation, *The Chronological Guide to the Bible* adapts the system of dates for the kings found in *The Mysterious Numbers of the Hebrew Kings* by Edwin R. Thiele.

In the later history of Israel, the dates are much more certain, though a few chronological

problems remain. Occasionally a biblical historian will recount some event out of chronological order, usually to make a theological point. For instance, the very last event described in the life of Hezekiah king of Judah is his entertaining of ambassadors from Babylon (2 Kin. 20:12–19; Is. 39:1–8). Evidence from both inside and outside of the Bible reveals that that event actually occurred earlier, certainly not just before Hezekiah's death (2 Kin. 20:21). The biblical historian evidently moved the account to the end because of the prophet Isaiah's warning about Babylon. During Hezekiah's reign, God had delivered Judah from Assyria, but the historian foreshadows a coming time when God would allow Judah to fall to Babylon. Emphasizing chronological order, *The Chronological Guide to the Bible* restores such temporal displacements to their probable chronological contexts.

The Prophets

Other biblical books also concern the time covered by the Samuel/Kings and Chronicles double history. In *The Chronological Guide to the Bible* most of the prophetic books are inserted at the appropriate historical points, according to the events which are narrated or prophesied, not according to the times when the books were written. The Book of Jonah, for instance, is often thought to have been composed some time in the Persian era (559–331 B.C.), but events in the book are set in the lifetime of the prophet Jonah, who lived centuries earlier, during the reign of Jeroboam II (793–753 B.C.). Thus, the Book of Jonah appears in the context of Jeroboam's reign.

Other prophetic passages speak of times later than the traditional date of composition for the passage itself. For example, parts of the Book of Isaiah refer to events that took place centuries after the prophet Isaiah lived. Though Isaiah prophesied in Jerusalem during the 8th century B.C., the passage of Is. 44:28—45:1 refers by name to Cyrus, a Persian king who lived in the 6th century B.C. For this reason, some chapters from the Book of Isaiah appear in the time of Cyrus (539–530 B.C.). While scholars disagree whether these chapters were written by Isaiah of Jerusalem or by a later prophet during the 6th century, they agree that the 6th century is the time to which these chapters refer.

The Book of Ezekiel provides many dates, most of which indicate when the prophet received a message from God. To calculate his dates Ezekiel began counting from the exile of Jehoiachin to Babylon in 597 B.C. Each date is expressed as a "year of King Jehoiachin's captivity" (Ezek. 1:2) or a "year of our captivity" (Ezek. 33:21). In providing modern equivalents for Ezekiel's dates, *The Chronological Guide to the Bible* follows the system of dates compiled in *Babylonian Chronology 626 B.C.–A.D. 75* by R. A. Parker and W. H. Dubberstein.

The Book of Jeremiah

The Book of Jeremiah, perhaps the most radically rearranged book in *The Chronological Guide to the Bible*, is a prime example of a book that lacks chronological order in its canonical form. As one of the most history-conscious of the prophetic books, Jeremiah refers specifically to individual kings and officials and even includes several historical narratives. At the same time, though, these history-minded oracles and historical narratives are not presented in anything resembling chronological order. Even the historical narratives of Jer. 25—29 and 32—40 skip back and forth in time (see Jer. 25:1; 26:1; 32:1; 36:1). Thus, although the Book of Jeremiah is only understandable in light of the historical events surrounding the destruction of Jerusalem in 586 B.C., simply reading the book from start to finish does not give the reader that necessary understanding.

Messianic Prophecies

Messianic prophecies raise a question as to the time period to which a particular prophecy refers. The New Testament takes great care to demonstrate that many Old Testament passages ultimately refer to the person and work of Jesus Christ. It would make sense to locate such Old Testament passages at pertinent places in the life of Jesus. This has not been done, however. Without denying that messianic prophecies are ultimately fulfilled in Christ, most of them also have significance for their original Old Testament time period. For instance, the promise in Isaiah 7:14, "Behold, the virgin shall conceive and bear a Son," is quoted in Matt. 1:23 as a reference to Christ's virgin birth. In the context of Is. 7, though, the promise is a part of the prophet Isaiah's larger message to Judah's king Ahaz, providing a sign that he should not fear the nations of Syria and Israel, for they would soon be destroyed (Is. 7:16). This prophecy has significance for more than one time period; and in *The Chronological Guide to the Bible*, it appears in its original context, during the reign of Ahaz, even though its prophetic significance extends to the later context at the birth of Christ.

Wisdom Literature and Psalms

Some of the most hotly contested debates among Old Testament scholars concern the date when this or that passage was composed. Fortunately, *The Chronological Guide to the Bible* only seeks to place biblical passages according to the setting described, a question about which there is more agreement. Even so, complete scholarly consensus still is not possible, and sometimes it is not certain to which time period various passages refer.

The wisdom literature of Proverbs, Ecclesiastes, and Job is an example of such chronological uncertainty. While most of the Old Testament is centered in history, these writings are an exception. Wisdom speaks of universal, practical matters that apply to all people of all nations in all ages. A proverb such as "Hatred stirs up strife, but love covers all sins" (Prov. 10:12), for example, applies just as well to every age. Most of the Book of Proverbs and all of the Book of Ecclesiastes are associated with the court of King Solomon, the revered head of the wisdom movement in Israel. So in *The Chronological Guide to the Bible* these passages appear in Solomon's time. Some sections of Proverbs and the whole Book of Job, however, defy chronological placement. For this reason, these writings are separated from the chronology and located, somewhat arbitrarily, in the Babylonian exile.

The psalms also intentionally resist chronological placement. For the most part, they do not refer to any one time, but rather speak in general language, providing words for worship in the temple. Some psalms have superscriptions that associate them with particular events and determine their placement. Most of the psalms, however, are timeless, and without a historical context to follow can be placed only in reaction to their content. David's hymns of praise appear, as a block, in a time when David praised God: when he brought the Ark of the Covenant into Jerusalem (1 Chr. 15:29). On the other hand, David's laments appear at a time when David lamented: during a plague (1 Chr. 21:30). Other psalms appear in other historical contexts, from the fall of Jerusalem (Ps. 89) to the Babylonian captivity (Ps. 137) to the rebuilding of Jerusalem under Nehemiah (Ps. 120—134).

The Gospels

A challenging task faces us when we attempt to arrange the Gospels into a chronological presentation of Jesus' life. If early Christian tradition is correct, Mark's Gospel was not written to provide a sequential account of the events in Jesus' life. If the other Synoptic Gospels—Matthew and Luke—are related to Mark, as most scholars believe, they are not organized primarily along chronological lines either. What has long been recognized about John's Gospel is probably also true of the Synoptic Gospels: the Gospel writers' theological interests and their communities' practical needs were more decisive than historical concerns.

The first three Gospels are called the Synoptic Gospels. The word "Synoptic" comes from two Greek words meaning "seen together." Matthew, Mark, and Luke tell the story of Jesus in essentially the same sequence and in nearly identical terms. The similarities are especially obvious when these three Gospels are compared with John. But equally striking are their conspicuous differences when compared closely with each other. This creates what scholars call the "Synoptic Problem": How can both the similarities and the differences be satisfactorily explained?

Similarities might be explained by appeal to the Gospels' divine inspiration. But this fails to account for their differences. Virtually all scholars today agree that the similarities among the Synoptic Gospels are so close as to require a literary explanation. That is, either all three copied from a lost earlier gospel or two of the Gospels depended on the third.

Other gospels did exist, which are called "apocryphal" because the church never accepted them. The apocryphal gospels were never widely used. Some were rejected because they seemed to promote false doctrines. Others were dismissed as merely fanciful speculations designed to answer the curious questions of those familiar with the canonical Gospels. In any case, none of the apocryphal gospels that survive explain the similarities among the canonical Gospels.

Various theories have been proposed to explain how the Gospels might have depended on each other. St. Augustine proposed the theory that Matthew was the earliest Gospel and that Luke and Mark used it in writing theirs. Many modern scholars espouse a similar view. But since the 19th century most scholars have presumed that Mark was the earliest Gospel. Even assuming that Mark was written first still does not account for all the similarities among the Synoptic Gospels. To offer more explanation, most scholars assume that, in addition to Mark, Matthew and Luke depended on a now-lost source. This hypothetical source is generally called "Q," an abbreviation for the German word *Quelle*, meaning "source."

Both ancient tradition and scholarly opinion seem to agree that Mark was the earliest Gospel. Since we cannot be certain of the exact sequence of events, the life of Jesus in *The Chronological Guide to the Bible* follows Mark's order. Additional information provided by the other Gospels is arranged in what seems to be the most plausible order around Mark's framework.

Acts of the Apostles

The second task in rearranging the New Testament books is to construct a chronology of important events that occurred during the lives of the apostles and during the early years of the Christian church. The Book of Acts and the New Testament letters serve as the basis for the chronology of the church age. References to the political leaders during this time help pinpoint certain dates.

The Book of Acts is the one book of the New Testament that traces the development of the early church after the ascension of Jesus. Standing between the Gospels and the New Testament letters, Acts is a bridge between the life of Jesus and the ministry of the apostle Paul. As such, the narrative of Acts is one source of historical information about the early church.

There is little doubt that the Book of Acts and the Gospel of Luke come from the same author. Since the author does not identify himself by name, scholars have ascribed the authorship of both books to Luke, the companion of Paul (2 Tim. 4:11).

Luke was closely associated with many events of Paul's mission, and this results in greater vividness in the latter half of Acts. At places (see Acts 16:10–17), the narrative changes to the first person ("we"), indicating that Luke was personally present. Nevertheless, some scholars believe that the books of Luke and Acts were written by an anonymous writer who was later identified with Luke. Also questioned is whether Luke is a reliable historian, since his primary motive for writing was not to record history, but to inform his audience of the triumphant course of the gospel, beginning in Jesus and continuing in the church (Acts 1:1). Thus, other scholars look to Paul's letters for a chronology of his ministry.

Paul's Letters

Paul the apostle was the earliest and most influential interpreter of Christ's message and teaching. As an early Christian missionary, Paul founded and corresponded with several early Christian churches. Using Paul's letters, however, to determine a chronology of events in his life is difficult. The letters do not provide any specific dates or a sequence of events, but only offer pieces of information that scholars try to relate to the narrative of Acts. To make the task more difficult, scholars cannot agree on the sequence in which Paul wrote his letters, or on whether all of the letters accredited to Paul were actually written by him.

The New Testament letters follow the general custom and form of letters that became an important form of communication in the Greek-speaking world about 300 years before the birth of Jesus. The Roman government provided postal service only for official documents, so private letters were sent by special messengers or friendly travelers. Letters normally were sent to designated parties, although some were "open" or circular letters. Paul's letters, with the possible exception of Ephesians, were addressed to specific congregations.

Ancient letters normally followed a pattern that included: (1) an introduction, listing the names of sender and recipient, followed by a formal greeting inquiring about the recipient's health and a thanksgiving formula; (2) a body, or purpose for writing; and (3) a conclusion, consisting of appropriate remarks and a farewell. Paul's letters follow this pattern, with some exceptions. Paul replaced the bland greeting of inquiry about health with a salutation combining Christian grace and Hebrew peace. His thanksgiving was likewise more than a formality; it was a sincere expression of gratitude for the well-being of his congregations. He also omitted the farewell in favor of personal greetings or a benediction.

Since Paul's letters do not provide a sequence of events, *The Chronological Guide to the Bible* follows the narrative sequence of Acts. In the Old Testament, books were rearranged based on the description of the narrative. Since the New Testament letters describe themselves as communication written from a particular sender to intended recipients, individual letters have been placed according to this description, if possible. In canonical Bibles, the Pauline letters are arranged in the New Testament according to length, from the longest (Romans) to the shortest (Philemon). In *The Chronological Guide to the Bible* they have been arranged, as much as possible, according to information given in the salutations, greetings, and bodies of the letters.

The Prison Epistles

The Book of Acts ends with Paul in prison in Rome. Four letters—Philippians, Philemon, Colossians, and Ephesians—are known as the Prison Epistles, since all make reference to Paul being in prison. Paul, however, was imprisoned in Caesarea and possibly in Ephesus, besides Rome, so the placement of any one of the Prison Epistles must be considered tentative.

The Pastoral Letters

The chronology from Paul's imprisonment on is drawn from inferences in the New Testament letters, which have been arranged in *The Chronological Guide to the Bible* according to their salutations, where possible. The Pastoral Letters—1 and 2 Timothy and Titus—have been placed according to the belief of some that Paul was released from Roman imprisonment to continue missionary work in Macedonia. If Paul was martyred while in prison, however, possibly in A.D. 64, these letters would have been compiled much later, by an unknown editor.

The Last New Testament Writings

The final books of the New Testament offer little help in determining a chronology. According to tradition, Peter was martyred in A.D. 64, so the letters of 1 and 2 Peter have been placed in *The Chronological Guide to the Bible* just before that time. Those who think one or both of the letters were written by an unknown author would place them later. Writings such as Hebrews and the letters of 1, 2, and 3 John indicate some time in the last half of the 1st century A.D., but a more precise dating is impossible. The Book of Revelation appears last in *The Chronological Guide to the Bible*. Its contents are not limited to a specific time; the author wrote about God's plan for his own day and for the far future.

EPOCH ONE

BEFORE THE PATRIARCHS

CREATION—2000 B.C.

The Bible begins its story with the accounts of creation and of humankind's earliest ancestors and history. The epoch extending from undatable creation to about 2000 B.C. witnessed the beginning both of life itself and of humankind's first civilizations. The very earliest part of this epoch is called "prehistory" because it covers the story of humans before there were recorded events. The advent of writing around 3000 B.C. marks the start of the historical era, as humans began preserving information concerning their economies, laws, and religions.

ARCHAEOLOGY AND THE PAST

Archaeologists arrange historical and cultural evidence according to the most vital metal of each period, such as stone, copper, bronze, or iron. The dates for these periods are approximate and are based on varying theories and interpretations of the biblical data.

The Stone Age (before 4000 B.C.) is subdivided into the Old Stone Age or Paleolithic period, an age of hunting and food-gathering in which people made implements of flint or chipped stone; the Middle Stone Age or Mesolithic period, a transitional stage to a food-producing economy with more developed civilization; and the New Stone Age or Neolithic period, which included the invention of pottery and advances in agriculture, textiles, and animal husbandry.

The Copper-Stone Age, or Chalcolithic period (4000 to 3000 B.C.), saw a transition to a significant use of copper. At some sites from this period, dwellings were underground, entered by shafts from the surface and connected by tunnels. Copper working was found in the many pits, ovens, and fireplaces common in such sites.

The Early Bronze Age (3000 to 2000 B.C.) is the period in which we leave "prehistory" and enter the "historical" period. This is the period in which written records appear. The Mesopotamians pioneered writing, but Egypt was quick to recognize the benefits of it. At the site of Arad in Palestine, archaeologists have uncovered a potsherd bearing the signature of Narmer, who is often identified with Menes, the pharaoh of Egypt's first dynasty.

THE PEOPLES AND GROUPS

The story of the Bible is linked with the histories of two great lands: Mesopotamia and Egypt.

The earliest known inhabitants of Mesopotamia lived in the southern part, the land of Sumer or southern Babylonia. Known as Sumerians, this culture greatly influenced the entire ancient Near East, including the Israelites. The Sumerians developed a township system of government, consisting of city-states, in which the temple of the local deity was the center of economic, cultural, and religious life.

In northern Babylonia lived the Accadians. This culture took its name from the town of Agade, also known as Accad. The Accadian culture did not develop the independent city-state system of the south, but seems to have existed as a single territory. While there were temples, the palace and household played the more important role in the Accadian economy. Around 2300 B.C. a northerner named Sargon of Agade was able to unify north and south Babylonia.

Egypt was a land divided into two kingdoms: Lower Egypt around the Nile Delta and Upper Egypt of the Nile Valley. Egypt's prehistory or predynastic period witnessed the development of rulership by pharaohs. This period ended around 3000 B.C. with the unification of Lower and Upper Egypt by the ruler Menes, resulting in the First Dynasty. During the following Archaic period, the country came to accept a divine monarchy in which the pharaoh was considered the incarnation of the sky god Horus. Later pharaohs of the Old Kingdom, beginning about 2700 B.C., became famous for their pyramids.

THE BIBLICAL LITERATURE

The Book of Genesis is usually divided at Gen. 12, where the story of the patriarch Abraham begins. The chapters 1—11, which concern the time before the patriarchs, are called "primeval history" because they relate the first ages of the world.

The major narratives of this primeval history give an account of creation, a great Flood, and the tower at Babel. The creation account (Gen. 1—3) describes the creation of all things, including humankind. The newly created humans rebel against God, resulting in their expulsion from the Garden of Eden. The Flood account (Gen. 6—9) tells of the continued evil in human hearts, and God's judgment upon humanity. The redemption of Noah's family offers a new beginning. Following the Flood, Gen. 11 narrates the spread of the human race and its arrogant attempt to build a tower to the heavens. God confuses their languages, forcing them to disperse.

THE BEGINNINGS OF HUMAN CIVILIZATION

Biblical and secular historians agree that human civilization began in the ancient Near East. The earliest large communities developed in Mesopotamia (modern Iraq and Iran) and in Egypt. Palestine, where biblical Israel is found, lies along the best road between Mesopotamia and Egypt, and so the Bible's own history appropriately begins with these two civilization centers.

The task of assigning specific dates to this ancient history is difficult and uncertain, but scholars have placed the first human settlements as early as 7,000 to 8,000 years before Christ. Although dating the early events of civilization is elusive, we can at least follow the general stages by which human communities developed.

Advances in technology made it possible for humans to live in large communities. First they developed stone tools, then discovered how to make clay vessels, how to extract and use copper ore, and, by about 3000 B.C., how to use bronze. In terms of food and support, humans moved from small family groups hunting and gathering their food to larger nomadic clans tending domesticated animals. Farming developed next, and by 3000 B.C. people in Mesopotamia and Egypt were using sophisticated irrigation techniques to harness the regular floods of the Tigris, Euphrates, and Nile rivers. Now for the first time, food could be produced in large supply, enough to support cities and even empires.

The period from 3000 to 2000 B.C. (called the Early Bronze Age) saw the development of several such empires: the civilizations of Sumer, Accad, and Ur in Mesopotamia and the Old Kingdom of Egypt. Towering monuments testify to the amazing technological sophistication of these cultures. This was the age of the great pyramids in Egypt and of similar structures in Mesopotamia, called ziggurats. These ancient peoples worshiped many gods, and writings from this time describe not only these gods, but also the creation of the world and a great flood.

EPOCH ONE
Chronological Reading Guide

- ❏ Genesis 1:1—11:32

THE BOOK OF GENESIS

The Old Testament as a whole chronicles the history of the nation of Israel. This nation does not emerge as an entity, though, until the Book of Exodus, when God appears to the twelve tribes at Sinai. Genesis, then, is the prologue to the history of Israel. Chapters 1—11 tell about the creation and earliest history of all humankind, and chs. 12—50 describe God's working within the chosen family of Abraham, from whom Israel descended.

Within the theological narratives of Gen. 1—11, there are several brief comments that reflect the advancing civilizations of Mesopotamia and Egypt. There are conflicts between hunters and shepherds and between shepherds and farmers. Humans develop technology and craftsmanship and establish the first cities. Chapter 11 describes humanity's technical skill (and vaulting ambition) in its account of a tower, or ziggurat, in the plains of Shinar (Mesopotamia).

Genesis, along with the books of Exodus through Deuteronomy, has traditionally been attributed to Moses. Many scholars retain this view today, but others, noting abrupt changes in vocabulary and style and certain perspectives that appear to come from a later time, argue that the book contains several sources and traditions, some much older than others. In either case, whether written entirely by Moses or composed from 900 to 400 B.C. of various ancient strands, the Book of Genesis is a recounting of Israel's origins by one who knew that all this was leading to God's choice of Israel as "a special treasure...above all people" (Ex. 19:5).

OUTLINE OF GENESIS 1–11

I. The Creation	**1:1—2:25**
A. Creation of the World	1:1—2:3
B. Creation of Man	2:4–25
II. The Fall	**3:1—5:32**
A. The Fall of Man	3:1–24
B. After the Fall	4:1—5:32
III. The Judgment of the Flood	**6:1—9:29**
A. Causes of the Flood	6:1–5
B. Judgment of the Flood	6:6–22
C. The Flood	7:1—8:19
D. Results of the Flood	8:20—9:17
E. After the Flood	9:18–29
IV. The Judgment on the Tower of Babel	**10:1—11:9**
A. Family Lines after the Flood	10:1–32
B. Judgment on All the Family Lines	11:1–9

THE CREATOR GOD IS NOT SUN OR MOON
(GEN. 1:16)

In Gen 1:16 the two great lights created by God are called the "greater light" and "lesser light." The words "sun" and "moon" were not omitted by accident from this verse. The writer of Genesis was aware that two prominent gods worshiped in the ancient Near East were the sun and the moon.

In Egypt the sun was associated with several important gods, including Amon-Re, Re, and Aton. Egyptians believed that the sun, as the god Re, created the world by his own personified power. One of Re's "eyes" was the moon god Tefnut. Another Egyptian god was Ptah, who was also considered the creator of all things. Ptah's two eyes were the sun and moon.

In Mesopotamia the sun god Shamash was worshiped as the benefactor of the oppressed. Night was seen as the passing of the sun to the netherworld or underworld. Ancient peoples prayed to the hidden sun for mediation between the dead and the living.

Canaanite worshipers knew the sun as Shemesh. The appearance of this god's name in place names, such as Beth Shemesh (1 Sam. 6:12), hints at the importance of Shemesh to the polytheistic Canaanites.

The author of Gen. 1:14–19 makes the case that the "greater" and "lesser" lights are simply creations of the creator God. No one should acknowledge the sun and moon as deities or confuse them with the true God.

WHERE WAS EDEN? (GEN. 2:10–14)

The Book of Genesis states that God planted a garden "eastward in Eden" (Gen. 2:8). For centuries biblical commentators have speculated on the location of Eden, which is associated with four rivers: Pishon, Gihon, Hiddekel, and Euphrates (2:10–14). The last two of these rivers are known, Hiddekel being the Hebrew name for the Tigris River. Thus the mention of the Tigris and Euphrates rivers would suggest a location for Eden somewhere in Mesopotamia.

Unfortunately, the other rivers, Pishon and Gihon, are obscure and defy absolute placement for the location of Eden. Pishon was in the land of Havilah (2:11), which has been associated with Arabia (Gen. 25:18), as well as with India. Gihon was in Cush (2:13), which was an ancient name for the area south of Egypt. Some scholars have argued that Pishon and Gihon represent the Indus and Nile rivers, but others contend that they may have been canals.

TIME CAPSULE	Prehistory to 2400 B.C.
5869	Carbon-14 dating of early fortification at Jericho
5500	Pottery is first known in Palestine
5000	Evidence of temple at Eridu, Iraq
4500	Sockets for hinging doors used in Sumer
4000	Casting of molten silver and gold in the Near East
3500	Sumerians develop advanced civilization in southern Mesopotamia
3200	Earliest writing, from Uruk in the Sumerian language
3000	Egyptians write in hieroglyphic script
2550	The Great Pyramid of Giza, 481 feet high
2450	Egyptians make copper pipes
2400	Elba, a Semitic city-state in northern Syria

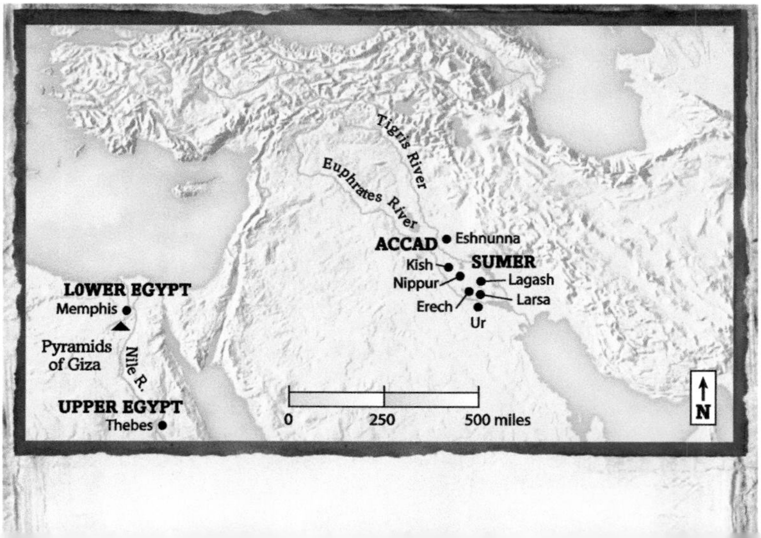

The Ancient Near East after 3000 B.C.
During the 3rd millennium Lower and Upper Egypt were united. Egypt's Old Kingdom (2700–2160 B.C.) produced the great pyramids, such as those at Giza. In Mesopotamia, the land of Sumer developed a system of independent city-states. Toward the end of the millennium this city-state rule was replaced by a more extensive territorial rule centered in Accad.

Records of the Descendants (Gen. 5:1—6:22)

Genesis 1—11 tells much of its story by means of genealogies. At the end of the Cain and Abel account is a list of eight descendants of Cain (Gen. 4:17–22), among whom are the ancestors of pastoral nomads (v. 20), musicians (v. 21), and metalworkers (v. 22). In Gen. 5 the line of Adam's descendants through Seth is given, breaking off just before the Flood. Finally, in Gen. 10 the peoples of the earth are listed under the three sons of Noah, categorized according to clans, languages, location, and nationality.

It is possible, using the numbers of these lists, to add up the years and thus date the creation of the world at about 4004 B.C. Such computations were published in A.D. 1650–1654 by the Archbishop James Ussher and are held to by some scholars today. Many scholars, though, argue that modern historical dating and chronological specificity were foreign to the ancient mind and suggest that the exact numbers should not be read so mechanically. Furthermore, the numbers themselves vary in different text traditions, showing many disagreements between the Hebrew Bible, Samaritan Pentateuch, and the Septuagint (Greek Old Testament). Thus different interpreters treat the genealogies in different ways, with many concluding that a date for the creation of the world is impossible to determine.

The Flood Through Other Eyes (Gen. 6—9)

Divine destruction of the world by means of a flood is a motif known in cultures from around the world. Most of these stories appear to have had their origin in the biblical account (Gen. 6:5—9:29). However, the ancient Near East has numerous myths of the great flood that are separate retellings of the same event. Mesopotamian stories of the flood are first found written in the Sumerian language, in the earliest known literature (3rd millennium B.C.). A variety of retellings produced a number of versions. The two most famous flood stories outside the Bible are the Gilgamesh Epic and the story of Atrahasis.

Both similarities and differences exist between the biblical Flood story and the legend known as the Gilgamesh Epic. Though the Gilgamesh flood story appears already in the mid-3rd millennium Sumerian stories, the epic account most widely known comes from the library of the Assyrian king Ashurbanipal (668–627 B.C.). The story is related by the flood survivor, Utnapishtim, at the edge of the world, where Gilgamesh (king of Uruk around 2600 B.C.) had sought him to discover how to become immortal.

There is no reason given in this account for the decision by the council of the gods to destroy the earth. However, Ea, the god of wisdom, realizing that destruction was a mistake, warns Utnapishtim that a flood is coming. Utnapishtim tears down his house and builds a boat, into which he gathers animals in pairs, seeds of all plants, his relatives, and skilled craftsmen. The deities unleash the flood, destroying everything that is not in the boat. After the flood ceased, the boat rested on a mountaintop in the Zagros Mountains. Utnapishtim releases first a dove, then a sparrow, both of whom return without finding a place to land, and lastly a raven, who does not return (similar to Gen. 8:6–12). The flood is finally over and everything is allowed to leave the boat and repopulate the earth.

The First World Empire (GEN. 10:8–10)

The city of Accad was one of the major urban centers in central Mesopotamia and one of the first cities in the kingdom of the legendary Nimrod (Gen. 10:10). Although the precise location has not been found, Accad was most likely near Babylon.

The Sumerian name of the city was Agade. A certain Sargon of Agade (c. 2350 B.C.) founded the city and made it the capital of an early Semitic dynasty. Sargon and his successors (notably his grandson Naram-Sin) were able to control the entire Tigris-Euphrates basin and claimed to have even reached the Mediterranean Sea. The dynasty of Agade lasted for about two centuries and was in fact the first world empire. Evidently the city was then destroyed and not subsequently reoccupied. A Sumerian text from the late 3rd millennium B.C., *The Curse of Agade*, commemorates the city's demise.

The First Major City (Gen. 10:10)

Erech is the biblical form of Uruk, a Sumerian city on the Euphrates River in ancient Mesopotamia. The name "Erech" is cited in Gen. 10:10 and Ezra 4:9, and its historical importance is that Uruk (Erech) played a role in the origin of urbanization.

Archaeological investigations have confirmed that the Ubaidian people, early inhabitants of Sumer, founded two villages in this area before 4000 B.C. By 3700 B.C. the two centers fused together to create Uruk, the first urban site in world history.

The first evidence of public architecture, cylinder seals, and the origins of writing come from this city. Building projects at Uruk included the earliest known ziggurat, a holy mound at the top of which was the White temple. Cylinder seals, which were used to mark ownership, spread from Uruk throughout the ancient world. Picture writing (dated to about 3200 B.C.) expressed ideas through a series of pictures. This writing would later evolve into the script known as cuneiform, used first by the Sumerians, early inhabitants of the Tigris-Euphrates valley.

Uruk had a long history, existing until Hellenistic times (the end of the 1st millennium B.C.). In the Bible it is mentioned very early as part of Nimrod's post-Flood kingdom (Gen. 10:8–10). Much later in time, it is one of the cities and nations writing against Jerusalem during the reign of the Persian ruler Artaxerxes I (465–424 B.C.; Ezra 4:9).

BABEL AND ITS TOWER (GEN. 11:1–9)

Babel was one of the chief cities in Nimrod's kingdom (Gen. 10:8–10). The term "Babel" is the Hebrew form of the name "Babylon," the city on the Euphrates River in central Mesopotamia.

The city has a very ancient past. It is first mentioned by the Accadian king Sargon (c. 2350 B.C.), who, according to tradition, burned it. Shar-kali-sharri (c. 2200 B.C.) restored its temple tower. Hammurabi (1792–1750 B.C.), a king of the 1st Dynasty of Babylon, made it his capital city. Unfortunately, archaeologists have been able to find evidence only as far back as the period of the Neo-Babylonian king Nebuchadnezzar II (605 B.C. and later). The rising water table in the area has prevented much research into earlier periods.

Babel has received much attention over its tower (Gen. 11:4, 5). It likely was a staged temple tower known by the Sumerian term "ziggurat." Ziggurats were developed in the 3rd millennium B.C. at Uruk (Erech) and Ur in Babylonia, as well as at Nineveh, and consisted of smaller and smaller stages or stories built on top of each other. Those who believe the tower at Babel refers to temple ruins from Mesopotamia point especially to Etemenanki, the ziggurat of the Marduk temple in Babylon. A Babylonian text describes it as having a base of 295 feet square with seven platforms over 108 feet high. The top platform had a temple where the god met with humanity. Access was achieved by ramps or stairways.

THE PATRIARCHS, ISRAEL'S ANCESTORS

2000—1500 B.C.

The term "patriarch" refers to the founder or ruler of a tribe, family, or clan. The Israelites traced their ancestry to one man—"the patriarch Abraham" (Is. 51:2; Heb. 7:4). They laid claim to Canaan based on the covenant God made with their first three patriarchs—Abraham, Isaac, Jacob—to "possess the land" (Deut. 1:8). The phrase "the patriarchs" eventually referred to Jacob's twelve sons as well (Acts 7:8, 9). Thus among figures of the Bible, the patriarchs were the ancestors of the Israelites from Abraham to Jacob's son Benjamin.

Exact dates for the period in which the patriarchs lived cannot be established. The events of the patriarchal narratives in Genesis cannot be synchronized with any events outside of the Bible. As a result, scholars have suggested dates for the patriarchs ranging from 2000 B.C. to as late as 1200 B.C. In the genealogy of Ex. 6:16–20, Moses is the great-great-grandson of Jacob, who himself was the grandson of Abraham. The line of descent—Abraham, Isaac, Jacob, Levi, Kohath, Amram, Moses—would set Abraham somewhere around 2000 to 1900 B.C.

ARCHAEOLOGY AND THE PAST

The Middle Bronze Age (2000–1500 B.C.) produced one of the more archaeologically rewarding sites that have been discovered in Mesopotamia. The city of Mari owed its importance to being a focal point on caravan routes crossing the Syrian desert and linking Mari with Syria and the Mediterranean coasts, as well as with Assyria and Babylonia. In addition to the temple of Ishtar, the Mesopotamian goddess, and a ziggurat (or temple tower), archaeologists found a royal palace containing almost 300 rooms.

Some 20,000 clay tablets, known as the Mari letters, were dug up, which shed much light on the ancient biblical world. These documents date from the time of Hammurabi (c. 1750 B.C.) and refer to terms often associated with the patriarchs. The term "Habiru," found both at Mari and in the Nuzi texts, has been compared to Abraham being named a "Hebrew" (Gen. 14:13). The seminomadic group called "Beneyamina" at Mari bears a similar name to the Israelite name "Benjamin." Mari also sheds light on the Amorites. Nahor, Haran, Mari, Qatna, and Ugarit all appear as Amorite cities with Amorite kings.

Another discovery related to the patriarchs dates from around the change from Middle Bronze (2000–1500 B.C.) to Late Bronze (1500–1200 B.C.). Numerous clay tablets from the city of Nuzi are thought to

illuminate customs and local practices found in the patriarchal narratives. Exact dates for Nuzi are difficult to determine, although the Nuzi tablets are usually dated between 1400 and 1330 B.C. The similarities of social and legal customs between the Nuzi texts and the patriarchal stories have led some scholars to place the patriarchs themselves after 1550 B.C. The Nuzi customs, however, may reflect social conditions of centuries before Nuzi, as well as those of much later times in the 1st millennium. Rather than demonstrating a date for the patriarchs, the Nuzi texts provide insights into cultural customs that help us understand daily life in the 2nd millennium B.C.

THE PEOPLES AND GROUPS

The dynasty of Sargon of Agade (c. 2350 B.C.) lasted for only about a century before it declined. Mesopotamia experienced a period of anarchy, partly caused by invasions of the Gutians, foreigners from the Zagros Mountains. The strongest dynasty to emerge during this unstable time was the 3rd Dynasty of Ur, founded by Ur-Nammu about 2112 B.C. The connections that existed between Ur and various Syrian cities form one possible setting for Abraham's journeys.

Eventually, Ur too declined. The Ur Empire collapsed with the invasion of the Elamites, bringing an end to Sumerian civilization. Tribes of Semitic peoples, called Amorites, migrated into Mesopotamia from the west in large numbers. Capturing major regions, they established Amorite dynasties in various city-states. Both Shamshi-Adad I (c. 1813–1781 B.C.), ruler of Asshur, and Hammurabi of Babylon (1792–1750 B.C.) were Amorite kings.

In Egypt, a period of decline and civil war ended gradually during the Middle Kingdom. King Amenemhet I of Thebes (1963–1934 B.C.) convinced the princes of the land to give their allegiance to him as the true heir to Egypt's throne. Another pharaoh, Sesostris III (1862–1843 B.C.) established a central government by restraining the powers of Egypt's provincial rulers and families.

Unity in Egypt continued for more than 200 years. Eventually, however, the country experienced a second period of weakness in which rival dynasties competed for control of limited areas. The most important of these dynasties was the Hyksos, who gained control of Lower Egypt, establishing a capital at Avaris. Toward the end of the Middle Bronze Age, King Kamose of Thebes broke the power of the Hyksos, and his younger brother Ahmose eventually drove them from Egypt.

THE BIBLICAL LITERATURE

The second part of the Book of Genesis (chs. 12—50), tells the stories of Israel's patriarchs. The events from the lives of Abraham, Isaac, and Jacob (chs. 12—38) take place primarily in Canaan, although Abraham originated in Mesopotamia (Ur and Haran). The traditions concerning these ancestors are grouped into cycles of stories around Abraham (12:1—25:18) and around Jacob (25:19—36:43). Isaac appears in the Abraham and Jacob cycles, with much of his story in Gen. 26.

Abraham enters into covenant with God and is given the promise that he and his descendants will become a blessing to all humanity. In the stories of Abraham and Sarah, Isaac and Rebekah, Jacob and Leah and Rachel, and Joseph, the fulfillment of God's promises takes concrete form. The life of Joseph (chs. 37—50) is set primarily in Egypt, and in that foreign place we see God's unfailing providence and His determination to keep His promise to Abraham.

THE CHANGING OF THE EMPIRES

After about 2200 B.C. the great empires of the Early Bronze Age fell apart. Political instability and unrest spread throughout Egypt and Mesopotamia at the close of this age and the beginning of the Middle Bronze Age (2000–1500 B.C.).

In Egypt, the Old Kingdom was followed by over a century of political and social disarray. During this time, known in Egyptian history as the First Intermediate Period (2160–2010 B.C.), bedouins from Asia were able to infiltrate the Nile Delta. Civil strife between Egypt's city-states ended in 2040, when Mentuhotep II from Thebes reunified the land and began the prosperous and stable Middle Kingdom, which lasted until about 1786 B.C.

In Mesopotamia, no great empire arose to replace the 3rd Dynasty of Ur after that city-state fell in 2004 B.C. Smaller kingdoms such as Isin, Larsa, Assyria, Mari, and Babylon took turns dominating one another for brief periods. The greatest of these was the kingdom of Hammurabi I of Babylon (1792–1750 B.C.), whose famous law code parallels many of the Israelite laws. Hammurabi eventually brought all of Mesopotamia under Babylonian control. Even this kingdom was brief, though, declining during the rule of Hammurabi's son.

The instability of the time resulted partly from the appearance throughout the ancient Near East of a new ethnic group, the Amurru, or Amorites. This large group of Semitic people had personal names and customs that resemble those of the biblical Hebrews. Their influence was so pervasive that even some Mesopotamian kings had Amorite names.

After 2000 B.C. Amorites inhabited Palestine. Some settled in villages and established their own city-states, others lived as seminomadic shepherds, and still others lived on the fringes of society as warlike outcasts. Such outsiders, referred to as "Habiru," usually served as slaves or mercenaries to others, but on occasion fought their own battles.

Amorites worshiped many gods, but each city or clan identified its own particular deity. In Mesopotamia, in cities influenced by the Amorites, there even appeared prophets of these local gods, using language very similar to that of the much later Old Testament prophets. Away from the cities, among the seminomadic shepherds, great stress was given to the god of the clan's forefathers. Worship usually involved animal sacrifice, but child sacrifice was also common.

EPOCH TWO
Chronological Reading Guide

❑ Genesis 12:1—36:43

THE BOOK OF GENESIS

The second part of Genesis focuses on God's dealings with one man, Abraham, through whom God promises to bring salvation and blessing to the world. Abraham and his descendants learn firsthand that it is always safe to trust the Lord in times of famine and feasting, blessing and bondage. Through Abraham's family God's promises begin to come to fruition in a great nation possessing a great land.

It begins with God's call to Abraham and Sarah to become the parents of a new people—a new nation. The three covenant promises God makes to Abraham (land, descendants, and blessing) are foundational to His program to bring salvation upon the earth. God renews His covenant with Isaac as the spiritual link with Abraham, then transforms Jacob from selfishness to servanthood and changes his name to Israel, the father of the twelve tribes. Jacob's favorite son, Joseph, suffers at the hands of his brothers and becomes a slave in Egypt. After his dramatic rise to the rulership of Egypt, Joseph delivers his family from famine and brings them out of Canaan to Goshen.

OUTLINE OF GENESIS 12—50

I. The Life of Abraham	**11:10—25:18**
A. Introduction of Abram	11:10–32
B. The Covenant with Abram	12:1—25:18
II. The Life of Isaac	**25:19—26:35**
A. The Family of Isaac	25:19–34
B. The Failure of Isaac	26:1–33
C. The Failure of Esau	26:34–35
III. The Life of Jacob	**27:1—36:43**
A. Jacob Gains Esau's Blessing	27:1—28:9
B. Jacob's Life at Haran	28:10—31:55
C. Jacob's Return	32:1—33:20
D. Jacob's Residence in Canaan	34:1—35:29
E. The Family Line of Esau	36:1–43
IV. The Life of Joseph	**37:1—50:26**
A. Joseph's Family	37:1—38:30
B. The Exaltation of Joseph	39:1—41:57
C. The Salvation of Jacob's Family	42:1—50:26

TIME CAPSULE	2166 to 2000 B.C.
2166–1991	Abraham's life (based on early Exodus)
2040–1786	The Middle Kingdom in Egypt
2004	City-state of Ur falls to the Elamites
2000–1500	Middle Bronze Age
2000	Drains and sewers are used in Knossos, Crete
2000	Egyptian rulers develop royal postal system

THE GREAT PYRAMID AT GIZA (GEN. 12:14)

The famous pyramids at Giza functioned as individual tombs for some of the monarchs of Egypt's Old Kingdom (2700–2160 B.C.). Earliest among the monumental pyramid tombs appears to have been the Step Pyramid of Pharaoh Djoser (c. 2650 B.C.). The monarchs of the 4th Dynasty (2600–2500 B.C.), Khufu and his successor, Khafre, built huge pyramids in imitation of the Step Pyramid. The Great Pyramid is slightly over 480 feet high, and each of the four sides at the base is about 756 feet wide. Such massive monuments demonstrate the great architectural precision and excellence of the Egyptian Old Kingdom.

The patriarch Abram traveled to Egypt during a time of famine in Canaan (Gen. 12:10). Exact dates for Abram's life are unknown, but scholars often place him around 2000 or 1900 B.C. Thus, the Great Pyramid at Giza was already centuries old when Abram and Sarai visited Egypt (Gen. 12:10—13:1).

Passing Between the Halves (Gen. 15:17–21)

There are no adequate modern parallels to the broad-ranging meanings of the term "covenant" as used in the Bible. The closest parallel probably resides in marriage, where a public gathering solemnizes an agreement between two people.

The type of covenant presented in the Bible is most often between two parties. The superior party was known as the suzerain; the inferior party as the vassal. Both the suzerain and vassal had specific responsibilities. Primarily, in ancient societies the suzerain provided protection for the vassal, while the vassal supported the suzerain with taxes and was loyal in time of war.

The Lord and Abram joined themselves in a suzerain and vassal covenant (Gen. 15:18). Like similar ancient Near Eastern covenants they held a public ceremony to ratify their relationship. The sacrifice of animals and a meal (15:9, 10) were typical components of covenant ceremonies, as were the promises of both parties. Abram's part of this agreement was to "believe" in the Lord (15:6), which meant to worship no other gods. The Lord promised Abram to make his descendants as numerous as the stars (15:5) and provide a homeland for them (15:18).

Two differences between ancient Near Eastern covenants and the Gen. 15 covenant are striking. Usually the list of the vassal's duties and responsibilities was much larger than that of the suzerain's. In fact, a covenant, including the duties of the vassal, was imposed on the vassal by the suzerain. In the Gen. 15 covenant almost nothing is said about Abram's responsibilities. The focus is on what the Lord promised to Abram, not what Abram promised the Lord.

In the second difference it was usually the vassal who cut the animals in two parts and walked between them (15:10, 17). The ritual symbolically demonstrated what would happen to the vassal if the covenant was broken. The "burning torch" passing between the pieces of flesh in the Gen. 15 covenant (15:17) was obviously a representation of the Lord. The symbolism of Him passing between the cut sacrifice implies that He would die before He would allow His covenant with Abram to fail.

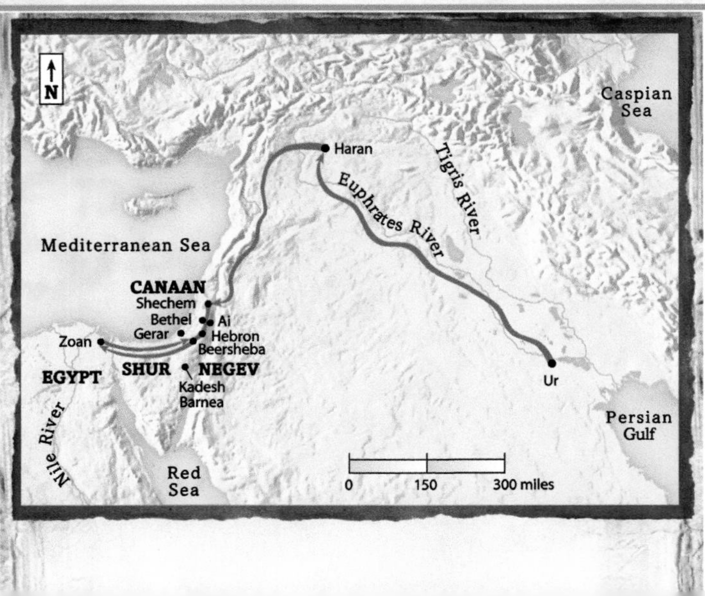

Journeys of Abraham

Abraham's birthplace has long been identified with Sumerian Ur in southern Mesopotamia. Ur may have sponsored colonies in northern Mesopotamia in the vicinity of Haran, from which Abraham's family possibly originated.

At Shechem in central Canaan, Abraham received the promise of God concerning the new land (Gen. 12:7). Famine, caused by unpredictable rains in Canaan, forced Abraham to move to Egypt, which was watered by the Nile River. Yet he would return to the land of promise.

The Birth of Ishmael (Gen. 16:1—20:18)

None of the events of the patriarchs can be synchronized with any dates known from nonbiblical sources. Nevertheless, Genesis does provide a brief chronological outline of Abraham's life. Abram was 75 years old when he left Haran in Mesopotamia and journeyed to Canaan with his wife, Sarai (Gen. 12:4, 5). After living 10 years in Canaan, Sarai made use of a typical ancient Near Eastern custom for a barren wife: she authorized her husband to obtain children by her personal slave (Gen. 16:3). Thus, Abram at age 86 fathered Ishmael through Sarai's maid Hagar (16:16). Sarai's barrenness continued for 13 more years, but God intervened before Abram, now 99 years old (Gen. 17:1), could announce Ishmael as his legal heir. Changing Abram's name to Abraham, and Sarai's to Sarah, God promised a child by Sarah (17:5, 15, 16).

Ancient marriage contracts obligated wives to provide a son for the married couple. Contracts dating from the mid-2nd millennium B.C. have been discovered in the city of Nuzi that specify that if a wife bore no male child she had the obligation to provide a child via a female servant. If a child was thus born to a servant, the child would be considered the child of the wife in regards to the contract. Thus, even a barren wife could fulfill her marital contract.

Abram's later reluctance to send Hagar away, when Sarai became jealous of her (Gen. 21:9–11), reflects another aspect of the Nuzi tablets. Servants who provided such children were not supposed to be sent away, but rather treated favorably. So it was that it took the voice of God to convince Abram to listen to Sarai's desire (21:12).

Circumcision (Gen. 17:10, 11)

Circumcision is a minor operation that removes a piece of skin from the male organ. It was practiced in several nations of the ancient Near East, including Egypt. But for Israel it was a sign of membership in the community and was required of every male. Traditionally it was performed with a flint knife.

TIME CAPSULE	1963 to 1700 B.C.
1963–1934	Amenemhet I rules Egypt during time of prosperity
1900	Mathematicians discover Pythagorean Theorem
1876	Jacob enters Egypt (based on early Exodus)
1834	Amorite tribe captures city-state of Larsa
1813–1760	The Mari tablets
1800	Musical notation used in Babylonia
1800	Wheel-thrown pottery in Greece
1792	Hammurabi ascends throne in Babylon
1790	Sumerian King List traces the history of Sumer and Accad from the flood to Hammurabi
1779	Earliest evidence of a wheel with spokes, from Syria
1760	Hammurabi destroys palace at Mari
1705	Jacob enters Egypt (based on late Exodus)
1700	Phoenicians develop alphabet of consonants only

The Birth of Isaac (Gen. 21:1—24:67)

Both Abraham (Gen. 17:17) and Sarah (18:11, 12) laughed in disbelief that a couple well past childbearing age should bear a son. Yet in fulfillment of God's promise, Abraham, age 100, fathered Isaac through his wife, Sarah, age 90 (Gen. 17:17; 21:1–5). Sarah's first concern was for her new son's status as Abraham's heir, a status threatened by Hagar's son Ishmael (21:9, 10). Ishmael was now about 14 years old, being 13 at his circumcision (17:24, 25).

An ancient Near Eastern law code describes the practice of giving one's maid as a second wife. The law provided protection for children born to the second wife. It prohibited the disinheriting of a firstborn son of a slave wife (Ishmael) in the event that the barren upper-class wife should later bear a son (Isaac). However, the upper-class wife's son would supersede the slave wife's son as the legal "firstborn." Furthermore, the slave wife and her children could be offered their freedom, in which case they forfeited their inheritance. Isaac did become Abraham's heir, representing one case in which a younger son received the inheritance and blessing.

ABRAHAM'S LIFE (EARLY EXODUS)

B.C. 2200 — 2150 — 2100 — 2050 — 2000 — 1950

- Abram is born 2166 B.C.
- Sarai is born 2156 B.C.
- Abram moves to Canaan (Gen. 12:4, 5) 2091 B.C.
- Ishmael is born (Gen. 16:15, 16) 2080 B.C.
- Ishmael is circumcised (Gen. 17:24, 25) 2067 B.C.
- Isaac is born (Gen. 21:2–5) 2066 B.C.
- Sarah dies in Hebron (Gen. 23:1, 2) 2029 B.C.
- Abraham dies and is buried in Hebron (Gen. 25:7–10) 1991 B.C.

My Servant Is My Heir! (Gen. 24:2, 3)

When God promised Abram that his descendants were to grow into a great nation, He was addressing Abram's complaint in Gen. 15:2, 3. Abram was childless, so his servant Eliezer, a man from Damascus, was going to be his heir—a common relationship for that time.

Tablets discovered in the ancient city of Nuzi reveal that childless couples regularly selected a servant as a replacement son. It was the duty of this servant to care for his adopted parents when they grew old and to perform the burial rites when they died. For his service the servant became the heir to the parents' property. Ancient contracts specify the duties of an adopted son and describe the relationship of the adoptee to any natural son born at a later time. Usually the natural son assumed the firstborn status. However, the adopted son was still treated well and not forsaken.

When Abram grew old, he made Eliezer his heir, probably with the usual stipulation that if a natural son was born, Eliezer would take second place. But even after the birth of Abram's sons, Ishmael and Isaac, Eliezer still maintained an important status in the household. He controlled all that Abram possessed (Gen. 24:2) and, as the oldest and most trusted of Abram's servants, even had the important task of selecting Isaac's wife (24:3).

The Mari Tablet Towns (Gen. 28:10)

Estimates for dating Abraham, Isaac, and Jacob range from about 2100 to 1800 B.C. Such dates would locate the patriarchal period sometime before, or simultaneous with, the Mari tablets, which themselves have been placed between 1813 and 1760 B.C.

Mari was once a powerful city located about halfway between Babylon and the Mediterranean Sea. Situated on the banks of the Euphrates River, Mari became rich through trading. More than 20,000 clay tablets written in the Accadian language were dug up at the excavation site. The Mari tablets frequently mention the cities of Nahor and Haran. Both Abraham (Gen. 11:31) and Jacob (27:43; 28:10) lived in Haran at separate times during their lives. Abraham's servant is reported to have traveled to Nahor (24:10). Since cities mentioned in the Mari tablets are also named in the patriarchal stories, it is possible that the tablets reflect aspects of the culture known by the patriarchs.

Jacob and Esau
by Francesco Hayez
c. 1844

ABRAHAM'S LIFE (LATE EXODUS)

B.C. 2000 — 1950 — 1900 — 1850 — 1800 — 1750

- Abram is born 1995 B.C.
- Sarai is born 1985 B.C.
- Abram moves to Canaan (Gen. 12:4, 5) 1920 B.C.
- Ishmael is born (Gen. 16:15, 16) 1909 B.C.
- Ishmael is circumcised (Gen. 17:24, 25) 1896 B.C.
- Isaac is born (Gen. 21:2–5) 1895 B.C.
- Sarah dies in Hebron (Gen. 23:1, 2) 1858 B.C.
- Abraham dies and is buried in Hebron (Gen. 25:7–10) 1820 B.C.

LABAN OF ARAM-NAHARAIM (GEN. 31:47)

Padan Aram, also known as Aram-naharaim, was the home of Laban, a descendant of Abraham's brother Nahor (Gen. 28:2). Meaning literally "Aram between the Rivers," Aram-naharaim was the geographic name for upper Mesopotamia—the region between the Tigris and Euphrates rivers. Egyptian sources, including the Amarna archives from the 14th century, referred to the region as Naharina (without the "Aram" prefix). English translations often translate it as "Mesopotamia" (Deut. 23:4).

Laban is described as an "Aramean" (Gen. 28:5, translated "Syrian" in the NKJV). The ethnic group known as the Arameans is not mentioned as inhabitants of this area until the 12th century B.C. But in the early 1st millennium B.C. numerous Aramean states were found in eastern Syria, and many individual Aramean tribes were causing great difficulty for both the Assyrian and Babylonian kingdoms in Mesopotamia.

When Laban speaks the words "Jegar Sahadutha," he is saying "Heap of Witness" in the Aramaic language (Gen. 31:47). Until the 1st millennium, Aramaic (a Semitic language closely related to biblical Hebrew) was spoken primarily by people from Aramean states. The Assyrians found Aramaic a convenient language for administering their conquered areas, thus it became an official language in portions of the Neo-Assyrian Empire from the 8th century on. The use of Aramaic spread until it later became the international language of commerce during the period of the Persian Empire's dominance (c. 559–331 B.C.).

The figure of Laban from upper Mesopotamia represents a people that had great influence on their world. The Arameans did not establish major kingdoms, as did the Assyrians and Babylonians. Nevertheless, the adjective "Aramean" was used long after the Aramean political states no longer existed. They left their mark through their language. Although Aramaic was later replaced by Greek in the Mediterranean world, the language continued to be used in the Near East by the Parthians (after 200 B.C.) and could be found as far east as India. It was the primary language of Palestine during the time of Jesus.

EGYPT IN THE MIDDLE BRONZE AGE

The spread of the Amorite peoples evidently reached even to Egypt. After several prosperous centuries, the Middle Kingdom of Egypt ended, and the land again began to break up politically. In the Second Intermediate Period (1786–1550 B.C.) of Egyptian history, as in the First Intermediate Period, foreigners entered Egypt from Asia and settled in the Nile Delta. Eventually, Egypt fell under the control of these outsiders, a Semitic people, known as the Hyksos (meaning "foreign chiefs"). Although much despised by the native Egyptians, the Hyksos maintained their control from about 1648 to 1540 B.C., even expanding Egypt's control north into Palestine, which became an Egyptian province.

EPOCH TWO
Chronological Reading Guide

- ❑ Genesis 37:1—50:26

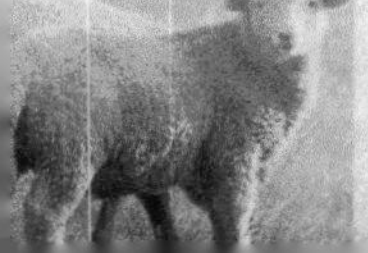

JACOB IN EGYPT (EARLY EXODUS)

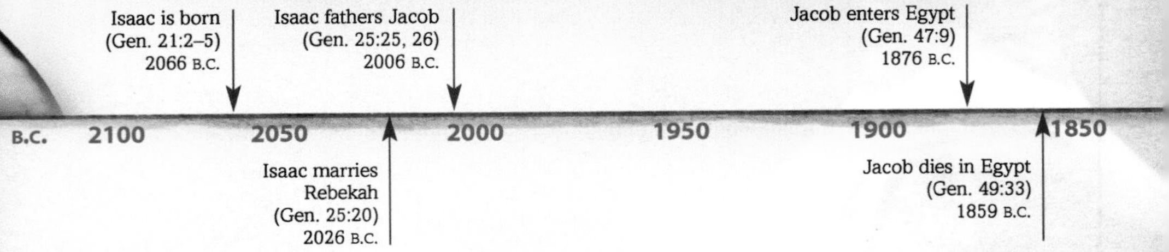

Joseph Goes to Egypt (Gen. 39:1, 2)

After arriving in Egypt, Joseph became a slave of the Egyptian officer Potiphar (Gen. 39:1), but this slave's fortunes changed dramatically. Joseph's rise to power saw him become first the overseer of Potiphar's house (39:4), but eventually a ruler over all of Egypt, second in power to the Egyptian pharaoh himself (41:39–43). One possible setting for the Joseph story is the period when the Hyksos people ruled Egypt.

Before the Hyksos arrived, Egypt had been a united country. Sometime after the 12th Dynasty the country began to fragment. Various rulers set up their own dynasties over portions of Egypt and ruled at the same time. The 13th Dynasty (1786–1633 B.C.) established a new capital at Thebes, while the 14th Dynasty (1786–1602 B.C.) consisted of several rulers in the Delta who proclaimed themselves "kings."

The political upheaval made Egypt ripe for the invasion of the Hyksos people, who subjugated the country and placed their own capital at Avaris in the Delta region. The Hyksos dynasty lasted more than a century (1648–1540 B.C.). The ethnic background of the Hyksos is one reason for setting the Joseph story during this period. These invaders were a mixture of Semitic and Asiatic peoples. In an Egypt ruled by such foreigners, it is possible that someone such as Joseph, himself being Semitic and foreign, could rise from a servant to a position of high office.

Storehouses (Gen. 41:48)

The Egyptians maintained large stone storehouses, primarily for grain. This protected them from famine and also helped stabilize prices. The granaries were often associated with temples. The ruler was regarded as divine, and the department devoted to grain was one of the most important in the fundamentally religious government of Egypt.

The Twelve Tribes of Israel (Gen. 46:1–27)

Each tribe was a social group composed of many clans and families, together with their dependents, outside the ties of blood kinship, who had become associated with the group through covenant, marriage, adoption, or slavery. Israel was an association of twelve tribes, designated by the names of the ancestors from whom they were descended (Deut. 27:12–13; Ezek. 48:1–35). Jacob, whose name was later changed to Israel (Gen. 32:28), was the father of 12 sons (Gen. 29:31—30:24; 35:18, 22–26). The sons of Jacob, excluding Levi and Joseph but including Joseph's sons, Manasseh and Ephraim, were the ancestors of the later tribal units in the nation's history. The development of the tribes begins with the events described in the Book of Exodus.

The sons of Jacob, together with their father and families, migrated to Egypt to join their brother Joseph and to escape the famine in Canaan (Gen. 46:1–27; Ex. 1:16). They grew significantly in number for the next 400 years (Gen. 15:13; Ex. 12:40). Then the descendants of Jacob's sons left Egypt in the Exodus under the leadership of Moses. They were joined by many who were not descendants of Jacob. The Exodus people are thus characterized as a "mixed multitude" (Ex. 12:38; Num. 11:4).

The number of dependents, those not of blood kinship, continued to increase as the tribal units developed. Moses' father-in-law, whose clan joined Israel in the wilderness, was a Midianite (Num. 10:29). Caleb, who figured prominently in the conquest of the land of Canaan, was called a Kenizzite (Josh. 14:13–14). Later the Calebites were given an inheritance among the tribe of Judah (Josh. 15:13).

The tribal confederation with its institutions reached its highest form during the period recorded in the books of Joshua and Judges. The rigidity of Israel's tribal structure did weaken somewhat with the establishment of the united kingdom under David and Solomon. But tribal organization and association was maintained throughout later biblical history (Luke 2:36; Acts 4:36; Rom. 11:1; Heb. 7:14).

JACOB IN EGYPT (LATE EXODUS)

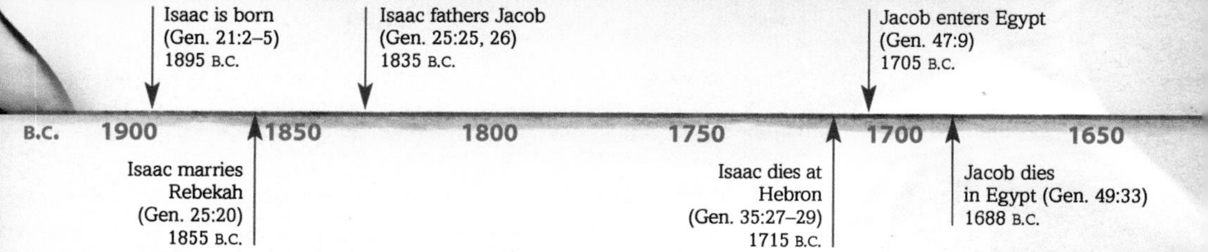

Jacob Enters Egypt (Genesis 47:1—50:26)

Jacob's journey from Canaan to Egypt is summarized in Gen. 47:27: "So Israel dwelt in the land of Egypt...and multiplied exceedingly." This event marks the move of the Israelite people from Canaan, the Promised Land, to Egypt, the land of slavery. As such, it became part of Israel's basic statement of faith. Israel's faith started with the retelling of her historical origins, often beginning with Jacob's descent to Egypt. For instance, the ritual retelling of Deut. 26:5–9 begins: "My father was a Syrian, about to perish, and he went down to Egypt."

Jacob was 130 years old when he entered Egypt (Gen. 47:9). This figure is sometimes used to relate Abraham to the Israelite sojourn in Egypt. Abraham fathered Isaac when he was 100 years old (Gen. 21:5). Isaac fathered Jacob 60 years later (Gen. 25:26). Adding the numbers makes a passing of 290 years between Abraham's birth and this entry into Egypt (100 + 60 + 130 = 290).

THE RISE OF A UNIFIED PEOPLE

1500—1200 B.C.

The Exodus marks the beginning of Israel as a people. The patriarchs were, at most, an extended family, rather than a people. More such families undoubtedly moved to Egypt either because of famine or because of the migrations of peoples all over the Middle East. When a dynasty of strong pharaohs returned to power, these "foreigners" were oppressed and put to forced labor. The escape of a large band of these slaves under the leadership of Moses was a new beginning for the Israelites. Their experiences in the years of wandering in the wilderness—along with the great covenant ceremony at Mount Sinai—began to mold them into both a distinct religious entity and the nucleus of a nation. Their entry into Canaan and the struggle to maintain a separate identity in the face of cultural and religious temptations strengthened their sense of being a people.

ARCHAEOLOGY AND THE PAST

The oldest written records of significance for Palestine come from the Late Bronze Age (1500–1200 B.C.). The Amarna letters were part of the royal archive of Amenhotep IV, also known as Akhenaten (1352–1336 B.C.). Akhenaten was more interested in religious reform than in foreign policy. He abandoned Egyptian activity in Palestine to pursue the introduction of monotheism, based on the worship of the sun god Aten.

Akhenaten's disinterest in administering the Egyptian empire resulted in turmoil and civil war in Palestine, and the Amarna letters reflect this disorder. Without the stabilizing influence of the Egyptian military, the kings of the city-states were increasing their own power at the expense of their neighbors. There were also raids by a people called the Habiru. Many of the Amarna letters appeal to the pharaoh for aid against the incursions of these Habiru.

Other writings from the Late Bronze Age reflect a time of Egyptian power. An inscription of Merenptah, who ruled Egypt from 1213 to 1203 B.C., includes the first mention of Israel in Egyptian documents. Merenptah commemorates his victories over the Libyans and other foreigners, boasting that all the peoples of Asia had submitted. One line reads, "Israel is laid waste, his seed is not."

THE PEOPLES AND GROUPS

Early in this period, Egyptian armies marched through Palestine into Syria, where they clashed with the Hurrians of Mitanni (in modern Iraq). The greatest political accomplishment of the Hurrians was the Mitanni Empire, which ruled Assyria and lasted until the reign of Shalmaneser I of Assyria (1273–1244 B.C.). They were even more important culturally, with their writings found from Assyria to Asia Minor to Egypt.

Later in the Late Bronze Age, there were wars between Egyptians and the Hittites of Anatolia (modern Turkey). The Hittite Empire captured towns and regions, such as Ugarit and Amurru, from under Egypt's control. Hostilities with the Egyptians erupted again during the reign of Pharaoh Ramesses II (1279–1213 B.C.), who fought the Hittites to a stalemate in Syria and kept Palestine under Egyptian rule. Around 1200 B.C. the Hittite Empire collapsed, partly because of attacks by the "Sea Peoples" from the Aegean and the rise of Assyria.

Two ethnic or political groups played roles in Israel's history during the Late Bronze Age—the Midianites and Canaanites. The Midianites lived in northwest Arabia, along the Gulf of Aqaba. They were shepherds but also copper miners and traders. Moses fled to the land of Midian, where he married into the family of Jethro, a priest of Midian (Ex. 18). Much later, a related tribe of Midianites were involved in the Israelite worship of Baal of Peor (Num. 25:16–18). The incident led to hostilities between Israel and Midian during the time of Moses (Num. 31:1–8).

The Canaanites were the inhabitants of Palestine west of the Jordan at the time of Joshua's invasion. They are first mentioned in an inscription of Amenhotep II (1427–1400 B.C.), and also in the Amarna letters. Originally, the term probably applied either to a Hurrian military aristocracy or to a class of merchants. By the time of Joshua, the Canaanites were a mixed group of people. In the Old Testament the term "Canaanites" sometimes refers to all the people who lived west of Jordan. Other times the term is restricted to the Phoenicians who lived along the coast.

THE BIBLICAL LITERATURE

The biblical books of Exodus, Leviticus, Numbers, Deuteronomy, and Joshua relate the rise of the Israelites from slaves in Egypt to a unified people. The theme of these books is God's mighty acts on behalf of His people in the historical and political events of the Late Bronze Age. Though the focus of the biblical books is on God's activity, and the response of Israel to that activity, we still catch glimpses of the larger world of the Late Bronze Age.

Several pivotal events shaped Israel as a people. The Book of Exodus focuses on their escape from Egypt under the leadership of Moses and the making of the great covenant at Mount Sinai. The books of Leviticus and Numbers continue with the covenant, relating more divine instructions from Mount Sinai. Numbers also narrates the experiences the Israelites faced before coming to the Promised Land, most significantly the wilderness wanderings. Finally they were at the doorstep of Canaan. The Book of Deuteronomy is written as Moses' farewell speeches to the people of Israel. They would enter the land under a new generation of leaders, which is the story of the Book of Joshua.

EGYPT AND THE EXODUS

At last an Egyptian dynasty arose to expel the hated Hyksos rulers and begin the last great period of prosperity for ancient Egypt, the New Kingdom (c. 1550–1069 B.C.). Perhaps from a desire to keep all foreigners at bay, the kings of this time were more expansionist than were previous Egyptian dynasties. King Thutmose III (1479–1425 B.C.), for instance, expanded Egypt's boundaries through Palestine as far as the Euphrates River. These gains in Syria were soon challenged by an enemy from the north, the empire of the Hittites in Asia Minor.

One of Thutmose's descendants, Amenhotep IV (1352–1336 B.C.), is an especially remarkable New Kingdom ruler. Rejecting the many gods of Egyptian religion, this king worshiped one god, the sun god named Aten. He changed his own name to Akhenaten and built a new capital at Amarna. Letters found in the ruins of Amarna show that the city-states of Palestine were in varying degrees of rebellion during Akhenaten's reign. His religious reforms died when he did.

Another New Kingdom ruler, Ramesses II (1279–1213 B.C.), was especially notable for his many building projects. Egyptian sources suggest that Ramesses expanded the old Hyksos capital Avaris and renamed it "Raamses" after himself. The city became the royal residence for the 19th and 20th Dynasties. Ramesses reigned for more than 60 years, but his successors inherited a weaker Egypt and never equaled his glory.

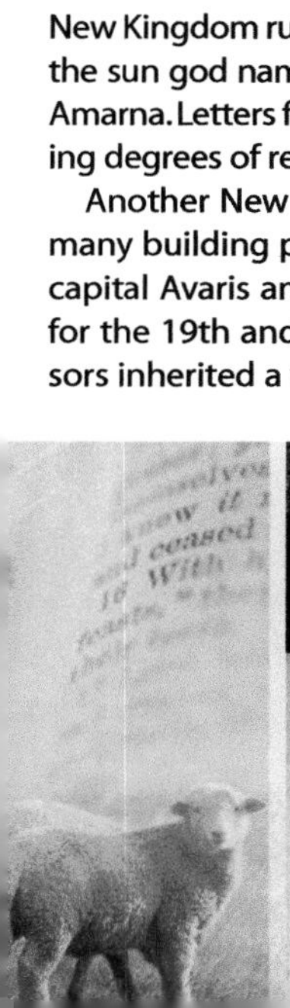

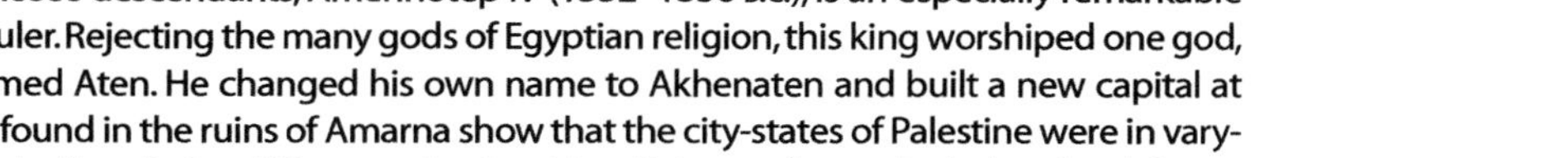

EPOCH THREE

Chronological Reading Guide

- ❑ Exodus 1:1—40:38
- ❑ Leviticus 1:1—27:34
- ❑ Numbers 1:1—36:13
- ❑ Deuteronomy 1:1—34:12
- ❑ Psalm 90

THE BOOK OF EXODUS

The Hebrews' exodus from bondage in Egypt is the defining event both in Israel's emergence as a nation and in the shape of that nation's faith. The Book of Exodus devotes about equal space to the events and to the ensuing covenant. The first half (chs. 1—19) tells the history, from Moses' birth through the Exodus itself up to Israel's climactic encounter with God on Mount Sinai. The second half of the book (chs. 20—40) consists mostly of God's instructions to His covenant people—both general, like the Ten Commandments, and specific, like the instructions for building the tabernacle, Israel's tent shrine.

It is no denial of the divine origin of this covenant to note how it is couched in the language and customs of its day. For instance, it is interesting to note that the covenant's emphasis on one God was preceded by the failed reforms of Akhenaten. Or again, the pattern for the giving of the covenant in Ex. 19—24 follows a very common Hittite treaty pattern, beginning with a prologue and continuing with a list of expectations (chs. 20—23), then concluding with a ratification ceremony (ch. 24).

Moses in Midian (Ex. 2:16—6:30)

Within the official boundaries of the Egyptian empire, in Palestine and the arid Sinai Peninsula, lived a diverse group called the Midianites. These people appeared sometime around the 13th century B.C. and were known as traders (cf. Gen. 37:36) and metalworkers. Less clearly known is their religion, but there is some evidence that they worshiped in tent shrines in the desert. The tabernacle that Moses was commanded to build (Ex. 26) may be related to Midianite practices. Moses' father-in-law (Ex. 2:18) was, after all, a priest of Midian.

OUTLINE OF EXODUS

I. The Need for Redemption from Egypt	**1:1–22**
A. Israel's Rapid Multiplication	1:1–7
B. Israel's Severe Affliction	1:8–14
C. Israel's Planned Destruction	1:15–22
II. The Preparation of the Leaders	**2:1—4:31**
A. Moses Is Saved	2:1–10
B. Moses Avenges a Wrong	2:11–22
C. Israel Calls upon God	2:23–25
D. God Calls Moses	3:1—4:17
E. Moses Accepts the Call	4:18–26
F. Israel Accepts Moses as Deliverer	4:27–31
III. The Redemption of Israel	**5:1—15:21**
A. Confrontation through Word	5:1—6:9
B. Confrontation through Miracles	6:10—7:13
C. Confrontation through Plagues	7:14—11:10
D. Redeemed by Blood	12:1—13:16
E. Redeemed by God's Power	13:17—15:21
IV. The Preservation of Israel	**15:22—18:27**
A. Preserved from Thirst	15:22–27
B. Preserved from Hunger	16:1–36
C. Preserved from Thirst Again	17:1–7
D. Preserved from Defeat	17:8–16
E. Preserved from Chaos	18:1–27
V. Revelation of the Covenant	**19:1—40:38**
A. The Ten Commandments	19:1—20:21
B. Various Laws for the People	20:22—23:33
C. Establishment of the Covenant	24:1–18
D. Design for the Tabernacle	25:1—31:18
E. Israel Breaks the Covenant	32:1–35
F. Renewal of the Covenant	33:1—34:35
G. Construction of the Tabernacle	35:1—40:38

From Egypt to Midian to Egypt (Exodus 7:1—12:36)

The life of Moses is viewed by tradition in three periods. The first period, beginning with Moses' birth, ended abruptly when he was forced to flee Egypt. The Book of Exodus defines this time only as "when Moses was grown" (Ex. 2:11). However, Stephen's sermonic survey of Israel's history makes Moses "forty years old" at this time (Acts 7:23).

The second period, during which Moses found refuge in Midian, ended with Moses' return to Egypt, accompanied by Aaron. The Book of Exodus reports Moses to have been 80 years old when he and 83-year-old Aaron first approached Pharaoh (Ex. 7:7). Stephen's sermon agrees, placing the burning bush experience 40 years after Moses fled to Midian.

The last period of Moses' life ends, of course, with his death. That Moses was 80 when he stood before Pharaoh, is consistent both with his age of 120 when he died (Deut. 34:7) and with the 40 years of wandering in the wilderness (Num. 14:33–35).

EGYPT AND THE NEW KINGDOM

The Egyptian priest Manetho (c. 305–285 B.C.) describes the destructive invasion of Egypt by the Hyksos people, who seized control of Egypt and made Avaris, in the Delta region, their new capital.

Second Intermediate Period	**The Dynasties**
1786–1550 B.C.	13th–17th Dynasties. The weakening of the 13th Dynasty (1786–1633 B.C.) began a period in which rival dynasties vied for power.
1786–1602 B.C.	In the Delta several rulers proclaimed themselves "kings," representing the 14th Dynasty.
1648–1540 B.C.	The Hyksos dynasty controlled only Lower Egypt, while the kings of the Upper Nile Valley stood firm in their own local domains.

The New Kingdom	**The Dynasties**
1550–1069 B.C.	18th–20th Dynasties. The Egyptian kings Kamose and Ahmose I expelled the Hyksos from Egypt, beginning Egypt's "New Kingdom."
1550–1295 B.C.	18th Dynasty. Amenhotep I named himself after the god Amen or Amon. This universal god was linked with the sun god Re, and worshiped as Amon-Re.
1295–1186 B.C.	19th Dynasty. Seti I began new wars of conquest that pushed Egypt into Palestine, driving back the Hittites.
1186–1069 B.C.	20th Dynasty. Ramesses III fought off invasions by the Sea Peoples.

DUELING DEITIES: Magic and Magicians in Egypt (Ex. 7:11)

Throughout the ancient Near East magicians were important members of royal courts. Magic was a means by which power could be transferred from the gods to humans. Magicians were well-educated, literate persons, who had studied the incantations and actions that were needed to cause gods or demons to honor human requests. Their official services were needed for understanding the will of the gods, bringing down curses on treaty-breakers, or creating catastrophes for enemies.

Egypt's magical traditions are the best known to us of all the traditions of the ancient world. This is partly because other civilizations were impressed by the Egyptian traditions, but mostly because a wealth of their magical texts has survived in the desert. The Egyptian magical texts extend in time from the Pyramid Texts (3rd millennium B.C.) to the end of the Roman Empire, and include incantations, amulets, secret signs, certain geometric shapes, acrostic word patterns, and the names of famous persons.

In Exodus, Moses is presented as directing the plagues in the same manner as the Egyptians understood their magic to work. Pharaoh's magicians were unimpressed with Moses and his God until they were unable to do the same tricks through their magical arts. When they could not produce gnats, the Egyptians expressed their admiration for Moses with the words "This is the finger of God" (Ex. 8:18, 19), which quotes an actual Egyptian magical phrase. In this way they acknowledged that Moses' God was greater than their gods.

TIME CAPSULE	**1648 to 1525 B.C.**
1648–1540	Hyksos dynasty controls Lower Egypt
1633–1550	Egypt's 17th Dynasty rules at Thebes
1625	Chariots used by the Hittites
1600	Chariots introduced to the Nile valley
1600–1400	The zenith of the Minoan civilization
1595	Hittite king Mursilis ends Old Babylonian dynasty of Hammurabi
1550–1069	The New Kingdom in Egypt
1540	Ahmose I expels Hyksos from Egypt
1525–1504	Amenhotep I, pharaoh of Egypt

TWO DATES FOR THE EXODUS

Two dating schemes have been proposed for the Exodus from Egypt—an "early" date and a "late" date. The early scheme considers the 480 years of 1 Kin. 6:1 to be a precise note of time; the late scheme considers it to be a symbolic figure, not an actual one.

A 15th–Century Exodus

When: Approximately 1446 B.C.
Ruling Pharaoh: Thutmose III (1479–1425 B.C.)
Reasons: 1 Kin. 6:1 states that the Exodus occurred 480 years before Solomon began building the temple.
Solomon, who reigned from 970 to 930 B.C., began the temple in the 4th year of his reign (about 966 B.C.).
The Exodus would then have occurred 480 years before 966 B.C., placing it in 1446 B.C.

A 13th–Century Exodus

When: Approximately 1275 B.C.
Ruling Pharaoh: Ramesses II (1279–1213 B.C.)
Reasons: Ex. 1:11 states that the Hebrew slaves built the supply cities, Pithom and Ramses.
Egyptian sources suggest that Pharaoh Ramesses renamed the city of Ramses after himself.
The 480 years of 1 Kin. 6:1 is a symbolic number, representing 12 generations of 40 years each.

Where Was the Red Sea? (Ex. 10:19)

The Hebrew slaves escaped Egypt by way of the Red Sea. In antiquity this Red Sea also included the Gulf of Suez and the Gulf of Aqaba, the two gulfs into which it splits. The precise location of the Exodus crossing has been debated by scholars since antiquity without any agreement on a possible site.

The Red Sea is called *Yam Suph* in Hebrew, which is often translated as "sea of reeds." The Sea of Reeds would refer to the marshes where bulrushes or reeds grow plentifully. In a number of Old Testament passages, *Yam Suph* is associated with the Gulf of Aqaba, which marked the southern tip of King Solomon's empire (1 Kin. 9:26; Ex. 23:31). Yet in other passages *Yam Suph* probably refers to the Gulf of Suez, since the narrative indicates a body of water bordering on Egypt (Ex. 10:19; 13:18). The majority of scholars favor a location somewhere in the eastern Delta region of Egypt, but the true location is still undetermined.

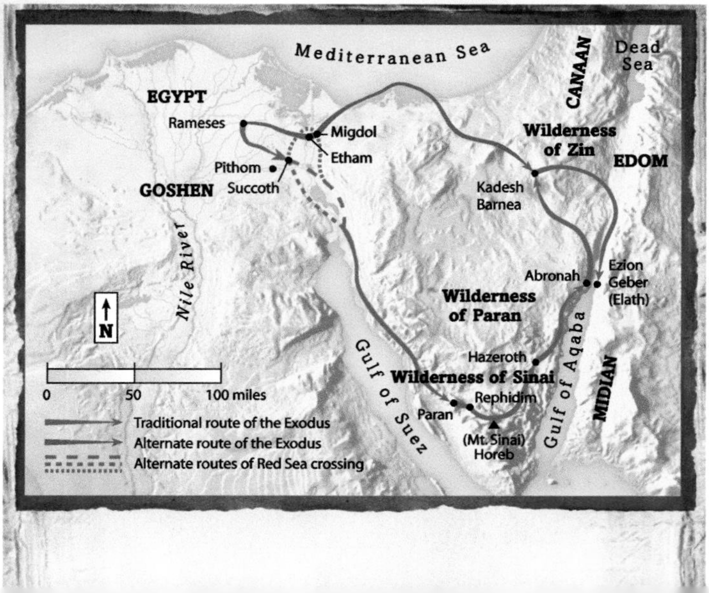

The Route of the Exodus
Two routes have been proposed for the exodus of the Israelites from Egypt. A northern route moves east from Rameses along the northern Sinai coast. The southern route passes Succoth, continuing to the lower region of the Sinai Peninsula.

ORIGINS OF THE PASSOVER MEAL (Ex. 12:8)
Certain elements of the Passover ritual can be traced to ceremonies that celebrated the new agricultural year in farming cultures. These elements include a sacrifice to be eaten by the community, the eating of the new crop, bitter herbs, unleavened bread, thanksgiving for not dying during the period between harvests, and, of course, a new start. The Israelites would have known about these celebrations from farming in the Nile Delta.

God revealed through Moses a new meaning for the Israelite meal. Now the feast would symbolize salvation from Egyptian slavery and from death. To this day the Passover Seder is celebrated by Jewish families throughout the world. It is prepared and eaten according to the rules of Ex. 12. As the meal is eaten, the story of Passover is related—not as something which happened long ago to ancestors, but always as happening now. It is now that God brings every person who partakes of the meal to freedom and to salvation. The feast establishes identity: we are the people of God, because God did these things for us. Anticipating the coming of God's Messiah, Jewish tradition added to the service a place at the table for Elijah should the prophet come "this year" to proclaim the advent of the Messiah.

Where the Gods Live: Sacred Mountains (Ex. 19:2, 3)

Where heaven and earth met, humans and deities could come together. On the physical landscape of the ancient world, this meant mountains. Since ancient people thought deities actually lived on the peak of a sacred mountain, they built temples or altars on or near the mountain in honor of the gods.

So it was all over the Near East. The Canaanites and Phoenicians believed their gods lived on actual mountains near their cities. At Ugarit, El lived on Mount Zaphon. In Ex. 19:20, Israel's God Yahweh lives on Mount Sinai. Later, the Judeans believed Yahweh took up His residence on Mount Zion in Jerusalem, while the Samaritans said He lived on Mount Gerizim near Samaria. In the flat river valleys of Mesopotamia, worshipers of various deities built their own mountains, called ziggurats.

The appearance of the deity (called "theophany") at the sacred mountain often was accompanied by thunder, lightning, earthquakes, clouds, loud noises, lesser deities, and terror. Many of these characteristics are present in the description of God coming down on Sinai (Ex. 19:16–19). Usually only priests were willing to risk experiencing such presence of the god. The actual appearance of the deity itself was thought to be dangerous to people who had not properly prepared themselves. The people of Israel were carefully prepared for the visit of God to the mountain (Ex. 19:10–13). Despite preparations, they were too terrified to actually meet God, and so Moses served as intermediary between God and the people (Ex. 19:23–25; 20:18–21).

The Code of Hammurabi shares parallels with scriptural laws recorded in Exodus, Leviticus, and Deuteronomy.

The Code of Hammurabi (Ex. 22:16,17)
Babylon's king Hammurabi (1792–1750 B.C.) is best known for his law code. The Code of Hammurabi contains 282 laws and has numerous parallels with Scripture. Hammurabi did not create these laws; rather, they appear to be a collection of diverse traditions.

The format of the Code of Hammurabi shows a similarity with laws in Exodus, Leviticus, and Deuteronomy. Both the Code of Hammurabi and the Covenant Code, found in Ex. 20:22—23:33, have a series of laws structured in an "if...then" format. These laws begin with the word "if," introducing a description of a potentially criminal situation. The format continues with the word "then," offering a description of the penalty. This format or style of law is often called case law since its format describes particular cases or situations.

The similarities of these two codes (and others) show there was a widespread legal tradition in the 2nd millennium B.C. In fact a number of situations mentioned in the Hammurabi code are virtually duplicated in the Mosaic code, often with different penalties.

MOSES AND THE PROMISED LAND (EARLY EXODUS)

B.C. 1550 — 1500 — 1450 — 1400 — 1350

- Moses is born 1526 B.C.
- Moses flees Egypt (Ex. 2:15; Acts 7:23) 1486 B.C.
- Caleb and others spy out the land (Num. 13:2, 3; Josh. 14:7) 1445 B.C.
- Aaron and Moses appear before Pharaoh (Ex. 7:7) 1446 B.C.
- Moses leads the Israelites from Egypt (Ex. 12:31, 37) 1446 B.C.
- Aaron dies on Mount Hor near Kadesh Barnea (Num. 33:38) 1406 B.C.
- Moses gives his final speeches on the plains of Moab (Deut. 1:3) 1406 B.C.
- Moses dies and is buried in Moab (Deut. 34:5, 6) 1406 B.C.
- Caleb receives Hebron as an inheritance (Josh. 14:7, 10, 13) 1400 B.C.

Calves, Cows, & Bulls Representing the Divine (Ex. 32:1–4)
The stories of Aaron molding the golden calf (Ex. 32:1–4) and Jeroboam building the golden calves for his new temples at Bethel and Dan (1 Kin. 12:28–31) are similar. But why make a calf? Cattle were common images for deities in the ancient Near East. In Egypt, Hathor, a very popular goddess, was represented as a cow, as a woman with cow horns or ears or both, and as a human with a cow's head. The usual manner of depicting a male deity in Syria-Palestine was to represent him either as a bull or with some features of a bull—usually horns. In Babylon the bull images of Hadad lined the main processional street.

The golden calf was possibly the representation of a Canaanite deity. Both El or Baal are connected with bulls in the Ugaritic texts. No large images of cattle deities have been recovered from Syria-Palestine, but a number of small bull images from the time of the Israelite occupation of the land demonstrate that larger statues could likely have been realistically fashioned in standing positions.

Forbidden Religious Objects (Ex. 34:13)
Altars, sacred pillars, and wooden images appear in the Bible as a recurring group of banned religious objects (Ex. 34:13). All three were common in the religious world of Syria-Palestine, including Canaan.

Altars were used for making sacrifices to the god of the area. They were constructed where the deity was felt to be present, sometimes along with a temple, a shrine, or an open sanctuary. Many of the numerous ancient altars discovered in Palestine are carefully carved with stone horns on the four top corners. A depression was often carved around the outer top area to catch blood so that it could be ritually sprinkled on the altar itself, a standard sacrificial ritual.

Sacred pillars were standing slabs of stone, sometimes carved, which stood in religious centers as representatives of deities. Such cultic items dating from the 3rd millennium B.C. have been recovered from Syria-Palestine. The tops often were shaped into a curve, and sometimes a divine symbol was carved into one of the flat surfaces. They functioned as divine images.

The Hebrew *Asherim*, translated as "wooden images," were representations of the goddess Asherah. Because of the impermanence of wood and the lack of Old Testament descriptions, the form of the Asherim is uncertain. Some suggest these items were sacred trees or representations of sacred trees. Others suppose they were wooden objects made by humans, possibly poles or images. Since the Asherim stood for the goddess Asherah, it is understandable that the Judahites and Israelites were told to cut down, splinter, and burn them (Deut. 7:5; 12:3).

MOSES AND THE PROMISED LAND (LATE EXODUS)

- Moses is born 1355 B.C.
- Moses flees Egypt (Ex. 2:15; Acts 7:23) 1315 B.C.
- Aaron and Moses appear before Pharaoh (Ex. 7:7) 1275 B.C.
- Moses leads the Israelites from Egypt (Ex. 12:31, 37) 1275 B.C.
- Caleb and others spy out the land (Num. 13:2, 3; Josh. 14:7) 1274 B.C.
- Aaron dies on Mount Hor near Kadesh Barnea (Num. 33:38) 1235 B.C.
- Moses gives his final speeches on the plains of Moab (Deut. 1:3) 1235 B.C.
- Moses dies and is buried in Moab (Deut. 34:5, 6) 1235 B.C.
- Caleb receives Hebron as an inheritance (Josh. 14:7, 10, 13) 1229 B.C.

B.C. 1400 1350 1300 1250 1200

A THRONE FOR GOD (Ex. 37:1–9)
The ark of the covenant was an object that reminded the Israelites of the presence of God in their midst. Although some nomadic peoples used small traveling casks for worship, no ancient people had a sacred object that compares to Israel's large box with its heavy adornment and sculptured cherubim on the lid (Ex. 37:1–9).

There are various ideas as to what the ark represents, often relating to each other in meaning. It has been described as a container or chest, as a portable throne for Israel's God, or as an extension of God's presence.

The construction of the ark is described in the shape of a chest, measuring 45 inches long by 27 inches wide by 27 inches tall (Ex. 37:1). As such, it served as a container to hold items. Similar to the temple thrones of gods in Egypt and the foundation deposits of temples in Mesopotamia, the ark also bore the words of the deity: the tablets of the Ten Commandments. Other items contained within the ark were Aaron's rod and a jar of manna (Heb. 9:4).

As a portable throne the ark provided the place where God would "sit" in the presence of the Israelites. The cherubim on the ark (Ex. 37:7) were not images of God, but rather divine attendants. They represented the type of throne that seated rulers and deities along the eastern Mediterranean coast as far back as the 2nd millennium B.C. A king sitting upon a cherubim throne is pictured in the sarcophagus of Ahiram, king of Byblos in the 10th century B.C.

The ark was a symbol of the invisible presence of God. The possession of the ark in battle represented both the presence and the favor of God (1 Sam. 4:3–7). Its capture by the Philistines meant that the favor of God had been lost as well (1 Sam. 4:19–22).

THE BOOK OF LEVITICUS

Leviticus continues God's covenant instructions on Mount Sinai, begun in Ex. 20. The name "Leviticus" comes from the many laws and regulations of the book that concern the rights and duties of priests (who were of the tribe of Levi).

Certain clearly defined bodies of laws can be identified in the book. The first seven chapters prescribe the laws of sacrifices; chs. 11—15 distinguish between what is clean and unclean; ch. 16 describes the Day of Atonement; and the various laws of chs. 17—26 are unified by the distinct refrain "You shall be holy, for I the Lord your God am holy" (Lev. 19:2).

The entire Book of Leviticus is set in a relatively brief period of time. Only a month and a half passes between the erection of the tabernacle at Mount Sinai and the Hebrews' departure from Sinai. However, its content extends beyond this short month and a half in the wilderness. Many of the laws clearly pertain to a time after the Israelites had entered their land; for instance, the laws for planting fields and cleansing houses. Partly for this reason, some suggest that at least the current form of the book was actually composed later than its context would suggest, perhaps from several different law codes. Of course, those who accept the traditional attribution of the first five books of the Bible to Moses disagree and understand these passages simply as laws given for a future time.

The animal sacrifices described so carefully in Leviticus fit properly in the historical context of the book. Animal sacrifice was universal in ancient Near Eastern religion, so Israel's sacrifice of animals is hardly surprising. More striking, though, is the absolute prohibition against the equally common practice of child sacrifice (see Lev. 18:21).

OUTLINE OF LEVITICUS

I. The Laws of Approaching God	**1:1—17:16**
A. The Laws of Sacrifice	1:1—7:38
B. The Laws of the Priests	8:1—10:20
C. The Laws Regarding Purity	11:1—15:33
D. The Laws of National Atonement	16:1—17:16
II. The Laws of Sanctification	**18:1—27:34**
A. For the People	18:1—20:27
B. For the Priesthood	21:1—22:33
C. In Worship	23:1—24:23
D. In the Land of Canaan	25:1—26:46
E. Through Vows	27:1-34

Ritual Uncleanness (Lev. 5:2)

The uncleanness treated in Leviticus is ritual uncleanness. Being unclean in this sense, means to be excluded from normal participation in acts of religion. A person could become unclean by touching a corpse (Lev. 5:2), although this is not an immoral or sinful act. The offerings provided the means for removing uncleanness in this and other cases.

Animals That Carry Away Sin (Lev. 16:7–10)

The Day of Atonement, observed on the 10th day of the 7th month, was the most sacred event in the year (Lev. 16:29, 34). One of the rituals for this annual day of fasting involved the cleansing of the sanctuary with blood. This was the only time in the year when the high priest entered the Most Holy Place to appear before the mercy seat (16:11–17). The other ritual involved the sending away of the scapegoat (16:7–10, 20–22).

In the scapegoat ritual, the scapegoat was sent into the wilderness. First, however, the priest placed his hands on the goat and confessed the sins of his people. The ritual symbolized the "removal" or "taking away" of the people's sin (16:21, 22).

The general form of the scapegoat ritual, as described in Leviticus, is not unique to Israel. Rituals from Anatolia and Mesopotamia attempt to appease an angry deity by using animals to carry away a plague or other evil suffering. A Hittite text from the mid-2nd millennium B.C.outlines the ritual that a monarch should do in case there is pestilence in his land caused by fighting in enemy territory.

In the Israelite ritual two goats were used. One was designated for the Lord and offered as a sin offering (16:9). The other goat, the scapegoat, bore the people's iniquities (16:22). In this ritual Israel released a live animal to carry away impurities, as other cultures did to eliminate sicknesses or sorceries.

Seeking Divine Knowledge (Lev. 19:26)

Ancient people considered it important to know the will of the gods—on demand, if necessary. So there were specialists in the art of determining a deity's will through rituals or through the specialists' deep knowledge of the secret meaning of natural phenomena. Such specialized practices, which included divination and soothsaying, were aimed at foretelling the future.

Most of what we know about divination and soothsaying comes from Mesopotamia—Babylonia and Assyria. Mesopotamian prophecy was carried out by highly educated, trained priests. A number of tablets tell how they tried to read almost any natural occurrence to determine the will of the gods. Mesopotamian priests could also obtain particular information by performing sacrifices. Archaeologists have found large numbers of clay models of livers taken from sheep sacrificed for the purpose of divination. By reading the bumps on the liver the priests could determine the answers to questions. The answers were then recorded on these clay models.

The peoples around Israel also sought knowledge from the gods. Sacred oracles from Syria-Palestine are found in Greek records such as *De Dea Syria* from the 2nd century A.D. These records indicate that answers to the questions of worshipers came through sounds from the openings of caves or from the flying of gods' statues (which skeptics claimed were rigged with ropes).

The Israelites themselves were forbidden to divine the will of God through "divination or soothsaying" (Lev. 19:26). They were allowed the oracular items called Urim and Thummim (Deut. 33:8; 1 Sam. 14:41), but for the Israelites the divine will would be disclosed by God through vision, dream, or prophet, and the Israelite worshiper was free to petition God for such revelation.

TIME CAPSULE	1504 to 1446 B.C.
1504–1492	Thutmose I, pharaoh of Egypt
1500–1200	Late Bronze Age
1492–1479	Thutmose II, pharaoh of Egypt
1486	Moses flees Egypt (based on early Exodus)
1470–1425	Thutmose III, pharaoh of Egypt
1450	Earliest Egyptian shadow clock
1446	Moses leads exodus from Egypt (based on early Exodus)
1446–1406	The 40 years of wilderness wandering (based on early Exodus)

Israel's Feasts (Lev. 23:1—24:23)

In addition to the Sabbath (Lev. 23:3), Lev. 23 describes seven sacred festivals of the Hebrew calendar that were observed before the Babylonian exile. These feasts were occasions for nationwide gatherings that called the people to public worship.

Passover (23:5) and the *Feast of Unleavened Bread* (23:6–8) occurred in Abib (also called Nisan), the 1st month (March-April) of the sacred year. Combined they were one of Israel's three annual pilgrimage festivals for which every adult male was required to present himself at the tabernacle, and later, the temple. Passover may have been celebrated for one day at the beginning of the week-long Feast of Unleavened Bread, as it is in modern Judaism.

Firstfruits (23:9–21) was celebrated twice during the year as an expression of gratitude to God for His provision in the harvest. The first celebration occurred on the day following the Sabbath at the time of the Feast of Unleavened Bread. This fell during the barley harvest, sometime between the 16th and 22nd days of the 1st month (Abib). The second celebration occurred 50 days later during the Feast of Weeks.

The *Feast of Weeks* (23:15–22), also known as *Harvest* (Ex. 23:16), occurred 50 days after the offering of firstfruits at the barley harvest. Held in connection with the wheat harvest, this one-day celebration during the 3rd month (Sivan) involved the firstfruits observation as well as other sacrifices. It was the second festival with required attendance at the temple.

The *Feast of Trumpets* (23:23–25) was the first of three holy days of the 7th month (Tishri). It was a sacred celebration of the new civil year, calling attention to judgment for sin and the need for penitence and forgiveness.

The *Day of Atonement* (23:26–32) was the second holy day of the 7th month. On this day sacrifice was made for the sin of the whole nation; thus, it was a time of true repentance and faith preparing for the Feast of Tabernacles.

The *Feast of Tabernacles* (23:33–36; or *Booths*, vv. 39–43), the third holy day of the 7th month, was celebrated at the end of the grape harvest in September-October. Also known as *Ingathering* (Ex. 23:16), it was a time for great joy when all harvests were completed. It was also the third feast requiring a pilgrimage to Jerusalem.

The Sabbath Years and Year of Jubilee (Lev. 25:1—27:34)

Every 7th year was the Sabbath Year, in which the land was to lie fallow (Lev. 25:4). Among other things this practice would prevent soil depletion and the subsequent impoverishment of the farmer. Although people might eat such produce in the fields (25:6, 7, 12), their regular meals were to come from the excess of the previous years (25:21).

Every 50th year was the Year of Jubilee (Lev. 25:11–13). The provisions of this sacred time were intended to maintain economic equality and prevent the concentration of wealth in the hands of a few. In the Jubilee year, if property were not already redeemed, it was to be restored to the original owner (25:25–28). This prevented the creation of great hereditary estates that would have reduced the families of small landholders to the status of serfs.

The concept of the Jubilee year in Lev. 25 bears a general similarity to the suspension of debts, which was a widespread phenomenon in the Old Babylonian period (c. 2017–1595 B.C.). While the Old Babylonian peoples lived a few centuries before Israel inhabited Canaan, they too were concerned about the equitable distribution of land and the resultant wealth.

An Old Babylonian literary text (in the form of a letter) describes the conduct of judges during the suspension of debts on behalf of the sun god Shamash. The judges of two city-states, Babylon and nearby Sippar, met at Sippar to read the lawsuits of Sippar citizens. Also to be read were the sale documents for fields, houses, and orchards, which became invalid during the suspension of debts (the jubilee).

In both cultures there was an awareness that the accumulation of land could result in the oppression of those who were socially and economically weak. In the Old Babylonian letter, an individual who had been subsequently wronged wrote to the officials, asking that "the weak not be handed over to the strong in the presence of my lord, and for the strong not to oppress the weak." Israel's God Yahweh included a command amongst the stipulations of the Jubilee year: "you shall not oppress one another" (25:14, 17).

THE BOOK OF NUMBERS

In the Hebrew Bible, this book is entitled "In the Wilderness." The name "Numbers" comes from the Greek translation of the Old Testament and refers specifically to the census figures given in two census reports: Num. 1:2–46 and 26:2–51.

The content of the Book of Numbers is diverse, moving back and forth between lists and laws and narratives, making it hard to identify any single outline or structure. The book begins in the same vein as Leviticus, with more divine instructions from Mount Sinai, still stressing priestly matters. These laws conclude in ch. 10, and the Israelites set out for the Promised Land.

Israel needed organization in order to reach that "land flowing with milk and honey," and God instructed Moses to take a census (Num. 1:2) so that the people would be organized both for travel and for warfare. This first census took place in the 2nd month of the 2nd year of the Exodus, either 1445 or 1274 B.C., depending on an early or late Exodus dating. In that same month and year, Moses and the people departed from Sinai (Num. 10:11–13).

The census numbers are surprisingly large, and interpreters have often been puzzled by them. For instance, how could 603,550 fighting men (Num. 1:45, 46) be intimidated by the tiny nation of Edom (Num. 20:14–21)? To answer such questions, many have noted that the Hebrew word for "thousand" is the same as the word for "clan." Understood that way, the numbers would be considerably lower.

The narratives of Num. 10—25 take up where those of Exodus leave off and in many ways parallel the accounts of Israel's grumbling against God in Ex. 16; 17. Indeed, the people appear even more dissatisfied in Numbers. In the end, God decrees that this complaining generation, including Moses himself, would not enter the Promised Land.

OUTLINE OF NUMBERS

I. Preparation to Inherit the Promised Land	**1:1—10:10**
A. The Organization of Israel	1:1—4:49
B. The Sanctification of Israel	5:1—10:10
II. Failures of the Old Generation	**10:11—25:18**
A. The Failure En Route to Kadesh	10:11—12:16
B. The Climactic Failure at Kadesh	13:1—14:45
C. The Failure in the Wilderness	15:1—19:22
D. The Failure En Route to Moab	20:1—25:18
III. Preparation of the New Generation	**26:1—36:13**
A. The Reorganization of Israel	26:1—27:23
B. The Regulations of Sacrifice and Vows	28:1—30:16
C. The Conquest and Division of Israel	31:1—36:13

CENSUS (NUM. 1:2)

A census is an official count of a population and is usually understood as an assertion of government power. Frequently its purpose is taxation. In Num. 1:2 it is a means of raising an army. By 1800 B.C. the city of Mari on the Euphrates River had a military census in its archives.

ORDEALS (NUM. 5:17–28)

An ordeal is a way of deciding whether a person is innocent or guilty. Whether the person is harmed or safe under a particular trial is supposed to reveal guilt or innocence. Ordeals were common in the ancient Middle East. The Bible describes only one ordeal (Num. 5:17–28). In it, the punishment as well as the determination of guilt is referred to God (5:21, 22, 27).

TIME CAPSULE  **1406 to 1350 B.C.**

1406	Israelites reach the plains of Moab (based on early Exodus)
1406	Aaron and Moses die (early Exodus)
1405	Joshua leads Israelite conquest of Canaan (early Exodus)
1400–1330	Nuzi tablets illuminate patriarchal customs
1400	Population of Egypt is about 4 million
1400	Population of Canaan is about 200,000
1363–1328	Ashur-uballit I is first ruler called "king of Assyria"
1352	Amenhotep IV introduces monotheism to Egypt
1350	Abdi-Hepa, king of Jerusalem, writes to Pharaoh Amenhotep IV in Egypt

Canaan Before the Conquest (Num. 13:1–33)

From Kadesh Barnea the Israelites made their first attempt to penetrate the land of Canaan (Num. 13:17–20). Before the arrival of the Israelites, Canaan was divided between dozens of small, relatively independent city-states, each with its own king. After the conquests of the Egyptian pharaoh Thutmose I (1504–1492 B.C.), these Canaanite city-states were officially provinces of Egypt, but as letters from Palestine to Pharaoh Akhenaten show, Egyptian control was not always very firm.

Many of the Canaanite peoples were of Amorite descent, as were the Israelites themselves, but later migrations had brought other ethnic groups into the land. Thus the Bible's frequent lists of the peoples to be conquered reflect a genuine ethnic mix. Nevertheless, the Bible often uses the term "Amorite" (or sometimes "Canaanite") in a general way, to refer to all or any of the peoples, nations, or tribes living in Palestine.

The city-states within Canaan were established and comparatively strong, while those to the east of the Jordan River were newer and weaker. Thus it makes sense that Israel established its control first in the east.

Israel in the Wilderness (Num. 14:1—20:13)

The story continues through the Israelites' tragic refusal at Kadesh Barnea to enter the Promised Land and through the consequent 40 years of wandering in the wilderness (Num. 14:33–35). The Book of Numbers describes the Israelites' journey from Sinai to Kadesh Barnea and then on to the plains of Moab; however, it reports almost nothing about the 40 years of wandering.

These gaps in the historical record arise because Numbers is not intended to be a history of the Hebrew people. It is a record of the faithfulness of God. Despite the failures of everyone, from the least of the people to Moses himself, God is faithful to His original promise to Abraham and his descendants. This does not mean that individuals escape the consequences of their sins, only that God's redemptive purposes in the world cannot be thwarted.

Thus the stagnant 40 years while the people were simply waiting are omitted as insignificant. Only the events occurring at the beginning and the end of the 40 years are mentioned: the Israelites' defeat when they tried to enter the land on their own strength (Num. 14:45), and their request for permission to pass through Edom (Num. 20:14). Between these events are only various laws and a few stories of the disobedience of key leaders.

THE WILDERNESS YEARS (EARLY EXODUS)

Thutmose III becomes pharaoh of Egypt 1479 B.C.

Tabernacle is finished, 1st month (Ex. 40:17) 1445 B.C.

Israelites cross the Jordan and celebrate Passover (Josh. 4:19; 5:10) 1405 B.C.

B.C. 1500 1475 1450 1425 1400

Exodus from Egypt, 1st month (Ex. 12:2, 31) 1446 B.C.

Israelites arrive at Mount Sinai, 3rd month (Ex. 19:1) 1446 B.C.

Israelites observe the Passover, 1st month (Num. 9:1–5) 1445 B.C.

Israelites depart from Mount Sinai, 2nd month (Num. 10:11, 12) 1445 B.C.

Israelites reach the plains of Moab (Num. 22:1; 33:48) 1406 B.C.

A Quick Cure for Snakebite (NUM. 21:4–9)

The bronze serpent on a pole that Moses made in the wilderness functioned as a cure for venomous snakebites (Num. 21:4–9). Scholars have suggested three explanations for what the people of Israel may have understood concerning this serpent.

One suggestion is that the image of the fiery serpent, representing the actual snake that bit the victim, was presented as a way of removing the poison from the snakebite. Magic amulets or charms for warding off and then curing illnesses and poisons were used everywhere in the ancient Near East. A number of copper and bronze serpent figures have been recovered, showing that the practice was widespread.

A second possibility is that the object symbolized God's power over the snakes. The "glance" toward the object would have been a plea or prayer to God for help. The bronze serpent was only an aid to the prayer, while the cure would have come from God.

Yet a third suggestion supposes the bronze serpent to have been an intermediary between God and the people. In the ancient Near East, the highest god of a pantheon could create new deities for specific purposes. The Israelites may have understood the bronze serpent as a lesser divine being created expressly to cure their particular kind of snakebites. Among the mythological texts of Ugarit (13th century B.C.) is the Legend of Keret. In this story the god El creates the goddess Shatiqatu solely to cure King Keret from an illness no other deity could handle.

This third understanding possibly explains what happened later as the bronze serpent was incorporated into the Israelite worship of God. It had been created by Moses and had been part of the religious world of Israel and Judah since before the settlement in Canaan. But by the time of Hezekiah (715–686 B.C.), Judahites worshiped it as Nehushtan (2 Kin. 18:4), possibly considering it a minor deity. The people's devotion to the bronze serpent was condemned by Hezekiah, who had it destroyed.

THE WILDERNESS YEARS (LATE EXODUS)

Ramesses II becomes pharaoh of Egypt 1279 B.C.

Tabernacle is finished, 1st month (Ex. 40:17) 1274 B.C.

Israelites reach the plains of Moab (Num. 22:1; 33:48) 1235 B.C.

B.C. 1300 1275 1250 1225 1200

Exodus from Egypt, 1st month (Ex. 12:2, 31) 1275 B.C.

Israelites arrive at Mount Sinai, 3rd month (Ex. 19:1) 1275 B.C.

Israelites observe the Passover, 1st month (Num. 9:1–5) 1274 B.C.

Israelites depart from Mount Sinai, 2nd month (Num. 10:11, 12) 1274 B.C.

Israelites cross the Jordan and celebrate Passover (Josh. 4:19; 5:10) 1234 B.C.

Balaam: Prophet for Hire (Num. 22:5, 6)

Balaam son of Beor is the famous prophet of Num. 22—24 whose services were requested by Balak, king of Moab. The Israelites were crossing through Moab at the time, and Balak was uncomfortable with such a large group of people in his land. So he called on the prophet to curse the Israelites in the name of God.

Normally a ruler would call on his own professional court prophets for such an undertaking. The blessing or cursing of neighboring kingdoms was standard duty for a court prophet. In contrast, prophets-for-hire were generally viewed unfavorably as unscrupulous persons who would say whatever their employer wished to hear. Nevertheless, Balak believed himself to be in sufficient danger to send for a famous and powerful prophet.

In the biblical traditions of Num. 22—24, Balaam is presented both favorably and unfavorably. Balaam, intending to keep his contract with Balak, attempted to curse the Israelites, but God kept him from doing so, insisting that Balaam bless them instead. In this way Balaam was a true prophet even in spite of himself and so, perhaps, was worthy of his fame. In a separate tradition (Num. 31:8, 16), Balaam is held responsible for the Israelite apostasy at Peor and reported to have been killed by Israel.

An 8th-century B.C. inscription from Jordan confirms that Balaam was a renowned prophet at the time of Judah's and Israel's monarchies. The text, found at Tell Deir 'Alla, displays a heavenly pantheon and tells how the prophet Balaam was called by the gods in the night through a vision or dream to witness to the divine will (see Num. 22:20). Thus Balaam's reliability as a prophet was remembered and recorded not only in the Bible, but also by the devotees who inscribed the Tell Deir 'Alla walls.

ISRAEL'S SACRED TIMES

Sabbath	Every 7th day was a solemn rest from all work. *Ex. 20:8–11; 31:12–17; Lev. 23:3; Deut. 5:12–15*
Sabbath Year	Every 7th year was designated a "year of release" to allow the land to lie fallow. *Ex. 23:10, 11; Lev. 25:1–7*
Year of Jubilee	The 50th year, which followed seven Sabbath years, was to proclaim liberty to those who were servants because of debt, and to return lands to their former owners. *Lev. 25:8–55; 27:17–24; Ezek. 46:17*
The New Moon	The 1st day of the Hebrew 29 or 30-day month was a day of rest, special sacrifices, and the blowing of trumpets. *Num. 28:11–15; Ps. 81:3*
Dedication (Lights or *Hanukkah*)	An 8-day feast in the 9th month (Chislev) commemorating the cleansing of the temple from defilement by Syria, and its rededication. *John 10:22*
Purim (Lots)	A feast on the 14th and 15th of the 12th month (Adar). The name comes from Babylonian *Pur*, meaning "lot." *Esth. 9:18–32*

THE BOOK OF DEUTERONOMY

Deuteronomy opens where the Book of Numbers closes: the Hebrew people are on the plains of Moab across the Jordan from Jericho (Num. 36:13; Deut. 1:1). The journey from Kadesh Barnea, which is reported to take 11 days (Deut. 1:2), was now over—after 40 years in the wilderness (1:3). Of the whole generation that refused to accept God's promise of the land of Canaan (Num. 14:26–32), only three persons were left: Joshua, Caleb, and Moses.

Except for a few introductory and concluding statements referring to Moses in the third person, the Book of Deuteronomy consists of Moses' speeches to the people of Israel on the eve of their crossing the Jordan River to capture the Promised Land. In his first speech (chs. 1—4) he reviews the history of the people's travels from Egypt to their current place on the eastern banks of the Jordan. His second speech (chs. 5—28) summarizes the commandments that God had given on Mount Sinai, including a second presentation of the Ten Commandments in ch. 5. The name "Deuteronomy," which is derived from Latin and means "second law," refers to this speech. The third speech (chs. 29—33) is Moses' farewell and includes exhortations, songs, and blessings.

The structure of the book can be compared to a common ancient Near Eastern treaty format, found especially among the Hittites (see "The Book of Exodus"). Such treaties began with a preamble and historical prologue (in Deuteronomy, the first speech), proceeded to the conditions and stipulations of the agreement (as in Moses' second speech), declared the blessings and curses that would result from obedience or disobedience (Deut. 27; 28), called on heavenly witnesses (31:28), and provided for the care of the treaty document (31:24–29). Again we see God and His representative speaking in language and forms that would have been familiar to the original ancient Israelite audience.

The huge influence of Deuteronomy on the rest of the Old Testament is indisputable. Its highly distinct style appears throughout the historical books and in several of the Prophets, and it was very probably the book discovered in the temple that prompted the reforms of King Josiah (2 Kin. 22). Some scholars accept Moses as the author while others do not (particularly the account of Moses' death in ch. 34). Nevertheless, even those who consider the earlier books of Genesis through Numbers to be carefully edited composites from different sources agree on the fundamental unity of Deuteronomy.

OUTLINE OF DEUTERONOMY

I. Moses' First Speech	**1:1—4:43**
A. Preamble of the Covenant	1:1–5
B. Historical Review of God's Acts	1:6—4:43
II. Moses' Second Speech	**4:44—26:19**
A. Introduction to the Law of God	4:44–49
B. Explanation of the Covenant Stipulations	5:1—11:32
C. Explanation of the Additional Laws	12:1—26:19
III. Moses' Third Speech	**27:1—34:12**
A. Confirming the Covenant	27:1—28:68
B. Establishing the Covenant	29:1—30:20
C. Changing the Covenant Mediator	31:1—34:12

TIME CAPSULE  **1323 to 1250 B.C.**

1323–1295	Horemhab, pharaoh of Egypt
1315	Moses flees Egypt (based on late Exodus)
1279–1213	Ramesses II, pharaoh of Egypt
1275	Moses leads exodus from Egypt (based on late Exodus)
1275–1235	The 40 years of wilderness wandering (based on late Exodus)
1274	Ramesses II suffers defeat against the Hittites, both sides using chariots
1273–1244	Shamaneser I of Assyria boasts of conquering the Hittites, Arameans, and Mittanni
1250	Hittite letter mentions the iron blade of dagger

How Is an Idol a God? (Deut. 5:8, 9)

The prohibition of Deut. 5:8, 9 reflects a world where bowing down to idols meant worshiping not just images, but deities. Representations of gods in human, animal, or abstract forms were everywhere in the ancient Near East. Scattered from Egypt through Syria-Palestine and throughout Mesopotamia were local temples housing these images.

Beliefs differed as to whether or not gods were really there in the statues. In Egypt the gods were understood to be always in heaven above the human world, yet always in the images as well. The statues were considered to be the body of the god into which the presence of the deity entered. For this reason the body was clothed, bathed, and fed as one would care for a ruler. Since heavenly deities were invisible, the statues were normally kept in the dark, inner room of the temples away from the eyes of the people. Except for feast days when the image was brought out on procession, only the attending priests were allowed into the image's presence.

In Mesopotamia the understanding of images was slightly different. The image was considered only wood, stone, or metal as long as it was being fashioned. However, once it was set up in the temple, a lengthy ritual called "opening the mouth" changed the nature of the image. Through this religious ritual the deity supposedly entered the statue so that the idol became the god and, at that point, could receive praise, bestow blessings, and grant favors. The image was understood to be a gift of the god who dwelt within it. Therefore, any image that was looted in warfare was taken as absolute proof that the favor of the deity had passed to the victors.

In contrast to the Egyptians and Mesopotamians, Israel's worship was to be imageless. The commandment in Deut. 5:8, 9 condemns the fashioning of any image: "any likeness of anything." Moreover, the commandment even forbids making an image of the God of Israel.

Pharaoh, King of Egypt (Deut. 7:8)

Although the term "Pharaoh" is well known from Scripture, it was not the most common designation used by Egyptians for their monarch before the New Kingdom period (c. 1550 B.C.). The Egyptian term for "Pharaoh" means literally the "Great House." Originally, it designated part of the large palatial complex at Memphis, one of the early capitals of Egypt in the 3rd millennium B.C. Soon thereafter, it denoted the Egyptian government itself—the king and his administration—not just the buildings from which they governed.

The process by which the king of Egypt became known as "Pharaoh" was gradual, involving various stages. In the first stage, sometime before Thutmose III became king (1479 B.C.), the title was occasionally applied to Egypt's monarch. A more advanced stage occurred before the end of the New Kingdom period (c. 1069 B.C.) when the use of "Pharaoh" referring to the king moved from everyday speech into the official language of the country. From the time of King Shoshenq I (or Sheshonk, 945–924 B.C.), "Pharaoh" was added to the king's official title.

The biblical writer uses the term as a common way of referring to the Egyptian king. God had delivered His people from bondage under "Pharaoh king of Egypt" (Deut. 7:8). This use reveals a knowledge of Egypt in the late 2nd and early 1st millenniums B.C.

The title "Pharaoh" highlights Israel's climactic experience with Egypt's king. The monarch of Egypt was considered the divine incarnation of Horus (the falcon god), as well as the son of Re (the sun god). Since Pharaoh was considered a god, the contest was between gods: the incarnate god of Egypt against the God of Israel, who spoke through His prophet Moses.

Annihilation of the Golden Calf
(Deut. 9:21)

Moses did not want the people to forget their failure to remain devoted to Yahweh. He recalled for them the calf idol they had made and that he had destroyed. Moses' actions appear to have a parallel within Canaanite ritual. Ritual annihilation of an enemy god was evidently common, at least in Canaan. A text from Ugarit (c. 1400–1200 B.C.), belonging to the Baal-Anath cycle of myths, describes a very similar destruction. The goddess Anath burns, grinds, and scatters the god Mot.

The Ugaritic ritual may not be the same ritual that is being described in Deut. 9:21. Nevertheless, the similarities suggest that Moses' annihilation of the idol calf was possibly a symbolic or ritualistic destruction known in Canaanite culture. It was not uncommon for Israelites and others to destroy enemy gods by breaking, burning, crushing, grinding, and scattering them, actions that possibly symbolized the utter defeat of the gods. In addition to Moses, two Judahite kings—Josiah (2 Kin. 23:4, 6, 15) and Asa (2 Chr. 15:16)—performed similar actions.

LAW CODES OF ANCIENT MESOPOTAMIA

The Hebrew laws of the Bible can be compared with several collections of laws (called "law codes") from other peoples of the ancient Near East. Many of the legal stipulations in the books of Exodus, Leviticus, Numbers, and Deuteronomy also appear in these other legal traditions.

Legal Collections in the Bible	Reference
The Ten Commandments	Ex. 20:2–17; Deut. 5:6–21
The Covenant Code	Ex. 20:22—23:33
The Book of the Law	Deut. 12—26
The Holiness Code	Lev. 17—26

Law Codes of Ancient Cultures	Date	Language
Code of Ur-Nammu	c. 2112–2095 B.C.	Sumerian
Code of Lipit-Ishtar	c. 1934–1924 B.C.	Sumerian
Laws of Eshnunna	c. 1900 B.C.	Accadian
Code of Hammurabi	c. 1792–1750 B.C.	Accadian
Hittite laws	c. 1750–1200 B.C.	Hittite
Middle Assyrian laws	c. 1132–1076 B.C.	Accadian

Appointing Just Judges (Deut. 16:18–20)

The qualifications for choosing judges and officials were considered a serious matter in ancient cultures. Both Israel and Egypt had stipulations regarding the conduct of judges, emphasizing that a system of justice is only as good as the people who administer it. Israel's law called for the selection of judges who would judge "with just judgment" (Deut. 16:18). The ideal of a just legal system was supported by prohibitions requiring that Israel's judges not "show partiality" or "take a bribe" (16:19).

The same ideal is evident in Egypt according to the Edict of Horemhab. Pharaoh Horemhab ruled for about 30 years (1323–1295 B.C.) in Egypt's 18th Dynasty. For the administration of justice, the monarch looked for "people discreet and of good character, knowing how to judge the inmost thoughts, obedient to the instructions of the palace, and to the laws of the throne hall." He claims to have taught these judges "the right course of life by guiding them to the truth." His advice to them was: "Do not associate with other people. Do not take bribes from others, for that will not turn out well." As the pharaoh advised his judges, he was clear in his warning concerning showing partiality: "Behold, (anyone) of you who makes common cause with another shall be for you as one who offends against truth."

The Curses of Disobedience (Deut. 28:30–34)

The various commandments and statutes established in the Law of Moses were to be obeyed. The solemn message of Deut. 28:15–68 is that disobedience would not be tolerated in Israel. They could enjoy blessings from God, or they could experience curses: their carcasses eaten by birds (28:26); their bodies plagued by incurable diseases (28:27); their wives raped (28:30). The list of miseries goes on throughout Deut. 28.

Curses were a part of covenants in the ancient world and were intended to enforce the stipulations of the covenant. What jars our modern concepts of God is Israel's belief that it was their deity who would cause these curses if they violated the covenant. Several times in Deuteronomy are the words, "The Lord will..." (28:20–22, 24, 25, etc.). Israel was not unique in these beliefs concerning covenant curses. The grave consequences for disobedience are formally similar to the consequences other peoples faced for breaking treaties with their monarchs.

Esarhaddon, king of Assyria (680–669 B.C.), required subject states to accept a treaty of fidelity to both Esarhaddon and his successor(s). The *Vassal Treaties of Esarhaddon* contain in explicit detail the consequences for breaking the oaths and reflect traditional curses found in Mesopotamian texts for at least 1,000 years before Esarhaddon.

A selection of gods in the Assyrian pantheon was called upon to enact various curses (very similar to Deut. 28) upon a disobedient vassal and his heirs. For example: Nergal would extinguish the life of the vassal, along with bringing carnage and pestilence; Ishtar would break the bow of the vassal in battle; Ninurta would kill the vassal with his bow and feed his carcass to the birds; the god Sin would clothe the vassal with leprosy; and Shamash would cause the individual to walk about in darkness. Last, all of the gods listed on the tablet would work to turn the vassal's soil into iron and turn the rain in the sky over his land into copper.

The Death of Moses (Deut. 34:1–12)

Though he could not enter, Moses was allowed to see the new land. He had been the great spokesman for God. There would be other prophets in Israel, but no one would ever hold the place of the man who led them out of Egypt to the Promised Land. As a crowning honor, he is called for the first time the name by which he is perhaps best remembered: "Moses the servant of the Lord" (Deut. 34:5). Moses died at the age of 120 years (Deut. 34:7).

THE CONQUEST OF CANAAN

Historians disagree as to when the Israelites left Egypt. The same historians disagree as to when Israel arrived in Canaan. Some place the invasion at the end of the 15th century; others at the end of the 13th. Archaeological support has been claimed for both dates, such as evidence that Jericho was destroyed at this or that era. But assigning specific dates to physical remains is difficult, and, ultimately, archaeology has not solved the question.

What can be agreed on, from evidence both within and outside of the Bible, is that the conquest of Palestine was not the unstoppable, crushing tide of invaders that is sometimes pictured. Despite sweeping statements that Joshua conquered "the whole land" (e.g., Josh. 11:16, 23), there are also descriptions of the land that "remains...to be possessed" (e.g., Josh. 13:1–6). Some of the Israelite conquests appear to have been by peaceful assimilation of the native peoples into the Israelites' own group, such as happened with the Gibeonites (Josh. 9).

The danger of such assimilation is that the Israelites' faith would be mixed with the religious beliefs and practices of Canaan. The Canaanites recognized many deities, two of the more prominent ones being El, the great sky god, and his female consort, Asherah. By the time of the conquest, the worship of El had been overshadowed by worship of a warrior storm god, Baal.

Canaanite worship practices included child sacrifice and fertility rites, often involving relations with cult prostitutes. Images of the gods were common in worship, as were the wooden poles or objects called "Asherim" after the goddess Asherah. Much of Israel's religious history dealt with the conflict between worshipers of the one God of the Exodus and worshipers of these Canaanite deities.

EPOCH THREE
Chronological Reading Guide

- ❑ Joshua 1:1—24:33

THE BOOK OF JOSHUA

Although the Book of Joshua tells of Israel's conquest of Canaan, it is not a typical war story: little space is given to accounts of actual fighting. Indeed, almost half of the book (chs. 13—21) details how the land would be divided between Israel's twelve tribes. Clearly the focus is God's fulfillment of His promise of land instead of on feats of arms.

God's command that Israel destroy every creature living in the land (Josh. 6:17, 21) poses a difficult ethical issue. This command is moderated somewhat in Josh. 8:2 but is still understandably troubling to many readers. We should not minimize the ethical question, but should understand that the reason given for the command involves the abominable and idolatrous Canaanite lifestyle. God ordains this total destruction so that Israel would not adopt the religious practices of the Canaanites (see Deut. 20:16–18).

The book concludes on the same theme. In a covenant renewal ceremony (chs. 23; 24), Joshua demands that Israel choose whether they will follow God or the gods of Canaan.

OUTLINE OF JOSHUA

I. The Conquest of Canaan	**1:1—13:7**
A. Preparation for the Conquest	1:1—5:15
B. Conquest of Canaan by Israel	6:1—12:24
C. Unconquered Parts of Canaan	13:1–7
II. The Settlement of Canaan	**13:8—24:33**
A. Settlement East of the Jordan	13:8–33
B. Settlement West of the Jordan	14:1—19:51
C. Settlement of the Religious Community	20:1—21:45
D. Conditions for Continued Settlement	22:1—24:33

TIME CAPSULE	1240 to 1208 B.C.
1240	Hittite Empire declines and vanishes by 1180 B.C.
1235	Israelites reach the plains of Moab (based on late Exodus)
1235	Aaron and Moses die (late Exodus)
1234	Joshua leads Israelite conquest of Canaan (late Exodus)
1213–1203	Merenptah, pharaoh of Egypt
1208	Merenptah defeats the Libyans and Sea People
1208	In the Israel Stele, Merenptah mentions Israel as one of his conquests

WHEN THE HEAVENS GO TO WAR (JOSH. 5:13–15)

Joshua met the Commander of God's army, who spoke for God whom He served (Josh. 5:13–15). Being aware that he had, in effect, met God in this divine servant, Joshua's reaction was to bow down and worship the heavenly being. The Commander's instruction for Joshua to remove his sandals reminds us of the same command to Moses at the burning bush (Ex. 3:5).

That heaven should have its own army would not have seemed strange in the ancient world. While there were specific gods and goddesses of warfare, entire armies of gods could be found in the mythology of the ancient Near East, serving the desires of their superior gods. Mesopotamian myths of the 2nd and 1st millenniums B.C. describe heavenly armies waging war against both divine and human enemies. In the Babylonian epic, Enuma Elish, the god Marduk conquers the army of the goddess Tiamat.

Human wars were fought under the direction of the deities of the land over which a king reigned. The ancients believed that wars were not just between human armies, but also between heavenly armies. The patron deities of the rival states had their own armies to back their people.

Joshua believed that he would not be fighting alone. Egyptian letters from the Amarna period (c. 1360–1333 B.C.) reflect the belief that the king of Egypt went to war as part of a divine army. In a similar fashion, Joshua, having been asked by God to take the Promised Land, met his heavenly counterpart. The notification "I have now come" (Josh. 5:14) informed Joshua that the human conquest of the land was only a part of the real action. Crucial events of the battle would take place in heaven.

Conquering the Canaanite Cities (Josh. 6:1—14:5)

The detailed accounts in chs. 1—5 of the preparation, the Jordan crossing, and the camp at Gilgal show Israel mobilized to enter the land. The crossing of the Jordan and the Passover celebration are dated in the 1st month (Josh. 4:19; 5:10), suggesting that Joshua readied the people in less than two months after Moses' death.

The conquest itself is described in three campaigns or stages: the thrust into central Canaan (Josh. 6:1—8:35), the southern campaign (9:1—10:43), and the northern campaign (11:1–15). The first stage relates the destruction of Jericho and Ai. Stages two and three present the long and complex military campaigns against coalitions of Canaanite cities.

The reader could easily assume that the whole operation took only a short time, whereas the process actually lasted several years. And even then the conquest was not complete (13:1).

Accursed and Under the Ban (Josh. 7:1)

All of the inhabitants of Jericho, humans and animals, were killed as a sacrifice to God. They were "doomed by the Lord to destruction" (Josh. 6:17). In addition, all of Jericho's property was placed off limits to the Israelites and destroyed, except for items of iron, bronze, silver and gold, which went into the sacred treasury (6:18, 19). All of these things—people, property, valuables—were considered "accursed." The Hebrew word translated "accursed" referred to things that were completely destroyed or set apart for sacred use.

Accursed things were given to God by either being totally destroyed or dedicated to sacred use. They were kept from the Israelites. They were for them "accursed" items. By not taking these items for themselves, the Israelites were acknowledging that such things belonged to God. God was the real conqueror of the city. Jericho was a kind of "tithe," the first city conquered in the Promised Land. Its possessions, therefore, belonged to God.

Achan's sin (Josh. 7:1) was that he took a "garment, two hundred shekels of silver, and a wedge of gold weighing fifty shekels" from Jericho, even though he knew that everything in Jericho had been dedicated to God. He thus stole from God. By taking an "accursed" item, he himself became cursed.

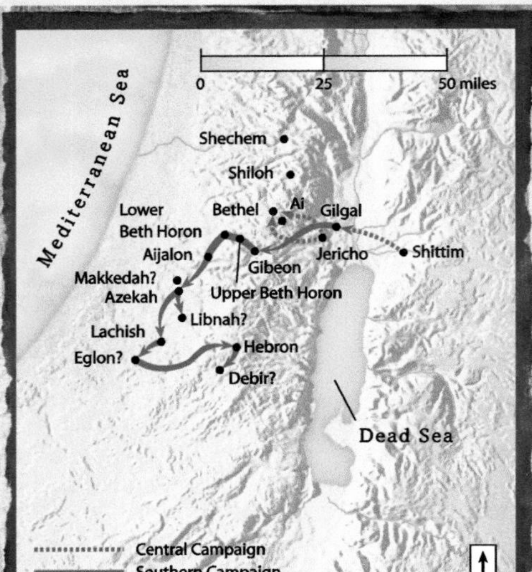

The Conquest of Canaan (Central and Southern Campaigns)

From the camp at Gilgal, Joshua launched two campaigns. Jericho fell in the central campaign, which continued with an ambush of Bethel and Ai. Joshua launched the southern campaign against the Amorites assembled near Gibeon and continued the assault all the way to Debir.

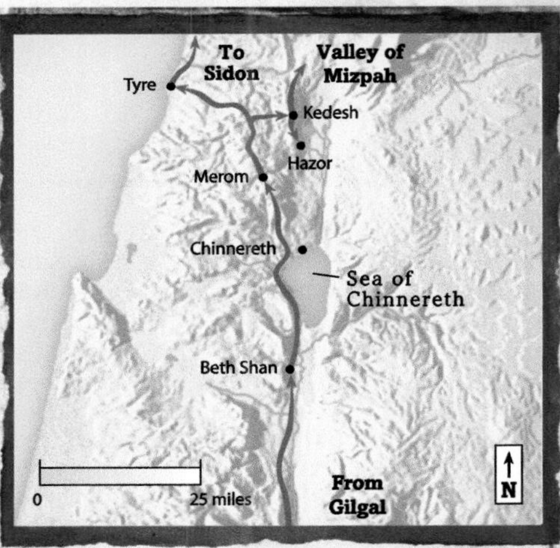

The Conquest of Canaan (Northern Campaign)

A large coalition of kings gathered at the waters of Merom to fight against Joshua. In a surprise attack, Joshua's armies drove the forces back, some toward Tyre and Sidon, others toward Kedesh. Joshua divided his forces, destroying Hazor along the way.

When God Listened to a Man (Josh. 10:12, 13)

Joshua's prayer, "Sun, stand still over Gibeon; and Moon, in the Valley of Aijalon" (Josh. 10:12), seems to request that God stop the sun or perform some other miraculous heavenly event to lengthen the day. Joshua did not pray late in the evening: the sun "over Gibeon" would be in the east, while the moon "in the Valley of Aijalon" would be in the west. This positioning of the sun and moon indicates early morning, and for Joshua to utter a request for a longer day at that time of day seems unusual.

Joshua's asking the sun and moon to "stand still" (10:12) is a request typical of celestial omen texts from Mesopotamia. These texts are concerned with the 1st day of the full moon that came at the middle of the month and was observable by the location of the sun and moon in the early morning on opposite horizons. In Mesopotamian omen texts the sun and moon are asked to "wait" on each other, so that they would be on their respective horizons on the 14th day of the month. When this positioning occurred, it was seen by the Mesopotamians as a sign of good fortune. For them it indicated that their calculations were accurate, that there would be exactly 30 days in the month, and that the days themselves would be full-length. On the other hand, when the sun and moon were on their respective horizons on any other day, it was considered a bad omen.

The position of the sun in the east (Gibeon) and moon in the west (Valley of Aijalon) suggests that this event occurred near the middle of the month. Joshua may be asking God to allow the sun and moon to "stand still" (10:12) or wait for each other so that they would be on their horizons on a day other than the 14th day of the month. That would cause the Canaanites to believe that that day was an evil day for fighting and give the Israelites the upper hand before the battle began. What made this occasion memorable is that "the LORD heeded the voice of a man" (10:14). God listened to Joshua, and the sun and moon were positioned for Israel's advantage—"the LORD fought for Israel."

THE SEA PEOPLES SETTLE IN PHILISTIA (JOSH. 13:2, 3)

The Philistines were a people group whose origins are not clearly known. New Kingdom Egyptian sources from the 13th and 12th centuries B.C. mention them as one of the Sea Peoples who unsuccessfully invaded Egypt. The inscriptions of Pharaoh Merenptah (1213–1203 B.C.) report that when the Libyans attacked Egypt, there were "foreigners from the sea" fighting within the ranks of the Libyan armies. Egyptian descriptions of Pharaoh Ramesses' battles against the Sea Peoples list the Philistines among the opponents.

Some scholars believe that the Sea People groups came from the western regions of the Mediterranean and Aegean Seas—from Greece and Crete. Cities, regions, and empires fell to these seaborne raiders: Cyprus, north Syria, the Hittite Empire, and Ugarit. The Sea Peoples continued down the eastern Mediterranean coastal areas toward Canaan until Egypt's Ramesses III (1184–1153 B.C.) stopped their advance in 1175 B.C.

Ramesses did not win decisively. Later Egyptian sources record the settlement of some of the Sea Peoples in southern Palestine, which was in the Egyptian sphere of influence. The group called "Philistines" organized a confederation of five major cities: Gaza, Ashdod, Ashkelon, Gath, and Ekron. The Sea Peoples' invasion spawned a new culture in Palestine, one that the Israelites would experience as "the Gazites, the Ashdodites, the Ashkelonites, the Gittites, and the Ekronites" (Josh. 13:3).

Pharaoh Merenptah

Jebus, City of the Jebusites (JOSH. 18:28)

In Josh. 18:21–28 the biblical writer lists the cities that made up the inheritance of the tribe of Benjamin. For one of those cities he adds identification in parentheses: "Jebus (which is Jerusalem)." Jebus was the pre-Israelite name for Jerusalem, capital city of Israel. The inhabitants of Jebus, the Jebusites, are listed as one of the Canaanite tribes who dwelt in the region of central Palestine (Ex. 33:2).

The name "Jebus" is not mentioned in any source outside of the Bible. We do not know whether the Jebusites received their name from the city Jebus, or whether Jebus was named after the Jebusites who dwelt there. The city's Hebrew name, Jerusalem, is found in the Egyptian Execration Texts (19th to 18th centuries B.C.) and in the documents from Tell el-Amarna in Egypt (14th to 13th centuries B.C.). Such evidence suggests that the city's name had been Jerusalem for several centuries. It is possible that David restored the earlier name, Jerusalem, when he became king of Israel and captured the city from the Jebusites (c. 1003 B.C.; 2 Sam. 5:6, 7).

The Covenant Renewed at Shechem
(Josh. 24:15)

The ancient fortified city of Shechem was the first capital of the northern kingdom of Israel. Its name means "shoulder," probably because the city was built mainly on the slope, or shoulder, of Mount Ebal. Shechem was an important city long before the Israelites occupied Canaan. The city has been destroyed and rebuilt several times through the centuries.

Shechem is first mentioned in connection with Abraham's journey into the land of Canaan. When Abraham eventually came to Shechem, the Lord appeared to him and announced that this was the land He would give to Abraham's descendants. Because of this incident, Shechem is an important place in the religious history of the Hebrew people.

After the Israelites conquered Canaan under the leadership of Joshua, an altar was built at Shechem. Its building was accompanied by a covenant ceremony in obedience to the command of Moses, given earlier in Deuteronomy 27:12–13. Because Shechem was situated between Mount Ebal and Mount Gerizim, this covenant ceremony took on a symbolic meaning. To this day Mount Gerizim is forested, while Mount Ebal is barren. Thus the blessings of faithfully keeping the covenant were proclaimed from Mount Gerizim, while the curses of breaking the covenant were proclaimed from Mount Ebal.

At the close of his life, Joshua gathered the tribes of Israel at Shechem (Josh. 24:1). Here he reviewed God's gracious dealings with Israel and performed a covenant-renewing ceremony on behalf of the nation. He closed his speech with his famous statement, "Choose for yourselves this day whom you will serve....But as for me and my house, we will serve the LORD" (Josh. 24:15).

FROM TRIBES TO A NATION

1200—930 B.C.

The conquest of Canaan under Joshua is pictured as a united effort by the Israelite people. Yet because of natural boundaries and local concerns, Israel became an increasingly fragmented people. This was a time when international power in the ancient world was at low ebb. Still the Israelite tribes were struggling to survive in the new land against such relatively insignificant peoples as the Moabites, Midianites, and Amalekites.

Israel's story makes a transition, however, from the loose-knit group of tribes to a highly organized monarchy. The tribes that were governed by divinely selected judges eventually became a kingdom ruled by a dynasty also chosen under divine guidance. This story is told through a dramatic sweep of events that produced the most powerful empire in the ancient Middle East, in the golden age under the leadership of David and Solomon.

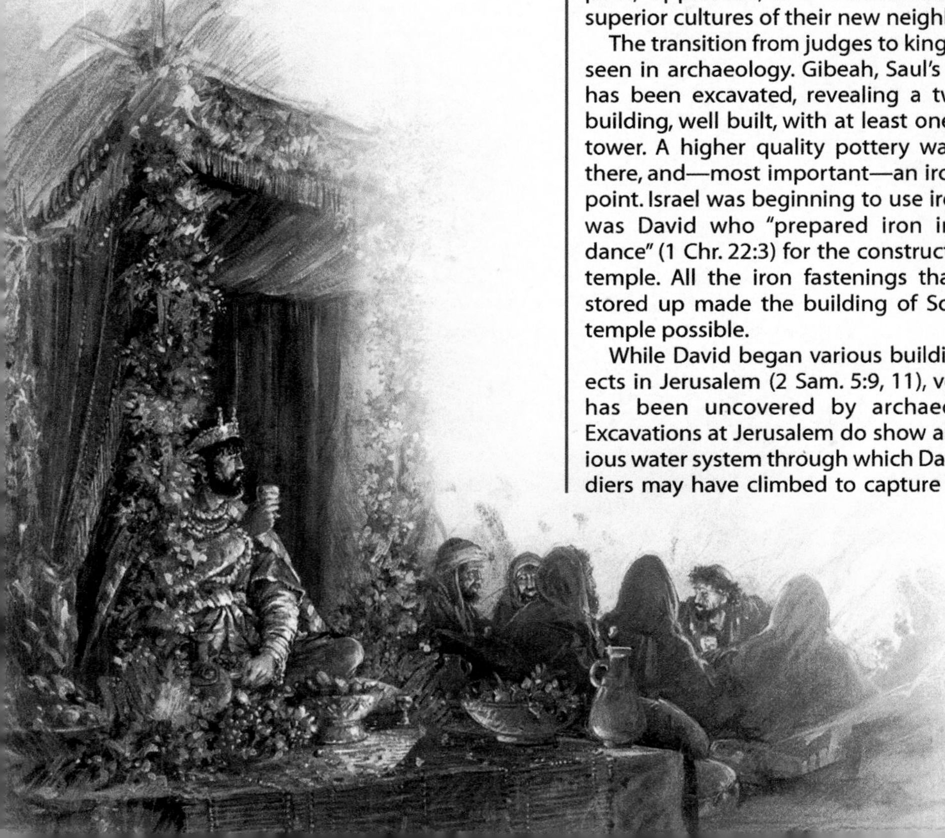

ARCHAEOLOGY AND THE PAST

Archaeological excavations reveal that such Canaanite cities as Bethel or Beth Shemesh were flourishing urban cultures. Houses were well built, with paved floors, and cities had public drainage systems and fortified walls. Sophisticated pottery, art, jewelry, and statues of gods are found in large numbers. The pottery and other goods discovered suggest that trade with Syria, Egypt, and the Aegean flourished. Stone bowls from ancient Egypt were found in the ruins, attesting to a trade in "antiques."

Archaeology offers a different picture of Israelite settlements during this period. Towns appeared in the hill country for the first time, including such places as Shiloh, Mizpah, and Gibeah, among others. The houses were built of stones stacked together, with no attempt to shape the stones to fit, and with no mortar to hold them together. Art and pottery were crude, and there are almost no signs of trade. This picture fits with that in the Book of Judges: the Israelites were poor, oppressed, and threatened by the superior cultures of their new neighbors.

The transition from judges to kings can be seen in archaeology. Gibeah, Saul's fortress, has been excavated, revealing a two-story building, well built, with at least one watchtower. A higher quality pottery was found there, and—most important—an iron plowpoint. Israel was beginning to use iron. Yet it was David who "prepared iron in abundance" (1 Chr. 22:3) for the construction of a temple. All the iron fastenings that David stored up made the building of Solomon's temple possible.

While David began various building projects in Jerusalem (2 Sam. 5:9, 11), very little has been uncovered by archaeologists. Excavations at Jerusalem do show an ingenious water system through which David's soldiers may have climbed to capture the city, when it was known as Jebus (2 Sam. 5:8). The situation changes, however, with David's son Solomon. Several archaeological finds lend support to the biblical picture of Solomon as Israel's first great builder.

Solomon was a trader in chariots and horses, buying chariots in Egypt and selling them farther north and east. Chariot cities built by Solomon include Megiddo, Hazor, and Gezer. All of these cities show evidence of fortifications dating to Solomon's time, particularly the six-chambered gates that were common in Solomon's building enterprises.

Excavations at Ezion Geber, on the Gulf of Aqaba, have uncovered the remains of a metal industry, apparently worked by slaves. Solomon controlled the mines of the Sinai and had a monopoly on the metal industry of his day. It was from these mines, most likely, that the great bronze doors and other metal trappings of the temple came. Ezion Geber was also a seaport, from which Solomon's ships went on trading expeditions to Africa every third year (1 Kin. 10:22).

Solomon's most significant building project was the temple and royal palace. The plan of Solomon's temple, as described in the Bible, is similar to plans of other temples in Canaan and Phoenicia. In fact, a temple dedicated to Yahweh has been excavated near the city of Arad in the Negev. It was part of a royal fortress from the time of Solomon and differs from the Jerusalem temple mainly in having a broad room, rather than the long holy place. The 20-year temple-palace enterprise (2 Chr. 8:1) was impressive testimony that Israel had made the transition from tribes to a great nation.

THE PEOPLES AND GROUPS

Much of Israel's history reflects the relative strength and weakness of Egypt and the empires of Mesopotamia. These major empires were weak during the reigns of David and Solomon, allowing both kings to expand their Israelite kingdoms. Yet other peoples interacted with Israel during the settlement and kingdom period.

The Sea Peoples were a great migration of seaborne groups coming out of Greece and the regions around the Aegean Sea. They overran ancient civilizations in Troy, Cyprus, and Asia Minor. They attacked Egypt by both land and sea, and Pharaoh Ramesses III (1184–1153 B.C.), while preventing their advance into Egypt, did allow them to settle in Egyptian strongholds on the Palestine coast. One of the Sea Peoples, the Philistines, controlled much of Palestine, and only under King David were the Israelites able to compete with and ultimately defeat the Philistines.

The Canaanites were a highly cultured people in the land when Israel arrived, with superiority in areas of building, art, trade, and economics. But their most important threat to Israel was in the area of religion. A nomadic people trying to settle in the land must have found it almost impossible not to think the gods of the Canaanites were powerful indeed, giving the Canaanite people such wealth and power. The documents found at Ugarit (Ras Shamra) include many of the myths, rituals, hymns, and prayers of the Canaanites.

The Arameans were the various tribes and kingdoms located in southern Syria, just northeast of Canaan. Cushan-Rishathaim, an unknown king from the early days of the judges (Judg. 3:8, 10), is sometimes identified as an Aramean. More definite references to Arameans (or Syrians), though, come from the time of David. Aram often refers to Aram-Damascus, the state whose capital was Damascus. David eventually conquered an alliance of Arameans from Damascus and from Zobah, an Aramean kingdom north of Damascus ruled by King Hadadezer (2 Sam. 8:3–8). Damascus regained its independence from Israel during Solomon's reign (1 Kin. 11:23–25).

Several nomadic or seminomadic groups raided the settled lands from time to time. The Amalekites are mentioned only in the Bible. The Midianites threatened Israel during the era of the judges and were opposed by Israel's judge Gideon (Judg. 6—8). What made such raids successful was the domestication of the camel, which freed travelers (and raiders) to range farther afield into the deserts. By David's reign these raiding groups were no longer serious threats.

THE BIBLICAL LITERATURE

Biblical books which relate Israel's transition to a kingdom include Judges, Ruth, 1 and 2 Samuel, 1 Chronicles, and parts of 1 Kings and 2 Chronicles. These books not only give data about the past, but they try to explain what the data mean and how God was active in the history of the people. Judges is a collection of narratives about tribal heroes and heroines in the period between the death of Joshua and the time of Samuel. Ruth is about a foreign woman through whom God works to bring forth King David. 1 and 2 Samuel report the end of the judges and the rise of the monarchy in Israel, including the lives of Samuel, Saul, and David.

The histories of Samuel, Kings, and Chronicles report the golden age of monarchy under David and Solomon. Many of Israel's writings were associated with these great kings. Traditionally, more of the Psalms were ascribed to David than to any other person. The glory years of Solomon are reflected in the love songs of the Song of Solomon, in the collections of sayings on the good life in Proverbs, and in the ultimate questions of life and death covered in Ecclesiastes.

A TRIBAL CONFEDERATION IN ISRAEL

Having established at least a foothold in the land of Canaan, Israel now organized itself into a loose confederation of independent tribes. The link connecting these clans was their God. The tribes celebrated common religious festivals at the shrine where the ark of the covenant was kept—most often located either at Gilgal or Shiloh.

The tribal confederation had military purposes as well. When an outside people invaded, the clans were to join in a holy war. Some leader would take the initiative and summon makeshift armies from the tribes to battle. These leaders, for the most part, we call the judges.

Through most of the period of the judges, Egypt and the countries of Mesopotamia were weak and preoccupied with internal problems. The wars of the Book of Judges are waged against unconquered Canaanites and small neighboring nations such as Edom, Midian, and Ammon.

Toward the end of the Late Bronze Age (1500–1200 B.C.), though, a new group began to arrive in the land of Canaan, evidently from across the Mediterranean. They had war chariots and knew how to use iron, giving them a military advantage over the Israelites, who only had bronze. The Sea Peoples, including the Philistines, settled the fertile land along the southern coast. Their presence helps to explain why the tribe of Dan, to whom Joshua allotted the coastland, never conquered any of its portion. Despite the uneven efforts of the Danite judge Samson, the tribe of Dan ultimately left the coast and found itself a new homeland far to the north (Judg. 18:1).

EPOCH FOUR
Chronological Reading Guide

- ❑ Judges 1:1—21:25
- ❑ Ruth 1:1—4:22
- ❑ 1 Samuel 1:1—7:17

THE BOOK OF JUDGES

The brief introduction of the Book of Judges (Judg. 1:1—2:6) makes it clear that the Israelite invasion of Canaan was incomplete. The major portion of the book (3:7—16:31) focuses on the judges, the men and women by whom God delivered His people from oppressors. Though the judges were usually military leaders, they also exercised administrative duties, and some of them are not reported to have led armies at all (such as the "minor judges"; cf. Judg. 10:1–5; 12:8–15).

By the end of the book, the confederacy appears ready to collapse. The tribes had never been entirely unified either in worship or war. Four of them, Reuben, Gad (Gilead), Dan, and Asher, seem not to have responded to Deborah's summons to assist the other tribes in battle (Judg. 5:16, 17). By the latter stages of the judges' period, the tribes had fallen into idolatry and civil war. The refrain of the final chapters—"In those days there was no king in Israel; everyone did what was right in his own eyes" (17:6; 21:25)—points ahead to 1 Samuel and the beginning of the monarchy.

OUTLINE OF JUDGES

I. The Deterioration of Israel	**1:1—3:6**
A. Failure to Complete the Conquest	1:1–36
B. God's Judgment for the Failure	2:1—3:6
II. The Deliverance of Israel	**3:7—16:31**
A. The Southern Campaign	3:7–31
B. The Northern Campaign	4:1—5:31
C. The Central Campaign	6:1—10:5
D. The Eastern Campaign	10:6—12:7
E. The Second Northern Campaign	12:8–15
F. The Western Campaign	13:1—16:31
III. The Depravity of Israel	**17:1—21:25**
A. Failure Through Idolatry	17:1—18:31
B. Failure Through Immorality	19:1–30
C. Failure Through Civil War	20:1—21:25

TIME CAPSULE 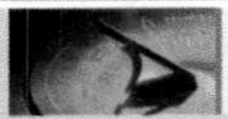 **1203 to 1180 B.C.**

1203	After Merenptah's death, Egypt declines into civil wars
1200–800	The Dark Age of Greece
1200–600	Iron Age
1200	Fall of Troy to the Greeks
1184–1153	Ramesses III, pharaoh of Egypt
1180	End of the New Kingdom of the Hittites

ARAD IN THE INSCRIPTIONS (JUDG. 1:16)

The southern region of Judah, a dry wilderness area, was known as "the Negev" (translated "the South"). Arad was a Canaanite town in the Negev, thus the writer of Judges employs the description "in the South near Arad." The site of Arad was a large fortified town during the Early Bronze Age (c. 3000 B.C.) and showed extensive trade connections with Old Kingdom Egypt. This Arad was destroyed about 2700 B.C.

Another Arad emerged later during the Iron Age (c. 1200–600 B.C.), as is known from various inscriptions. Pieces of broken pottery (called by the Greek name *ostraca*) were used as inexpensive writing material, being inscribed with pen and ink. The name "Arad" appears on these pottery fragments or potsherds, as well as being mentioned in the records of Shishak, the Egyptian pharaoh (945–924 B.C.).

Over 200 ostraca have been found at the site of Arad. One inscription mentions a "House of Yahweh," using the personal name of Israel's God. This shrine or temple has in fact been found, containing a number of stone altars. The inscriptions also list a number of Hebrew names of priestly families.

Pharaoh Shishak claims to have captured Arad during a raid of Palestine in 925 B.C. An inscription on the walls of the temple of Karnak, listing over 150 towns that Shishak captured, includes the citadel of Arad. Archaeological excavations show that Arad was destroyed by fire during Shishak's time.

Organizing a Pantheon of Many Gods
(JUDG. 2:11–13)

When the Israelites "served the Baals" (Judg. 2:11), they were buying into the mythological structure of the universe understood by the local culture. The gods of the religious world of Syria-Palestine were formed into a four-level hierarchy not unlike a small, localized bureaucracy.

The highest authorities of the Canaanite universe were the deities El and Asherah, the parents of all the other gods—the actual rulers of the cosmos and the final court of appeal for both gods and humans. As highest rulers, they assigned each of their offspring responsibility for specific tasks in governing the world.

The second level of deities was an especially rowdy group, as the myths recovered from Ugarit demonstrate. These gods were the powers behind the forces of nature, the political fates of cities and empires, and even behind abstractions, such as justice. Very powerful, they ordered the universe, promoted the welfare of their worshipers, and advanced themselves against other deities. Conflicting interests of their divine wills explained for devotees why the world did not always operate as it ought.

A third level of gods served as craftsmen and artisans for the higher deities. As specialists in the professions their expertise was unsurpassed. They might contradict and even argue with higher-level gods when ordered to do things they themselves knew to be folly. While they obeyed orders, they were not averse to mocking their superiors for the inferior knowledge those gods had of the work at hand.

At the bottom of the divine hierarchy were the messenger deities—the angels, the slave labor of the Canaanite heaven.

Israel's temptation to "try out" some of these deities sometimes was too great (Judg. 2:12). Besides Asherah (3:7), they knew of second-level gods and goddesses, such as Baal (3:7) and Anath (3:31). The idol that Hezekiah called Nehushtan (2 Kin. 18:4) represents a healing deity of the third level.

THE ERA OF THE JUDGES (EARLY EXODUS)

B.C.	Event
1406 B.C.	Israel conquers King Sihon of Heshbon (Num. 21:25, 26)
1405 B.C.	Joshua leads Israelite conquest of Canaan (Josh. 4:19)
	Jephthah approximates a period of 300 years since Israel dwelt in Heshbon (Judg. 11:26)
1125 B.C.	Abimelech destroys Shechem and its tower (Judg. 9:45–49)
1125 B.C.	Deborah composes her song of victory over Sisera (Judg. 5)
1125 B.C.	Eli serves as both priest and judge for 40 years (1 Sam. 4:18)
1050 B.C. or 1020 B.C.	Saul becomes Israel's first king (1 Sam. 11:15)

B.C. 1415 1315 1215 1115 1015

How Long Was the Era of the Judges? (Judges 3:7—21:25)

After Joshua's death, conditions changed quickly for the Israelite tribes. Their experiences are described in Judg. 2:11—3:6 as a recurring cycle of apostasy, oppression, supplication, and deliverance. The collection of stories in 3:7—16:31 reports the exploits of Israel's judges during 7 cycles of oppression and deliverance.

The book provides various numbers for the years of the judges' period. Three types of chronological information indicate the number of years (1) that Israel was oppressed (e.g., Judg. 3:8), (2) that Israel had peace following a deliverance (e.g., Judg. 3:11), and (3) that particular individuals served as judge (e.g., Judg. 10:2). When tabulated, the total of these years is 410, but this figure does not necessarily represent the length of this period. Interpreting the numbers is complicated by the possibility of overlapping time periods and of symbolic numbers.

It was common to list periods chronologically that were either contemporaneous or overlapping. Since most of the judges were confined to particular tribes or regions, it is reasonable to assume considerable overlapping of the periods and events. The report that in one period Israel was oppressed by both Philistia and Ammon (Judg. 10:7) could suggest that Jephthah and Samson may have been living and working at the same time.

Many of the numbers in the Book of Judges may be symbolic, rather than chronological. Twelve judges are mentioned, although a detailed account is given for only six. While there were possibly many more judges than these, the number 12 speaks in symbolic fashion of the whole of an era. The same is true for the 7 cycles of oppression and deliverance, with 7 also depicting a sense of completeness. Also the duration of leadership ascribed to many of the judges is in units or multiples of 40, a number frequently denoting a generation of unspecified length.

An exact, precise dating of the judges' period will remain unknown. No references to contemporary events of this period are available. All that can be said with certainty is that the period of Israel's judges stretches from the entry into Canaan (around 1406 or 1235 B.C.) until the establishment of the monarchy with Saul (around 1050 or 1020 B.C.).

BAAL, GOD OF STORMS (JUDG. 6:25–32)

Of all the deities of Canaan, the Israelites were most drawn to Baal. Gideon's family had been devotees of the god (Judg. 6:25). The seriousness with which some Israelites took their devotion to Baal is seen in their desire to kill Gideon for tearing down Baal's altar (Judg. 6:28–30).

In Hebrew, "Baal" is the title "lord." This title was given to the storm god Hadad, who is widely known from Syria, Mesopotamia, and Egypt through inscriptions dating from the mid-3rd millennium to the last century B.C. Usually Hadad was simply called "Baal" and was understood to be the god of storms.

Since Baal brought rain, he was also credited with bringing the annual crops that were dependent on the rain. The gifts of rain and crops were so important that there were many sites devoted to the worship of Baal, each using the local version of the god's name.

In the Ugaritic myths Baal is portrayed as a mighty, lustful, and ambitious deity, but also as a god with decidedly more muscles than brains. His worshipers clearly enjoyed a good story about Baal charging into a situation through sheer bravado only to discover too late that it was a really dumb thing to do. Baal relied primarily on his sister Anath to rescue him from these difficulties of his own making, though others, such as Kothar-and-Hasis (a skilled artisan deity), Shapshu (the sun goddess), Asherah and El (rulers of the pantheon), helped him as well.

Shechem in the Amarna Letters
(Judg. 9:6–31)

Nearly 400 cuneiform tablets (mostly letters) were found in Egypt at Tell el-Amarna (ancient Akhetaten) in the "office-house of the Pharaoh." These texts, called the Amarna letters, cover about a 30-year period (c. 1360–1333 B.C.) during the reigns of pharaohs Amen-hotep III and Akhenaten. Most of the letters are written in Accadian, an East Semitic tongue that was the international language during this period.

Descriptions of Canaan in the Amarna letters fit well with the biblical portrayal. The land was politically decentralized, divided into separate, politically organized communities settled around larger cities and surrounding villages. The most prominent of these city-states were Gezer, Shechem, and Hazor. Some sites named in the Bible for this period, such as Hebron, Jericho, and Ai, are not mentioned in the Amarna letters. Jerusalem, however, is depicted as a modest city and relatively unimportant.

The city of Shechem that is described for Abimelech's time (Judg. 9) bears similarity to the Canaanite town described in the Amarna letters. The Shechem of the Amarna letters has city lords and a mayor. Similarly, the city lords of Judg. 9, called the "men of Shechem," exercise the power to make Abimelech king (9:6), then later challenge his rule (9:23). The mayor who administered Shechem's affairs on behalf of King Abimelech was the city magistrate Zebul (9:30, 31).

The Amarna letters provide important information about the social and political world of Palestine during the era of Israel's judges. Often mentioned are the Habiru, roving bands of mercenaries, who are named in the Amarna letters as employed by Shechem. Similarly, a band of Habiru hired by the "men of Shechem" in Judg. 9 is represented as "Gaal and his brothers" (9:26, 41).

Gods' Lands, Gods' Peoples
(Judg. 11:24)

People of ancient cultures believed that the gods owned territory and could give it to whomever they wished. The gods also took care of particular peoples. When any ruler went out to battle, he proclaimed that he was fighting alongside his god or gods. The outcome of the battle was in the hands of the gods who were leading the kings. These two notions—gods giving lands and gods protecting their people—collide when two deities, Chemosh and Yahweh, are thought to possess the same land (Judg. 11:24).

Jephthah explained to the king of Ammon how Israel came to control the land that it then inhabited. The long explanation (Judg. 11:14–28) describes the entrance of Israel into the Promised Land. Jephthah's theological language was familiar throughout the ancient Near East. The God of Israel actually took the land from other gods and gave it to Israel.

Chemosh was the national god of Moab (Num. 21:22), but apparently he was worshiped also by the Ammonites. The disagreement between Jephthah and the Ammonite king centered on what territory Chemosh had given the Ammonites (Judg. 11:24). The Ammonites claimed that they should have the land held by Israel; but Jephthah argues that the issue of land ownership was already decided, and the outcome of any battle was already decided. Israel had not broken faith with either Yahweh or the Ammonites. The land that Israel possessed was given to them by Yahweh, not to the Ammonites by Chemosh.

Samson the Nazirite (Judg. 16:17)

Besides his extraordinary physical strength and his spectacular wildness of character, Samson had one other unique distinction: he was a Nazirite (Judg. 16:17). The word "Nazirite" means one who is consecrated (or separated or devoted) to something. More specifically, a Nazirite was one who had taken a vow "to the Lord" (Num. 6:2).

The peculiarities of the Nazirite vow were defined by very clear parameters. Nazirites were to avoid any produce from grapevines: juice, fresh grapes and raisins (Num. 6:3, 4). In addition, they were not to cut their hair (Num. 6:5) or come in contact with a dead body, even if it was a close relative (Num. 6:6, 7).

The Nazirite vow was considered very solemn. Indeed the Samson stories open with an angel telling Samson's mother that her child would be a Nazirite from his birth and instructing her on the details of the Nazirite lifestyle (Judg. 13:3–5). Even Samson's mother was to keep herself from grapevine produce and food considered unclean (13:13, 14).

While Samson is the only Old Testament person specifically identified as a Nazirite, it is likely that many prophets were also Nazirites. The prophet Amos mentions prophets and Nazirites together (Amos 2:11, 12), and Samuel is an example of someone who was both. His mother Hannah made a vow that Samuel's hair would never be cut (1 Sam. 1:11). The Septuagint (the Greek translation of the Old Testament) adds to 1 Sam. 1:11 that Samuel would also abstain from grape juice. While not specifically said to be a Nazirite, it seems likely that, since Samuel followed the Nazirite rules, he was a Nazirite.

THE ERA OF THE JUDGES (LATE EXODUS)

B.C. 1235 — 1180 — 1125 — 1070 — 1015

- Israel conquers King Sihon of Heshbon (Num. 21:25, 26) 1235 B.C.
- Joshua leads Israelite conquest of Canaan (Josh. 4:19) 1234 B.C.
- Abimelech destroys Shechem and its tower (Judg. 9:45–49) 1125 B.C.
- Jephthah approximates a period of 300 years since Israel dwelt in Heshbon (Judg. 11:26)
- Deborah composes her song of victory over Sisera (Judg. 5) 1125 B.C.
- Eli serves as both priest and judge for 40 years (1 Sam. 4:18)
- Saul becomes Israel's first king (1 Sam. 11:15) 1050 B.C. or 1020 B.C.

THE BOOK OF RUTH

The Book of Judges, like many histories, presents only the wars and battles of its time. The Book of Ruth deals with what average people were doing between those wars. It describes a stable society, governed by wise elders, in which the laws of the covenant are respected and kept. For instance, the law demanded that if a man died before his wife had borne him children, his nearest male relative should marry the widow and raise up an heir to the one who had died (Deut. 25:5–10). Under this law Ruth eventually marries Boaz.

The book also pictures more peaceful relations with Israel's neighbors than does Judges. Naomi moves back and forth between Israel and Moab, and her sons take Moabite wives. This intermarriage alone is surprising, but even more startling is that the mixed marriage of Ruth and Boaz is blessed by God and produces Israel's greatest king, King David (Ruth 4:18–22).

TIME CAPSULE	1175 to 1120 B.C.
1175	Sea battle between Ramesses III and the Sea Peoples
1175	The Philistines settle on southern coast of Palestine
1169	Sea Peoples depicted in horse-drawn carts
1130	Egyptians lose control of southern Canaan
1125	Deborah composes her song of victory over Sisera
1125	Archaeological remains at Shechem show Abimelech's destruction of the city and its tower (Judg. 9:45–46)
1120	Nebuchadnezzar I conquers Elam and returns statue of Marduk

OUTLINE OF RUTH

I. Ruth's Love Is Demonstrated	**1:1—2:23**
A. Ruth's Decision to Remain with Naomi	1:1–18
B. Ruth's Devotion to Care for Naomi	1:19—2:23
II. Ruth's Love Rewarded	**3:1—4:22**
A. Ruth's Request for Redemption by Boaz	3:1–18
B. Ruth's Reward of Redemption by Boaz	4:1–22

Naomi's Close Relative (RUTH 2:20; 4:1–10)

Naomi recognizes God's kindness in the person of Boaz, who is one of her "close relatives" (Ruth 2:20). The Hebrew word *goel*, translated "close relative," means "to redeem." Such relatives were redeemers because they had a legal obligation under the Law of Moses to redeem or buy back the property of destitute relatives from foreclosure (Lev. 25:25).

The close relative could redeem various types of obligations through a monetary payment. Individuals could reclaim their land or house. An indentured servant could be redeemed from servitude. A religious offering could be reclaimed. Yet some redemptions were not made with a sum of money. The closest male relative of a murdered Israelite was a "blood redeemer." This "avenger of blood" (2 Sam. 14:11) was required to avenge the blood of the dead kinsman with the life of the murderer.

The closest adult male relative of a deceased person was required to assure the economic welfare of the deceased's kin. In this case, the legal custom of the close relative was very similar to another legal custom—the levirate marriage (Deut. 25:5–10). *Levir* is the Latin word for "brother-in-law." If a man died without leaving a male heir, his widow was to marry within the husband's family. Moreover, the husband's brother was required to marry the woman and produce a son.

Preserving the family line was important in Israel. The levirate marriage was linked to laws of inheritance, so any offspring from the husband's brother were considered children of the deceased. The firstborn son would take the name of the dead former husband.

If the brother-in-law refused to perform the levir's duty, the woman was to perform the ceremony of the removal of his sandal (Deut. 25:8–10). A woman had a right to bear children to her deceased husband. If her brother-in-law refused her that right, she could publicly humiliate him. She was then allowed to marry outside of the family.

The primary purpose of the levirate marriage law was to protect the widow and help compensate the deceased husband's family for their personal loss. In Naomi's case, since she was beyond childbearing age, the levirate marriage would be to her widowed daughter-in-law Ruth. Naomi's closest relative was not willing to assume this obligation (Ruth 4:6). In the sandal ceremony of Ruth 4:6–8 there seems to be no disdain for the relative who declined to perform the duty of the levir. The significance of taking off the sandal seems to imply the passing of one's legal rights to another. Boaz thus gained the right to clear the property against any future claims and to marry Ruth (4:9, 10).

THE BOOKS OF SAMUEL

The books of Judges and Ruth point toward the beginning of an Israelite monarchy; in the books of Samuel the monarchy takes shape. In general terms, 1 Samuel tells of the beginning of the kingdom to the end of the reign of the first king, Saul. Then 2 Samuel is devoted to the career of David, Israel's second, and greatest, king.

First Samuel begins not with a king, but with the imposing figure of Samuel. Samuel is priest and prophet and judge, indeed everything except king. It is from Samuel that the people seek a king. It is Samuel whom God sends to anoint first Saul, then David. It is Samuel who announces God's rejection of Saul (ch. 15), and when Saul's kingdom totters, it is from Samuel's ghost that Saul seeks advice (ch. 28).

The books of Samuel never identify an author and may have been constructed from several different sources. For instance, the history from 2 Sam. 9 to 1 Kin. 2 gives such intimate detail of the inner workings of David's court that many have called it an independent eyewitness account. If so, it has been connected with other, more general, historical sources to form the present books.

OUTLINE OF 1 AND 2 SAMUEL

I. Samuel, the Last Judge	1 Samuel 1:1—7:17
A. Transition of National Leadership: Eli-Samuel	1:1—3:21
B. Judgeship of Samuel	4:1—7:17
II. Saul, the First King	8:1—31:13
A. Transition of National Leadership: Samuel-Saul	8:1—12:25
B. Reign of King Saul	13:1—16:13
C. Transition of National Leadership: Saul-David	16:14—31:13
III. The Triumphs of David	2 Samuel 1:1—10:19
A. Political Triumphs	1:1—5:25
B. Spiritual Triumphs	6:1—7:29
C. Military Triumphs	8:1—10:19
IV. The Transgressions of David	11:1–27
A. Sin of Adultery	11:1–5
B. Sin of Murder	11:6–27
V. The Troubles of David	12:1—24:25
A. Troubles of David's House	12:1—13:36
D. Troubles of David's Kingdom	13:37—24:25

RITUAL FOR AN AUDIENCE WITH GOD (1 SAM. 1:8–18)

In the ancient Near East people believed that the gods would appear to you if you went to a sacred site. Worshipers followed a ritual that included a sacrifice, a meal dedicated to the god, and a prayer of petition, then spent the night in the holy place. Often the deity appeared to the worshiper in a dream (see 1 Kin. 3:5), but sometimes through the priests or a direct vision.

According to a text from about 2150 B.C., Gudea, king of Lagash, slept at the site of a proposed shrine. Gudea asked permission of the god Ningirsu to build a temple for the deity at that site. Ningirsu appeared to Gudea in a dream, giving him not only permission to build, but also the plans for the building itself. Other examples of this kind of prayer are found in Mesopotamia, Asia Minor, Egypt, Phoenicia, and the Greco-Roman world (including the epics of Homer).

Each year Elkanah and his wife Hannah visited the holy sanctuary of Yahweh at Shiloh (1 Sam. 1:3, 7), where Elkanah made a sacrifice for her (1:4, 5). After eating what was possibly a meal dedicated to Yahweh, Hannah made her prayer of petition (1:9–11). She was answered by Eli, God's priest, in God's name, and her request was granted in the birth of Samuel (1:20).

Dagon Breaks Before God
(1 Sam. 5:1–5)

The Philistine community at Ashdod adopted one of the most widely worshiped gods arising from the middle Euphrates region. Dagon was known as a deity at two of the Philistine's five principal cities: Gaza (Judg. 16:21, 23) and Ashdod (1 Sam. 5:1–5). Dagon's temple at Ashdod still existed as late as the Hellenistic period (2nd century B.C.) when the city was known as Azotus (1 Macc. 10:83, 84).

The worship of Dagon is first recorded in the records of Sargon of Accad (c. 2350 B.C.), long before the time of the Philistines. The central temple of the cult was situated at Terqa, located just below the junction of the Habor and Euphrates rivers. A lack of narrative materials makes it difficult to describe Dagon. The most reasonable theory—that he is the deity of grain—was suggested by Philo of Byblos, a 2nd-century A.D. Greek historian. The Hebrew noun *dagan* simply means "grain," and the central place of grain in the diet of all the cultures of the area might explain the popularity of the deity. A less likely, yet popular, theory connects Dagon to fish (Hebrew *dag* means "fish").

The Mari tablets (c. 1813–1760 B.C.) describe the activities of Dagon. As a ruling god, he led his people in warfare, provided for the fertility of the land and populace, protected the territory from human and divine encroachment, and took special care of the royal family. More interestingly, Dagon kept contact with his people by means of prophetic communication. Professional and nonprofessional prophets would report the will of the deity through those whom the god seized for such communication.

By Samuel's time the cult of Dagon had spread throughout Mesopotamia, Syria, and Palestine. Following ancient practice, a victorious Philistine city would bring booty taken from Israel's deity and place it before the image of their own deity. The breaking of Dagon's image in the presence of the ark of God (1 Sam. 5:3, 4) demonstrated the power Israel's God had over the Philistines' Dagon.

THE UNITED MONARCHY IN ISRAEL

In the larger scope of ancient Near Eastern history, no time was more propitious for Israel to establish a monarchy. No great empire existed that might challenge a new kingdom. Assyria, the dominant power in Mesopotamia, was going through a temporary, but lengthy, period of weakness. Egypt's powerful New Kingdom (1550–1069 B.C.) was ending, and Egypt would never again be as strong.

Israel's major rivals during the united monarchy were the smaller kingdoms around Palestine. Of these, the Philistines on the coastal plain remained the greatest threat. Indeed, it was the Philistine threat that led the people to call for a king; and their first king, Saul, died fighting the Philistines. Not until Saul's successor, David, was this enemy finally subdued (2 Sam. 5:25).

David's rise to power as king attained high points in two events. First was his capture of the Jebusite city, Jerusalem (2 Sam. 5:6, 7). The city was well suited to be the capital of David's united nation. Second was his defeat of the Philistines, which enabled him to extend his rule across the Jordan River into Edom, Moab, and Ammon, and north into Syria (2 Sam. 8).

By the reign of Solomon, David's son and successor, Israel's borders had expanded to their greatest extent ever. Solomon consolidated his father's modest empire. By means of diplomatic ties, especially with the merchant city of Tyre to the north, Solomon became very successful in international trade. Within Israel, the loose confederacy of independent tribes was replaced by a highly organized central bureaucracy, including military conscription and forced labor. Even Israel's worship center changed, from a movable tent shrine to a permanent temple, with the king himself performing some sacred functions. Israel received what they had asked for in 1 Sam. 8:5: a king "like all the nations."

EPOCH FOUR
Chronological Reading Guide

- ❑ 1 Samuel 8:1—16:23
- ❑ Psalm 23
- ❑ 1 Samuel 17:1—19:17
- ❑ Psalm 59
- ❑ 1 Samuel 19:18—21:15
- ❑ Psalms 56, 34
- ❑ 1 Samuel 22:1—23:29
- ❑ Psalms 52, 63
- ❑ 1 Samuel 24:1–22
- ❑ Psalms 57, 142
- ❑ 1 Samuel 25:1—30:31
- ❑ Psalm 54
- ❑ 1 Samuel 31:1–13
- ❑ 2 Samuel 1:1–27
- ❑ Psalm 18
- ❑ 2 Samuel 2:1—7:29
- ❑ 1 Chronicles 9:35—15:29
- ❑ Psalms 8, 19, 29, 32
- ❑ Psalms 65, 68, 103, 108
- ❑ 1 Chronicles 16:1–43
- ❑ Psalms 138, 96, 105, 106
- ❑ Psalms 39, 50, 62
- ❑ Psalms 73—83
- ❑ 1 Chronicles 17:1–27
- ❑ Psalm 88
- ❑ 2 Samuel 8:1—14:33
- ❑ Psalm 51
- ❑ 2 Samuel 15:1–37
- ❑ Psalm 3
- ❑ 2 Samuel 16:1—20:26
- ❑ Psalm 7
- ❑ 2 Samuel 21:1—23:39
- ❑ 1 Chronicles 18:1—20:8
- ❑ Psalm 60
- ❑ 2 Samuel 24:1–25
- ❑ 1 Kings 1:1—2:46
- ❑ 1 Chronicles 21:1–30
- ❑ Psalms 4—6, 9—14, 16
- ❑ Psalms 17, 22, 25—28
- ❑ Psalms 31, 35, 36, 38
- ❑ Psalms 40, 41, 53, 55, 58
- ❑ Psalms 61, 64, 69—71
- ❑ Psalms 86, 102, 109
- ❑ Psalms 139—141
- ❑ Psalms 143, 37
- ❑ 1 Chronicles 22:1—26:19
- ❑ Psalms 30, 15, 24
- ❑ Psalms 42—49, 84, 85
- ❑ 1 Chronicles 26:20—29:30
- ❑ Psalms 87, 2, 20, 21, 72
- ❑ Psalms 93—99
- ❑ Psalms 101, 110, 144
- ❑ 1 Kings 3:1—4:34
- ❑ Proverbs 1:1—22:16
- ❑ 1 Kings 5:1—10:29
- ❑ Ecclesiastes 1:1—12:14
- ❑ 1 Kings 11:1–8
- ❑ Song of Solomon 1:1—8:14
- ❑ 1 Kings 11:9–43
- ❑ 2 Chronicles 1:1—9:31

Saul and David (1 Samuel 9:1—12:25)

The Bible contains two separate histories of the Israelite monarchy. The first is found in the books of Samuel and Kings, and the second in the books of Chronicles. Although the account in Chronicles is based on the earlier history of Samuel and Kings and often quotes directly from it, the two accounts tell the history from very different perspectives—whereas Samuel and Kings are especially interested in prophets and prophecy, Chronicles is much more concerned with the temple and its priests.

The prophetic account begins with the prophet Samuel's meeting with Saul, the man from the tribe of Benjamin who would become the first king. At that time, the Philistines along the Mediterranean seacoast dominated the scene, but Saul was well suited to command Israel. He proved this by leading a military campaign against Ammon (1 Sam. 11). In this battle, Saul behaves like one of the judges of earlier years and is consequently accepted by both northern and southern Israel.

The account of Saul's career is woven together with the rise to power of Israel's next king, David. Saul's last years were clouded by periods of depression and gloom. By the time the young David entered Saul's court with his soothing music (1 Sam. 16:19–23), he had already been anointed Saul's successor (16:1, 13).

SAUL OF ISRAEL AGAINST THE PHILISTINES

Saul wars with the Philistines throughout his reign (1 Sam. 13:1–3; 31:1–3)

B.C. 1200 — 1150 — 1100 — 1050 — 1000

- Pharaoh Ramesses III stops the advance of the Sea Peoples 1175 B.C.
- One of the Sea Peoples, the Philistines, settles on southern coast of Palestine 1175 B.C.
- Large, prosperous Philistine settlement at Ashdod 1050 B.C.
- Saul's coronation, accepting the 40-year reign of Paul's sermon (Acts 13:21) 1050 B.C.
- Saul's coronation, estimating a reign of 10 years (1 Sam. 11:15) 1020 B.C.
- David rules as king of Judah at Hebron (2 Sam. 2:4) 1010 B.C.

THE EVIL HIGH PLACES (1 SAM. 9:12)

High places were a regular part of religious life in Canaanite society. The Israelites were also attracted to these facilities, making them a common feature in their cities, both in Israel (2 Kin. 17:9) and in Judah (2 Kin. 23:5, 8).

The fullest description of a high place is of one near a city in the region of Zuph (1 Sam. 9:5). At this high place there was a hall large enough to hold at least 30 people (9:22), which was used, at least sometimes, as a place for eating (9:13). A cook was stationed there, which means the high place probably also had some type of kitchen and, presumably, storage rooms (9:23, 24). An altar was also present, allowing Samuel to attend a sacrifice at this high place (9:12).

Because of the word "high," many have assumed that high places were necessarily built on isolated hills or mountaintops. Nevertheless, high places were probably just as often built within the walls of cities. The location of high places is said to be "in the cities" (2 Kin. 23:5) or "at the gates" of a city (2 Kin. 23:8). If cities most often were built on hilltops, it could mean that the highest point of a city may have been reserved for a high place.

On the other hand, archaeologists have discovered figurines and other cult objects in and around raised platforms, not so prominently located within cities. Small rooms and cooking areas have been found associated with these raised platforms, which possibly were the "high places" of Old Testament cities, even though not located on hilltops.

Worship in high places became centers for the worship of foreign gods, where the Israelites engaged in evil practices (Jer. 19:4, 5). Hezekiah is reported to have been a good king partly because, among other things, he "removed the high places" (2 Kin. 18:4).

SAUL THE KING? (1 SAM. 11:14, 15)

Gilgal held special significance for the relationship between Israel and her God Yahweh. It was there that the Israelites renewed their covenant with Yahweh before entering the Promised Land (Josh. 5:10). It was also at Gilgal that Saul was made king (1 Sam. 11:15). Yet despite the coronation ritual and celebration, a question hung over the new king: What kind of kingdom did he really have?

His standing army was relatively small and divided into two units, both of which were stationed within Benjamin, Saul's own tribal territory (1 Sam. 13:2). Before his coronation, Saul acted like a judge, calling together troops for a specific need (1 Sam. 11:7). Even though Samuel had already proclaimed Saul's kingship, the king-to-be met with opposition and rejection (10:24–27).

It appears that Saul's kingdom was an act of desperation on the part of the Israelites. The Ammonites were moving in on the tribes of Reuben and Gad (11:1–3), while the Philistines were controlling the heartland of Israel (13:3). The Israelites were ill prepared for war, lacking swords and spears, as well as a way to sharpen them, if they had them (13:19–22).

Saul's reign was one of defense and struggle. He is pictured as spending much of his time chasing David. The Bible says nothing about any building activities. Saul spent all of his time building a kingdom, with no time to build a palace. While there was great rejoicing in Gilgal at Saul's coronation (11:15), such things as palaces and royal cities would have to wait until the reign of his successor, David.

From Copper to Bronze to Iron (1 Sam. 13:19–22)

The first metals used by humans were gold, silver, and copper. Gold and silver were too soft to be used for tools or weapons. Copper is also soft, although it was hammered into a harder form. However, sometime around 3500 B.C. metalworkers discovered that copper hardened when alloyed with tin to produce bronze or with zinc to produce brass.

The harder bronze was not only a better metal for producing tools, but also resulted in more effective weapons. During the Early Bronze Age, from about 2300 B.C., bronze swords and ax heads were produced by bronzeworkers with increasing skill. Bronze instruments of warfare, such as the spear (2 Sam. 21:16), the bow (2 Sam. 22:35), and shield (2 Chr. 12:10), were still in use at the time of Israel's monarchy.

The next advance in metal technology came with the discovery of smelting to separate iron from its oxides. The ironworking process was slow to develop. Before 1200 B.C. iron was used mostly for jewelry and ceremonial weapons; however, there are a few examples of military use. An Accadian text from Nuzi in northern Mesopotamia, dating from about the 15th century B.C., gives evidence of a coat of iron scale armor made for a horse. When the Israelites first arrived in Canaan, they were faced with the superiority of their opponents' iron-reinforced chariots (Judg. 1:19; 4:3).

Ironworking demanded the skill of a blacksmith. A letter of the Hittite king Hattusilis III, dating around 1250 B.C., shows that the Hittites had developed skills in the production of smelted iron. When Saul became Israel's king (1050 or 1020 B.C.), Philistine ironsmiths were able to control the actual working of iron in Canaan. They would sharpen the Hebrews' iron tools, but would not teach them to "make swords or spears" of iron (1 Sam. 13:19, 22).

David in Saul's Court (1 Sam. 17:1—19:17)

David's arrival in Saul's court as musician and armorbearer (1 Sam. 16:14–23) is followed immediately by a second arrival, this time as the boy slayer of the Philistine giant (1 Sam. 17). Though some details of these two accounts are puzzling, such as why Saul does not seem to recognize his own armorbearer (1 Sam. 17:55), the "two arrivals" are appropriate to David's character. He will always be remembered as both a great warrior, the lion of Judah, and as the sweet singer of Israel, the man after God's own heart.

Saul's and David's victories over the Philistines gave heart to Israel, but the Philistines continued pressing inland. Saul would spend the rest of his life at war with them. That strain, along with his jealousy of David's popularity, helped to overset an already troubled mind.

How Big Is a Giant? (1 Sam. 17:4)

The height reported for the Philistine Goliath, "six cubits and a span" (1 Sam. 17:4), indicates a very big man: approximately 9 feet, 9 inches tall. If such a height seems tall now, it was much taller in ancient times. Biblical people averaged about 5 feet in height, judging from skeletons uncovered by archaeologists.

Other Old Testament sources offer a different measurement for Goliath's height. Some manuscripts of the Septuagint (the Greek Old Testament) and one of the Samuel manuscripts from the Dead Sea Scrolls read "four cubits and a span" in 1 Sam. 17:4. This height—about 6 feet, 9 inches—would still make Goliath a giant among warriors for David's time. It cannot be known which of these manuscripts preserves the original number.

Jonathan Transfers Claim to the Throne (1 Sam. 18:1–4)

After he killed Goliath, David became a member of Saul's court. Jonathan, Saul's son and heir, took an immediate liking to David and saw this new friend as an equal. This was central to the rise of David to the throne.

When Saul had offered David his armor and sword (1 Sam. 17:38, 39), David returned them. Jonathan handed over to David his robe and his military gear, including his sword and bow (1 Sam. 18:4). As with Saul's offer, Jonathan's offer entailed more than the clothes. With David's acceptance of the sword of Jonathan, David became who Jonathan was. David was now the heir apparent to the throne of Israel. In this action the already established heir, Jonathan, acknowledged that God's decision had been made: David was to rule rather than himself, and he was willing to step aside.

Both Saul and Jonathan knew what had happened with this transfer of royal insignia (1 Sam. 20:30, 31). Saul began sending out David to battles he had previously fought himself or had sent Jonathan to fight (18:5). After this time, in another indication of David's new status, Saul began to refer to David as "my son" (1 Sam. 24:16; 26:21).

ANGEL: MESSENGER AND PRESENCE OF GOD (Ps. 34:7)

Angels do the will of God. Both the Hebrew and Greek words for "angel" mean "messenger." In the ancient Near Eastern cultures' pantheons of gods, the angels were the lowest denizens of heaven—the slave messengers who did only what they were commanded to do by their superiors. The gods of the pantheons could disagree with and disobey the authoritative deities of their own divine hierarchy.

However, the official religion of Israel accepted no other divine beings than God, save the angels. The psalmists knew of no disagreement in heaven, since God is in control of all divine beings (Ps. 89:6, 7). The angels do the work of heaven in harmony with the will of God. In narratives of the Bible and of the texts from Ugarit (1400–1200 B.C.), divine messengers carry messages in the form of living letters. The messengers repeat word for word what they are told to report to other gods or to humans. In this way the message given by an angel in the name of another deity was indeed the very words of the deity who sent the messenger.

An angel of any given deity was so closely associated with the god as to represent the actual presence of the god. Thus, as Moses experienced at the burning bush (Ex. 3:2–4), to speak with an angel was actually to speak with the deity. The Bible presents a similar situation with the activity of angels. Since the messenger could do only as ordered by God, whatever an angel did in the name of God was done by God. So in Israel's psalms, it is God who protects the faithful, even though the actual divine being standing guard is God's angel (Ps. 34:7).

Who Will Succeed Saul as King? (2 Samuel 2:1—4:12)

Most ancient Near Eastern kingdoms had established dynasties in which successive rulers came from the same family. The practice of dynastic succession meant that when a king died, his eldest son normally reigned in his place. But dynastic succession was foreign to Israel. During the earlier tribal confederacy, the judges had been inspired specifically for times of crisis, and their inspiration was not transferred to their sons. When Gideon was asked to reign, he refused, saying, "I will not rule over you, nor shall my son rule over you; the LORD shall rule over you" (Judg. 8:23).

When Israel's first king died, the question of succession became crucial. Some favored a dynastic succession, placing Saul's son Ishbosheth on the throne (2 Sam. 2:8–10). Others, perhaps remembering the pattern of the judges, preferred to crown the man who had shown himself most able, David (2 Sam. 2:10, 11).

In addition, both Ishbosheth and David had ambitious generals. Abner, who was commander of Saul's army, as well as a cousin of Saul, naturally supported Ishbosheth. In the same way, Joab, commander of David's army and the son of David's sister Zeruiah, was a powerful element in David's campaign for the throne. In the ensuing years of civil war, the plots and maneuverings of these generals became extremely significant.

Equally significant are the brief lists in 2 Sam. 3:2–5 and 5:13–16 of the sons born to David. The question of royal succession would apply to the next generation as well. David's first and third sons, Amnon and Absalom (3:2, 3), would prove themselves unworthy of the throne and be eliminated (2 Sam. 13—18). Two other sons, Adonijah (3:4) and Solomon (5:14), would later challenge each other for their father's throne (1 Kin. 1; 2).

The Sort-of Wife (2 Sam. 3:7)

The word "concubine" is difficult to define for people of western culture since there is no analogous relationship in Western European society. In the ancient Near East a concubine was a woman who had legal status within a family and who shared the sexual attentions of the husband, while having somewhat lesser authority than a wife. The presence of concubines in a household was openly acknowledged without any pejorative implication (2 Sam. 19:5). The sons of a concubine were treated as heirs, though with, perhaps, somewhat lesser status (Gen. 25:6).

For one to take another man's concubine was seen as usurping the husband's authority. This was especially true of a king's concubines. To gain possession of a king's harem was to gain title to the king's throne. After David became king, he took possession of Saul's concubines (2 Sam. 12:8). When Absalom usurped his father David's rule of Jerusalem, one of his first acts to publicly claim royal authority was to establish sexual relations with David's concubines (2 Sam. 16:21, 22).

After Saul died, his son Ishbosheth struggled to secure his position as Saul's successor. There were battles between Ishbosheth's Israel and David's Judah (2 Sam. 3:6). In light of Ishbosheth's shaky kingship, it is quite natural that he would be alarmed at the possibility of anyone, especially the army commander Abner, having relations with Saul's concubine, Rizpah (3:7).

THE BOOKS OF CHRONICLES

While Chronicles has a different emphasis than Samuel and Kings, the Chronicler often quotes the other histories, especially Kings. But Chronicles also extends further in time. Whereas Kings ends during the Babylonian exile, Chronicles concludes with the Persian king Cyrus's proclamation that allowed the exiled Jews to return to Jerusalem.

Although the books of Chronicles are especially concerned with the monarchy, they begin much earlier, with Adam. In the historical shorthand of genealogies of 1 Chr. 1—9, the Chronicler covers the time span between Adam and a good deal beyond King Saul. These genealogical lists actually go as far as the postexilic period and provide an important backdrop for that era.

The final genealogy (1 Chr. 9:35–44), however, covers Saul's family and introduces the narrative of his tragic death in 1 Chr. 10. Within the list are what were probably the original names of Saul's son (Esh-Baal, 9:39) and grandson (Merib-Baal, 9:40). The prophetic story of Saul's family in 2 Samuel consistently spells these names as Ishbosheth (2 Sam. 2:8) and Mephibosheth (2 Sam. 4:4). The author of Samuel replaced the name of the Canaanite god Baal with *bosheth*, the Hebrew word for "shame."

OUTLINE OF 1 AND 2 CHRONICLES

I. From Adam to Saul	1 Chronicles 1:1—9:44
A. Family of Adam	1:1–27
B. Family of Abraham	1:28–54
C. Family of Israel	2:1–55
D. Family of David	3:1–24
E. Descendants of the Israelite Tribes	4:1—8:40
F. Descendants of the Remnant	9:1–34
G. Family of Saul	9:35–44
II. The Reign of David	10:1—29:30
A. David Becomes King	10:1—12:40
B. Removal of the Ark	13:1—17:27
C. Military Victories of David	18:1—20:8
D. Preparation for the Temple	21:1—27:34
E. Last Days of David	28:1—29:30
III. The Reigns of Solomon	2 Chronicles 1:1—9:31
A. Succession of Solomon as King	1:1–17
B. Completion of the Temple	2:1—7:22
C. Glory of Solomon's Reign	8:1—9:28
D. Death of Solomon	9:29–31
IV. The Reigns of Selected Kings of Judah	10:1—36:23

THE FIRST KINGS OF ISRAEL

Ishbosheth is assassinated (2 Sam. 4:5–8) 1003 B.C.

David is anointed king of all Israel (2 Sam. 5:3) 1003 B.C.

Rehoboam succeeds his father Solomon as Israel's king 930 B.C.

B.C. 1030 — 1005 — 980 — 955 — 930

Saul's death (if Ishbosheth did not immediately rule) 1010 B.C.

David is anointed king of Judah at Hebron (2 Sam. 2:4) 1010 B.C.

David's reign reported to be 40 years (1 Kin. 2:11) 1010 B.C.

Saul's death (if Ishbosheth immediately succeeded Saul) 1005 B.C.

Ishbosheth, Saul's son, becomes king of Israel (2 Sam. 2:10) 1005 B.C.

Solomon succeeds his father David as Israel's king (1 Kin. 2:12) 970 B.C.

Solomon's reign reported to be 40 years (1 Kin. 11:42) 970 B.C.

THE BOOK OF PSALMS

The psalms, almost without exception, are difficult to tie to a specific historical context. They are the worship songs of Israel and are intended to apply to the needs of all worshipers across time. Some psalms do have historical superscriptions that make it possible to associate them with specific events, but these make up only about ten percent of all the psalms.

The rest of the psalms must follow some other criteria by which to read them within the history of Israel. One criterion is to place the psalms ascribed to David (or Solomon or Moses) during the life of that person. A second criterion is to place psalms according to their type.

While there are various classifications of psalm types, two prominent types are hymns and laments. Hymns are songs of praise to God, and laments are appeals for God's help in times of trouble. In the Bible, the psalms are arranged in five distinct books (perhaps to parallel the five books of the Pentateuch). In general, the movement through the five books progresses from lament (in the early books) to praise (in the fifth book).

There was joy and shouting and music as David and Israel moved the ark to Jerusalem (1 Chr. 15:25–28). Such a setting favors the reading of psalms that are hymns of praise, and which are ascribed to David. Several psalms (Ps. 8; 19; 29; 32; 65; 68; 103; 108; 138) are appropriate for the context of David's joyous entry into Jerusalem before the ark. A psalm of thanksgiving, such as Ps. 32, expresses gratitude to God for deliverance. The joy that accompanies God's deliverance could also reflect the joy of the ark event.

OUTLINE OF PSALMS

I. Book 1	Psalms 1—41
II. Book 2	42—72
III. Book 3	73—89
IV. Book 4	90—106
V. Book 5	107—150

King of the Universe (Ps. 29:10, 11)

The last two verses of Ps. 29 are a classic ending for hymns in the ancient world. They define Yahweh as the God who rules above all other gods. Cultures that believed in pantheons of many gods commonly honored one deity as the ruler of all the others. While the official religion of Israel considered Yahweh to be the only God, hymns could reflect Yahweh's power over the gods of popular religion.

The heavenly throne room is pictured much like the throne room of a human ruler. The king sat upon a throne raised above all others in the reception hall. Similarly, the psalmist describes Yahweh as King, sitting above "the Flood" forever (29:10). For ancient people the Flood meant the waters of chaos that still surround the created order. The waters of chaos were terrifying; they were the waters unleashed in the Flood. But as long as God reigns, He keeps them in check.

The power that is described in Ps. 29 as belonging to Yahweh is also given to God's people (29:11). Just as rulers empower people who live under their rule, so the Israelites, God's chosen people, are promised the strength of Yahweh. The psalm ends with a sense of order, kept for the benefit of Israel.

KINGDOMS OF SYRIA AND PALESTINE

Syria refers to the region north of Palestine, which was associated with the city-state of Damascus. In ancient times Syria was known as Aram. Since Syria and Palestine rarely knew political unity, various kingdoms inhabited these regions.

Kingdom	Approximate Period	Important Rulers
Ebla	2400–2250 B.C.	Igris-Halam, Irkab-Damu
Alalakh	1800–1400 B.C.	Yamhad, Yarim-Lim, Idrimi
Ugarit	1400–1180 B.C.	Niqmaddu II
Sea Peoples	1200–1050 B.C.	Seafaring peoples including the Philistines
Aram-Damascus	1050–732 B.C.	Rezon, Hadad-ezer (Ben-Hadad), Hazael
Phoenicia	1050–340 B.C.	Hiram I, Ethbaal I
United Israel	1050 (or 1020)–930 B.C.	Saul, David, Solomon
Israel	930–722 B.C.	Jeroboam I, Ahab, Jehu
Judah	930–586 B.C.	Rehoboam, Hezekiah, Josiah

Music in the Temple (1 Chr. 16:1–43)

One aspect of the Chronicler's emphasis on the temple is his interest in the different priestly duties, particularly in the musical service. In the genealogical introduction to 1 Chronicles (1:1—9:34), more space is given to the Levitical musicians than to some entire tribes.

The prophetic account in 2 Sam. 6:12–19 mentions the sound of music when the ark was brought to Jerusalem. The Chronicler, however, provides much more detail about that music and stresses the role of the Levites in this event. There were Levites carrying the ark, as well as singing and playing instruments (1 Chr. 15:2, 15, 16, 28). Once the ark was in Jerusalem, David began to organize the service of the Jerusalem sanctuary. One of his first actions was to appoint the Levitical musicians and their three leaders: Asaph, Heman, and Jeduthun (1 Chr. 16:37, 41, 42; see 2 Chr. 5:12).

TIME CAPSULE	1086 to 1003 B.C.
1086	Ussher's date for the birth of David
1076	Assyria's power declines after death of Tiglath-Pileser I
1069	End of New Kingdom in Egypt
1050	Philistines have prosperous settlement at Ashdod
1050	Saul becomes first king of Israel (or 1020)
1010–1003	David rules as king of Judah at Hebron
1003–970	David rules as king of Israel at Jerusalem

There Are gods and Then There Is God (Ps. 96:5)

Hymns of praise in the ancient Near East often declared the god being praised to be superior to all other gods. The Bible occasionally uses that kind of language, but more often goes beyond it and says that Yahweh is the only god.

One way of dismissing other gods was to say they were only statues. The supposed "gods of the peoples" are nothing more than the inanimate idols themselves (Ps. 96:5). Yahweh is declared the true deity because only He created the world—"the LORD made the heavens" (96:5). All other gods are impotent and unworthy of adoration; they should be ignored. People who could mistake stone, metal, or wood for a real god are foolish.

A second way of dismissing other gods was to leave open the possibility they existed, yet maintain that they had no serious power and therefore were not to be taken seriously. The prophet Jeremiah, for example, says that other gods did not create the world and will therefore cease to exist (Jer. 10:11). Their insignificance is stressed by their being placed lower than Yahweh in divine authority.

In this way, the Hebrew poets were able to adapt the usual language of Near Eastern hymns into the worship of Yahweh. To Israel and Judah only Yahweh mattered. The other deities either did not exist or were so meaningless that whether they existed was irrelevant. Yahweh was "to be feared above all gods" (Ps. 96:4).

WORSHIPING ANCESTORS AS GODS (Ps. 106:28)

The deification of ancestors was common throughout the ancient world. The mythological texts from Ugarit (1400–1200 B.C.) make reference to "rulers" in the netherworld who formerly had been monarchs in the human realm. These deceased humans were treated as minor deities, having religious feasts held in their honor. Even in ancient Palestine, the excavations of graves have sometimes uncovered tubes built into the ground so that communication and food could be delivered to the deceased.

Ancestor worship is not common in the Bible. There is one Canaanite practice mentioned, however, by which famous or important dead persons had become deities of the underworld. The psalmist reports that the Israelites "ate sacrifices made to the dead" (Ps. 106:28). The practice is associated with the "Baal of Peor" incident, indicating that the Israelites encountered the custom as they moved toward the Promised Land.

The Law of Moses made it unacceptable to treat any human as a god, whether living or dead (Ex. 20:2; Deut. 26:14). The Israelites who engaged in the regional religious belief of eating sacrifices for the dead were considered to have turned away from the one true God and "provoked Him to anger" (Ps. 106:29).

Cherubim, the Divine Guardians (Ps. 80:1)

The religious and royal art of ancient Near Eastern civilizations shows a number of winged, mythological creatures being depicted as composites of several different animals. These supernatural beings appear as guardians for thrones, gateways, palaces, and temples, as well as serving as stands for the images of deities.

The cherubim of the Bible are representatives of these creatures. They acted as guardians of the Garden of Eden (Gen. 3:24); they formed the moving throne of God (Ezek. 1—3); their likenesses were molded at the top of the ark of the covenant (Ex. 25:18). In the Most Holy Place of Solomon's temple were two large cherubim, and images of cherubim were carved into the temple walls by order of Solomon (1 Kin. 6:23–29). Clearly, the artistic representation of the cherubim was associated with the worship of God in Jerusalem.

Cherubim are always described in the Bible as having wings, but we lack a full description of their appearance. From similar creatures found in the art of Phoenicia, Mesopotamia, and even in the Samaritan ivory fragments (not to mention Egyptian sphinxes), cherubim appear to have animal bodies with human heads and a pair of wings extending from the shoulders. While human heads appear on all examples, as well as wings, the bodies may be those of lions or bulls or a combination of both. Phoenician artistic examples exist from the 2nd millennium B.C. through the biblical period.

In religious art cherubim formed mounts, guardians, or companions of the deities, but did not represent the gods themselves. Likewise, the cherubim in Solomon's temple were not intended to be images of God, but were displayed to demonstrate the holiness of the sanctuary and the majesty of the deity worshiped there. Ps. 80:1 reflects the place where God's presence was most revered: in the temple, dwelling between the cherubim of the mercy seat (see Num. 7:89).

David's Reign (2 Samuel 8:1—12:15a)

When Saul died, the Philistines must have assumed that their victory over Israel was complete. The government of Ishbosheth, Saul's son, had virtually no power, and David's rule over Judah was probably condoned by the Philistines. After all, David had been living in their land, and they considered him their man.

If those were the Philistines' assumptions, they were wrong. Within an astonishingly brief time, David had constructed an impressive empire. First, he drove the Philistines from Israelite territory (2 Sam. 5). Then, responding to an insult from Ammon, he sent his armies across the Jordan. By the time he was done, he had defeated the Ammonites, several Aramean (Syrian) kingdoms, Moab, and Edom (2 Sam. 8; 10). He was aided, no doubt, by the decline of the empires of Egypt and Mesopotamia, but his achievements are still impressive, by any standards.

In typical fashion, the biblical history pays scant attention to such feats of arms. Instead, the text focuses on David's behavior while his armies were off at war—especially on his affair with Bathsheba. This incident and its aftermath form the heart of what is often called the "Succession Document" (2 Sam. 9—1 Kin. 2). The history of the "Succession Document" gives a unified and very detailed record of events in David's court up until Solomon, the son of Bathsheba, was crowned David's successor.

Ashes of Sorrow (2 Sam. 13:19)

People of biblical times often figuratively expressed their feelings. For example, distraught people sometimes tore their clothes in a dramatic expression of their feelings. We should remember that long before the industrial revolution every piece of clothing was handmade. This only reinforces how much sorrow a person must have felt to tear a garment, especially if it was a precious one.

Tamar's tragic story is one of a sister being sexually violated by her brother Amnon, even though she pled with him that "no such thing should be done in Israel" (2 Sam. 13:12). In disgrace she tore her robe, a special possession as indicated by its description as "of many colors." In addition, Tamar, as was true of other ancient persons (Esth. 4:1; Job 2:8; Dan. 9:3), put "ashes on her head" (2 Sam. 13:19), which were refuse and dirty. By tearing her beautiful robe and covering her head in ashes, she expressed, even better than with words, how distraught she was.

David the Sweet Psalmist (2 Sam. 23:1)

The last words of David are introduced by the epitaph, "the son of Jesse...the man raised up on high, the anointed of the God of Jacob, and the sweet psalmist of Israel" (2 Sam. 23:1). David and psalms are ever considered together in the tradition of Israel.

Psalms are often thought of as poems or songs. In the Hebrew tradition the psalms are known as "songs of praise." While other themes are exhibited in the psalms, praise is the most pronounced feature. Music was a regular part of ancient life, accompanying mourners at funerals, priests at temples, brides at weddings, and the solitary individual in contemplation. Within this musical culture, the psalms were Israel's worship songs, offering reflection on the experiences of life.

In the stories that surround David, psalms are shown to be an integral part of his life (2 Sam. 1:17). His skill at playing the harp was widely known and highly appreciated (1 Sam. 16:16–23). When David became king, he appointed professional singers to perform religious duties (1 Chr. 6:31, 32; 15:16–24). David himself rendered "songs of praise" at special religious occasions (1 Chr. 16:7–36). In these services, music was used as a vehicle for prophesying (1 Chr. 25:1).

The Book of Psalms is often associated with David because the superscriptions (or psalm titles) ascribe a large number of the psalms to David or to an event in his life. After his death, David's fame as a psalmist grew ever larger. While the Hebrew Bible associates David with 73 psalms, later translations increase the number of psalms ascribed to him. The Dead Sea Psalms Scroll claims that David wrote 4,050 psalms and songs.

GATES AND FORTIFIED CITIES (1 CHR. 19:9)

Battles were often fought near the gate of a city, which was its most vulnerable defensive feature. City gates were made of wood, so it was easier for enemies to gain access to the city by beating them down or setting them on fire, than by storming or undermining the stone walls. For this reason a number of developments were added to city gates to make them a stronger part of a fortified city's overall defense (2 Chr. 8:5).

One building strategy was to make the approach to the city a long narrow ramp. Such ramps ran parallel to one of the city's walls and were often built along the wall from right to left. Enemy soldiers carrying shields and being mostly right-handed were forced to turn nearly backward to defend themselves. Furthermore, this process exposed them to observation and attack from the city's defenders.

Cities also had more than one gate in the gatehouse or main-gate complex. The outer gate was built well outside the city and at a right angle to the city. It was placed directly in front of the approach ramp and was the first major obstacle for attackers.

These gatehouses were part of a castlelike building similar to towers. Defenders were stationed on the roofs of these complexes and behind the doors. If enemy soldiers succeeded in gaining entrance, they found themselves confined to a narrow passage that made a sharp right turn toward the main gate. Of course, defenders were not only blocking the passage but were also stationed above on the walls of the passage. If enemies survived this gauntlet, they still faced the city's primary gate.

The main gate was a multichambered structure resembling an extra-large tower. It consisted of up to four separate sets of gates, behind which were chambers for defending soldiers. The roofs of these gate structures were designed so that the defenders had clear aim at the attackers.

THE BOOKS OF KINGS

Although the books of Kings present a unified history, they clearly consist of many smaller strands, woven together by an editor. These strands include a detailed account of Solomon's court, a history of the kings of both the northern and southern kingdoms, and narratives about the prophets Elijah and Elisha.

All these strands are woven together and unified by theological comments that interpret the history. The interpretations evaluate the different kings and kingdoms in terms of the requirements found in the Book of Deuteronomy. For instance, 2 Kin. 17, which explains in some detail why God allowed the northern kingdom to be destroyed, uses thoughts and even specific expressions from Deuteronomy. For this reason, Kings is often described as part of a "Deuteronomistic History."

The history concludes during the Babylonian exile, with the last recorded event occurring in 561 B.C. (2 Kin. 25:27–30). However, there is no mention of the Persian king Cyrus and his edict of 539 B.C. that freed the exiled Jews (see 2 Chr. 36:22, 23). Therefore, it is reasonable to assume that the editing process was done sometime between 561 and 539 B.C.

The Book of 1 Kings begins with the story of how Solomon became David's successor instead of Adonijah, the crown prince. An exact date for when Solomon began his reign is impossible to determine. The 40 years given as the length of his reign (1 Kin. 11:42) could be a symbolic number, and, furthermore, it is not known how long Solomon ruled as a coregent while his father, David, was still alive (1 Kin. 1:32–35; 2:10). Accepting these uncertainties, we can set the date for Solomon's enthronement at approximately 970 B.C.

OUTLINE OF 1 AND 2 KINGS

I. The United Kingdom	**1 Kings 1:1—11:43**
A. Establishment of Solomon as King	1:1—2:46
B. Rise of Solomon as King	3:1—8:66
C. Decline of Solomon as King	9:1—11:43
II. The Divided Kingdom	**12:1—22:53**
A. The Division of the Kingdom	12:1—14:31
B. Reigns of Two Kings in Judah	15:1–24
C. Reigns of Five Kings in Israel	15:25—16:28
D. Reign of Ahab in Israel	16:29—22:40
E. Reign of Jehoshaphat in Judah	22:41–50
F. Reign of Ahaziah in Israel	22:51–53
III. The Divided Kingdom Continued	**2 Kings 1:1—17:41**
IV. The Surviving Kingdom of Judah	**18:1—25:30**

Satan, Initiating Evil for Israel
(1 Chr. 21:1)

The Chronicler uses "Satan" as the proper name of a celestial being who is operating independently of Yahweh. This Satan, who "stood up against Israel, and moved David to number Israel" (1 Chr. 21:1), is related to the divine functionary who appears as an adversary or accuser of humans (Job 1:6; 2:1; Zech. 3:1). The Chronicler's Satan, however, differs by being a divine being in opposition to the will of God.

Ancient Near Eastern civilizations had many demons, as well as deities who often did horrendous things to humans. The only deity, though, who can reasonably be compared to the figure of Satan (as developed in early Judaism and Christianity) is found in Persia's dualistic religion, Zoroastrianism.

The Iranian prophet Zoroaster lived possibly between the 10th and 6th centuries B.C. He taught that the cosmos was divided into two warring factions, one good and one evil. Those who struggle on behalf of good worship Ahura Mazda, the god of light; those seeking evil worship Angra Mainyu (also called Ahriman). These two deities, with their followers, were destined to vie for control of the universe until a final cosmic battle in which good will triumph over evil. Those humans who served Ahura Mazda would find rewards in heaven; those who served Angra Mainyu would be cast into a burning hell.

Zoroastrianism became the official religion of the Persian Empire during the Achaemenid Dynasty (c. 559–331 B.C.). It was publicly declared the royal faith in a huge inscription by Darius I (522–486 B.C.). The Chronicler wrote during the approximately 200 years that Judah was a territory within the Persian province called "beyond the River" (1 Chr. 19:16), and his notion of Satan as the evil counterpart of God compares to the evil Angra Mainyu of Zoroastrianism.

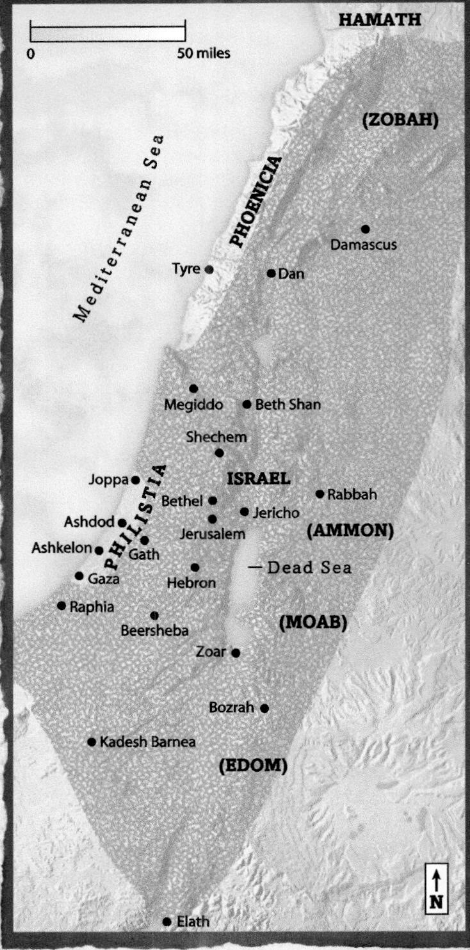

The Davidic Kingdom
The military successes of David against the Moabites and Edomites expanded and solidified his control to the east and south of Jerusalem. He also succeeded in isolating the Philistines to a few coastal cities. Victories against Zobah and the Arameans in the northeast and against the Ammonites in the central region greatly extended his borders.

SOLOMON AND HIRAM BUILD THE TEMPLE

B.C. 975 — 970 — 965 — 960 — 955

- Solomon begins coregency with his father David (1 Kin. 1:32–39) 973 B.C.
- Solomon becomes sole ruler on Israel's throne (1 Kin. 2:12) 970 B.C.
- 12th year of Hiram (if Carthage was founded in 825 B.C.) 968 B.C.
- Solomon lays the foundation of the temple (1 Kin. 6:1) 966 B.C.
- Hiram's builders help with the construction of the temple (1 Kin. 5:18)
- All work is completed on the temple (1 Kin. 6:37, 38) 959 B.C.
- 12th year of Hiram (if Carthage was founded in 814 B.C.) 957 B.C.

THE SLEEP OF DEATH (Ps. 13:3)

Death is a universal dilemma. In one ancient Near Eastern story, the Gilgamesh Epic, the hero Gilgamesh is suddenly struck by the pain of death, when his friend Enkidu dies. Gilgamesh then begins a long journey in search of the secret of eternal life. Even when he finds it in a thorny plant, it is stolen from him, and Gilgamesh concludes that seeking immortality is useless because all must die.

The Israelites had a unique focus on the here and now. While the Egyptians prepared elaborate tombs, including paintings and figures that would supposedly benefit the dead one, the Hebrew Scriptures stressed the importance of living life to its fullness because death was the end of human activity. Hebrew wisdom offered this advice: Find joy in the daily rounds of life, "for there is no work or device or knowledge or wisdom in the grave where you are going" (Eccl. 9:10).

Death was often equated with a kind of sleep, thus the psalmist uses the image of "the sleep of death" (Ps. 13:3). When the kings of Israel died, we are told they went to sleep or "rested" with their fathers (1 Kin. 2:10; 11:43; 14:31).

The Hebrews described death with visual imagery as the abode of the dead. A person who dies goes to Sheol (sometimes translated as "hell," "grave," or the "pit"), which clearly represents the grave (Job 21:13; Prov. 7:27). In Sheol there is no human activity, not even the praising of the Lord (Ps. 146:3, 4; 115:17); or as the author of Ecclesiastes wrote, "For the living know that they will die; but the dead know nothing" (Eccl. 9:5).

Death was not to be dreaded; it was the expected, normal end of life. Indeed, death was considered good for the person who was "full of years" and had reached "a good old age" (Gen. 25:8; Job 42:17).

PROPHETS BETWEEN GOD AND HUMANITY (1 CHR. 25:5)

Prophets were common in the ancient Near East. In most royal courts, they were specialists whose occupation was to act as a mediator between God (or the gods) and the human world. These prophets were understood to have been seized by the divinities who used them to convey their very words to the human listeners. Kings employed court prophets in order to be informed of the divine will any time it was deemed necessary. Some of these professional prophets were not trustworthy, since they might claim as divine word whatever would advance their own positions in court.

A historical note in the Book of 1 Samuel indicates that the prophet had earlier been known as a "seer" (1 Sam. 9:9). The term "seer" refers to the experience of the prophet being allowed to see the deliberations of the divine council and to relate the decisions made there in accurate detail. Thus one who was called a "seer," a term related to the prophet's vision, came to be called a prophet, a term related to the public proclamation of the message.

In David's court Heman is described as "the king's seer" (1 Chr. 25:5). This Heman was also one of David's temple musicians (1 Chr. 16:42).

Kings as Vice-Regents (Ps. 2:7)

The position of king in the ancient Near East was the point at which heaven and earth came together. The Egyptians believed their pharaoh was divine and returned to the gods when he died. From about 1500 B.C. the pharaoh was thought to be the son of the god Amon-Re, as well as the "image of god," both physically and in his actions. Egyptian kings had their own priests, and their palace was treated as a temple. The pharaoh counted on the help of the other gods in ruling his kingdom.

In Mesopotamia, rulers were not considered divine, but they were understood to have been appointed king by the patron deity of their city or empire. Since the god had chosen him, the king ruled as vice-regent of the god and was accountable to the god for all his actions. As long as the king did what was expected of a good ruler, the gods would protect him and guarantee victory over his enemies.

Such ancient Near Eastern theology was used by Judah to celebrate the crowning of Davidic kings in Jerusalem. The psalmist describes Yahweh speaking to Judah's new king in words parallel to the Mesopotamian royal texts: "You are My Son, today I have begotten You" (Ps. 2:7). The early Christians understood Ps. 2 to be referring to Jesus as the messiah (Acts 4:25, 26; 13:33). But originally Ps. 2:7 meant that Judah's king was the legitimate heir to the throne (other rulers were "adopted"). The king was the vice-regent of Yahweh, seated at His right hand, and Yahweh would guarantee victories for the king over Judah's enemies.

Solomon Marries Pharaoh's Daughter (1 Kin. 3:1)

Marriage was an effective means for creating alliances among ancient nations. The idea behind such marriages was that two nations, by marriage, became one larger extended family. The hope was that one would deal more kindly with kin than with strangers.

No greater evidence of Solomon's importance among the nearby countries could be given than to record his marriage to an Egyptian pharaoh's daughter. As policy, Egypt's pharaohs did not give their daughters in marriage to foreign kings. In one tablet from Tell el-Amarna, Egypt (1360–1333 B.C.), the Egyptians respond to a request by a Babylonian king for one of pharaoh's daughters: "From of old a daughter of the king of Egypt has not been given to anyone." At the same time, the pharaohs themselves did marry royal, foreign wives. Solomon's marriage to one of pharaoh's daughters (1 Kin. 3:1; 9:16) is a major testimony to Solomon's unusual esteem.

On the other hand, in the time of Solomon Egypt had seen its better days. Solomon's Egyptian father-in-law is not named, but Siamun (978–959 B.C.), who reigned during Egypt's Third Intermediate Period, is the likely pharaoh. This period was characterized by weakness and instability. The pharaohs were so politically weak that they did all they could to assure support from important Egyptians, including allowing the marriage of their daughters to Egyptian commoners. In the case of Solomon, Siamun sought the support of Israel by doing the extraordinary—marrying one of his daughters to a foreign king.

THE BOOK OF PROVERBS

The wisdom tradition of Israel influences several different biblical books, but its heart is in the Book of Proverbs. The proverbs are short, poetically matched comments on the world. They do not claim to be universal truth, but rather situational advice to be applied to different contexts. (For instance, two adjacent proverbs in Prov. 26:4, 5 give directly contradictory advice.)

The Book of Proverbs is actually several different collections of proverbs. Chapters 1—9 contain relatively long strings of interconnected proverbs and a few extended "wisdom poems." The sayings of Prov. 10:1—22:16 are a less unified collection of individual proverbs, though there is some organization around themes. Other collections in the Book of Proverbs are to be dated later than Solomon's reign.

Both of the first two collections are ascribed to Solomon. Many interpreters suggest that the attributions in Prov. 1:1 and 10:1 do not necessarily refer to authorship but are rather tributes to Solomon, the greatest of all the wise. The longer poems of chs. 1—9 have especially been considered to be later than Solomon's time. Other interpreters, though, accept the attributions of 1:1 and 10:1 as simple statements of fact. In either case, it is appropriate to read these wise sayings following the comment of 1 Kings that Solomon was "wiser than all men" (1 Kin. 4:31).

OUTLINE OF PROVERBS

I. The Purpose of Proverbs	1:1–7
II. Proverbs to Youth	1:8—9:18
III. Proverbs of Solomon	10:1—22:16
IV. Proverbs Concerning Various Situations	22:17—24:34
V. Proverbs of Solomon Copied by Hezekiah's Men	25:1—29:27
VI. The Words of Agur	30:1–33
VII. The Words of King Lemuel	31:1–9
VIII. The Poem About the Wise Woman	31:10–31

The Person of Lady Wisdom (Prov. 8:22–31)

God's first possession, which He possessed before the universe was created, is the figure of Wisdom (Prov. 8:22). In Prov. 8:1—9:12 Wisdom is portrayed as a woman who seeks to teach all humans how to live properly in this world in accordance with the will of God and in harmony with the design of creation. She knows from direct involvement both God's will and creation's design, for it was by Wisdom that God created the world (8:27–31) so that humans can understand it and live well in it.

The poem in Proverbs insists that acquiring wisdom is easy, since Wisdom herself seeks out persons, both wise and foolish, to teach them (8:1–4). The ways of God are not hidden, neither are the ways that lead to a good human life. Anyone who wishes to succeed is welcomed to learn this way of life. For wisdom, it is asserted, leads to a good life, while foolishness leads to death.

The Hebrew Bible represents God's wisdom as a person, the feminine figure of Wisdom, but not as a separate deity. Wisdom became increasingly identified with God and with the Torah, the first five books of Israel's Scripture. Her traits accumulated through a tradition of poems written later than Proverbs, such as Ecclesiasticus (Wisdom of Jesus ben Sirach), Baruch, and the Wisdom of Solomon. By the time the Wisdom of Solomon was written, Wisdom could be portrayed as creator of the world, the giver of life, and even the source of eternal life. Later, these same notions appear in the prologue of the Gospel of John (John 1:1–18), describing the preexistence of Christ, the divine Word.

FOUNDING SOLOMON'S TEMPLE (1 KIN. 6:1)

According to 1 Kings, the construction of the Jerusalem temple began in the 4th year of Solomon's reign. The Jewish historian Josephus (A.D. 37–100) lived long after Solomon, but wrote in his work titled *Against Apion* concerning the date of the temple's foundation.

Josephus's accounts of Hiram, king of Tyre, provide information that could be instrumental in approximating a date for the building of the temple, as well as for Solomon's own rule. Josephus quotes from a lost work of the historian Menander of Ephesus, who provided a list of Tyrian kings.

Scholars debate whether Josephus's chronological information is reliable. In addition to the list of kings, Menander wrote that the time from Hiram's coronation as king to the founding of the North African city of Carthage was 155 years and 8 months. Josephus also tells us, via Menander, that the temple of Jerusalem was built in Hiram's 12th year. Unfortunately, Josephus's own calculations do not add to his totals.

We cannot obtain a precise date for Solomon's 4th year from Josephus's information. Scholars do not agree on when Carthage was founded: some say 825 B.C.; others say 814 B.C. Combining Josephus's calculations would date Solomon's temple building in either 968 or 957 B.C. In the absence of absolute chronological data, Solomon's 4th year is usually estimated to have been about 966 B.C.

Building the King's Palace (1 Kings 7:1—9:14)

The construction of the temple was a 7-year process, lasting from 966 to 959 B.C. (1 Kin. 6:37, 38). The palace complex, however, took longer to complete because it included several buildings south of the temple. The House of the Forest of Lebanon (1 Kin. 7:2–5) served as a treasury and armory (1 Kin. 10:17, 21; Is. 22:8). Other buildings were the Hall of Pillars (7:6), the Hall of Judgment (7:7), and residences for Solomon and Pharaoh's daughter (7:8).

The account in 1 Kings records the length of time it took Solomon to complete the temple and palace. In addition to the 7 years of temple construction was another 13 years for the palace (1 Kin. 7:1). Thus, these two major projects covered a period of 20 years (966–946 B.C.; see 1 Kin. 9:10).

Solomon and His Architecture (1 Kin. 9:15)

Three cities that were rebuilt by Solomon—Hazor, Megiddo, Gezer—provide one of the most striking correlations between archaeology and the Bible (1 Kin. 9:15). At each of these cities, archaeologists have dug down to layers that are assigned to Solomon's time period. They have uncovered a striking similarity in the fortifications that these cities had at that time.

Hazor, Megiddo, and Gezer all had nearly identical six-chambered gates. The chambers were part of a gate complex and part of a larger tower structure. They were constructed by building four parallel piers on each side of the entranceway. These piers were connected and made into rooms by an outside wall on each set of piers. There were, then, three rooms on each side, with an aisle down the middle.

Wooden gates were placed between the piers, which meant that the entire gate complex had four separate gates. The multiple gates and chambers behind each gate assured a difficult access for those trying to take the city by force.

At both Hazor and Gezer, a casemate wall was connected to the unique gateways. Casemate walls were two closely parallel walls that were subdivided into rooms. While these walls were rather narrow and not very thick, dirt from within the city could be quickly placed between the walls, transforming the two walls into one thick, strong wall. The architectural similarities found at Hazor, Megiddo, and Gezer suggest that six-chambered gates and casemate walls were characteristic of Solomon's building strategy.

Ruins of the six-chambered gate at Megiddo.

THE BOOK OF ECCLESIASTES

No book in the Bible is more surprising than this one. In its secular worldview, its purely philosophical approach to reality, and especially its thoroughgoing pessimism, it is unlike any other biblical text. To be sure, it concludes with an orthodox statement of faith (Eccl. 12:13, 14), but this glimmer of faith follows chapter upon chapter of anguished doubt.

Perhaps equally surprising is the book's attribution to Solomon. Though Solomon's name is not mentioned, the author calls himself "the Preacher, the son of David, king in Jerusalem" (1:1; see 1:12). Because of this identification, and even more because of Solomon's traditional position as the master sage and model wise man, some scholars suggest that the Preacher's words are indeed Solomon's. Other scholars, however, note that except for the references to the Preacher's wisdom and wealth (2:4–9), the book hardly fits the Bible's portrait of Solomon. This fact, along with the late style and grammar used in the book, suggests to them that someone else wrote the book, assuming the role of Solomon.

Whether it is Solomon or another writer, the author who appears in the pages of the book is, above all, a teacher. The Hebrew word for "Preacher," Qoheleth, means "one who leads an assembly." The Book of Ecclesiastes consists of the words of this preacher (12:9, 10). He diligently produced many proverbs (12:9) and other words of truth (12:10), so that the people might be admonished. He was a wise man, a teacher, a skilled writer, a seeker of truth, and an exhorter of his flock (12:11, 12).

Regardless of whether Solomon wrote the original, the book can be read in light of Solomon's greatness. Read in this way, Ecclesiastes offers a striking contrast between Solomon at the peak of his power and worldly success and this bleak and weary book. The writer's thesis is "Vanity of vanities, all is vanity" (1:2). There are inexplicable mysteries about life that defy easy solutions. Human wisdom is only partial; it cannot fathom the mysteries of God's creation. Only at the end, almost as an afterthought, does the Preacher appear to make his peace with his world and his God (12:13).

OUTLINE OF ECCLESIASTES

I. "All Is Vanity"	1:1–11
A. Introduction	1:1–3
B. Illustrations of Vanity	1:4–11
II. The Proof That "All Is Vanity"	1:12—6:12
A. Proof from Experience	1:12—2:26
B. Proof from Observation	3:1—6:12
III. Counsel for Living with Vanity	7:1—12:14
A. Coping in a Wicked World	7:1—9:18
B. Counsel for Life's Uncertainties	10:1—12:8
C. Conclusions	12:9–14

What the Dead Know (Eccl. 9:5, 10)

Necromancy was the contacting of the dead on behalf of the living. It is found in ancient literature from the Sumerian period (late 3rd millennium B.C.), such as the Mesopotamian story of Gilgamesh and Enkidu in the netherworld. Heroes would make their way to the edge of the land of the dead to speak with those who had passed into the land of Death. Or they consulted a medium who connected them to the spirit to whom they wished to speak. Hebrew wisdom literature, however, presented a different view: "the dead know nothing" (Eccl. 9:5).

The Law of Moses forbade such practices (Deut. 18:11). Nevertheless, a famous case of an Israelite seeking information from the spirits of the dead is that of Saul asking the medium of En Dor to call up the ghost of Samuel. Saul, desperate for information from God, thought he could learn the will of God from the dead Samuel (1 Sam. 28:8–19).

What did the dead know? Sometimes it appears from ancient literature that the dead were expected to know the future or events that were happening at a great distance. Gilgamesh asked Enkidu about the meaning of life and the possibility of avoiding death, but the query was of no avail, only confirming Gilgamesh's mortality. The usual conversation between the living and the dead seems to involve the desire of a living person to learn the fates that relatives and loved ones faced in the afterworld. The Hebrew Scriptures not only prohibited consulting the dead, but said it was futile. The dead have no "knowledge or wisdom" whatsoever (Eccl. 9:10).

THE SONG OF SOLOMON

This book is an extended dialogue between two lovers (the Shulamite and her beloved), written in sumptuous and often erotic poetry. The speakers are not identified by name in the text, but in the Hebrew it is clear when a speech is addressed to a man and when to a woman.

Solomon is mentioned by name, not only in the superscription (1:1) but also in the speeches (3:7–11; 8:11, 12). Some suggest that the book is actually a three-person conversation, with Solomon being one of the speakers. This is uncertain, as indeed are most things about this book, where luxurious description overpowers plot and logic. Jews and Christians alike have often interpreted the poem as an allegory of God's love affair with His people. Many, though, read it literally and accept it as the Bible's blessing on the delights of human love.

The superscription does not necessarily mean that Solomon wrote the book. The Hebrew construction of Song of Solomon 1:1 is ambiguous and could mean "to Solomon," "for Solomon," or simply "in the manner of Solomon." The other references to Solomon are in the third person, which make it possible that the book is in honor of an "ideal Solomon," and refers to the style in which Solomon may have composed love songs (1 Kin. 4:32).

Regardless of whether the book was authored by Solomon or compiled late, it nevertheless reflects the setting of Solomon's era. The pomp and circumstance described in the book calls to mind Solomon's royal court. His association with the song warrants reading it in light of his relations with women described in 1 Kin. 11:1–8.

OUTLINE OF SONG OF SOLOMON

I. The Beginning of Love	1:1—5:1
A. Falling in Love	1:1—3:5
B. United in Love	3:6—5:1
II. The Broadening of Love	5:2—8:14
A. Struggling in Love	5:2—7:9
B. Growing in Love	7:10—8:14

HIRAM, KING OF TYRE (2 CHR. 2:11)

Hiram, who became king of Tyre in either 980 or 969 B.C., had a special relationship with Solomon, king of Israel (2 Chr. 2:11). They were business partners in several efforts. This association continued a friendship that had existed previously between Solomon's father and Hiram (2 Sam. 5:11).

A treaty between Hiram and Solomon involved several acts of cooperation (1 Kin. 5:12). One was the rebuilding of Jerusalem, the capital of Israel. Craftsmen of Israel and Tyre worked together in building the temple, Solomon's palace, and other projects (1 Kin. 5:18; 2 Chr. 2:12–14). The two kings were also joint participants in a commercial shipping business (1 Kin. 10:11, 22).

Additional information about Hiram comes from Josephus, the Jewish historian of the 1st century A.D. Josephus in turn draws information from a historian named Dius, whose work has not survived to modern times.

One might suppose that Hiram was helping Solomon only because of his friendship with David (1 Kin. 5:1). In fact, Hiram was helping, at least in part, because of the wealth it brought him. Not only did he receive a yearly payment in kind (1 Kin. 5:11), but, at the end of the major building projects, Solomon gave Hiram 20 cities, which were probably located on the Mediterranean coast (1 Kin. 9:11). Indeed, the Phoenicians became one of the wealthiest people in the 1st millennium B.C.

TIME CAPSULE  **1000 to 930 B.C.**

1000	Growth of coast trade under Phoenicians
1000	Hebrew and Greek alphabets develop from Phoenician
980	Hiram becomes king of Tyre (or 969)
975	The temple of Hera is constructed at Olympia in Greece
973	Solomon is coregent with David
970–930	Solomon, king of Israel
966–959	Solomon completes the temple
945–924	Shishak, pharaoh of Egypt
945	The term "Pharaoh" is added to Egyptian king's official title
934–612	Neo-Assyrian period
934	Ashur-dan, king of Assyria, fortifies city of Asshur
930	Solomon dies and is succeeded by his son Rehoboam

Chariots and Chariot Cities (2 Chr. 8:5, 6)

The first chariots were apparently four-wheeled wagons or carts used to transport soldiers into battle. Pictures of such vehicles have been found from as early as 3100 B.C. The Egyptians, the Assyrians, and the Romans all used chariots in war. They were symbols of mobility and power.

In its classic form, the chariot is a two-wheeled, horse-drawn vehicle from which a soldier rides and fights. Through the centuries, most chariots carried two passengers, a driver and a fighter, and were drawn by two horses. The best chariots were made in Egypt starting about 1500 B.C., before the Hebrews' Egyptian service. Several complete Egyptian chariots from this time were recovered in A.D. 1922 from the tomb of Tutankhamun, one of the pharaohs whose goods were buried with him.

Tutankhamun's chariots are made of carefully shaped wood, glued and tied together with rawhide. The platform carried two riders side by side; it was a wooden frame with woven straps of leather for the floor. All this made the chariot light in weight, very strong, and as springy as engineering would allow. The "chariots of iron" driven by Israel's enemies (Josh. 17:16, 18; Judg. 1:19; 4:3, 13) were probably wood with iron tires or metal reinforcement at certain points.

Chariot forces became a crucial part of an adequate defense in the ancient Near East. King David confiscated chariots from his conquered enemies (2 Sam. 8:3, 4). But it was his son Solomon who realized the military potential of the chariot. He not only imported Egyptian chariots, but also established "chariot cities" (2 Chr. 8:6). Archaeological excavations at Hazor, one of the cities fortified by Solomon (1 Kin. 9:15, 17–19), shows the remains of chariot enclosures dating to Solomon's time.

SOLOMON THE BUILDER

Solomon is reported to have laid the foundation of the temple in the 4th year of his reign (1 Kin. 6:1). It took 7 years to build the temple (1 Kin. 6:37, 38) and an additional 13 years to build the king's palace (1 Kin. 7:1). In all, Solomon spent 20 years in two great building projects (1 Kin. 9:10; 2 Chr. 8:1). These chronological figures are possibly symbolic, rather than actual, but they do stress the architectural accomplishments of one of Israel's great leaders.

Year	Event
970	Solomon becomes king (1 Kin. 1:32–40; 1 Chr. 29:22)
966	Solomon begins to build the temple (1 Kin. 6:1; 2 Chr. 3:1)
959	Solomon completes construction of the temple (1 Kin. 6:37, 38; 2 Chr. 5:1)
946	Solomon completes construction of the royal palace (1 Kin. 7:1; 2 Chr. 8:1)
930	Solomon dies and is succeeded by his son Rehoboam (1 Kin. 11:43; 2 Chr. 9:31)

SOLOMON AND THE QUEEN OF SHEBA (2 CHR. 9:1–9)

The queen of Sheba who visited Solomon at Jerusalem (2 Chr. 9:1) is otherwise unnamed in Scripture. Presumably, Sheba was a land in the southwestern Arabian Peninsula and was known in native sources as Saba. The kingdom of Saba was a complex society by the end of the 1st millennium B.C.

The term "Saba," referring to the people called Sabeans, is mentioned in the inscriptions of two Assyrian kings: Tiglath-Pileser III (744–727 B.C.) and Sargon II (721–705 B.C.). Although these Sabeans were in northern Arabia, it is possible that they had originated in south Arabia (in Sheba) and later expanded along important northern trade routes.

Sabean civilization appears to have been sophisticated, having large urban centers, irrigation systems, and a myriad of trade connections throughout the Near East and southern Asia. Sabean merchants (or "merchants from Sheba") were well known for their trade items (Is. 60:6; Ezek. 27:22, 23).

It is possible that the queen of Sheba came to Jerusalem, not only to visit socially with Solomon, but also to strengthen trade relations with him. Solomon had just built a cargo fleet that traversed the Gulf of Aqaba (1 Kin. 9:26–28), and the queen's abundant gifts to him (1 Chr. 9:9) may have been in exchange for trade concessions.

THE FALL OF TWO NATIONS

930—586 B.C.

The brokenness of God's people led to brokenness in the world. Solomon's empire broke apart partly because Solomon and Rehoboam failed to be instruments of justice for their people. The many positive accomplishments of the united monarchy slowly unraveled, eventually resulting in the division of Solomon's kingdom into Israel (north) and Judah (south).

The story of the divided monarchy is one of gradual decay, with only brief interludes of hope. The two little nations of Israel and Judah spent most of their existence as vassal states, serving first the Neo-Assyrian Empire (934–612 B.C.) and then the Neo-Babylonian Empire (626–539 B.C.). Israel was destroyed by the Neo-Assyrians; Judah by the Neo-Babylonians.

ARCHAEOLOGY AND THE PAST

The Iron Age (1200–600 B.C.) spans the united and divided monarchies, and remains and records of this age often relate to the Bible. For example, Pharaoh Shishak I left inscriptions listing the cities and towns that he conquered in Palestine after the division of the kingdoms. While Egypt was not a strong force in the region, the records of other empires, especially those of Assyria, provide more details to supplement the biblical accounts.

Israelite kings built a new capital for the northern kingdom at Samaria. Excavations there have revealed great city walls on bedrock, dating from this period. Large numbers of ivory inlays from furniture were also found, reminding us that the ruling classes in Israel were incredibly wealthy. The prophets criticized the upper classes because their "houses of ivory" (Amos 3:15) were built by exploiting the poor.

King Ahab rebuilt the stables at Megiddo and made it once again a great city. He also built a palace at Hazor as part of the renovation of that city. His economic power made him an international force. According to an inscription of Shalmaneser III of Assyria, "Ahab the Israelite" brought 2,000 chariots and 10,000 infantry to the battle of Qarqar (853 B.C.). Ahab apparently had picked up on Solomon's trade in horses and chariots. Certainly he was a force in halting Assyria's advance toward Palestine.

Israel appears in other important inscriptions of the period. The famous Moabite Stone tells how King Mesha of Moab rebelled successfully against Israel in the 9th century B.C. The Black Obelisk of Shalmaneser III (841 B.C.) shows, in a series of carvings, conquered kings paying tribute to the Neo-Assyrian emperor.

King Jehu of Israel is shown kissing the feet of Shalmaneser.

Records and annals of Assyrian kings reveal contact between the Neo-Assyrian Empire and the divided kingdoms of Israel and Judah. King Azariah (Uzziah) of Judah is listed in the records of Tiglath-Pileser III as leading a revolt against Assyria. Both Assyrian inscriptions and excavated cities in Israel record that Tiglath-Pileser overran Israel (about 732 B.C.), laying waste cities, making Galilee an Assyrian province, and deporting the population to other parts of his empire.

Ironically, one of the more important archaeological finds related to the fall of Israel is found to the south, in Jerusalem. The "Broad Wall" of Judah's king Hezekiah was a city wall built on the western hills of Jerusalem. It tells us that, at this time, Jerusalem was greatly enlarged, partly to handle the flood of refugees from Israel.

Judah herself experienced Assyrian power through Assyria's king Sennacherib. Hezekiah undertook a massive water project to carry water from the Gihon spring, outside the city walls, through a tunnel into the city. The tunnel was dug to ensure the water supply at the time of Sennacherib's invasion in 701 B.C. Sennacherib also left a long document describing his siege of Jerusalem. The carvings on Sennacherib's palace walls included large pictures of the siege and destruction of Lachish, an important Judahite fortress. The carvings show both the siege process, the storming of the city, and the surrender of the citizens.

The Neo-Assyrian Empire fell around 612 B.C., but in its place the Neo-Babylonian Empire arose, which would ultimately destroy Jerusalem and carry the kings of Judah into exile. From the period of the Babylonian invasions are the Lachish Letters. These messages are written on pieces of broken pottery to the military commander at Lachish (which had been rebuilt). In them, an officer describes how he can no longer see the signals from other outposts, a sign of the advance of the Babylonian army.

In Jerusalem itself, recent excavations in the City of David have uncovered what is called the House of Ahiel, a 6th-century house that was destroyed by the Babylonians in their attacks on the city. The house had been burned, and there were Babylonian arrowheads in the ruins.

On a more peaceful note are the many seals and seal impressions from this period found in Jerusalem. One seal belongs to Gedaliah, the governor, who may have been the governor put in place by the Babylonians after they destroyed Jerusalem. Another fascinating seal impression bears the name of Baruch, son of Neriah, the name of the prophet Jeremiah's friend and scribe.

THE PEOPLES AND GROUPS

The Assyrians were one of the great superpowers of the ancient world, with an empire centered on the Tigris River. One of the keys to Assyrian power was a large, permanent army, with soldiers trained in every specialty needed for war. Artists were important in Assyria, and literature and architecture flourished. The most spectacular work was stone carving, and Assyrian palaces and monuments are filled with carvings, showing the nation at war, at work, and in the daily round of life. On the other side of their character, the Assyrians were unspeakably cruel and tortured prisoners as a regular practice. The Assyrian Empire was overthrown by the Medes and Babylonians in the years between 612 and 609 B.C.

The other superpower in the East was Babylon. One of their greatest kings was Nebuchadnezzar, whose armies destroyed Jerusalem in 586 B.C. In addition to his military and political ambitions, Nebuchadnezzar rebuilt Babylon to make it one of the most beautiful cities in the world. The Ishtar Gate was a double gate, faced with enameled bricks, in patterns of flowers, animals, and dragons. The palace was also built of enameled bricks and contained one room decorated with bricks of gold and blue. The "hanging gardens," a set of gardens built on terraces that thrust up into the air, is one of the wonders of the ancient world. Babylon was taken by the Persians in 539 B.C.

THE BIBLICAL LITERATURE

Biblical books that relate this period come from three groups, the first consisting of portions from Kings and Chronicles. The history of the kingdoms of Judah and Israel shows their alternation between faithfulness and faithlessness in their relationships with Yahweh.

A second group relates to the Neo-Assyrian period and includes the prophetic writings of Amos, Hosea, Isaiah, Micah, Jonah, and Zephaniah. Amos and Hosea preached in Israel, with an emphasis on social and economic justice. They warned of the coming punishment of Yahweh because of Israel's failure to keep the covenant. Isaiah was a counselor to the kings of Judah. He worked through two major international crises, which he saw as signs of God's rule over the nations and of God's displeasure over Judah's failure to bring about social justice. Micah was a rural contemporary of Isaiah who also preached against injustice, but lifted up a vision of a day of peace and salvation. Zephaniah began preaching sometime after 640 B.C., condemning idolatry and injustice. All these prophets were conscious of God's concern for justice and the failure of their nation to bring justice to the people.

The third group relates to the Neo-Babylonian period. Parts of the Book of Daniel tell the story of a Jewish youth exiled to Babylon, while the Book of Lamentations mourns the destruction of Jerusalem. Also included are prophecies from Jeremiah, Habakkuk, Nahum, Ezekiel, and Obadiah. Jeremiah lived through the destruction of Jerusalem in 586 B.C. He continued to call for social justice and loyalty to Yahweh, but also introduced the vision of a new covenant and of hope. Habakkuk records the pain of seeing the Babylonians on the march and wonders where God is in these events. Nahum rejoices over the defeat of Assyria. Ezekiel was the first prophet to write from exile in Babylon. He first preached a message of doom and judgment but, after the destruction of Jerusalem, began to preach hope. Obadiah is a song of anger against the people of Edom for their part in the destruction of Jerusalem.

THE DIVIDED MONARCHY IN ISRAEL

Israel was more united under the monarchy than ever before, but the old tribal loyalties remained, at least under the surface. Saul, from the tribe of Benjamin, had surrounded himself with other Benjamites (1 Sam. 22:7), as had David with members of his own tribe of Judah. These two tribes remained rivals throughout the united monarchy. While resentment over the forced labor imposed by Solomon precipitated the division of Israel into different parts (1 Kin. 12:1–17), the divisions were there already.

The division of Israel into two kingdoms led to some resentment and even the threat of war, but war was averted and before long the two new nations were diplomatic allies. However, the glory years of Solomon's united monarchy were ended, replaced by a divided monarchy—a northern kingdom, which from this time on assumed the old name "Israel," and a southern kingdom of Judah.

The division of the kingdom left David's empire in shambles. Not only was Israel split, but the other nations that David had conquered soon achieved independence. The continuing weakness of the Egyptian and Assyrian empires allowed the weakened land of Israel to survive, but Aram-Damascus (Syria) to the northeast was a growing threat.

EPOCH FIVE
Chronological Reading Guide

- ❑ 1 Kings 12:1—16:20
- ❑ 2 Chronicles 10:1—16:14
- ❑ 1 Kings 16:21—22:50
- ❑ 2 Chronicles 17:1—20:37
- ❑ 1 Kings 22:51–53
- ❑ 2 Kings 1:1—10:36
- ❑ 2 Chronicles 21:1—22:9
- ❑ 2 Kings 11:1—14:22
- ❑ 2 Chronicles 22:10—25:28

The Kingdom Divides (1 Kin. 12:1–24)

The books of Kings are an anonymous writer's reflections on the history of the Israelite monarchy from the accession of Solomon to the end. The story of the uneasy coexistence of Israel and Judah continues from 1 Kin. 12:1 until the fall of the northern kingdom in 2 Kin. 17:41). The unity between North (Israel) and South (Judah) under Saul, David, and Solomon had been held together by the charisma and strength of its leaders. Now the tribes went separate ways, following separate leaders: Jeroboam I for the northern tribes and Rehoboam, Solomon's son, for the southern tribes of Judah and Simeon.

First Dynasty of the Northern Kingdom (1 Kin. 12:25—14:20)

Israel in the north was much larger and stronger than the southern Judah. But Israel was less unified than Judah. Not only did it include more tribes, but it had neither a central shrine, such as the temple in Jerusalem, nor the ark of the covenant. To remedy this lack, Israel's first king, Jeroboam I, built replacement shrines at Dan and Bethel. These were probably dedicated to Israel's one God, but the golden calves Jeroboam set there were soon regarded as idols (1 Kin. 12:25–33).

The visit of the "man of God" to Bethel reflects the interest in prophecy by the historian of Kings. This man of God is presented as a true prophet who makes a distant prophecy (1 Kin. 13:1, 2). He prophesies events to occur during the reign of Josiah (640–609 B.C.), 300 years after the time of Jeroboam (930–909 B.C.). But Jeroboam rejected the warnings from this prophet and became the stereotype of the sinful king (13:33, 34).

TIME CAPSULE	930 to 900 B.C.
930	Kingdom of Israel splits into northern Israel and southern Judah
930	Rehoboam becomes king of Israel; Jeroboam I becomes king of northern Israel
930–722	The northern kingdom of Israel
930–586	The southern kingdom of Judah
925	Pharaoh Shishak sacks the temple in Jerusalem
913	Abijah becomes king in Judah
910	Asa becomes king in Judah
909	Nadab becomes king in Israel
908	Baasha assassinates Nadab and becomes king in Israel
900	Phoenicians establish trading colonies as far away as Spain

HOLY COWS (1 KIN. 12:28)

The act of Jeroboam in crafting images of cows for worship was not unique. Not only did he repeat the actions of Aaron by creating a golden calf, but he imitated the words of Aaron from Ex. 32:4 when he said, "Here are your gods, O Israel, which brought you up from the land of Egypt" (1 Kin. 12:28).

Exactly which god was represented by the calves is not known. The Hebrew word for "calves" in 1 Kin. 12:28 suggests that the animal was a young bull, as was used for sacrifices (Mic. 6:6). A number of small bull images have been found by archaeologists, testifying to the common worship of such images. Calf worship was still prominent among the Israelites of the northern kingdom when Hosea prophesied (Hos. 8:5; 10:5, 6), during the reign of Jeroboam II (793–753 B.C.).

Jeroboam I placed his two idol calves in the two geographical extremes of his empire (1 Kin. 12:29). Bethel, just a few miles north of Jerusalem, means "house of god" and had been a traditional place of worship since the days of the patriarchs (Gen. 31:13). Dan lies in the most northerly extreme of Israel. In so doing Jeroboam made sure that one of his worship centers was closer to the Israelites than was Jerusalem.

To completely separate the Israelites from the worship of God in Jerusalem, Jeroboam even began a new priesthood. In Israel's covenant the Levites were assigned as priests for the nation's worship (Num. 3:5–10), but Jeroboam appointed non-Levitical priests, causing the Levites to flee to Judah (1 Kin. 12:31; 2 Chr. 11:14, 15). He even inaugurated separate feasts (1 Kin. 12:32). By encouraging the worship of the golden bull Jeroboam hoped to keep the hearts of his people from returning to King Rehoboam, the grandson of David (12:26, 27).

REHOBOAM AND JEROBOAM DIVIDE THE KINGDOM

The discontent and unrest that existed in Solomon's kingdom was like a powder keg awaiting a spark. When Solomon died, the occasion for the explosion came because of the foolish insensitivity of his son Rehoboam. The 10 northern tribes revolted against Rehoboam and appointed Jeroboam as their king.

Israel (northern kingdom)

Jeroboam established his capital at Tirzah. He was succeeded by his son Nadab, but the dynasty was soon cut off by Nadab's assassination.

Nadab besieged the Philistine city of Gibbethon, but during the siege was assassinated by his successor Baasha (1 Kin. 15:27).

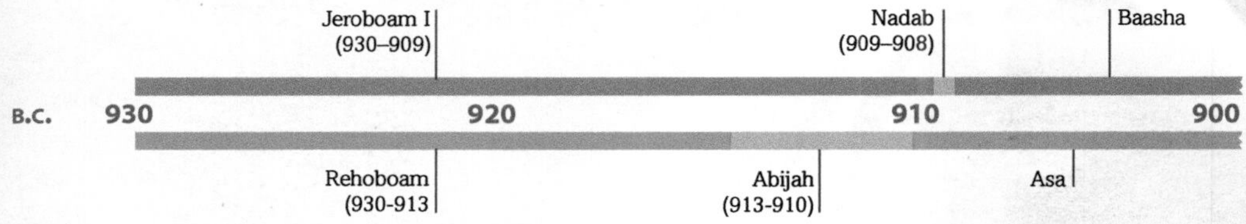

Judah (southern kingdom)

Rehoboam fought border wars against Jeroboam, probably over the territory of Benjamin which was a buffer zone between the two kingdoms (1 Kin. 14:30).

Abijah (or Abijam), son of Rehoboam, continued the border wars against Jeroboam (1 Kin. 15:7).

The Davidic Dynasty in Judah (1 Kin. 14:21—15:24)

The descendants of David continued to rule in Judah during the divided monarchy, represented first by Solomon's son Rehoboam. During Rehoboam's reign (930–913 B.C.), the Egyptian pharaoh Shishak marched against Judah and Jerusalem, taking tribute from the temple and palace (1 Kin. 14:25, 26).

In the first account of Judah during the divided kingdom, the historian of Kings presents three kings: Rehoboam, Abijam (or Abijah, 913–910 B.C.), and Asa (910–869 B.C.). He dates each king by synchronizing his accession year with the reign of the monarch in the other kingdom (see 1 Kin. 15:1, 9).

Because Kings alternates between accounts of Israel and Judah, some unusual historical sequences result. For example, the border wars between Asa and Israel's Baasha (15:16–21) are discussed before Baasha is formally introduced (15:27–30). During the 9th century B.C. Damascus (Syria) allied itself with various Aramean kingdoms and became a serious threat to Israel's northeast. Asa enticed Ben-Hadad I of Aram-Damascus to invade Israel, hoping to relieve Israel's military pressure on Jerusalem.

SHISHAK CAMPAIGNS AGAINST SOLOMON'S SON (2 CHR. 12:2, 9)

Shishak (also spelled Sheshonk or Shoshenq) was the founder of the 22nd Dynasty of Egypt. He claimed descent from a series of Libyan chiefs who had migrated generations earlier to the Delta region of Egypt. From Egyptian sources, Shishak is first known as the commander in chief of the Egyptian army under Psusennes II (959–945 B.C.), the last pharaoh of the 21st Dynasty. One of Shishak's sons had married a daughter of the pharaoh, which possibly allowed Shishak to claim Egypt's throne when Pharaoh Psusennes died.

A statue of Shishak has been found at Byblos, a Phoenician city on the Mediterranean Sea. The statue indicates possible Egyptian dominance on the Phoenician coast, and Shishak's activity so close to Israel may explain why political dissidents under Solomon's rule, such as Jeroboam, fled to Egypt (1 Kin. 11:40). Egypt's acceptance of these dissidents may imply an antagonistic relationship between Egypt and Israel late in Solomon's reign.

After Solomon's death, in the 5th year of his son Rehoboam's reign (925 B.C.), Shishak invaded Palestine (2 Chr. 12:2, 9). Archaeologists have uncovered evidence of that invasion at settlements in both Israel and Judah, which show signs of tremendous destruction. An inscription in the temple of Amon at Karnak tersely describes the campaign, listing over 150 towns that are said to have been destroyed. Not on the list is Jerusalem, having been spared because Rehoboam apparently paid Shishak with treasures from the temple and palace (1 Kin. 14:26; 2 Chr. 12:7–9).

Shishak's reign (945–924 B.C.) was the beginning of over two centuries of Libyan rule in Egypt. He erected a victory stele at Megiddo, thus reasserting Egyptian domination in Palestine.

Asherah, Queen Mother of the Gods (2 Chr. 15:16)

King Asa of Judah removed his mother Maachah from her position as queen mother of Judah because she made sacred objects for the goddess Asherah (2 Chr. 15:16). The worship of any deity beside Yahweh was forbidden, so Asa was fulfilling the cultic laws by removing his mother from the royal precinct.

Asherah was a widely worshiped goddess throughout Syria-Palestine and even into Egypt. In the myths recovered from Ugarit, she is the spouse of El, head of the pantheon, and thus the queen mother of the gods. She chose which deities were to be established in what positions of authority in the cosmos. In the chain of authority she was the final resort for petitions to El. Unquestionably, Asherah was the most politically powerful goddess in the Canaanite pantheon.

It appears that at times Judahites worshiped Asherah as the spouse of Yahweh, who was also called El (Gen. 33:20; 35:7). Inscriptions dating from the time of the divided monarchy (after 930 B.C.) name Yahweh and refer to "His Asherah." These inscriptions were found in northeast Sinai at Kuntillet 'Ajrud and within Judah's borders at Khirbet el-Qom. The goddess clearly was popular in the land among populace and royalty alike, who continued worshiping her even down to the reign of Josiah (640–609 B.C.; 2 Kin. 23:4).

Ahab the Religious Compromiser (1 KIN. 16:28–33)

Ahab was the second king of a dynasty founded by his father Omri in the northern kingdom of Israel. He ruled from 874 to 853 B.C. and is possibly alluded to in a royal inscription, called the Moabite Stone, from c. 850 B.C. The Moabite king Mesha claims to have freed the Moabites from Israelite domination during the reign of the "son of Omri."

Much of Ahab's reign saw tension between Israel and the Aramean kingdom of Damascus to the northeast. Continuing his father's policies of thwarting the Aramean presence in Israel, Ahab sought a series of alliances with neighboring Judah to the south and with Phoenicia on the coast. His alliances were strengthened by political marriages. His daughter Athaliah was married in 867 B.C. to Jehoram, the son of Judah's King Jehoshaphat (2 Kin. 8:16–18; 2 Chr. 21:5, 6). The marriage helped to end hostile relations between Israel and Judah.

Ahab solidified peace with Phoenicia through his marriage to the infamous Phoenician princess Jezebel, whose father Ethbaal ruled the Phoenician kingdom including Tyre and Sidon (1 Kin. 16:31, 32). This foreign queen remained true to her foreign background: the historian Josephus reports that her father was also a priest in the Phoenician cult of Baal; his name "Ethbaal" means "with Baal." The writer of Israel's history strongly condemned Ahab for supporting Jezebel's worship of the Phoenician and Canaanite god and compromising the Israelite worship of Yahweh (1 Kin. 16:30–33).

KINGS OF THE DIVIDED MONARCHY

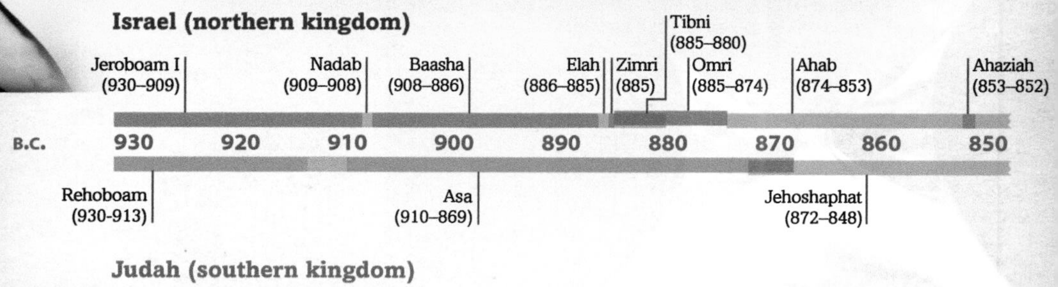

Mocking Canaanite Religious Ritual (1 Kin. 18:17–29)

The confrontation between Elijah and the 450 prophets of Baal on Mount Carmel (1 Kin. 18) demonstrates the power of Israel's God Yahweh over against the weakness, even unreality, of the god Baal. After King Ahab married Jezebel, the princess of Sidon, the foreign queen promoted the worship of her Sidonian god, Baal (1 Kin. 16:31, 32). The goddess Asherah, symbolized by trees or wooden images (16:33), was also part of this cult, being represented by 400 prophets of her own (18:19).

The prophets of Baal and Asherah are said to "eat at Jezebel's table" (18:19), meaning they were on the government payroll. Professional prophets were standard personnel in many courts; though the number of prophets in Jezebel's court (850) suggests either a rich kingdom or extravagance on her part.

Elijah chose a ritual for the contest that was common to the opposing prophets. An animal sacrifice (18:23) was a central cultic ritual used to honor deities, and bull sacrifices are well known from the clay tablets found at Ugarit. Both Yahweh and Baal were worshiped by the proper sacrifice of bulls.

Elijah's request that each deity light the fire for its own sacrifice (18:24) may reflect the staging of "miracles" in Phoenician temples. The 2nd-century A.D. writer Lucian from Samosata records in *De Dea Syria* how Phoenician priests would rig idols with hidden ropes. Pulling on the ropes would make the idols appear to move and thus amaze worshipers. On the mountain, at a new altar, there would be no chance to fool people with a staged "miraculous" divine intervention.

The prophets of Baal cried aloud and cut themselves in a cultic frenzy (18:28). Self-laceration and mutilation, considered a sign of submission to the deity, appears in a number of religious cult activities. Lucian of Samosata reports worshipers of the goddess at Hierapolis falling into a frenzy and cutting off parts of their own flesh in honor of the deity. On Mount Carmel such actions failed to elicit any divine response (18:29).

Jezebel (1 Kin. 19:2, 3)

The marriage between Israel's king Ahab and Sidon's princess Jezebel was politically motivated. Unfortunately, the union had an ill effect on Israel's worship of Yahweh. Even today, the name "Jezebel" is associated with all that is evil.

Jezebel killed the prophets of Yahweh (1 Kin. 18:13). She was also the one who frightened Yahweh's prophet Elijah so much that he fled for safety (1 Kin. 19:2, 3). She also caused the man Naboth to be killed so her husband could possess Naboth's field (1 Kin. 21:8–13). Her evil deeds led Elijah to predict that Jezebel would be eaten by dogs after her death (1 Kin. 21:23; 2 Kin. 9:35–37).

That Jezebel's influence came from being the queen is true but not the whole story. She was also the daughter of Ethbaal, the king of Sidon (1 Kin. 16:31). During Ahab's time Sidon was one of the most powerful and certainly richest areas in and around Israel. The material culture of the Sidonians is one of the highest of those found in ancient Canaan. Their ceramic dishes are artistically beautiful, making the typical pots of the Israelites look clumsy and backwoodish.

As a princess from Sidon, Jezebel might have been the original "uptown" girl. She came from the richest and most advanced culture, as the daughter of a king, to Israel, a simple hill-country kingdom. Her aristocratic presence overwhelmed those around her; all eyes and hearts turned in her direction. They swooned in following her god Baal and deserted Yahweh, God of Israel. Not surprisingly, this original "uptown" girl also influenced her husband Ahab's worship of Baal (1 Kin. 16:31).

KINGS OF THE DIVIDED MONARCHY (CONTINUED)

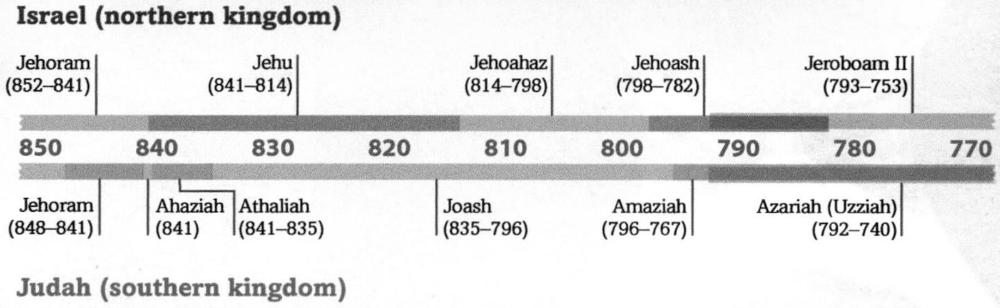

Ahab Wars with Damascus (1 Kin. 20:1—22:40)

Towards the end of Ahab's reign, one of Israel's primary threats was the state of Aram (or Syria), with its center in Damascus. In 853 B.C. Damascus led a coalition of Syro-Palestinian states (including Ahab and Israel) that was able to resist an advancing Assyrian army at the town of Qarqar. Ahab and Damascus were allies in that encounter with Assyria, but they became enemies soon afterward. The wars that Ahab fought against Aram-Damascus are recounted in 1 Kin. 20; 22.

The identity of King Ben-Hadad who led the Aramean (Syrian) forces against Israel (1 Kin. 20:1) is uncertain. Since the Arameans' main deity was Hadad, god of rain, several of Aram's kings were named "Ben-Hadad," meaning "son of Hadad." Some think that Ahab's opponent was the same Ben-Hadad who aided Judah's King Asa (1 Kin. 15:18), or possibly the King Hadad-ezer of Damascus who led the coalition at Qarqar. Others even suggest that the name "Ben-Hadad" reflects the Aramean king of 2 Kin. 13:24, 25. Thus the actual events surrounding Ahab's death in 853 B.C. remain unidentified.

Heaven Plans an Assassination (2 Chr. 18:18–22)

Ahab, king of Israel (874–853 B.C.), asked Jehoshaphat, king of Judah, to join him in an attack on Syria (2 Chr. 18:3). The two kings then consulted the professional court prophets, inquiring about the will of the deity in the matter. This was normal practice throughout the ancient Near East, especially during military campaigns.

The 400 professional prophets who answered Ahab spoke with one voice (18:5). Prophets usually determined the will of the deity by means of set observations that were written down in manuals. This kept individual interpretation to a minimum. However, one prophet, Micaiah, spoke independently for Yahweh, claiming to have seen and heard the heavenly court procedure.

Usually the divine council was made up of gods. In Canaanite religion, El, the head of the pantheon, would be in charge of such a council, but the deities in attendance were the ones who debated the course of action. Once a plan was determined, these lesser deities were also the ones to carry out the action in the world. In Micaiah's vision Yahweh is the head of the council (18:18), and the members are called spirits. The spirit who devised the plan to lead the king of Israel into a battle where he would die was also the one assigned to carry out the plan (18:21).

Neo-Assyrian texts show that court prophets continued to be consulted by the Assyrian kings Esarhaddon (680–669 B.C.) and Ashurbanipal (668–627 B.C.). The prophets, who are called "proclaimers," reported oracles to the king from such Assyrian deities as Asshur, Ishtar, and Ninlil. The oracles themselves were preserved in the official royal annals.

KINGS OF THE DIVIDED MONARCHY (CONTINUED)

Israel (northern kingdom)

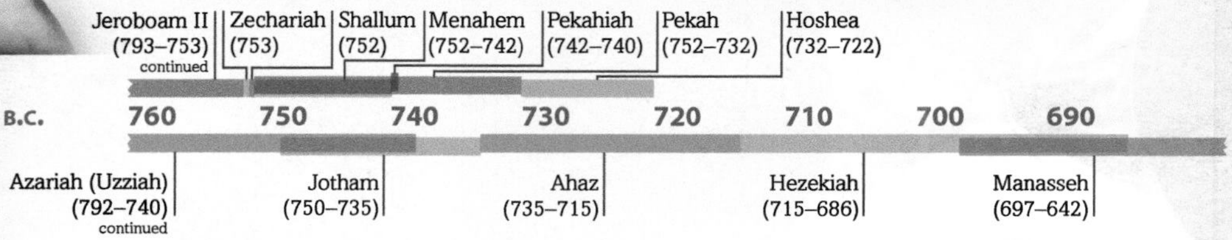

Judah (southern kingdom)

THE LORD OF THE FLIES (2 KIN. 1:2–16)

Baal-Zebub, a Philistine deity at Ekron, is unknown outside of 2 Kin. 1:2–16. The deity is often confused with Beelzebub (or Beelzebul) mentioned in the New Testament (Matt. 12:24). The name "Baal-Zebub" means "lord of the flies," and a deity by this name likely was worshiped in the Philistine city of Ekron. One method by which professional prophets determined the will of the gods was to watch the ways in which flies swarmed. So probably Baal-Zebub was a god from whom knowledge of future events was sought by means of the flight of insects.

Ahaziah, due to an accidental injury (2 Kin. 1:2), did not rule long as king of Israel (853–852 B.C.). Having been wounded, he sent messengers to the deity Baal-Zebub, seeking information about his chances of recovery, just as people from all over the ancient world visited the Greek shrine at Delphi to inquire of the oracle there.

Elijah, the prophet of Yahweh, stopped the messengers from consulting Baal-Zebub and then confronted Ahaziah with his lack of faithfulness. This was a demonstration that Yahweh is all Israel needs; there is no need for foreign gods (1:6). That the king did not trust the God of Israel enough to inquire of Him was enough to cause the king to die. The ancients believed that rulers were given their kingdoms by their patron gods. When a king abandoned his patron god, he risked being abandoned by the god.

Jehu Encounters Shalmaneser and Hazael (2 KIN. 9:13)

Jehu was the individual who became king after overthrowing the dynasty of Omri in Israel. To complete his bloody revolution he attempted to eradicate the Baal cult from Samaria. Followers of Baal would have naturally supported the Omri-Ahab family, and thus would have been a constant threat to Jehu (2 Kin. 10:18–27).

The Assyrian king Shalmaneser III conducted his fourth campaign against Syro-Palestine in 841 B.C., the first year of Jehu's reign (841–814 B.C.). Jehu was apparently part of a coalition of kings that included King Hazael of Aram-Damascus. The Assyrians wreaked great havoc in the area, but they did not take either Damascus or Samaria.

Details of Shalmaneser's campaign are found in Assyrian inscriptions. Among the annals and on the Black Obelisk of Shalmaneser are records that Jehu was reduced to vassaldom and was required to pay a heavy tribute to the Assyrian monarch. The Assyrian writings describe Jehu as the "son of Omri." Either the Omri dynasty enjoyed an international reputation or the Assyrians were ignorant of the hostile relationship between Jehu and the Omri royal family.

Shalmaneser carved a scene on his Black Obelisk depicting Jehu bowing in submission to the Assyrian ruler, bringing with him many articles of tribute. Jehu, by submitting to the Assyrians, gained protection against Aram-Damascus. In fact, Shalmaneser invaded Damascus again in 838 B.C. but failed to overthrow Hazael.

No Assyrian sources mention Jehu again, implying that he had been successfully subjugated, requiring no further Assyrian incursions. Years later, however, as the Assyrian Empire declined, Hazael of Aram-Damascus attacked Israel, conquering parts of Jehu's kingdom (2 Kin. 10:32, 33).

Black Obelisk of Shalmaneser III

KINGS OF THE DIVIDED MONARCHY (CONTINUED)

Israel (northern kingdom)

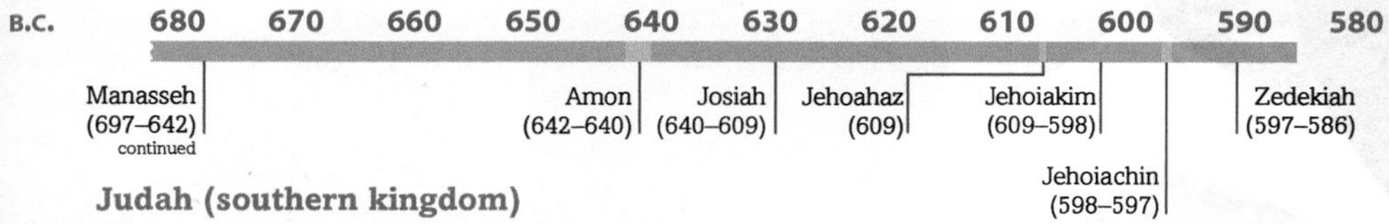

TIME CAPSULE	900 to 853 B.C.
900	Earliest example of laminated steel
895	Asa leads covenant renewal celebration in Judah
895	Osorkon I of Egypt invades Palestine
887	Ethbaal I, priest of Astarte, seizes throne of Tyre
883–859	Ashurnasirpal II of Assyria campaigns every year of his reign
879	King Omri of Israel builds city of Samaria and makes it Israel's new capital city
874	Ahab becomes king of Israel
869	Jehoshaphat becomes sole king in Judah
858	Assyrian Empire reaches to the Mediterranean
853	Anti-Assyrian coalition fights against Assyria's Shalmaneser at the battle of Qarqar

TIME CAPSULE	842 to 752 B.C.
842–800	Hazael, king of Aram-Damascus
841	The Black Obelisk of Shalmaneser III
841	Shalmaneser forces King Jehu of Israel to pay tribute
838	Shalmaneser invades Damascus but fails to overthrow Hazael
835	Athaliah is killed, and Joash becomes king of Judah
814	Jehoahaz becomes king in Israel
798	Jehoash (or Joash) becomes king in Israel
796	Ben-Hadad of Damascus pays tribute to Adad-nirari III of Assyria
763	City of Haran rebels against Assyrians and is destroyed by Asshur-dan III
752	Menahem assassinates Shallum and becomes king in Israel

Priests Wielding Political Power
(2 Chr. 24:1–3)

In the power structures of the ancient Near East, priests carried both political and religious authority. They were consulted by rulers and free citizens to determine the will of the gods. They were responsible for teaching the moral rules decreed by the gods. In both Mesopotamia and Egypt, priests controlled large tracts of land and their temples played the role of modern banks for storing money and making loans. At times in Egypt the priests were said to wield more power than the pharaoh. So priesthoods were able to bring both political and sacred authority to bear on the rulers of their societies.

In Israel and Judah priests also exercised power in relation to kings and rulers. The most important office of the priest was as the intermediary between God and the people; this meant also between God and the king. Priests were expected to bring up future rulers in the proper service and worship of God.

The potential political power of the priesthood is witnessed in the Jerusalem priest Jehoiada. He organized the palace guard to bring about the downfall and execution of Queen Athaliah, resulting in the enthronement of Joash (Jehoash) as king (2 Kin. 11:4–21). Since the new king was so young, the priest Jehoiada served in the influential position of regent and advisor to the king, even securing wives for him (2 Chr. 24:1–3).

THE NEO-ASSYRIAN EMPIRE

Most of Israel's national history took place in a power vacuum. The New Kingdom of Egypt, from which the Israelites had escaped in the Exodus, faded away shortly after Ramesses II (1279–1213 B.C.). The Egyptian dynasties that followed were much weaker. In Mesopotamia, the major power was Assyria, but Assyria remained too busy with internal problems to worry about outlying nations such as Israel.

A few times Assyria seemed to revive and look beyond its borders, such as when king Shalmaneser III (858–824 B.C.) swept through Israel and forced the Israelite king Jehu to pay tribute to Assyria. Such triumphs were rare, though, until the Assyrian Tiglath-Pileser III (744–727 B.C.) came to power during the reigns of Uzziah in Judah and Jeroboam II in Israel. Tiglath-Pileser quickly established his supremacy over Mesopotamia, even over Assyria's old rival Babylon, and began to expand Assyria's borders.

Few armies were as hated as the Assyrian army. Even in a time and culture that was not known for respecting human life, Assyrian tactics and policies toward their enemies were notoriously brutal.

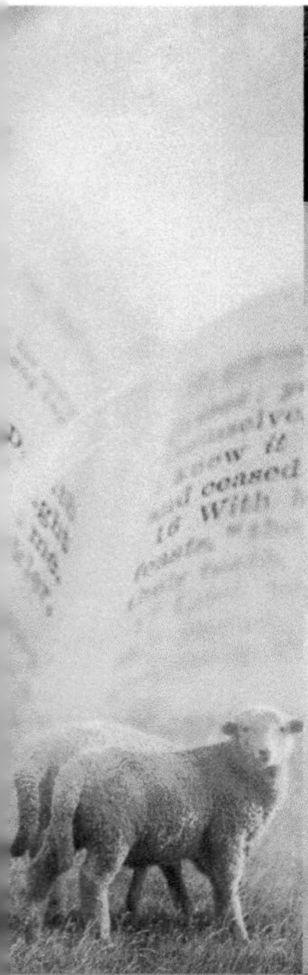

EPOCH FIVE
Chronological Reading Guide

- ❑ 2 Kings 14:23–29
- ❑ Jonah 1:1—4:11
- ❑ Amos 1:1—9:15
- ❑ Hosea 1:1—14:9
- ❑ 2 Kings 15:1–7
- ❑ Isaiah 6:1–13; 1:1—5:30
- ❑ 2 Chronicles 26:1–23
- ❑ 2 Kings 15:8—16:9
- ❑ Isaiah 7:1—10:4
- ❑ Isaiah 17:1–14; 14:24–32
- ❑ 2 Kings 16:10–20
- ❑ Micah 1:1—7:20
- ❑ 2 Chronicles 27:1—28:27
- ❑ 2 Kings 17:1–4
- ❑ Isaiah 28:1—29:24
- ❑ 2 Kings 17:5—18:12
- ❑ Isaiah 10:5—12:6
- ❑ Proverbs 25:1—29:27
- ❑ Isaiah 18:1—20:6
- ❑ Isaiah 15:1—16:14
- ❑ Isaiah 22:15–25
- ❑ Isaiah 30:1—32:20
- ❑ 2 Kings 20:1–11
- ❑ Isaiah 38:1–22
- ❑ 2 Kings 20:12–19
- ❑ Isaiah 39:1–8
- ❑ 2 Kings 18:13—19:7
- ❑ Isaiah 36:1—37:7
- ❑ 2 Kings 19:8–37
- ❑ Isaiah 37:8–38
- ❑ 2 Kings 20:20, 21
- ❑ Isaiah 22:1–14
- ❑ Isaiah 23:1—27:13
- ❑ 2 Chronicles 29:1—31:21
- ❑ 2 Chronicles 32:24–31
- ❑ 2 Chronicles 32:1–23
- ❑ 2 Kings 21:1–18
- ❑ 2 Chronicles 32:32, 33
- ❑ 2 Kings 21:19—22:20
- ❑ Zephaniah 1:1—3:20
- ❑ 2 Kings 23:1–25
- ❑ 2 Chronicles 33:1—35:19
- ❑ Psalms 33, 66, 67, 100

Jeroboam and Azariah (Uzziah) (2 Kin. 14:23–29)

The prophetic history found in 2 Kings places particular emphasis on the history of the northern kingdom and kings, such as Jeroboam II. Jeroboam was the fourth generation of the Jehu dynasty in Israel, following his grandfather Jehoahaz and father Jehoash to the throne. His long reign of about 41 years (793–753 B.C.) began with an 11-year coregency, during which time Jeroboam ruled together with his father. Upon the death of Jehoash (Joash) in 782 B.C., Jeroboam "sat on his [father's] throne" (2 Kin. 13:13), now a king in his own right.

It was a good time to take leadership in Israel. The Assyrian Empire led by Shalmaneser III had forced Jeroboam's great-grandfather Jehu to pay tribute in 841 B.C. But that empire was now greatly weakened. During the years from 782 to 745 B.C., Assyria was fragmented into various governor-ruled states and threatened by an expanding kingdom of Urartu to its north. Assyria's weakness allowed Jeroboam to pursue an expansionist policy himself, restoring territory on Israel's northern border (2 Kin. 14:25).

THE BOOK OF JONAH

Jonah the son of Amittai is mentioned in 2 Kin. 14:25, prophesying a victory for the Israelite king Jeroboam II. The book devoted to this prophet does not mention Jonah's activities in Israel. Instead, it tells of a message God gives Jonah to deliver to Nineveh, the capital of Assyria.

Certain details of the Book of Jonah have troubled historians. Leaving aside Jonah's extraordinary encounter with the great fish, scholars have noted that Assyrian records do not mention a mass repentance in Nineveh at this time. Also the title "king of Nineveh" (Jon. 3:6) seems rather small for the ruler of an empire. For these reasons, many have treated the book as an extended parable, not intended to be read as history. Others though, not troubled by accounts of God doing miracles, find no reason to doubt the book's facticity.

Jonah is distinct among prophetic books in that it is a narrative, not a collection of poetic oracles. The message of the book, that God is concerned with all His creation, not just with Israel, is not unique, though. It also appears with other prophets, including Jonah's contemporary Amos.

Two features stand out in the book's theology. One is the universal love and compassion of God for all nations. Another is the sovereignty of God. The relatively unimpressive title "king of Nineveh" serves above all to humble Nineveh's great monarch before the power of Israel's God.

OUTLINE OF JONAH

I. First Commission of Jonah	**1:1—2:10**
A. Disobedience to the First Call	1:1–3
B. Judgment on Jonah	1:4–17
C. Prayer of Jonah	2:1–9
D. Deliverance of Jonah	2:10
II. Second Commission of Jonah	**3:1—4:11**
A. Obedience to the Second Call	3:1–4
B. Repentance of Nineveh	3:5–10
C. Prayer of Jonah	4:1–3
D. Rebuke of Jonah by God	4:4–11

Jonah Sails for Tarshish (JON. 1:3)

When Jonah decided to flee from God, he boarded a "ship going to Tarshish" (Jon. 1:3). The narrative about Jonah indicates that Tarshish was in an opposite direction from Nineveh, but the specific direction is not given.

Tarshish is mentioned over thirty times in Scripture, yet its exact location is uncertain. The kings Jehoshaphat and Ahaziah built ships at Ezion Geber, near the Red Sea, which were intended to "go to Tarshish" (2 Chr. 20:36, 37). Nevertheless, the location of Tarshish was not necessarily in the vicinity of the Red Sea.

The most likely candidate for a location is the Phoenician colony Tartessus in southwestern Spain. This colony was known to the Greek historian Herodotus and the Latin writers Strabo and Pliny. Their writings refer to its rich metal resources. Assyrian records from the 7th century B.C. also mention a place called Tarsisi, but its location is unknown.

Some scholars suppose that the term "Tarshish" may well describe an activity associated with a place rather than a specific geographic location. Besides Strabo and Pliny, the prophets Jeremiah (Jer. 10:9) and Ezekiel (Ezek. 27:12) also knew that Tarshish was a source for metals. In the Hebrew language the word "Tarshish" often refers to a precious stone, usually translated as "beryl" (Ex. 28:20; Ezek. 28:13). Possibly then, "Tarshish" did not identify one specific location, but rather several places where the activity of metalworking took place.

In the Bible, ships are frequently called "ships of Tarshish" (Is. 23:1, 14; 60:9). Tarshish ships were often found in the Mediterranean area, carrying goods from Tyre (Ezek. 27:25). We may never know whether the destination of the Tarshish ship in the Jonah story was one site known as "Tarshish" or one of several sites referred to by that name.

THE BOOK OF AMOS

Two of the minor prophets, Amos and Hosea, spoke to the northern kingdom of Israel during the rise of the Neo-Assyrian Empire. Both took the Assyrian threat very seriously, but their messages were unheard. Comparative prosperity in Israel during the reign of Jeroboam II (793–753 B.C.) had fed complacency.

Amos spoke harshly about this complacency. Although he himself was from Tekoa in the land of Judah (Amos 1:1), Amos was sent by God to prophesy to Israel (see 7:10–17), and he brought with him a deep intolerance for oppression. He raged against the lavish lives of the rich (4:1–3), the oppression of the poor (5:11–15), and the ostentatious religious ceremony of the oppressors (5:21–24).

Even more startling, Amos belittles Israel's precious Exodus heritage. Yes, Israel was chosen from among all the nations, he says, but that just means God will judge Israel more harshly (3:1, 2). Besides, Amos adds, God works among other nations, too (9:7). Given Amos's message, it is not surprising that he was eventually sent home to Judah (7:12, 13).

OUTLINE OF AMOS

I. Introduction to Amos	1:1–2
II. The Eight Judgments	1:3—2:16
III. The Three Sermons of Judgment	3:1—6:14
A. Israel's Present	3:1–15
B. Israel's Past	4:1–13
C. Israel's Future	5:1—6:14
IV. The Five Visions of Judgment	7:1—9:10
V. The Five Promises of Restoration	9:11–15

Confrontation with Amaziah (Amos 7:10—9:15)

The account in Amos 7:10–17 of Amos's encounter with Amaziah, the priest of Bethel, includes the message that Amaziah sent to Jeroboam II (7:10, 11). The message reports a prophecy in which Amos predicts that Jeroboam will die violently and that Israel will go into exile. This prophecy thus dates Amos's ministry sometime before the end of Jeroboam's reign in 753 B.C.

Attempts have been made to date Amos's ministry by an earthquake which occurred during the reign of Judah's King Azariah (or Uzziah), but which was still remembered hundreds of years later (see Zech. 14:5). Amos received his vision "two years before the earthquake" (Amos 1:1).

Unfortunately, an exact date for this earthquake is uncertain. Archaeological work at the city of Hazor shows evidence that it happened sometime in the mid-8th century B.C. The Jewish historian Josephus connects the earthquake with the violation of the priest's office by Azariah (2 Chr. 26:16–20). When Azariah's violation resulted in leprosy, his son Jotham governed with him as coregent (2 Kin. 15:5). Jotham's 10-year coregency with Azariah began in 750 B.C., so following Josephus would place Amos's ministry a few years before 750.

God Is the God of All Peoples (Amos 9:7)

The prophet Amos recognized that Israel was not the only people who had received Yahweh's mercy. In a series of short poetic statements, Amos describes the universal power of Yahweh and reminds the Israelites that God is not concerned with them alone (Amos 9:7).

The prophet cites examples of three other peoples for whom Yahweh cares. His mercy reaches to a distant people (the Ethiopians), as well as to Israel's neighboring enemies (the Philistines and Syrians). He has brought to Canaan people from the centers of differing cultures: from Egypt (Egyptian cultural sphere), from Caphtor (East Mediterranean cultural sphere), and from Kir (Mesopotamian cultural sphere). Yahweh's concern is for all people.

This places the sin of Israel in a much broader context. It is not important to Amos that none of the other three peoples worshiped Yahweh. Israel had been called to be God's special people and to worship Yahweh alone, but had not done so. Now, as easily as God had brought these peoples into the land, He would scatter the Israelites from out of the land and into the world.

THE BOOK OF HOSEA

The names of five kings indicate the historical period during which Hosea prophesied. According to Hos. 1:1, his ministry is dated by the reign of Israel's Jeroboam II (793–753 B.C.) and by Judah's kings Uzziah, Jotham, Ahaz, and Hezekiah. The total period of the Judahite kings was from about 792 to 686 B.C., although there is no reason to believe Hosea's ministry extended past the fall of Israel in 722 B.C.

Hosea is the only native northern Israelite among the writing prophets. Although active at the same time as Amos, Hosea's message is quite different in its focus. Where Amos spoke about oppression, poverty, and injustice, Hosea speaks against the worship of the Canaanite deities, such as Baal and Asherah. These religions stressed rituals that were designed to promote the fertility of the land; among these rituals was sexual intercourse with official cult prostitutes.

Prostitution, or harlotry, becomes a major theme in Hosea, partly through the prophet's own family experience (Hos. 1—3). Israel is the bride of God, and once the marriage was happy (Hos. 2:14, 15; 11:1). By worshiping other gods, though, Israel has become a harlot. God alternately rages against His unfaithful wife and tenderly longs for reconciliation (6:4; 11:8, 9). The book ends with an impassioned appeal for Israel to "return" and a promise that, if she will, then God will become the true fertility God to His wayward people.

The words of Hosea are not arranged in the book chronologically, but rather by thematic and poetic connections. Moreover, it is almost impossible to suggest a chronology for Hosea's oracles, since they are vague concerning their historical context. Most could apply to any of a number of historical situations. Knowing some details about the last years of the northern kingdom, however, does help to illuminate a few of Hosea's many obscure passages.

OUTLINE OF HOSEA

I. The Adulterous Wife and Faithful Husband	**1:1—3:5**
A. Prophetic Marriage of Hosea to Gomer	1:1—2:1
B. The Application of Adultery of Gomer	2:2–23
C. The Restoration of Gomer to Hosea	3:1–5
II. The Adulterous Israel and Faithful Lord	**4:1—14:9**
A. Spiritual Adultery of Israel	4:1—6:3
B. Refusal of Israel to Repent	6:4—8:14
C. Judgment of Israel by God	9:1—10:15
D. Restoration of Israel to the Lord	11:1—14:9

TIME CAPSULE  **750 B.C.**

750	Jotham serves as coregent with Azariah (Uzziah) in Judah
750	Clay tablets presents Gilgamesh story as a drama
750	Greek city-state culture in Aegean
750	Iliad and Odyssey come from oral tradition

Hosea and Israel's Kings (Hos. 7:1—14:9)

"All their kings have fallen" (Hos. 7:7). This was an appropriate description of instability in the declining northern kingdom. Within 20 years, four of Israel's kings had been assassinated: Zechariah in 753 B.C., Shallum in 752, Pekahiah in 740, and Pekah in 732. After the Syro-Ephraimite War ended in 732, Israel was in its final years as a kingdom.

Hoshea (732–722 B.C.) was the last king of northern Israel. He led a pro-Assyrian conspiracy against Israel's king Pekah, assassinating him and seizing the throne himself (2 Kin. 15:30). At first Israel, under Hoshea, became a vassal of Assyria (Hos. 5:13; 14:3). Sometime after the death of the Assyrian king Tiglath-Pileser III in 727 B.C., Hoshea stopped paying tribute and turned to Egypt for help (2 Kin. 17:4). The prophet Hosea warns that an alliance with Egypt will be of no avail (Hos. 7:11, 16).

Hoshea's refusal to pay tribute to Assyria had dire consequences. The Assyrian king Shalmaneser V (726–722 B.C.) laid siege to Samaria from 725 to 722 B.C. and, at some point, imprisoned Hoshea. Samaria lost her king (Hos. 10:3, 7; 13:10, 11). The policy pursued by King Hoshea to lean upon Egypt for help against Assyria would not succeed in preserving the nation from destruction (11:5, 6; 13:16).

The Assyrians Make a Comeback (Hos. 11:5)

Assyria originated around the city of Asshur along the Tigris River and is first mentioned in Accadian sources in the late 3rd millennium B.C. The Assyrians evidently forged an independent state in the early 2nd millennium B.C. (c. 1800 B.C.) but did not become a lasting political force until the 14th century B.C. The reign of Ashuruballit I (c. 1363–1328 B.C.) marked the beginning of a stable empire. It was not until the 9th century B.C. that Assyria threatened Syria-Palestine, primarily under Shalmaneser III (858–824 B.C.) and his successors.

After Shalmaneser, the Neo-Assyrian Empire declined to a low point. By 745 B.C. its political structure was fragmented, and the kingdom of Urartu threatened its northern territory. At this crucial time for the empire a new king took power, beginning a revival of Assyrian strength. From 744 to 681 B.C. four Assyrian kings, all of whom appear in the Bible, led Assyria to its greatest period of imperial power: Tiglath-Pileser III, Shalmaneser V, Sargon II, and Sennacherib.

The revived Assyria threatened the very existence of the small states to the west. In 734 B.C. Tiglath-Pileser III mounted a ferocious offensive against the western states. This campaign culminated in the conquest of Damascus in 732 B.C. and forced most other states to pay tribute to Assyria. A decade later the Assyrians laid siege to Samaria, the capital of Israel, and ended its existence. Shalmaneser V conducted a 3-year siege, climaxing in Samaria's fall in 722 B.C. Sargon II succeeded Shalmaneser in that same year and probably was the king who carried the Israelite people into exile. Israel experienced the reality of Hosea's prophecy: "The Assyrian shall be his king" (Hos. 11:5).

Assyria had come back as a major power, and she would flex her new strength quickly. Sennacherib (704–681 B.C.) seized most of the major towns in Judah in his campaign of 701 B.C., and then he destroyed Babylon in 689 B.C.

THE BOOK OF ISAIAH

Few books have inspired more debate in terms of their historical context. Isaiah the prophet lived in Judah in the 8th century B.C., the time of Assyria's resurgence. He prophesied in Jerusalem, especially to kings Ahaz (735–715 B.C.) and Hezekiah (715–686 B.C.), and many of his prophecies speak clearly of the political situation of their time. His message to both kings, in brief, was that no human power could stand in the way of Assyria. Thus Judah was not to rely on alliances with Egypt or any other nation. Judah's only hope was faith in God's power to protect Zion, His chosen city.

The judgments recorded in Is. 1—35 can almost all be placed in this 8th-century Assyrian context. Chapters 36—39 are a historical narrative about that time period, almost identical to 2 Kin. 18:13—20:19. The setting changes, however, in Is. 40—55. These chapters are oracles of salvation that specifically speak of Cyrus the Persian and the restoration of Jerusalem in 538 B.C., some 200 years after Isaiah's time. Another change of setting occurs in Is. 56—66, chapters that appear to speak of the restored temple during Persian rule (c. 538–515 B.C.).

For almost a thousand years, some scholars have noted these shifts and suggested that the Book of Isaiah is the work of at least two different prophets. One would have been the prophet Isaiah himself, but the other an anonymous prophet of the late Babylonian exile (Cyrus's time) who consciously traced his spiritual roots to the original Isaiah. Other scholars, while acknowledging that chs. 40—66 speak of a later time, maintain that they are still the work of the prophet Isaiah, a divine vision of the salvation to come in the distant future.

But historical context concerns more than just the question of authorship. The sense of the various chapters of Isaiah should be considered in the context of which they speak. During Isaiah's own lifetime the threat was Assyria, and the prophet had to speak forcefully to his people and their kings, because they tended to trust in their own political and military maneuverings rather than in the power of God. This is the setting for most of Is. 1—39.

The prophecies of Is. 40—66 demonstrate that Judah's God is superior to other nations that would come. God promises to deliver His people, His chosen servants, from their captivity in Babylon. He will do something unheard of: through the mighty Persian emperor Cyrus, God will set an exiled people free to go home. Beyond all this, God will prepare His people to make His glory known to the Gentiles, who will come to the Lord's house to learn His ways (49:6; 56:3–8). These later chapters of Isaiah should be read in this context.

The first five chapters of Isaiah contain many representative oracles and may be intended as a thematic introduction to the book. Chronologically, though, Isaiah's ministry begins with his call, recounted in Is. 6. The prophet's call consists of a vision of God which he received "in the year that King Uzziah died" (6:1), about 740 B.C.

ASSYRIA REVIVES UNDER TIGLATH-PILESER III

B.C. 745 — 740 — 735 — 730 — 725

- Tiglath-Pileser III ascends to the throne of Assyria 744 B.C.
- Tiglath-Pileser wins battle against Sarduri II, king of Ararat 743 B.C.
- King Menahem of Israel pays tribute to Tiglath-Pileser (2 Kin. 15:19) 742 B.C.
- Tiglath-Pileser lays siege to capital of Ararat 735 B.C.
- King Ahaz of Judah pays tribute to Tiglath-Pileser (2 Chr. 28:19–21) 734 B.C.
- Rezin, king of Damascus, leads rebellion against Assyria 733 B.C.
- Tiglath-Pileser conquers Damascus and kills Rezin (2 Kin. 16:9) 732 B.C.
- Tiglath-Pileser defeats armies of Pekah, king of Israel 732 B.C.

OUTLINE OF ISAIAH

I. Prophecies of Condemnation	**1:1—35:10**
A. Prophecies Against Judah	1:1—12:6
B. Prophecies Against Other Nations	13:1—23:18
C. Prophecies of the Day of the Lord	24:1—27:13
D. Prophecies of Judgment and Blessing	28:1—35:10
II. Historical Material	**36:1—39:8**
A. Hezekiah's Deliverance from Assyria	36:1—37:38
B. Hezekiah's Deliverance from Sickness	38:1–22
C. Hezekiah's Sin	39:1–8
III. Prophecies of Comfort	**40:1—66:24**
A. Prophecies of Israel's Deliverance	40:1—48:22
B. Prophecies of Israel's Deliverer	49:1—57:21
C. Prophecies of Israel's Glorious Future	58:1—66:24

TIME CAPSULE	747 to 735 B.C.
747–664	Cushite Era in Egypt
747–539	The Babylonian Chronicle
744–727	Tiglath-Pileser III of Assyria (2 Kin. 15:19)
742–630	Period of Assyria's greatest imperial power
740	Isaiah's call consists of a vision of God
737–735	Rezin of Damascus leads coalition against Assyria
735–732	The Syro-Ephraimite War

Isaiah Encounters the Seraphim
(Is. 6:2–7)

In Judaism and Christianity the seraphim have been considered to be angels high in the heavenly court. The only account in the Bible where seraphim appear (Is. 6:2–7) suggests they were guardians of the throne room of Yahweh.

The translation "seraphim" comes from the Hebrew word *saraph*, which often refers to a "fiery flying serpent" (Is. 14:29; 30:6). Therefore some scholars assume that the flying beings that Isaiah saw guarding the throne of Yahweh had some type of serpents' bodies.

Ancient Near Eastern mythologies commonly present snakelike creatures guarding deities and their possessions. In Egypt the uraeus ("fiery snake") was not only a guardian of the god-king, but also a symbol of divine-kingship itself. The artifacts of Elam are rich in cobra symbolism. Mesopotamian artists used a serpent with legs liberally in public artwork. Further to the east, Indian mythology had nagas guarding the food and treasures of the gods. These cobra people could appear either as snakes or humans, or even with aspects of both. They also shot fire from their eyes and mouths.

The six wings of the seraphim (Is. 6:2) correspond to the six wings of the god El. The Greek writer Philo of Byblos (A.D. 64–141) explains in his *History of Phoenicia* that these wings represent eternal vigilance, mind, and understanding—all appropriate attributes for those closest to Yahweh.

The seraphim in Isaiah act for God and stand in God's presence, giving God glory and praise. They also act for God in relationship to the prophet. Inspiring both reverence and awe, the seraphim were able to make Isaiah acceptable in the presence of Yahweh (2:7), an activity that reflects their position as throne room guards.

THE FALL OF SAMARIA

Shalmaneser V ascends to the throne of Assyria 726 B.C.

Shalmaneser is killed in a revolution 722 B.C.

Sargon transports Samaria's inhabitants to Assyria 721 B.C.

B.C. 735 730 725 720 715

Hoshea ascends to the throne of Israel (2 Kin. 17:1) 732 B.C.

Hoshea of Israel pays tribute to Shalmaneser (2 Kin. 17:3) 725 B.C.

Shalmaneser lays siege to Samaria (2 Kin. 17:5) 725 B.C.

Samaria falls to the Assyrian army (2 Kin. 17:6) 722 B.C.

Sargon II usurps the throne of Assyria 722 B.C.

THE BOOK OF MICAH

Micah, like Isaiah, prophesied in Judah during the reigns of Jotham, Ahaz, and Hezekiah (Mic. 1:1). Indeed, there are even some parallels between the two prophets. Both spoke of God's plan for Zion (Jerusalem) and said that salvation would come through the line of David (cf. Is. 11:1–5; Mic. 5:2–5). There is even one shared prophecy: Is. 2:2–4 is almost identical to Mic. 4:1–3.

Micah has a few distinctives, however. Perhaps because he is not from Jerusalem itself, he is less convinced of Jerusalem's invulnerability than Isaiah seems. Micah prophesies Jerusalem's destruction (Mic. 3:12; see Jer. 26:17–19 for the results of this prophecy). In addition, Micah rejects religious hypocrisy and calls for the protection of the helpless in language that is more like that of Amos than that of Isaiah (Mic. 6:1–8).

OUTLINE OF MICAH

I. Prediction of Judgment	**1:1—3:12**
A. Introduction	1:1
B. Judgment of the People	1:2—2:13
C. Judgment of the Leadership	3:1–12
II. Prediction of Restoration	**4:1—5:15**
A. Promise of the Coming Kingdom	4:1–5
B. Promise of the Coming Captivity	4:6—5:1
C. Promise of the Coming King	5:2–15
III. The Plea for Repentance	**6:1—7:20**
A. First Plea of God	6:1–8
B. Second Plea of God	6:9—7:6
C. Promise of Final Salvation	7:7–20

A Prophet Prophesies Against the Prophets (Mic. 3:5–8)

Kings usually employed the services of professional prophets, who kept the king informed of the will of the gods. Yet despite the prevalence of such court prophets, it was widely believed that gods could use any human, from slave to ruler, as a prophet. The Mari tablets (c. 1813–1760 B.C.) record a prophecy from the deity Dagon as it was spoken by a slave woman who served one of the princesses. The prophetic frenzy of King Saul is an example of prophetic actions on the part of royalty (1 Sam. 19:23, 24).

Those persons who were seized by God and forced to speak the divine word are known as ecstatic prophets. For example, Amos insists that God had made him speak, though he was definitely not a prophet, only a sheepbreeder (Amos 7:14, 15). Similarly, Micah received power to prophesy "by the Spirit of the LORD" (Mic. 3:8). Yet Micah's prophecies denounced the professional prophets and seers who themselves could obtain "no answer from God" (Mic. 3:5–7).

Generally, the ecstatic prophets were different individuals from the professional court prophets, and the Bible distinguishes between true and false prophets. The true prophet was forced to speak the very word supplied by God whether or not the human wished to do so, as was Jeremiah's prophetic experience (Jer. 20:7–9). To hear the words of a true prophet was to hear the very word of God. False prophets, however, made up their own prophecies and then spoke them as if they were from the divine world. One seldom actually encountered a court prophet who was also ecstatic, though such was the prophet Micaiah in King Ahab's court (1 Kin. 22:8, 14).

Assyrians Worship Yahweh (2 Kin. 17:25, 28)

In the theology of the ancient world, gods owned territory. When Assyria overran Samaria, it was understood that Asshur, god of Assyria, was then in control of an empire that included Israel. Since the land of Israel still technically belonged to Yahweh, in the eyes of the Assyrians Yahweh was now a lesser deity in their pantheon, who would serve their god Asshur.

The Assyrians desired to be on good terms with the deities who owned the territories that Asshur and the Assyrian armies had conquered. It was important, therefore, to acknowledge Yahweh as God of Israel. Immediately after the conquest, however, busy with the resettling of peoples from other parts of their empire into Israel, the Assyrian army failed to retain the official rites in honor of Yahweh. As would any slighted god in the ancient world, Yahweh responded with a "gentle" reminder not to ignore the real power of the land; lions were sent which attacked people (2 Kin. 17:25).

Assyria attempted to correct this slight by finding among the exiled Israelites an official priest of Yahweh and returning him to Samaria. The king of Assyria hoped that the people who had been resettled in Israel would learn the proper religion for the territory they now inhabited. This would ensure that the local God, Yahweh, would remain happy with Assyria.

The people whom the Assyrians had forcibly relocated to Israel did what the Judeans would do approximately 136 years later when they were exiled to Babylonia. The new transplanted inhabitants brought their own gods with them to Israel and continued the worship they had practiced in their previous home territories (2 Kin. 17:29–33).

Tophet Burns with Much Wood (Is. 30:33)

Tophet (or Topheth) was a cultic site installed in the Valley of the Son of Hinnom (2 Kin. 23:10). It was connected to the worship of the god Molech and involved rituals that allowed children to be burned with fire (Jer. 7:31). The Valley of Hinnom runs roughly in a curving form, east-west, on the south side of the city of Jerusalem. To this day, no archaeological evidence of Tophet has been found.

The prophets often mentioned the fire of Tophet that was used to destroy children, but for the prophets Tophet was symbolical of the judgment God would bring on those not faithful to Him. Jeremiah proclaims that God would make Jerusalem and the towns around it like Tophet—like a place of burning—because their inhabitants had "stiffened their necks" against God's will (Jer. 19:12–15).

Another prophet, Isaiah, announces that a similar punishment would befall Assyria (Is. 30:31–33). Tophet is pictured by Isaiah as a funeral pyre that God had prepared "of old," ages before Assyria existed. It was "deep and large," a place of burning "with much wood," certainly adequate to punish Assyria (30:31) and its king (30:33).

The rites of child sacrifice at Tophet left their mark long after worship at that spot had been forgotten. By New Testament times, the Aramaic term *gehinnam*, meaning "Valley of Hinnom," was known in Greek as Gehenna, the "hell fire" (Matt. 5:22). In Jesus' warnings about hell fire (Matt. 18:9), Gehenna would be a fiery judgment, recalling the judgment and burning at Tophet proclaimed by Isaiah.

Sennacherib's Invasion (Is. 36:1; 2 Kin. 18:13–16)

After flirting with the idea for years, King Hezekiah finally rebelled against Assyria. The Assyrian king, Sennacherib (704–681 B.C.), promptly attacked Judah.

The chronology of Sennacherib's invasion is difficult. The 14th year of Hezekiah (2 Kin. 18:13; Is. 36:1) would be 701 B.C., but the siege was interrupted by an attack from Tirhakah of Egypt (2 Kin. 19:9; Is. 37:9), whose reign (690–664 B.C.) did not begin until about 10 years after this date. Some suggest that the Bible uses the name "Tirhakah," the most famous of the Ethiopian pharaohs, for a different and less well known king. Others argue that Hezekiah actually rebelled against Sennacherib twice, and the two accounts have been compressed into one narrative.

The suggestion that there were two invasions would also explain why there are two different reasons given for Jerusalem's deliverance. Hezekiah rebelled and was invaded in 701 B.C. He survived this first invasion only by paying exorbitant tribute to Sennacherib (2 Kin. 18:14–16). This payment is corroborated by Assyrian records, but interestingly enough, the parallel passage in Isaiah does not mention Hezekiah's tribute (Is. 36:1, 2).

A Second Invasion (2 Kin. 18:17—19:7; Is. 36:2—37:7; 2 Kin. 19:8–37; Is. 37:8–38; 2 Kin. 20:20, 21)

Hezekiah survived his rebellion of 701 B.C., but some 12 or 13 years later he tried again. Maybe around 688 B.C. Sennacherib again invaded and laid siege to Jerusalem (Is. 36:2—37:7). This time Tirhakah, the Ethiopian king of Egypt, interrupted the siege briefly but was driven back. This time there was no tribute paid; Jerusalem was spared by a miraculous plague that swept the Assyrian camp (Is. 37:8–38). A second invasion by Sennacherib is not recorded in Assyrian annals, but it has been suggested by scholars to account for the appearance of Pharaoh Tirhakah, who was not yet in power when Sennacherib invaded Judah in 701 B.C.

TIME CAPSULE	732 to 701 B.C.
732	Hoshea becomes king in Israel
732	Ahaz becomes sole king in Judah
725–722	Shalmaneser lays siege to Samaria
722	Fall of Samaria to the Assyrians
721–705	Israelites transported to Assyria during early years of Sargon's reign
720	After a victory at Qarqar, Sargon II marches through Gaza and Israel to Egypt's border
715	Hezekiah becomes king in Judah
705	Hezekiah revolts against Assyria
704–681	Sennacherib of Assyria faces alliance of Chaldeans, Arameans, and Elamites early in his reign
701	Sennacherib seizes major towns in Judah and besieges Jerusalem

HEZEKIAH'S TUNNEL (Is. 22:11)

Beginning in the 8th century B.C. the kingdoms of Judah and Israel were continuously threatened by the Neo-Assyrian Empire. Assyrian kings came to Canaan to collect taxes and to intimidate the local rulers. In 722 B.C. Samaria, the capital of Israel, was destroyed (2 Kin. 17:6), and those Israelites who could, fled toward Jerusalem. Upon becoming king of Judah in 715 B.C., Hezekiah did his best to prepare Jerusalem for the eventual attack by the Assyrians. His most lasting project involved water.

Rain in Judah usually comes only in the winter. Thus, Judahites built their cities near perennial springs, and in Jerusalem the main water source was the Gihon spring (1 Kin. 1:33, 38). Like most springs, the Gihon flowed in the valley, while the city sat on the hill above. Thus the spring that served Jerusalem water was at the foot of the hill, outside the walls of the city. That location would be a problem if an enemy army surrounded the city.

Hezekiah camouflaged the spring and ordered that a tunnel be carved into the hillside to bring the water under the city. Shafts were then dug down to the flowing water in the tunnel, which when finished was 1,750 feet long and emptied into the Pool of Siloam (2 Chr. 32:2–4, 30).

A dedication inscription was discovered in A.D. 1880 near the southern exit of the tunnel. Called the Siloam inscription, it describes the 8-month effort of two teams of diggers working toward each other from opposite ends of the tunnel. As the workmen came close together they could hear the other team, and they dug, according to the inscription, "pickaxe against pickaxe" until the water flowed from the spring to the reservoir.

Hezekiah's tunnel was a remarkable building project. The height of the tunnel varies greatly but averages 6 feet, and the water is most often less than knee deep. Even today, visitors to Jerusalem can wade through the s-shaped tunnel in the cool waters of the Gihon spring. Hezekiah was successful in securing the city's water supply. But the prophet (Is. 22:9–11) warns Judah's leaders that dependence on defense projects would not be sufficient to secure the city itself.

Hezekiah Brings Revival to Judah (2 CHR. 30:26)

King Hezekiah of Judah (715–686 B.C.) is given very high marks as a monarch by the writer of 2 Kings. The works of this king (2 Kin. 18:3) and those of Josiah (2 Kin. 22:1, 2) are favorably compared with those of their ancestor King David. Hezekiah is credited with sweeping reforms of Judah's temple worship (2 Chr. 29—31). The Passover observance that he restored was such a time of joy that the Chronicler reports, "Since the time of Solomon the son of David, king of Israel, there had been nothing like this in Jerusalem" (2 Chr. 30:26).

A Bird in a Cage (2 Chr. 32:9, 21, 22)

In the 8th century B.C. the Assyrians were the dominant power in the Near East, so it is no wonder that several books report about the Assyrian period: Isaiah, Jonah, Nahum, 2 Kings, and 2 Chronicles. One of the most amazing accounts is that of the confrontation between Hezekiah and Sennacherib. What makes this incident so unusual is that it is mentioned not only in the Bible but also by the Assyrians in the annals of Sennacherib.

Sennacherib, the Assyrian king, invaded Judah in 701 B.C. He conquered Lachish, one of Judah's strongest cities, and was plaguing the entire area (2 Kin. 18:13, 14). The seriousness of this threat to Judah can be seen from Sennacherib's records where he claims to have destroyed 46 walled cities and to have conquered smaller towns "without number." In addition, Sennacherib boasted of taking 200,150 people captive. Undoubtedly, the Assyrian conquest was a catastrophic blow to Judah.

Whether in 701 B.C. or later, as some scholars suppose, in 688 B.C., Sennacherib finally focused his attention on Jerusalem. After surrounding the city, the Assyrian Chief of Staff Rabshakeh tried to convince the city's leaders to petition King Hezekiah for peace (2 Kin. 18:17–19). Sennacherib's records report about Hezekiah, "Himself, like a caged bird, I shut up in Jerusalem, his royal city."

Though the city was terrified, Isaiah prophesied the ultimate demise of Sennacherib and retreat of his army (2 Kin. 19:6, 7). The Chronicler records the destruction of Sennacherib's army as the work of the angel of the Lord (2 Chr. 32:21). Sennacherib himself, in his own records, does not say why he did not complete his conquest of Jerusalem. He only states that he had made preparation to do so, but then went away.

SHOULD WE CORRECT A CULT GONE ASTRAY? (2 KIN. 22:8–20)

Josiah was confronted with the "Book of the Law," revealing that the temple cult in Jerusalem had been corrupted (2 Kin. 22:8). His response was to check with the prophetess Huldah to find out if this was truly the word of God (22:13). The caution of the king appears to be part of standard cult reform procedure in the ancient Near East.

The Assyrian king Sennacherib demolished the city of Babylon in 689 B.C. Later, his son Esarhaddon ruled Assyria and undertook the rebuilding of Babylon and the temple cult of the god Marduk. According to inscriptions relating the events of Esarhaddon's reign (680–669 B.C.), Marduk caused omens to appear to the king, revealing that the cult should be reinstated. The king, however, worried about such an undertaking since it was Marduk himself who had ordered his own city destroyed. Following Mesopotamian customs, the king went to the temples of the deities in charge of omens, Shamash and Adad, as well as to Marduk, and kneeled before them. Each deity supplied yet more omens to confirm that the temple reform should be instigated.

In the same way, the Babylonian king Nabonidus (556–539 B.C.) observed an eclipse of the moon, which was interpreted (by means of an omen book) to mean that the moon god, Sin, wished a new high priestess and a refurbished cult. As with Esarhaddon and Josiah, Nabonidus wanted to confirm the message. The king checked three times with the gods Shamash and Adad, the omen deities, to confirm the need for a new high priestess, the restoration of the Sin temples throughout Babylonia, and the choice of his daughter for priestess of Sin.

THE BOOK OF ZEPHANIAH

The superscription to the Book of Zephaniah (Zeph. 1:1) places this prophet during the reign of Josiah (640–609 B.C.). Although Josiah's reforms are not mentioned specifically within the book, Zephaniah clearly sympathizes with Josiah's aims. In one oracle, the prophet pronounces doom on the idolatrous priests and pagan worshipers that Josiah sought to destroy (Zeph. 1:4–6). Zephaniah may have been one of the prophetic voices that encouraged the reform efforts (2 Kin. 23:2, 3), and his prophecies were probably delivered before the reforms of 622 B.C.

Zephaniah's message, however, extended beyond Judah. He also pronounces judgment on foreign nations, most significantly on Ethiopia (which had controlled Egypt until about 664 B.C.) and on Assyria itself. The "day of the LORD," Zephaniah declares, will come to all the nations. Jerusalem itself is not exempt (Zeph. 3:6, 7), but in the end God will establish justice and comfort for His city.

OUTLINE OF ZEPHANIAH

I. A Warning of Impending Judgment	**1:1–18**
A. Judgment Announced	1:1–6
B. Judgment Defined	1:7–13
C. Judgment Described	1:14–18
II. A Call to Repentance	**2:1—3:8**
A. Invitation to Repentance	2:1–3
B. Warning of Judgment	2:4—3:8
III. A Promise of Future Blessing	**3:9–20**
A. Promise of Conversion	3:9–13
B. Promise of Restoration	3:14–20

Josiah Keeps the Passover (2 Kin. 23:1–25)

The historian of Kings describes Josiah's religious reforms in some detail, and in 2 Kin. 23:25 gives Josiah by far the most complimentary evaluation of any of Judah's kings. Josiah's reign brought great hope to Judah, first to the priests and prophets who hoped to see a genuine renewal of worship. The celebration of the Passover in 622 B.C. formed a climax to Josiah's religious reforms (2 Kin. 23:21–23).

Josiah's reign also gave hope to Judahites with more secular goals. There were evidently many who dreamed of reunifying Israel. Josiah began to expand Judah's borders into what had been the northern kingdom of Israel before Assyria captured it. In these efforts, Josiah was helped by the sharp decline of the Assyrian Empire, which created a power vacuum in the area of the former northern kingdom. Among other actions, Josiah destroyed the idolatrous Israelite shrine of Bethel from which the prophet Amos had been expelled over a century before (Amos 7:10–17).

THE TEMPLE PANTHEON OF JERUSALEM (2 CHR. 34:31, 33)

Josiah's covenant with Yahweh meant that there would be only one deity worshiped in Judah, for Josiah "removed all the abominations" from the country (2 Chr. 34:31, 33). The reform began in 622 B.C. by removing the idols that had been placed in the Jerusalem temple. These images, representing gods such as Baal and Asherah (2 Kin. 23:4), were of Syro-Palestinian (Canaanite) origin. The expression "host of heaven" (2 Kin. 23:4) referred to an entire pantheon of gods.

Through the reigns of Manasseh and Amon, Josiah's predecessors, the local gods had been incorporated into the royal temple. Probably both Canaanite and Assyrian deities were worshiped, for Assyria was then the ruling power over the vassal state of Judah. Many of the traditional Canaanite gods had been worshiped in the northern kingdom, and an association of these gods with Israel may explain why Josiah took the cult images to Bethel for disposal (23:4). Bethel had been a national temple of Israel.

The sanctity of the temple space was retained during the reform efforts. Only priests were allowed to clean out the images. Hilkiah had been the high priest of the cult involving all these deities, but, under orders from the king (23:4), he removed the gods that he had served.

THE NEO-BABYLONIAN EMPIRE

The events of the approximately 30 years following Josiah's reform of 622 B.C. lie behind a wide range of biblical books. The most important are probably the books of Jeremiah and Ezekiel, but other prophetic books, historical accounts, psalms, and poems also refer to this critical era. The catastrophes of this time would completely reshape both the faith of the Judeans and the Bible itself. These disasters were even more staggering in that they came so suddenly after the optimistic years of Josiah's reign in Judah (640–609 B.C.).

Under Ashurbanipal (668–627 B.C.) the Assyrian Empire that had once made the world its own had grown old and surprisingly weak. Constant rebellions from outlying provinces had sapped its resources. Egypt, for instance, had effectively declared its independence and appeared to be regaining some of its former strength. Even more disturbing for Assyria, though, were rebellions closer to home. After Ashurbanipal died, Babylon rebelled once more, joined by the northeastern nation of Media. This time Assyria would not be able to quell the revolt.

The effect of these stirring events on Judah was virtually to give King Josiah complete independence from his official overlords in Assyria. He could pursue his religious reforms and expand his political boundaries at will.

EPOCH FIVE
Chronological Reading Guide

❑ 2 Kings 23:26, 27
❑ Jeremiah 1:1—6:30
❑ Nahum 1:1—3:19
❑ 2 Kings 23:28–34
❑ 2 Chronicles 35:20—36:4
❑ Jeremiah 22:10–17
❑ Habakkuk 1:1—3:19
❑ 2 Kings 23:35–37
❑ Jeremiah 7:1—8:3
❑ Jeremiah 26:1–24
❑ Jeremiah 11:1—12:17
❑ Jeremiah 47:1–7; 13:1–14
❑ Jeremiah 46:1–12
❑ Jeremiah 18:1–17
❑ Jeremiah 36:1–10
❑ Jeremiah 25:1–14
❑ Jeremiah 36:11–32
❑ Jeremiah 15:10–21
❑ Jeremiah 45:1–5
❑ Jeremiah 14:1—15:9
❑ Jeremiah 16:1—17:27
❑ Jeremiah 8:4—10:16
❑ 2 Kings 24:1–4
❑ Jeremiah 35:1–19
❑ Jeremiah 23:9–40
❑ Jeremiah 18:18—20:18
❑ 2 Kings 24:5–9
❑ Jeremiah 13:15–27
❑ Jeremiah 22:18–30
❑ 2 Kings 24:10–17
❑ 2 Chronicles 36:5–10
❑ Jeremiah 24:1–10
❑ Daniel 1:1—4:37
❑ 2 Kings 24:18, 19
❑ Jeremiah 27:1–11
❑ Jeremiah 48:1—49:39
❑ Jeremiah 52:1–2
❑ Jeremiah 25:15–38
❑ Jeremiah 27:12—29:32
❑ Jeremiah 50:1—51:64
❑ 2 Chronicles 36:11–12
❑ Ezekiel 1:1—3:21
❑ 2 Kings 24:20—25:3
❑ Jeremiah 52:3–6
❑ Jeremiah 10:17–25
❑ Jeremiah 21:1—22:9
❑ Jeremiah 34:1–22
❑ Jeremiah 46:13–28
❑ Jeremiah 37:1–21
❑ Jeremiah 30:1—33:26
❑ Jeremiah 23:1–8
❑ Jeremiah 38:1–28
❑ 2 Chronicles 36:13–16
❑ Ezekiel 8:1—11:25
❑ Ezekiel 13:1—18:32
❑ Ezekiel 20:1—21:17
❑ Ezekiel 22:1–22; 23:1–49
❑ Ezekiel 21:18–32
❑ Ezekiel 24:1–27
❑ Ezekiel 3:22—7:27
❑ Ezekiel 29:1–16
❑ Ezekiel 30:20—31:18
❑ 2 Kings 25:4–7
❑ Jeremiah 52:7–11
❑ 2 Kings 25:8–21
❑ Jeremiah 39:1–7
❑ Jeremiah 52:12–27
❑ Jeremiah 39:8–10
❑ Lamentations 1:1—5:22
❑ 2 Kings 25:22–26
❑ Jeremiah 39:11—44:30
❑ 2 Chronicles 36:17–21
❑ Ezekiel 12:1–28
❑ Psalm 89
❑ Ezekiel 19:1–14
❑ Ezekiel 33:21–33
❑ Ezekiel 22:23–31
❑ Ezekiel 25:1—28:26
❑ Ezekiel 32:1–32
❑ Psalm 137
❑ Obadiah 1:1–21
❑ Jeremiah 52:28–30

THE BOOK OF JEREMIAH

No prophet is more important in this crucial time period than Jeremiah. He was from a priestly family, from the small town of Anathoth near Jerusalem. He may have been a descendant of David's priest Abiathar, who had been banished to Anathoth by King Solomon (1 Kin. 2:26). In any case, Jeremiah's relationship with the Jerusalem establishment—temple, priests, prophets, and kings—was strained, to say the least. Unlike Isaiah, who was evidently acknowledged and respected throughout Jerusalem in his day, Jeremiah's long ministry was marked by persecution, banishment from the temple, and threats of death.

Jeremiah's very unpopular message was that Jerusalem had sinned so long and so grievously that God was about to destroy the temple, the city, and the land. In language very close to that of the northern prophet Hosea, Jeremiah called for the people to turn from their wickedness. Even after almost all of Jeremiah's prophecies had been fulfilled, though, few listened.

No book in the Old Testament presents more difficulties to chronological arrangement. In its usual order, the book is divided into three general sections: oracles against Judah and Jerusalem (chs. 1—25), narratives about Jeremiah (chs. 26—45), and oracles against other nations (chs. 46—51). The final chapter (ch. 52) is an almost exact reproduction of 2 Kin. 25. Not one of these three general sections follows a chronological arrangement, however. Even the historical narratives of the central portion skip back and forth in time. As for the oracles of the first section, it is almost impossible to decide the time period to which some of these refer.

Any attempt to arrange chronologically the various portions of Jeremiah must be both very different from the usual order and very tentative. On the other hand, no other Old Testament book benefits more from such a rearrangement. To read Jeremiah's words in light of his life and the history of his land is a completely new experience.

The first chronological difficulty concerns the beginning of Jeremiah's ministry. In Jer. 1:2 the prophet is reported to have received the word of the Lord in the 13th year of Josiah's reign (627 B.C.). If this is when he began his prophetic task, then the time of his ministry spans all of Josiah's reforms. It is odd then that Jeremiah never mentions these reforms or any other sign of religious faithfulness in Jerusalem.

The year 627 B.C. marks a beginning for this prophet, but was it the beginning of his ministry? Some think this is when Jeremiah became aware of his divine calling, and not necessarily when he began to prophesy. Others suggest that Jer. 1:2 actually refers to the date of Jeremiah's birth, noting that Jeremiah was called as a prophet even before he was born (Jer. 1:5). If he was born in 627, Jeremiah could have begun his prophetic ministry near the end of Josiah's reforms, when he was between the ages of 12 and 18. Many of the oracles found in chs. 1—6 rebuke the people and the priests for backsliding, perhaps indicating that Josiah's reforms were falling apart even during Josiah's reign.

The end of Jeremiah's ministry is dated by Jer. 1:3 in King Zedekiah's 11th year (586 B.C.). This prophet continued his work until Jerusalem fell and the city's people were exiled.

Broken Cisterns (Jer. 2:13)

In Old Testament times cisterns were an everyday part of life. The seasonal rainfall of the Bible lands necessitated extraordinary strategies for securing water. In some cities virtually every household had its own cistern, arranged so as to collect runoff water from the streets as well as from the roofs of the houses.

Cisterns were dug into the bedrock foundation of the houses and could be plastered or unplastered depending on the type of rock into which they had been dug. Sometimes two or more cisterns were connected by water channels. In the middle of many of these cisterns were stone-carved sumps where the larger impurities could be collected and periodically removed. Even in the best of times, however, the stored waters, while usable, were not very pleasant.

In Jer. 2:13 the prophet makes a contrast between the true God and the false gods of Canaan. He describes Israel's God as fresh, sweet water from a living or moving spring that could give life to all. The Israelites are charged with ignoring this refreshing source and turning instead to water from a cistern.

The irony of Jeremiah's prophecy is even greater. The cisterns from which the Israelites were seeking satisfaction were broken cisterns that really could not collect water. Jeremiah's contrast would be understood by those who daily sought drinking water from cisterns. God is a living sustaining water source that satisfies, while the false gods of Canaan are like broken, unusable cisterns that promise refreshment but leave those who try to drink there thirsty and without hope.

OUTLINE OF JEREMIAH

I. The Call of Jeremiah	**1:1–19**
A. Jeremiah's Call	1:1–10
B. Jeremiah's Signs	1:11–16
C. Jeremiah's Assurance	1:17–19
II. The Prophecies to Judah	**2:1—45:5**
A. The Condemnation of Judah	2:1—25:38
B. The Conflicts of Jeremiah	26:1—29:32
C. Jerusalem's Future Restoration	30:1—33:26
D. The Present Fall of Jerusalem	34:1—45:5
III. The Prophecies Against the Gentiles	**46:1—51:64**
IV. The Fall of Jerusalem	**52:1–34**
A. The Capture of Jerusalem	52:1–11
B. The Destruction of Jerusalem	52:12–23
C. The Exile to Babylonia	52:24–30
D. The Release of Jehoiachin	52:31–34

Avoiding Ungodly Alliances (JER. 2:18)

In the years between 627 and 605 B.C. many important events occurred in Judah. For instance, King Josiah undertook his reforms to centralize all worship of Yahweh at the Jerusalem temple and outlawed all idolatrous worship (2 Kin. 23:1–25). On the international scene, major changes were under way as well.

For over a century, the Assyrian Empire had reigned supreme throughout the ancient Near East. At the beginning of the 7th century B.C., the Assyrian king Sennacherib had conquered all of Judah, except for Jerusalem, which miraculously withstood his siege (2 Kin. 18:13—19:37). By the late 7th century, however, Assyria's influence had begun to wane. King Josiah took advantage of Assyria's loss of power to exert Judah's independence.

The Babylonians quickly arose to contest the Assyrians for control of Mesopotamia. In an attempt to hold on to power and stop the Babylonians, Assyria entered an alliance with a more distant power—Egypt. They hoped this alliance with the pharaohs of the 26th Dynasty (664–525 B.C.) would change the balance of power back into their favor.

While all these events happened far from Judah, no doubt Assyrian, and possibly also Egyptian, diplomats lobbied in Jerusalem for the Judahites to join with them. The Egyptian pharaoh Psammetichus II even visited Judah in 591 B.C. The offer to join forces with the two oldest and most powerful, prestigious states in that century would have looked very tempting. Surely this was the path to security and prosperity for the kingdom of Judah!

Jeremiah did not think so. The "road to Egypt" and the "road to Assyria" were dead ends. Help would not come from the part of the Nile River known as Sihor (or Shihor, Is. 23:3), nor from Assyria's Euphrates River (Jer. 2:18). Political alliances were not the way to security, but rather faithfulness to Yahweh and Yahweh alone. Rather than entering an alliance with the Assyrians and the Egyptians, Jeremiah counseled Judah to maintain the independence achieved during the reign of King Josiah (640–609 B.C.).

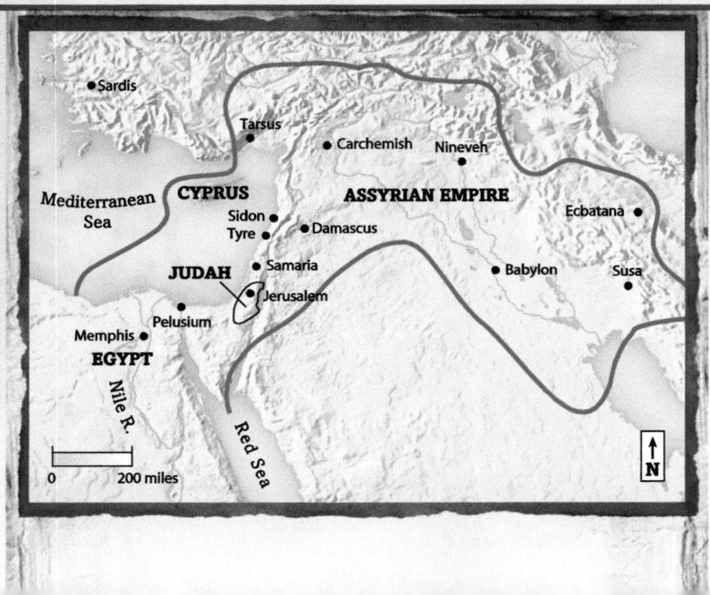

The Neo-Assyrian Empire
By 650 B.C. the Assyrian Empire, with its capital in Nineveh, stretched from the Persian Gulf in the east throughout the fertile crescent into Palestine and beyond, embracing for a short time all of Egypt in the southwest. Judah, while a free zone, still paid tribute to Assyria. The prophet Nahum mentions Assyria's victory over Thebes (or No Amon, Nah. 3:8). But Nahum also prophesies the destruction of Nineveh, Assyria's great capital (Nah. 3:18).

THE BOOK OF NAHUM

In 612 B.C. the rebel alliance of the Babylonians and the Medes, under the leadership of the Babylonian king Nabopolassar (626–605 B.C.), drove the Assyrians out of their own capital, Nineveh. The Assyrians were not entirely defeated, and they were able to regroup in the northwest, at the ancient city of Haran. Nevertheless, Nineveh, once a symbol of Assyrian splendor, was gone. The nations that had once been so terrorized by Assyria could only be delighted.

Nothing is known of the prophet named Nahum or of the exact time of his prophecy. It is clear, however, that the book speaks of the events of 612 B.C., when the Medes and Babylonians drove the Assyrians out of Nineveh. Nahum's glee at Nineveh's downfall can sound vindictive to modern ears, but it is understandable. Assyria's reputation for brutality and torture was well established; Nineveh was referred to as "the bloody city" (Nah. 3:1). More than one person had wondered how such cruelty could go unpunished, including the prophet Habakkuk (see "The Book of Habakkuk"). Nahum's delight comes primarily from seeing that the Lord does punish the wicked after all (see Nah. 1:2, 3).

Nahum's mention of "No Amon" (3:8) refers to Thebes, the Egyptian capital which Assyria herself had sacked in 664 B.C. Nahum recalls that Assyrian victory as a warning that Assyria also must face judgment and would fall as had her victims.

OUTLINE OF NAHUM

I. The Destruction of Nineveh Is Decreed	**1:1–15**
A. Principles of Divine Judgment	1:1–8
B. Destruction of Nineveh	1:9–15
II. The Destruction of Nineveh Is Described	**2:1–13**
A. The Call to Battle	2:1–2
B. The Destruction of Nineveh	2:3–13
III. The Destruction of Nineveh Is Deserved	**3:1–19**
A. Reasons for the Destruction	3:1–11
B. Destruction Is Inevitable	3:12–19

TIME CAPSULE	689 to 622 B.C.
689	Assyrian King Sennacherib demolishes Babylon
686	Manasseh becomes sole king in Judah
676	Edom, Moab, and Ammon become vassals of Assyria
668–627	Ashurbanipal rules in Assyria
650	Greeks use molds for making things out of clay
648	Ashurbanipal captures Babylon
640	Josiah becomes king of Judah
630	All of Philistia comes under Egyptian control
626–539	Neo-Babylonian Empire
625	Earliest coinage, found in Ephesus
622	The reforms of Josiah

Assyria's Capital Is Destroyed (Nah. 1:1)

Nineveh was the chief city of the Assyrian Empire in the last century of the empire's power (c. 705–612 B.C.). It is this 7th-century Nineveh that is known from accounts in the books of Nahum and Jonah. Yet the city had a very long history, and there are substantial archaeological material remains of Nineveh from the New Stone Age (c. 5000–4000 B.C.).

The city is not mentioned in written records until the mid-3rd millennium B.C. when it was under control of the Accadian kings. Nineveh was incorporated into Assyria during the reign of Ashur-uballit I (1363–1328 B.C.). The city thus played a prominent role in the Middle Assyrian Empire after 1273 B.C., and Assyrian kings spent much time in building activity there.

The Nineveh against which Nahum prophesies was more than just a major city. The Assyrian king Sennacherib (705-681 B.C.) decided to make Nineveh the capital of Assyria, and it was then transformed into the capital of a world state. Like the Babylonian king Nebuchadnezzar II a century later, Sennacherib spent a great deal of time in monumental building projects at the site.

Despite being protected by an enormous city wall, Nineveh was captured and destroyed by an alliance of Medes and Chaldeans in 612 B.C. The fall of this great city, which was recorded in the Babylonian Chronicle and described in Nahum's prophecy (Nah. 2:3–13), effectively ended the Assyrian Empire.

Josiah's Last Years (2 Chr. 35:20—36:4)

The Chronicler's account of Josiah's death in 609 B.C. is very close to the account in Kings. One difference is the curious note that Pharaoh Necho fought "against Carchemish" (2 Chr. 35:20). An important battle was fought by Assyria and Babylon at Carchemish in 605 B.C., 4 years after Josiah's death, but in 609 B.C. Necho was advancing to fight at Haran. The Chronicler may be referring to Necho's plans in 609 to join the Assyrian army near Carchemish on the Euphrates River and use that city as a base of operations for the siege of Haran.

Chronicles also provides more detail about Josiah's death. The Chronicler reports that God accomplishes His purposes even through a foreigner, the Egyptian pharaoh Necho (35:21). The tragedy of Josiah's death is accentuated by the lamentations of Judah and of the prophet Jeremiah, mourning for the king whose reign would be remembered forever as the kingdom's last moment of glory.

THE BOOK OF HABAKKUK

In the final years of Josiah's reign, while Assyria fought the Babylonian alliance in Mesopotamia, the prophet Habakkuk pondered the forces behind these events. Like Nahum, Habakkuk felt the injustice of Assyria's power. In a dialogue with God, he asks how such violence could go unpunished. Unlike Nahum, though, Habakkuk is not satisfied with Assyria's punishment at the hands of Babylon. Is Babylon any better than Assyria, after all? How can a pure God use such impure tools? In reply, God tells Habakkuk to wait, for in such faithful waiting is true righteousness (Hab. 2:4).

Habakkuk's forthright questioning has earned him the title "the philosopher prophet." He might just as well be described as a priestly prophet. He uses priestly language (ch. 3 is a psalm, complete with musical directions). Even the questions he asks of God sound priestly, very similar in tone and content to the questions asked by the psalmist of Ps. 73, a psalm associated with the priestly singer Asaph.

OUTLINE OF HABAKKUK

I. Habakkuk's First Complaint	1:1–4
II. God's First Response	1:5–11
III. Habakkuk's Second Complaint	1:12—2:1
IV. God's Second Response	2:2–20
V. Habakkuk's Prayer	3:1–19

CHALDEANS BECOME BABYLONIANS (HAB. 1:6)

As early as the 9th century B.C. the Chaldeans as a people are known from cuneiform records, the wedge-shaped characters etched in blocks of clay with styluses. The Chaldeans originally inhabited the southern portion of Babylonia on the west border of Elam. There was possibly a relationship between them and the Arameans, but that relationship is not clear. Both were tribal groups in southern Babylonia, and there is no difference between Aramean and Chaldean personal names. Yet the Arameans and Chaldeans were often described as distinct peoples.

For over 2 centuries of the Neo-Assyrian period (934–612 B.C.) the Chaldeans were at odds with the powerful Assyrians in the north. They often successfully waged guerrilla warfare against this foe. Merodach-Baladan II was a Chaldean king who twice occupied the throne of Babylon (721–710 and 703–702 B.C.). Evidently he also enlisted the support of Hezekiah, king of Judah, during a revolt against the Assyrians (Is. 39:1, 2).

By the 7th century B.C., the Chaldean tribes were able to control Babylonia and its capital city, Babylon. At that point, the terms "Babylonian" and "Chaldean" appear to be synonymous. Thus, Scripture uses these terms interchangeably: Nebuchadnezzar II, king of Babylon (c. 605–562 B.C.) and the destroyer of Jerusalem, was himself a Chaldean (see Ezra 5:12).

Jeremiah's Temple Sermon (Jer. 26:1–6; 7:1—8:3; 26:7–24; 11:1—12:17)

Jeremiah's ministry entered its most active stage when Jehoiakim became king in 609 B.C., when Jeremiah was (by one proposed chronology) about 18 years old. In Jehoiakim's first year, Jeremiah preached what is known as his Temple Sermon. The events surrounding this sermon and a short version of the sermon itself are recounted in Jer. 26. A much longer version of the sermon appears in Jer. 7:1—8:3. That Jeremiah was from Anathoth, not from Jerusalem, may explain why he was so scornful of those who put their trust in "the temple of the LORD, the temple of the LORD" (7:4). It may also explain why the Jerusalem hierarchy reacted so strongly to his condemnations.

At various points in the first half of the Book of Jeremiah the prophet's complaints to God appear concerning the difficulty of his calling. These are usually called Jeremiah's Confessions. They are couched in the language of the psalms, and like the psalms give few clues as to their precise historical context. These laments can be read where complaints would be appropriate. The first of these, Jer. 12:1–17, is appropriate in the context of Jeremiah's near execution after preaching his Temple Sermon (Jer. 26:8–19).

The Battle of Carchemish (Jer. 47:1–7; 46:1–12; 13:1–14; 18:1–17)

In Jehoiakim's 4th year (605 B.C.), the exiled nation of Assyria again made an alliance with Egypt and attacked the Babylonian army, which was led by the crown prince of Babylon, Nebuchadnezzar (also spelled Nebuchadrezzar). On the way through Canaan, Pharaoh Necho evidently attacked Gaza and Ashkelon in the Philistine coastlands.

The battle, fought at Carchemish on the northern Euphrates River, was a rout. Nebuchadnezzar's armies destroyed the Assyrians once and for all and sent Necho fleeing back through Palestine toward Egypt. Nebuchadnezzar was unable to follow up his advantage, however. Receiving word that his father Nabopolassar had died, Nebuchadnezzar returned to Babylon to assume the throne, now the undisputed ruler over all Mesopotamia.

Jeremiah was a keen observer of world events and frequently spoke to and about the nations around Judah. His announcements of judgment against Philistia (Jer. 47:17) and Egypt (46:1–12) may have referred to the events surrounding the battle at Carchemish. His political advice to Jehoiakim, which the king invariably ignored, was to accept Babylonian supremacy and reject alliances with Egypt.

Jeremiah's essential theme, though, was that all these events were part of God's plan, and that God was working through all the nations to perform His will. The object lessons of the ruined linen sash (13:1–11), the bottle filled with wine (13:12–14), and the potter's clay (18:1–17) illustrated clearly that no nation, not even Judah, could escape His judgment.

Jeremiah's Scroll (Jer. 36:1–10; 25:1–14; 36:11–32; 45:1–5; 15:10–21)

By the 4th year of Jehoiakim's reign (605 B.C.), when Babylon affirmed its supremacy at the battle of Carchemish, Jeremiah was well known to the Jerusalem leadership. Indeed, his constant condemnations of Judah's leaders had led them to banish him from the temple. There would be no more sermons at the temple gates. Jeremiah was not so easily silenced, though. The prophet dictated a message to his friend and scribe, Baruch, and sent him to read the scroll on the day of fasting (Jer. 36:1–10). Baruch had to wait over a year before a day of fasting was proclaimed. The 9th month of Jehoiakim's 5th year (36:9, 22), following the Babylonian calendar, would place the fast in December 604 B.C.

The exact contents of this scroll are uncertain, although it may have contained large portions of what is now Jer. 1—25. The message of Jer. 25:1–14 must have been a part of the scroll, since the superscription (25:1) dates these verses in Jehoiakim's 4th year, and the phrase "this book" (25:13) may refer to the scroll. Jeremiah reminds the people (25:3) that 23 years have passed since his calling in the 13th year of Josiah's reign (627 B.C.), and he has spoken to them repeatedly.

The second of Jeremiah's Confessions (15:10–21) can be read as an appropriate response to the king's rejection and burning of Jeremiah's written oracle (36:11–32). Jeremiah's friend Baruch also suffered and made his complaint, to which Jeremiah responds strongly (45:1–5). Baruch's brother, Seraiah, served as a high official under King Zedekiah. Baruch had good reason to believe that he, too, could have gained a responsible position in Judah's court (both were sons of Neriah, 32:12; 51:59). He forfeited that dream by siding with Jeremiah and alienating Judah's rulers.

A Faithful Friend and Scribe (JER. 36:4, 32)

Jeremiah dictated his prophetic message to a certain Baruch, the son of Neriah (Jer. 36:4). When temple officials forbade Jeremiah to enter the temple with his message of judgment, Baruch took the scroll into the temple courtyard and faithfully read it there (36:9, 10). Ultimately, the king destroyed the scroll, only to have Jeremiah dictate another to Baruch (36:20–24, 32). For his efforts, Baruch received a warrant for his arrest and had to go into hiding (36:26).

Throughout the Book of Jeremiah, Baruch is pictured as Jeremiah's loyal friend, scribe, and lawyer. Baruch witnessed and sealed the legal transaction for Jeremiah's purchase of land and personally held the deed for Jeremiah (36:12–16). When the military forced Jeremiah to move to Egypt as a refugee following the destruction of Jerusalem, Baruch went with him (43:5, 6). Baruch was evidently Jeremiah's "right-hand man."

Yet Baruch was also a very important person in Jerusalem's society. A seal impression reading "Belonging to Berechiah, son of Neriah, the scribe" has been found in a royal archive. This seal of "Berechiah" (the long form of the name "Baruch") identifies Baruch's profession as a scribe, yet also suggests that he was probably a royal scribe from a prominent scribal family.

Not just anyone had a seal, only those with wealth and influence. Such a seal was a ring used to grant legal status to documents and transactions. Pressed into soft clay, it made the document legally binding based upon the status and character of the person. Baruch's seal impression matches two imprints, or bullae, which were made by the seal. Apparently, Jeremiah's friend and scribe had important connections within Jerusalem's society.

A Prophet Without a Family (Jer. 16:2)

A prophet's life often characterized the message that God had given that prophet to proclaim. The symbolism of the single life takes on dark overtones for Jeremiah (Jer. 16:2–13). God prohibited Jeremiah from marrying, and thus from having children (Jer. 16:2). By prohibiting marriage, God emptied the prophet's life of any future significance from the perspective of his society.

Israelite society was grounded upon the social institution of the family. Not only did the family provide stability for the present, it also carried the status of the family into the future. The man governed the family, and heirs provided the means for his "name," his status and honor, to continue into new generations.

By depriving Jeremiah of a family, God symbolically pronounced the depth and extent of His judgment upon Israel. Even without a family, Jeremiah would be better off than his peers. The children of his peers would die "gruesome deaths" (16:3, 4) so frequently that even the parents would not observe the proper mourning rituals (16:5–7). Given the depth of destruction, even celebrations, such as those at weddings, would not occur (16:9). Such would be the price for Judah forsaking Yahweh and walking after other gods (16:10, 11).

ORACLES IN HEAVEN (JER. 10:2)

Jeremiah dismisses the idea of reading the future by looking at the skies. Even though Gentile nations studied the "signs of heaven" and were "dismayed at them" (Jer. 10:2), Judah was not to follow their example. Ancient people had two ways of trying to read the future in the skies: one way studied atmospheric conditions; the other, the movement of planets and stars.

The atmospheric method looked to various weather-related conditions as indicators of what events would occur on earth. The way the wind blew, how the rain fell, the formation of clouds, or the color of the morning or evening sky were recorded and checked against the omen books to see what they meant.

More famous, because it has been retained to the present age, is the reading of the stars and planets. Early forms of astronomy and astrology merged to tell both time and the future. By the 1st Dynasty in Egypt (c. 3000 B.C.) scribes associated the flooding of the Nile with the rising of the star Sirius. From the 9th Dynasty (c. 2160 B.C.) onward a series of stars (known as "rams" in Egypt) were thought to control individual destinies.

The zodiac and other familiar forms of astrology were developed in Mesopotamia. The earliest Mesopotamian astrological references date from the Dynasty of Accad (c. 2300 B.C.). The Old Babylonian period (c. 2017–1595 B.C.) provides the first extensive series of celestial "charts," collected in a work entitled *Enuma Anu Enlil*.

At first the system was used to predict events for the nation itself and for the royal family. By the Neo-Assyrian period (934–612 B.C.) all the elements that now make up the zodiac appeared in an Assyrian text. The formal 12-sign, 4-season structure appeared later in the Neo-Babylonian (626–539 B.C.) or early Persian (539–530 B.C.) periods. The prophets dismissed the endeavors of astrologers and stargazers as meaningless (Jer. 10:2; Is. 47:13).

True or False Prophet? (Jer. 23:16–27)

Jeremiah relentlessly proclaimed a message of God's judgment, warning that the Babylonians would come and completely devastate Judah and Jerusalem. The sufferings he described of the Babylonian siege and subsequent victory were terrifying (Jer. 18:21). To say the least, this did not exactly make him a popular speaker in Jerusalem. People then, as now, wanted an optimistic, upbeat message. Jeremiah, therefore, often had conflict with others, especially the aristocracy of Jerusalem, over the content of his prophecy. Among other things, Jeremiah once ended up in stocks outside the temple as the leaders of Jerusalem tried to get him to change his vision of the future (Jer. 20:1–6).

Jeremiah, however, was not the only prophet at work in Jerusalem at that time. Other prophets worked the streets as well and were much more popular. These other prophets recalled that the prophet Isaiah had correctly prophesied that God would save Jerusalem from the Assyrians merely a century earlier (Is. 37:21–35). From this they concluded, and publicly prophesied, that God again would save Jerusalem and His temple from defeat. Even though the Babylonians pressed near, there would be "peace" (Jer. 23:17).

In Jeremiah's time it was not easy to distinguish between a false prophet and a true prophet: Which prophet had really received counsel from God? The key difference, claimed Jeremiah, was moral: the false prophets' oracles had brought about no change in the Judahites' evil lifestyle (23:22). This indicated that these prophets spoke "a vision of their own heart, not from the mouth of the Lord" (23:16).

The Book of Daniel

Among the exiles taken to Babylon was the young man Daniel, who began immediately his training to become a courtier in Nebuchadnezzar's court (Dan. 1). His long life as a faithful Jew in a pagan land is told in chs. 1—6 of the Book of Daniel, while chs. 7—12 consist of Daniel's symbolic visions of the future.

The Book of Daniel presents many difficulties to chronological arrangement. To begin with, Dan. 1:1 places Nebuchadnezzar's siege and the beginning of Daniel's exile in the "third year of the reign of Jehoiakim" (605 B.C.). No other text describes a siege and captivity in that year, which was Nebuchadnezzar's 1st year. To resolve the difficulty, some scholars favor an otherwise unknown siege in 605 B.C. when, it is suggested, Nebuchadnezzar sent Chaldean (Babylonian) armies against Judah (2 Kin. 24:2), bound Jehoiakim in chains, and carried off vessels from the Jerusalem temple (2 Chr. 36:6, 7), along with Daniel and other exiles. Then final siege in 597 B.C. led to the much larger deportation described in other biblical accounts.

Other interpreters are more skeptical about an unknown event in 605 B.C. The historian of Kings recounts only the sieges of 597 B.C. (2 Kin. 24:10, 11) and of 588 B.C. (2 Kin. 25:1, 2). The prophet Jeremiah summarized the deportations of Judeans from Jerusalem (Jer. 52:28–30), recording three deportations that possibly correspond to 597, 586, and 581 B.C. Jeremiah does not list a deportation for 605 B.C.

It is difficult to imagine why both Kings and Jeremiah neglect to mention such an important event as an invasion and deportation. Perhaps the dates given in Dan. 1:1; 2:1, locating these narratives at the beginning of King Nebuchadnezzar's reign, serve a thematic purpose—to shift the focus away from Judah's history to Babylon's. Indeed, in many ways, the main character in Dan. 1—4 is not Daniel but Nebuchadnezzar.

The first large deportation, and thus the beginning of the Babylonian exile, occurred in Nebuchadnezzar's 8th year (597 B.C.; 2 Kin. 24:12), when Jehoiachin was taken captive to Babylon. Regardless of when Daniel was deported, the experiences of this most famous Judean exile can be read in that context.

A second chronological difficulty has to do with identifying the times referred to in the visions of Daniel (chs. 7—12). On the one hand, the visions themselves say that they refer to the "latter time" (8:19), and they are even today very often interpreted as referring to events that have not yet occurred. On the other hand, the more explicit visions (chs. 10—12) quite clearly refer to the end of the Persian Empire and the rise of the Greek Empire of the 4th through 2nd centuries B.C. (e.g., 11:2, 3).

To say that Daniel's visions speak specifically of events in the Persian-Greek period does not, however, mean that they cannot also refer to the "latter time." Daniel's visions are densely packed with obscure and surprising images; they resist being restricted to any single meaning. For this reason, many scholars understand them to have multiple fulfillments. Thus, Dan. 7—12 can be read in light of historical events at the end of the 1st millennium B.C., while keeping in mind the possible references

DEPORTATIONS FROM JERUSALEM TO BABYLON

The armies of Babylon under King Nebuchadnezzar besieged Jerusalem on different occasions, taking parts of the population away into exile. The Babylonian Chronicle records the campaigns of Nebuchadnezzar between the years 616 and 594 B.C., including the siege of Jerusalem in 597 B.C.

A Proposed Early Deportation

605 B.C. Nebuchadnezzar besieges Jerusalem, captures King Jehoiakim, and deports captives, including Daniel, into exile.

Source: The Book of Daniel is the only record of a deportation in this year. Dan. 1:1, 2 dates the siege in Jehoiakim's 3rd year, which according to the Babylonian method of counting would be 605 B.C. Some think that 2 Chr. 36:6, 7 refers to this event. (Jeremiah, writing in Judah and using the Judean method of counting, reckons 605 B.C. as Jehoiakim's 4th year, Jer. 46:2.)

The Deportation of Jehoiachin

597 B.C. Nebuchadnezzar captures King Jehoiachin, loots the temple treasures, and deports captives, including Ezekiel, into exile.

Source: The Babylonian Chronicle, as well as 2 Kin. 24:10–16; 2 Chr. 36:10; and probably Jer. 52:28. The reason for the large difference in the numbers of deported captives is not known.

The Fall of Jerusalem

588 to 586 B.C. Nebuchadnezzar besieges Judah's cities, including Jerusalem, during these years. In 586, his army captures King Zedekiah, burns down the temple, and deports Jerusalem's people into exile.

Source: The Lachish Letters, as well as 2 Kin. 25:1–21; 2 Chr. 36:17–20; and probably Jer. 52:29.

A Final Deportation

581 B.C. Nebuzaradan, captain of the guard for the Babylonians, deports 745 persons from Jerusalem.

Source: The Book of Jeremiah (Jer. 50:30) is the only record of a deportation in this year. It could have been a reprisal for the murder of the governor Gedaliah, who was appointed by the Babylonians.

to an ultimate fulfillment. See "The Apocalyptic Visions of Daniel."

Because the visions describe the events of the Greek era so clearly and in such detail, scholars often suggest that they were actually written during Greek times and attributed to the historical figure of Daniel. Other scholars, though, less puzzled by such explicit foretelling of future events among the prophets, accept the traditional attribution of the book to Daniel himself.

OUTLINE OF DANIEL

I. The Personal History of Daniel	**1:1–21**
A. Carried Away to Babylon	1:1–7
B. Faithfulness in Babylon	1:8–16
C. Daniel's Reputation in Babylon	1:17–21
II. The Prophetic Plan for the Gentiles	**2:1—7:28**
A. Nebuchadnezzar's Dream	2:1–49
B. Nebuchadnezzar's Image of Gold	3:1–30
C. Nebuchadnezzar's Vision of a Great Tree	4:1–37
D. Belshazzar and the Handwriting on the Wall	5:1–31
E. Darius' Decrees	6:1–28
F. Daniel's Vision of the Four Beasts	7:1–28
III. The Prophetic Plan for Israel	**8:1—12:13**
A. Vision of the Ram and Male Goat	8:1–27
B. Vision of the Seventy Weeks	9:1–27
C. Vision of Israel's Future	10:1—12:13

THE FALL OF JERUSALEM

- Nebuchadnezzar deposes King Jehoiachin (2 Kin. 24:10–15) 597 B.C.
- King Zedekiah is summoned to Babylon (Jer. 51:59) 593 B.C.
- The siege is interrupted by Pharaoh Hophra (Jer. 37:5) 587 B.C.
- King Zedekiah rebels against Babylon (2 Kin. 24:20) 588 B.C.
- Nebuchadnezzar begins a new siege against Jerusalem 588 B.C.
- Nebuzaradan deports more captives from Jerusalem (Jer. 52:30) 581 B.C.
- Nebuchadnezzar enters Jerusalem and burns temple (2 Kin. 25:4, 9) 586 B.C.
- The people are taken captive to Babylon (2 Kin. 25:11) 586 B.C.

B.C. 610 595 590 585 580

NEBUCHADNEZZAR, KING OF BABYLON (DAN. 3:1)

Nebuchadnezzar II reigned from 605 to 562 B.C., becoming the second and most famous king of the Neo-Babylonian or Chaldean dynasty (Dan. 3:1). As crown prince, he orchestrated the victory over the Egyptians at the crucial battle of Carchemish in 605 B.C.

The Chaldean king spent a great deal of effort in campaigning to the west—in Syria and Palestine—primarily to check Egyptian influence in the region. The Babylonian Chronicle, the primary historical source for the early periods of the Chaldean kingdom, records how Nebuchadnezzar laid siege to Jerusalem in 597 B.C. and deposed King Jehoiachin of Judah.

The destruction of Jerusalem in 586 B.C., related by the historian of Kings (2 Kin. 25:1–21), is not mentioned in cuneiform records, since the Babylonian Chronicle breaks off after 594 B.C. The Jewish historian Josephus (A.D. 37–100) does record Jerusalem's end in an account that apparently depends upon the Book of 2 Kings as a source.

Nebuchadnezzar was also known for his great building projects, especially in Babylon. These included a summer palace, a fortification of the city, the ziggurat (sometimes associated with the tower of Babel described in Gen. 11), and the famous royal hanging gardens.

This Chaldean king is also well known from later Greek, Latin, and Jewish sources. The classical writers were impressed with his monumental building activity, while the Jewish writers, understandably, condemned him for his destruction of Jerusalem and the temple.

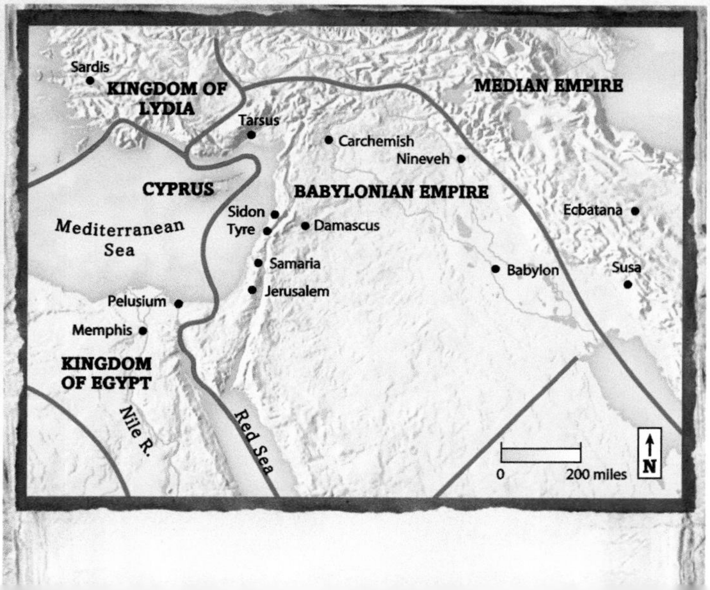

The Neo-Babylonian Empire

In 605 B.C. Nebuchadnezzar's 2-year siege of Carchemish proved successful, and most of the Assyrian Empire rapidly became the Babylonian Empire. In 586 B.C. Nebuchadnezzar conquered all of Judah, besieging and destroying Jerusalem and the Jewish temple in the process. At its zenith in 560 B.C. Babylon ruled the entire Fertile Crescent and Arabia, although Egypt regained autonomy.

THE BOOK OF EZEKIEL

The second great prophet of Jerusalem's last days, along with Jeremiah, was Ezekiel. When Nebuchadnezzar captured Jerusalem in 597 B.C., the young priest Ezekiel was one of the Judeans taken into exile in Babylon. Though he would visit Jerusalem in visions (Ezek. 8:3), he appears to have spent the rest of his life in Babylon.

Being a part of the Jerusalem priestly establishment, Ezekiel must have known of Jeremiah's preaching, and may even have joined the other priests in opposing it. If so, he changed his mind in Babylon. Ezekiel's message to the exiles was much the same as Jeremiah's to those who remained in Jerusalem. To those who felt that this exile would be brief and that soon all would be restored in Jerusalem, Ezekiel prophesied that Jerusalem and even the temple itself would be destroyed. Not until that destruction had taken place (in 586 B.C.) would Ezekiel speak of a future restoration. His oracles of judgment appear in chs. 1—24, followed by his oracles concerning other nations (chs. 25—32). The book concludes with Ezekiel's words of salvation (chs. 33—48).

Ezekiel's priestly heritage shines through his prophecies, especially in his focus on the temple. Judah's sins are sins against true worship and ritual purity, particularly in the temple (see chs. 8—11). Judah's greatest punishment comes when the glory of God leaves the temple (11:23). After that, the temple's destruction is inevitable. Judah's true salvation appears in the form of a new, heavenly temple, to which God's glory would return (chs. 40—48, especially 43:1–5).

TIME CAPSULE	612 to 581 B.C.
612	Fall of Assyria to the Medes and Babylonians
610–595	Pharaoh Necho II of Egypt is foe of Babylon
609	Pharaoh Necho kills King Josiah of Judah at Megiddo
605–562	Nebuchadnezzar II is 2nd king of Chaldean dynasty in Babylon
604	Baruch reads Jeremiah's scroll at the temple
601	King Jehoiakim of Judah rebels against Babylonian rule
598–597	Nebuchadnezzar besieges and captures Jerusalem
597	The prophet Ezekiel is among Judeans deported to Babylon
592	Ezekiel has vision of the Jerusalem temple
588	King Zedekiah revolts against the Babylonians
588–586	Nebuchadnezzar besieges and conquers Jerusalem
586–538	The exile of Judah to Babylon
581	Babylonian official Nebuzaradan deports captives from Jerusalem

OUTLINE OF EZEKIEL

I. Prophecies of Coming Judgment	**1:1—24:27**
A. The Call of Ezekiel	1:1—3:27
B. Overthrow Predicted	4:1—7:27
C. Sin and Fate of Jerusalem	8:1—11:25
D. Moral Necessity of the Captivity	12:1—19:14
E. Inevitable Downfall of Israel	20:1—24:27
II. Oracles Against Foreign Nations	**25:1—32:32**
A. Ammon	25:1–7
B. Moab	25:8–11
C. Edom	25:12–14
D. Philistia	25:15–17
E. Tyre	26:1—28:19
F. Sidon	28:20–26
G. Egypt	29:1—32:32
III. Prophecies Concerning Israel	**33:1—39:29**
A. The Prophet's Role	33:1–33
B. Message to the Shepherds	34:1–31
C. A Fruitful Israel	35:1—36:38
D. The Vision of Dry Bones	37:1–28
E. The Lord Will Defend Israel	38:1—39:29
IV. Vision of the Future	**40:1—48:35**
A. Description of the New Temple	40:1—43:27
B. A New Service of Worship	44:1—46:24
C. Israel Reorganized	47:1—48:35

A Prophet in Exile (Ezek. 1:1–3)

The River Chebar was located in Babylon, probably a few miles from the city of Nippur. It was there that Ezekiel began his prophetic work as a prophet "among the captives" (Ezek. 1:1)—the Judeans whom the Babylonians had exiled from Judah.

Ezekiel was among a group of Judeans who were deported along with King Jehoiachin by the Babylonians in 597 B.C. (2 Kin. 24:14–16). Taking the king and many of Judah's skilled citizens would discourage their relatives back home in Judah from further rebellion.

Ezekiel, therefore, prophesied to a group away from home who most likely had hopes of returning to Jerusalem. If they looked to Ezekiel to fuel this hope, they were disappointed. Rather than hope, Ezekiel saw nothing but God's judgment upon Jerusalem as long as the city stood (Ezek. 15; 16).

The Exiles Return to Samaria (Jer. 31:5, 6)

Originally "Samaria" was the name for the capital of the northern kingdom of Israel. The city had been built by King Omri in the early 9th century B.C., presumably to establish his kingship after a period of civil war and unrest in Israel. Later the name "Samaria" would also be associated with the northern kingdom itself.

An earlier name for the region of Israel had been "Ephraim." After the Syro-Ephraimite War (735–732 B.C.), Israel lost some of its outlying territories to Assyria. Under the Assyrian king Tiglath-Pileser III, these areas became Assyrian provinces known as Dor, Megiddo, and Gilead, each being named after the city from which the Assyrian-appointed governor ruled. Israel's borders were reduced to a territory that had belonged to the tribes of Manasseh and Ephraim during the era of the judges. So now what was left of the region of Israel was often called "Ephraim."

After the Assyrian conquest of the city of Samaria in 722 B.C., the Assyrian king Sargon II established another Assyrian province. Following the Assyrian practice of naming a province after its chief city, the name "Samaria" was now used for the region where the city had been.

The prophet Jeremiah mentions "the mountains of Samaria" as well as "Mount Ephraim" (Jer. 31:5, 6). The hill country of Samaria is a harsh, mountainous land full of fissures and valleys. Mountain passes make Samaria's hills accessible. In a message of hope, Jeremiah prophesies that God will return the exiles to the hill country known as Ephraim and Samaria. There they will settle, plant, and travel to Jerusalem (Zion) for worship.

A God Consuming Human Flesh (Jer. 32:35)

The god Molech was worshiped by sacrificing human children. The ancient world in general was horrified by this practice, and the sacrifice of children to a deity became widely known as a "Molech sacrifice."

Whether the name of this deity was actually "Molech" remains uncertain. The scribes of the Hebrew Bible were so appalled with the worship of Molech that they used the vowels of the Hebrew word *bosheth* (meaning "shame") with this deity's name. The original name apparently meant "king" and could have been understood as a divine title. But it could also have been the actual name of the deity. The prophet Jeremiah mentions Molech together with the god Baal, whose name means "lord" (Jer. 32:35).

While 1 Kin. 11:7 associates the worship of Molech with the Ammonites, it is the Phoenicians and the Judahites who show evidence of practicing child sacrifice. Literary and archaeological sources point to rituals involving the sacrifice of children at the Phoenician colony of Carthage from around 700 to 200 B.C. The central ritual of worship appears to have included the sacrifice of infants and small children, the burning of their bodies, and the burial of the cremated remains.

Jeremiah condemned both the practice of child sacrifice and the city of Jerusalem for allowing it (Jer. 7:30–32; 19:13). The Tophet was a cult site set up in the Valley of Hinnom, near Jerusalem, for human sacrifice. Two Judahite kings, Ahaz (2 Chr. 28:1–3) and Manasseh (2 Chr. 33:1, 6), are reported to have sacrificed children there. The prophet considered it an abomination (Jer. 32:35).

A Consultation with a Prophet (Ezek. 20:1–3)

Ezekiel pursued his prophetic ministry in public. He continuously went out into the public realm to proclaim a message from God or to engage in symbolic actions that communicated the divine message to the exilic community.

A different situation occurs when the "elders of Israel" approach Ezekiel. These elders, who were the leaders of Ezekiel's exilic community in Babylon, came to the prophet in order to "inquire of the Lord" (Ezek. 20:1).

"Inquiring of a god" recalls the professional prophets that existed throughout the ancient Near East, including Babylon. For a fee individuals or groups could approach a prophet to receive oracular advice in the form of an omen from their deity. Often the prophet, "possessed by the spirit of the god," would enter a trance before presenting the message of the god by offering the appropriate response.

Interestingly, the leaders of Ezekiel's exilic community perceived him this way. Indeed, they "sat before" Ezekiel, as if waiting for a "spirit" to take possession of the prophet (20:1). God, however, rejected this model for Ezekiel. In keeping with God's prohibition (Ezek. 14:1–3), Ezekiel refused to prophesy in answer to the elders' questions. He was not a prophet-for-hire. Rather, the elders received a stinging indictment from God for their behavior (20:4–32), along with God's refusal: "I will not be inquired of by you" (20:3, 31).

Ezekiel's Prophetic Theater (Ezek. 5:1–4)

As ancient Near Eastern prophets proclaimed a message from the gods, they often used more than words to get their message across. Often their very actions and lives illustrated the prophetic oracle. For no prophet was this more true than the prophet Ezekiel.

In one of his acted-out prophecies or sign acts, Ezekiel undergoes a haircut and a shave. The razor in this case, however, was to be a sword (Ezek. 5:1). Ezekiel then was to divide the hair into three parts: one-third to be burned in the midst of the city; a second third to be hit by a sword; another third to be scattered into the wind (5:2). Finally, from the last third, a small amount of hair was to be wrapped in Ezekiel's clothing, and later some of this would be thrown into a fire (5:3, 4).

Such symbolic actions seem bizarre, yet are significant for the prophet's message. First, the cutting of an adult male's hair and beard was a sign of humiliation. Using a sword as the razor, Ezekiel symbolically lived out with his own body the military humiliation that the Jerusalemites would face when the Babylonians conquered their city.

Yet the symbolism was even more precise. The burning of hair in the midst of the city and striking of hair with a sword signified the destruction of people when the Babylonians actually attacked Jerusalem. The scattered hair dramatically portrayed the fleeing of people into the countryside following the attack. The final third showed the destruction of the people after the attack. Only a few hairs, or people, wrapped into Ezekiel's clothing, would survive. Ezekiel's "haircut," thus portrayed an entire drama of death and destruction brought on by the Babylonian attack upon the city.

It is not known where Ezekiel undertook these activities. From his other prophetic behavior, however, we can assume that he performed these actions very much in the public eye, proclaiming Yahweh's message through the most effective media.

THE BOOK OF LAMENTATIONS

The Book of Lamentations consists of five separate poems on the destruction of Jerusalem in 586 B.C. These funeral songs and prayers describe both the horrors of the extended siege (e.g., Lam. 4:4, 5) and the destruction itself. No other book captures so vividly the despair of seeing Zion destroyed, of seeing the holy city and its temple become a mockery to the nations.

Lamentations is traditionally attributed to Jeremiah, which explains its usual placement after the Book of Jeremiah, but the book itself does not name an author. Whether by Jeremiah or an unknown poet, the book is surely an eyewitness account of those wretched days. The five poems were penned, probably not long after Jerusalem's fall in 586, by someone who had seen the slaughter of many of his people, the enslavement of others, and the abject despair of the few survivors.

OUTLINE OF LAMENTATIONS

I. Grief After the Destruction of Jerusalem	1:1–22
II. Personal Suffering After the Destruction	2:1–22
III. Hope in the Face of Adversity	3:1–66
IV. The Siege of Jerusalem	4:1–22
V. Remembering That God Still Reigns	5:1–22

Jeremiah mourns over the destruction of Jerusalem
Rembrandt Harmensz van Rijn
c. 1630

Temple Afire
(Lam. 2:5–7)

Temples were the focal point of civic life and the target for invaders. The patron deities of the city were believed to dwell in the temples. Festivals were held around temples, and valuables were deposited in them (they were the earliest banks).

For invaders, the capture of the central temple served several purposes, not the least of which was obtaining the wealth stored there. To take the temple was also to show that the gods of the city had chosen the conquerors over the local inhabitants. This meant that the conquerors were now the legitimate rulers of the people, land, and any possessions.

The burning of the central temple was a declaration of unconditional victory. Only if the gods of the city had abandoned that city to its fate would they allow their own home to be destroyed. When Sennacherib destroyed Babylon and the temple of Marduk in 689 B.C., he claimed to have done so on behalf of Marduk, who wished to punish his people for their evil behavior.

The captors were understood to have free rein with the city and its populace. The defeated city had no gods to whom they might appeal for mercy and no hope for a change in their fate. Their gods were believed to have moved to the capital of the victors, where they became patrons of the kings of that city.

The Book of Lamentations says the same thing about Nebuchadnezzar II burning Jerusalem and its temple in 586 B.C. (2 Kin. 25:9). Yahweh Himself had become Judah's enemy (Lam. 2:5) and destroyed His own temple—His "tabernacle" and "place of assembly" (2:6). With Yahweh's permission, Judah's enemy now "made a noise in the house of the LORD" (2:7).

Gedaliah the Governor
(2 Kin. 25:22–26; Jer. 39:11—44:30)

Nebuchadnezzar had had enough of kings in Jerusalem. Even his chosen servant Zedekiah had rebelled. Now there would be no more royalty. Instead, Nebuchadnezzar appointed a governor, named Gedaliah (2 Kin. 25:22). Archaeological finds indicate that this Gedaliah had been Zedekiah's chief minister, but he was not from the line of David. With Jerusalem a heap of rubble, Gedaliah set up his seat of government at Mizpah, while Nebuchadnezzar took still more of the people of Judah into exile to Babylon.

In the confusion of rounding up captives, it seems Jeremiah was arrested by mistake. He was taken to Ramah, a small town a few miles north of Jerusalem, where he was identified and released (Jer. 39:11—40:6). The prophet was offered the chance to leave his land and his people and have full provisions. He chose rather to stay with Gedaliah and the poor survivors.

Gedaliah's father, Ahikam, had once saved Jeremiah's life (Jer. 26:24), and Gedaliah was clearly disposed to follow Jeremiah's advice: he would humbly serve the king of Babylon (Jer. 40:9). Even after all Jeremiah's prophecies had been proven true, though, this advice remained unpopular. Only about 2 months passed (2 Kin. 25:8, 25) between Gedaliah's appointment as governor and his assassination by a certain Ishmael (Jer. 40:7—41:15).

The people, led now by a Judean army commander named Johanan, feared a reprisal by the Babylonians. Despite Jeremiah's prophetic word that they should stay in Judah, they fled to Egypt, taking Jeremiah and Baruch with them (Jer. 41:16—44:30). The last recorded messages of Jeremiah come from Tahpanhes in Egypt. His prophecies concern Pharaoh Hophra's loss of his throne in 570 B.C. to the Egyptian general Amasis (44:30) and Nebuchadnezzar's campaign against Egypt in 567 B.C., during which Hophra was killed (43:8–13).

MYTH AND THE PRINCE OF TYRE (EZEK. 28:2–10)

Ezekiel's prophecy against the prince of Tyre (Ezek. 28:2–10) brings together elements from the religious and mythological writings of the eastern Mediterranean. The sarcastic description Ezekiel offers of the prince's attitude reflects the cosmopolitan character of the Phoenicians.

Phoenician rulers were seen as subordinate partners with the patron deity of the city. The idea of the ruler himself being a god found some place in Phoenician royal ideology, having been incorporated from Egyptian culture. Thus, the prince of Tyre could boast, "I am a god" (Ezek. 28:2). Ezekiel, however, considered such pretensions to divine status to be merely self-delusion.

One Ugaritic myth presents another example of someone trying to move up the divine hierarchy, though not worthy. The god Athtar attempts to sit on Baal's throne, but Athtar is not equal to the throne, as Baal was, and has to step down. Ezekiel suggests that such is the case with the prince of Tyre: he is not even capable of retaining his royal position, let alone being a god. He is "a man, and not a god" (28:2).

The prince thought much of himself, his heart being "lifted up" (28:5). In Greek mythology, such exaggerated pride or self-confidence is known as hubris and angers the gods. The myth of Arachne demonstrates the dangers of hubris. Arachne was so good at weaving that she threatened the self-esteem of the goddess Athena. Athena turned her into a spider as punishment. Similarly, Ezekiel warns the prince that God will require his life in payment for his conceit (28:9, 10).

THE BOOK OF OBADIAH

Obadiah's name means "servant of the Lord," but beyond that, nothing certain is known about this prophet. The book's message, though, is clear: judgment upon Edom. The Edomites had acted treacherously against the inhabitants of Jerusalem during their darkest hour. They laughed at Judah's sorrow, probably looted the hapless people, and helped the Babylonian soldiers find fleeing refugees. Edom, descended from Israel's brother Esau, had betrayed that brotherhood. Now Edom would be punished.

The date of the book is not completely certain; it could be referring to any number of times that Edom opposed Judah. Various verses, however, fit particularly well with the time after the fall of Jerusalem in 586 B.C. Not only does Obadiah refer to the destruction of Jerusalem and a captivity (Obad. 1:11, 12), but he also appears to quote from a prophecy of Jeremiah's (Obad. 1:5; Jer. 49:7–9).

OUTLINE OF OBADIAH

I. Predictions of Judgment on Edom	1–9
II. Reasons for Judgment on Edom	10–14
III. Results of Judgment on Edom	15–16
IV. Possession of Edom by Israel	17–21

Various Deportations to Babylon (Jer. 52:28–30)

In Jer. 52:28–30 is a historical summary of the various deportations of Judeans from Jerusalem to Babylon. This summary does not occur anywhere else in the Bible. It differs both in dates and numbers of deportees from accounts given by the historian of Kings.

The summary lists three deportations, occurring in the 7th, 18th, and 23rd years of Nebuchadnezzar. The 7th year could refer to the exile of Jehoiachin in 597 B.C., while the 18th year could refer to the exiles deported at Jerusalem's fall in 586. The difference in dates from those reported in 2 Kin. 24:12 and 25:8 could result from different methods of reckoning the 1st year of a king.

The third deportation (52:30) is reported as carried out by Nebuzaradan in 581 B.C. (Nebuchadnezzar's 23rd year). There is no evidence beyond Jeremiah for a deportation in that year. Some scholars suggest that this may have been Babylon's response to the assassination of Gedaliah, the governor appointed by Nebuchadnezzar (Jer. 41:16–18). The amount of time that passed between Jerusalem's fall in 586 and Gedaliah's murder—2 months or 5 years—is not known.

Little is certain about Jeremiah's summary. The vastly greater numbers of deported Judeans given in 2 Kin. 24:14, 16 may be round numbers including women and children. On the other hand, Jer. 52 may refer to smaller deportations that were separate from those of 597 and 586. What the summary does offer is one more reminder of how greatly the inhabitants of Judah suffered in the fall of their nation.

EPOCH SIX

EXILE AND RETURN

586—332 B.C.

Judah experienced a time of great tragedy when Jerusalem was destroyed and nearly all of Judah's leaders were taken into exile in Babylon. It was a time of despair in Judah's relationship with Yahweh, as well. "How shall we sing the LORD's song in a foreign land?" (Ps. 137:4) was a cry from the heart. What had happened between the exiled people and their God Yahweh?

Chief among the problems facing the Judeans was the question of identity. Prior to the Babylonian exile, they had been an independent, political state, to some extent secured by military power, and with a God-ordained Davidic king on the throne. All this was taken as proof that their God was the true God, the King of the universe. Now, none of these conditions existed. They were a powerless, subject people in a great empire whose rulers thought Yahweh was only one petty god among many.

With their lives now controlled by the Babylonians, the Judeans experienced tremendous temptation to surrender all their previous claims to having an exclusive revelation from God. In addition, they were tempted to surrender those behaviors that had been designed to separate them from the surrounding pagan cultures. Thus, there was a real danger that they would become assimilated into those cultures, preserving some Judean customs, but surrendering the covenants God had made with them.

That this did not happen was largely due to the labors of the prophets Haggai, Zechariah, and Malachi; the priest Ezra; and the governor Nehemiah. Each of these individuals filled a distinctive role, and together they made it possible for the Jews to come to a new understanding of themselves. These five men showed them that their identity was to be a nation of priests, serving God and declaring Him before the world. Their constitution was not to be some political arrangement, but the Law of God. Their covenant with Him was what made them a people. This would be a time in which the faith of Israel would become a universal faith, one in which Yahweh would be seen as the saving God of all peoples.

ARCHAEOLOGY AND THE PAST

Various Babylonian remains elaborate on this period. The Babylonian Chronicle, a collection of documents written on baked clay tablets, describes events leading up to Judah's tragedy. This historical source of the Chaldean kingdom records how Nebuchadnezzar laid siege to Jerusalem in 597 B.C., deposed Jehoiachin of Judah, and appointed a new king in his place. The Babylonian Chronicle pictures Babylon as the new superpower in the Middle East; Judah lived only on sufferance from Babylon. But that relationship did not last, and archaeological surveys reveal that many cities and villages in Judah were destroyed in 586 B.C.

The Babylonian Chronicle recounts nothing after 594 B.C. Another Babylonian record, however, includes receipts for oil and other goods issued to Jehoiachin and his family. These Babylonian cuneiform texts, dating between 595 and 570 B.C., suggest that Judah's royal family, though in exile, lived in relative comfort and freedom at Babylonian expense.

Archaeology also witnesses the Judean return from the Exile. The Cyrus Cylinder, a baked clay document, states that Cyrus was chosen by Marduk, the chief god of Babylon, to be ruler over Babylon and to restore the true worship of the gods. The cylinder clarifies that the return of exiles and freedom of worship were key parts of Cyrus's policy. The language and content of the Cyrus Cylinder is very close to the decree in Ezra 1:2–4.

A document found in Egypt tells of a Persian inquiry into the religious practices of the Jews in Egypt near the end of the 5th century B.C. The letter, known as the Passover Papyrus, is one of the writings sent to the Jewish colony at Elephantine, and is dated in the 5th year of Darius II (419 B.C.), bearing his royal authority. It reminds us that the Persian rulers took an interest in the religious practices of subject peoples and were not above sending commissioners to assure that those practices were observed properly. Such a mission was given to the priest Ezra concerning religious practice in Jerusalem.

Coins and seals further testify to the restoration of Jerusalem. A series of jar handles show seal impressions reading "Judah," "Jerusalem," and "belonging to the king." The language reveals that Hebrew was giving way to Aramaic, which became the common language of the Persian Empire. Before the Persian period, gold and silver were weighed out on scales. Coins, however, made trade and business much simpler. During the second half of the 5th century, coins with Hebrew letters, bearing the name "Judah," appear. The Persian policy of allowing considerable local autonomy to Persian provinces included the right of provinces to strike their own coins.

THE PEOPLES AND GROUPS

During the reign of Babylon's last king, Nabonidus (556–539 B.C.), forces were building that spelled the end of the Babylonian Empire. Cyrus the Great ascended the throne of Persia in 559 B.C. The Persian Empire, founded by Cyrus, became the great superpower of its day. Between 539 B.C., when Cyrus entered Babylon, and 525 B.C., when Cyrus's son Cambyses conquered Egypt, all the Middle East became Persian. At least two Persian emperors tried to capture Greece. Darius I was defeated at Marathon in 490 B.C.; Xerxes I at Salamis in 480.

The Persian emperors were great builders as well as imperialists. Excavations at Susa have uncovered the palace begun by Darius and finished by Xerxes. The rock carvings on Persian palaces, tombs, and triumphal monuments show the power and splendor of the Persian kings. Their empire lasted until 331 B.C., finally being defeated by the Macedonian armies of Alexander the Great.

When the exiles returned to Judah, they encountered other peoples already there. Sanballat (Neh. 2:19) is identified as the governor of Samaria in documents from Elephantine. Samaritans were descendants of the mixed marriages between Israelites and peoples whom the Assyrians had imported. When the Jews enjoyed prosperity, the Samaritans were quick to acknowledge their blood relationship. But when the Jews suffered hard times, the Samaritans disowned such kinship, claiming to be descendants of Assyrian immigrants.

Samaritan hostility was coupled with that of the Ammonites in the east and the Arabians in the southeast. Tobiah the Ammonite (Neh. 2:19) may have been the Persian governor of Ammon, just as Nehemiah was governor of Judah. His family was powerful in the Transjordan from the 5th century to at least the 2nd century. Geshem the Arab (Neh. 2:19) was also a governor under Persian rule. The name "Geshem," appearing in inscriptions from Arabia and from a site near the border of Egypt, is associated with peoples of the northwest Arabian Peninsula.

THE BIBLICAL LITERATURE

Much of this period is related in the Bible by various prophets, as well as by some of the historical books. The prophetical books include Ezekiel, parts of Isaiah, Haggai, Zechariah, Malachi, and Joel. Ezekiel was taken to Babylon in 597 B.C., where he prophesied. He preached hope to the exiles, based on God's own nature and purpose. His book ends with a great vision of a future restoration of the temple. Isaiah's oracles of salvation in Is. 40—55 promise a return from exile and a rebuilding of Jerusalem and the temple. The final chapters (Is. 56—66) presumably speak of the second temple, built during the Persian era.

The second temple is the concern of Haggai and Zechariah, preaching in Jerusalem about 520 B.C. They insisted that the temple had to be rebuilt at all costs. Once done, God would restore the power of the house of David in the person of Zerubbabel, the last known prince of David's line.

Little is known of Joel and Malachi, but it seems they prophesied when a temple was standing, possibly the second temple. Malachi accused the people and priests of indifference, doubt, and immorality. Joel saw a great locust plague as the beginning of the judgment of God, and thus called for national repentance.

Events of the period are narrated in the historical books of Ezra and Nehemiah. The Book of Ezra records the mission of Ezra the priest to inspect religious life in Judah, insisting on ritual purity.

The Book of Nehemiah tells of the rebuilding of Jerusalem's walls under the leadership of this Judean governor appointed by the Persians.

The picture of this time is colored by other books. The Book of Esther relates the story of a Jewish heroine who becomes queen of Persia and saves her people at the risk of her own life. Two chapters of the Book of Daniel are set in the reigns of kings of this period: Babylon's Belshazzar, a coregent of Nabonidus (Dan. 5), and Persia's Darius (Dan. 6). Along with these books, we can read various psalms, the wisdom literature of Job and some proverbs, and the genealogical lists of 1 Chronicles.

EXILE IN BABYLON

Soon after Nebuchadnezzar, king of Babylon, destroyed Jerusalem, the entire ancient Near East fell under the control of the Neo-Babylonian Empire. In the early years of the conquest, the Babylonians were aided by Media, a nation located in the mountainous regions northeast of Babylon. Indeed, Cyaxares, king of the Medes, had been a part of Babylon's overthrow of Nineveh in 612 B.C. (see "The Book of Nahum"). Later on, in 550 B.C., the Medes themselves were conquered by Cyrus the Great and absorbed into Cyrus's Persian Empire. Median troops reinforced the Persian forces that brought about Babylon's downfall. That event of 539 B.C. was still years away.

Nebuchadnezzar became king in 605 B.C., shortly after defeating an Assyrian-Egyptian coalition at Carchemish in Syria. He reigned until 562 B.C., being succeeded by his son Amel-Marduk (the Bible's Evil-Merodach, 2 Kin. 25:27). In 560 B.C., Amel-Marduk was displaced by his brother-in-law Neriglissar (perhaps the Nergal-Sharezer who had been present at the fall of Jerusalem, Jer. 39:3, 13). Neriglissar also reigned only briefly, and his son and successor was deposed by the powerful Babylonian official Nabonidus (556–539 B.C.).

By the end of Nabonidus's reign, the empire was ready to fall apart. Nabonidus was not himself from the city of Babylon, and he did not worship that city's god, Marduk. Instead, he promoted the worship of the moon god Sin, thus angering the official priests of Babylon. Nabonidus moved his capital to an oasis in the Arabian Desert and left his son Bel-shar-usur (the Belshazzar of Dan. 5) as his regent in Babylon itself. Seeing Babylon's internal problems, nations on the edges of the empire began to assert their independence from Babylonian influence. The most significant of these was Babylon's former ally, Media.

Under the Medes' last king, Astyages (585–550 B.C.), Media became large enough to be called an empire in its own right. Internal problems developed, however, and in 550 B.C. Astyages was overthrown by a young general named Cyrus, from the Median province of Persia. In 539 B.C., Cyrus the Persian marched almost unopposed into the city of Babylon, thus ending the reign of Nabonidus and conquering the Neo-Babylonian Empire.

The accession of Cyrus also marked the end of the Judean exile in Babylon. That exile had lasted only about 70 years, but those years witnessed important changes in the faith of the Judeans. No longer able to identify the center of their faith in the temple, the exiles focused on Scripture—specifically the Torah, the first five books of the Old Testament. Their worship, meeting in the small gatherings that would later be called synagogues, stressed the reading of the Torah. A new class of religious leader arose, the scribe, whose function was to learn and interpret the Torah. The exiled Judeans became the people of the Book.

Moreover, the exiles had to adapt to their new position as a minority faith. In Babylon, they could not expect the king or the official priesthood to preserve correct worship. They had to define their faith themselves. This they did by emphasizing those laws that distinguished Judeans from other peoples, such as Sabbath observance, dietary laws, and above all the command: "You shall have no other gods before Me" (Ex. 20:3).

EPOCH SIX
Chronological Reading Guide

- ❑ Ezekiel 33:1–20; 34:1—48:35; 29:17–21; 30:1–19
- ❑ 2 Kings 25:27–30
- ❑ Jeremiah 52:31–34
- ❑ Isaiah 13:1—14:23; 21:1–17; 33:1—35:10
- ❑ Daniel 5:1–31
- ❑ Isaiah 40:1—55:13
- ❑ 2 Chronicles 36:22, 23

Ezekiel's Message of Hope (Ezek. 33:1–20; 34:1—37:28)

Because of the Judeans' new emphasis on the Scriptures, Judah's faith in God survived its shattering grief over the destruction of the temple (see Ps. 137). Indeed Judah's faith did not just survive; it was reborn, in a different form but stronger than ever. That rebirth is already evident in the work of Ezekiel, whose ministry took a new shape after Jerusalem and the temple were destroyed.

Ezekiel begins, in effect, a second ministry, inaugurated by a second vision of the watchman (Ezek. 33:1–20), a vision that had been a part of his original call experience (Ezek. 3:16–21). This second ministry still includes oracles of judgment—against the shepherds of Israel, against Mount Seir (Edom)—but these judgments are followed now by oracles of hope.

Judah was victimized by those closest to her. Kings are often portrayed as shepherds of the people, but many of Judah's kings had enriched themselves at the people's expense (ch. 34). Hope now presented itself in the promise of a true shepherd (34:23, 24). The Edomites were descended from Esau, yet Judah was treacherously attacked by this nation with close kinship ties (ch. 35; see "The Book of Obadiah"). Hope now came through the prophecy of restoration—both physical (36:1–15) and spiritual (36:16–38). Judah's restoration is illustrated by the vision of the valley of dry bones (37:1–14) and by the parable of the two sticks (37:15–28).

The Sacred and Profane (EZEK. 36:22–26)

While Ezekiel is known chiefly as a prophet, he was also a priest. In fact, priestly concerns, concepts, and terminology fill the Book of Ezekiel. The prophet-priest Ezekiel used terminology related to the temple and its rituals to describe the present situation and future salvation of Israel.

The Jerusalem temple was considered the point where the divine intersected with the earth. As such, the temple, together with its space, utensils, and personnel, was characterized by purity and holiness. To be sanctified or holy was to be set apart from everyday use, devoted solely to the service of God. To use a sanctified object for other reasons or outside the temple was to profane it, thus rendering it impure for use in the temple.

This priestly language makes up the imagery used by Ezekiel (Ezek. 36:22–26). Through the destruction of Jerusalem by the Babylonians in 586 B.C. Israel had come into contact with the nations. Yahweh's name, His status and honor, had been "profaned among the nations" (36:23). Israel's service was no longer confined to Yahweh and Yahweh alone. Contaminated by the nations, Israel had become impure, no longer qualified to enter into the temple area.

Yet Ezekiel saw a different day coming. First, God would again separate Israel from among the nations, returning her to her own land (36:24). Yet Israel's profanity, her impurity, had to be removed. In accordance with legislation in the Book of Leviticus, Ezekiel proclaimed that God would cleanse Israel through sprinkling with clean water (36:25). Purified by the ritual cleansing, Israel was sanctified, holy, again set apart for the service of God within the Jerusalem temple.

Ezekiel's Apocalyptic Prophecies (Ezek. 38:1—39:29)

Chapters 38 and 39 of Ezekiel are in many ways different from the rest of the book. Their message, the ultimate victory of God over the nations, is perfectly consistent with the preceding chapters, but the manner of describing that victory is distinct. Indeed these chapters are often noted as an early example of what would later be called "apocalyptic" writing, which is best represented in the Bible by Dan. 7—12 and the Book of Revelation.

Apocalyptic literature generally consists of vision reports (the word "apocalypse" comes from a Greek word meaning "revelation"). These visions usually involve a great many symbols, often quite obscure. While the original audience may have had the key to the symbols, such a key is usually left unstated. The primary purpose of apocalyptic writing appears to be to comfort the persecuted. The message is that while things may be bad now, and indeed may get much worse, in the end God will establish His eternal kingdom and will right all wrongs.

Fitting within this pattern of hidden symbolism is Ezek. 38; 39, which describe the attack and ultimate defeat of the mysterious Gog from the land of Magog. No nation by that name is known. Some have suggested that Ezekiel might have been referring to King Gyges (685–652 B.C.) of Lydia in Asia Minor. Others, noting that Gog comes from the north (Ezek. 38:6), think the name might refer to the Scythians, a band of barbarous raiders from the area around the Black Sea, north of Babylon.

These very different suggestions refer to groups that Ezekiel himself might have known. Because nothing in the Bible text itself favors one solution more than any other, though, the question remains open to further interpretation. Every generation, since Ezekiel himself, has had its own understanding of this passage, seeing the victory over Gog as a prophecy of victory over that generation's own enemies. While this makes the certain identification of Gog still more puzzling, perhaps it is that for which the prophecy calls. God's victory over an unidentifiable enemy implies God's victory over any and every enemy.

Not knowing exactly to what the prophecy refers makes it difficult to place the oracle chronologically. It is possible simply to read these chapters in their biblical context, as a part of Ezekiel's second, hopeful ministry. God will no longer use the Gentile nations to punish Israel. Instead, in a future battle God will personally fight for His people and utterly destroy Israel's enemies (38:22). No aggressor can stand against God. Ezekiel's hope includes reunification: God will bring together the once-divided northern and southern kingdoms (39:25).

Ezekiel's Second Temple Vision (Ezek. 40:1—42:20)

The 25th year of the Babylonian captivity (Ezek. 40:1) was perhaps April, 573 B.C. Nebuchadnezzar was still king, and the power of Babylon was growing greater each year. But to Ezekiel the turning point had already come, and he saw salvation arriving to replace Israel's shame and punishment. It is appropriate that Ezekiel, who would never forsake his priestly roots, should describe the ultimate salvation with a vision of a new, and better, temple.

Ezekiel's vision of the perfect temple is a companion piece to his earlier temple vision of chs. 8—11 (see "Ezekiel's Temple Vision"). In that vision, Ezekiel saw abominations and idolatry, and the vision concluded with the glory of God departing from the temple (Ezek. 11:22, 23). This time, Ezekiel sees only perfection. The crowning moment is when "the glory of the LORD came into the temple by way of the gate which faces toward the east...and behold, the glory of the LORD filled the temple" (Ezek. 43:4, 5).

Chapters 40—48 contain a great deal of symbolism. Most of the symbols seem to indicate the absolute perfection of the future temple, but more specific meanings are certainly possible. These chapters too can be described as early "apocalyptic" writing. In fact, the most extensive apocalyptic book in the Bible, the Book of Revelation, also contains an extended vision of a perfect temple in the future, phrased in language very similar to that of Ezekiel (Rev. 21).

These chapters, like chs. 38; 39 before them, are difficult to place chronologically. What temple is referred to here? If it is the actual rebuilt temple mentioned in Ezra 6:14–16, then the prophecy could be associated with that event; but the stunning, perfect temple described in this vision bears little resemblance to the disappointing structure mentioned at that time (see Ezra 3:12). Perhaps, as is the case with the temple vision of Rev. 21, Ezek. 40—48 is a vision of a future perfection, to come at an unspecified end. Thus it is not intended as a blueprint for an earthly, physical fulfillment. Rather it pictures the purity and spiritual vitality of the ideal place of worship and those who will worship there.

THE PRINCE IN THE TEMPLE (EZEK. 46:2)

As part of his prophecy of hope, Ezekiel envisioned that a "prince" will rule in the restored Jerusalem. The prince will have certain prerogatives, such as owning special property in Jerusalem around the holy space of the temple (45:6, 7). More significantly, only the prince may enter the east gate (44:1–3), the gate through which God's glory had reentered the temple (43:4).

The prince will be the civil ruler, but also a part of the religious organization. He will lead the people in their proper worship. During the Sabbath sacrifices, the prince offers burnt and peace sacrifices via the east gate, itself a large room, while the people look on from the outside (Ezek. 46:2). Additionally, the sacrificial duty of the prince extends to the monthly New Moon sacrifice (46:6, 7), as well as voluntary burnt and peace offerings (46:12).

Yet the prince must also be along when the people offer their sacrifices. The people are not free to roam in the temple courts; they enter via the north or south gate, escorted by the prince, and leave via the opposite gate (46:9, 10).

In the restored Jerusalem of Ezekiel's vision, then, the prince combines in his own body the civic and the sacred role to maintain the city in purity and righteousness. He orders the life of the people around the temple, which again will be filled with the glory of the Lord.

A FAILED ASSAULT ON HEAVEN (Is. 14:12–15)

The prophet Isaiah uses mythological language in a proverb mocking the king of Babylon (Is. 14:4, 22). His references to the Day Star, the ascent into heaven, the mount of the congregation, and to Sheol (or the Pit) would all have been familiar to his readers from the myths of the ancient Near East.

The name "Lucifer" (Is. 14:12) is a Latin translation of the Hebrew word *helel*, meaning "shining one." Lucifer refers to the Day Star, Venus, and the prophet further identifies him as "son of the morning" (14:12). Similar language appears with the Ugaritic deities Shahar and Shalim. Shahar was the god of dawn or morning; Shalim, the god of dusk or evening. In another Ugaritic text, Shahar (morning) appears together with Athtar, the star deity who is also identified with Venus. So the ancient myths possibly had made Isaiah's readers familiar with the Day Star whose father was the god of morning.

Isaiah's taunt of the Day Star for wanting to ascend into heaven (14:13) may reflect the Ugaritic myth of Athtar, the Venus star deity. Athtar attempts to ascend to the throne of Baal, but is not able and is forced to return to his own, lower position in the pantheon. Athtar was not storming heaven, only sitting on the vacated throne of Baal. He excuses himself from the position upon realizing that he is too small. Nevertheless, a Day Star ascending to heaven was known in Canaanite myth.

In Isaiah's proverb, the Day Star desires to sit on "the mount of the congregation" located "on the farthest sides of the north" (14:13). Similarly, Canaanite myths spoke of the mountain home of Baal on Saphon (the Hebrew word translated "north"), and also of a mount of assembly.

In Isaiah's proverb, the Day Star fails to ascend to heaven and is brought down to Sheol, the netherworld also called the Pit (14:15). Similarly in ancient Near Eastern mythology gods could die and be sent to Mot's netherworld. The reason that Baal's throne was vacant in the Ugaritic myth was that Mot had vanquished Baal and taken him to the realm of the dead.

Daniel and Belshazzar (Dan. 5:1–31)

Babylon's might declined fastest during the reign of Nabonidus (556–539 B.C.), who left the city of Babylon to live in an oasis in the Arabian Desert and worship the moon god Sin. His son, Bel-shar-usur, was left as regent over the city of Babylon.

The Book of Daniel, which spells Bel-shar-usur as "Belshazzar," refers to Nebuchadnezzar as Belshazzar's father (Dan. 5:2). This could be a metaphorical reference to Nebuchadnezzar as the father (or founder) of the kingdom; Belshazzar was not even related to Nebuchadnezzar. Daniel also calls Belshazzar "king" (5:1), which he never was officially. Still, while his father Nabonidus was absent, he was the closest thing to a king that Babylon had.

Belshazzar served as coregent in Babylon for his father Nabonidus sometime around 545 B.C. Nothing more is heard of Belshazzar after 543 B.C., when Nabonidus returned from Arabian Tema and took sole control of Babylon. Daniel's contempt for this "king," as well as the unflattering comparison made between Belshazzar and the great Nebuchadnezzar (Dan. 5:18–22), suggest that Nabonidus's son was far from deserving his borrowed title.

Isaiah and Cyrus the Persian (Is. 40:1—45:25)

The Babylon of King Nabonidus began to totter. In 550 B.C. Cyrus the Persian captured Ecbatana, the capital of the Median Empire, and began to look south toward Babylon. To a Babylonian population disgusted with the absentee king Nabonidus and his coregent Bel–shazzar, the prospect of a Persian conquest was quite attractive. In 539 B.C. Cyrus marched into Babylon as a conqueror, greeted by shouts of joy from the conquered.

The latter chapters of the Book of Isaiah have for centuries been recognized as different from the earlier chapters (see "The Book of Isaiah"). The language and style of Is. 40—55 are distinct, but the most remarkable difference is the tone. Whereas Is. 1—39 spoke almost exclusively of judgment and disaster, the new section begins with God's call: "Comfort, yes, comfort My people!" (40:1). These chapters declare not judgment but salvation, hope, and restoration.

It is not difficult to identify when this salvation is to be: Israel will return from the Babylonian exile. In these chapters, Jerusalem is spoken of as uninhabited and in ruins, the temple itself as destroyed; but both city and temple will be rebuilt (44:26–28). Israel's return from Babylon is pictured as a second exodus, with God making a way in the wilderness (40:3, 4; 43:19) and causing water to spring up in the desert (43:20; 44:3; 48:21).

God promises to deliver His people from Babylon. Furthermore, through the prophet, God even names the one through whom this great salvation would come about: Cyrus "My shepherd"

(44:28; 45:1). These words of comfort seem directed to the Judean exiles in Babylon just before the city of Babylon fell to Cyrus's Persian armies.

There is little argument, then, concerning the time spoken of in Is. 40—55. There is much more disagreement as to when and by whom these chapters were written. Many scholars hold that these oracles came from an unknown prophet who lived during the Babylonian captivity and predicted the approaching end of the Exile. This prophet, often called "Second Isaiah," would have considered himself a disciple of the great Isaiah of Jerusalem. Indeed, some scholars suggest that Second Isaiah may have been the one who preserved the collection of Isaiah's oracles found in Is. 1—39.

Others, though, accept the traditional association of these words with the original Isaiah. The two parts of the book (chs. 1—39 and 40—55) always appear together in the ancient manuscripts, and several key themes appear in both parts. Regardless of who wrote Is. 40—55, these chapters speak of a future event: the glorious return from exile that will be authorized by Cyrus the Persian.

Can God Really Do This "New Thing"? (Is. 43:19)

If the exiles were to return to Jerusalem, they somehow had to escape the political and military control of the Neo-Babylonian regime. Yet the prophet claims that this is precisely what will happen: God will do "a new thing" (Is. 43:19)—a subtle reference to the military defeat of the Babylonians (43:14, 15). The prophet invokes images of the Exodus from Egypt when the Lord defeated Pharaoh and freed the Israelites from slavery (43:16, 17). This time the Lord would lead the exilic community back across the wilderness to their ancestral home in Judah (43:19). What a hopeful announcement this was for the Judeans in Babylon!

Yet because the Judeans were still subject to Babylonian power, the announcement was also risky. The message rang of subversion and rebellion, qualities that the Neo-Babylonian regime met with brutal and violent displays of power in their subjected communities. Perhaps this explains why the community did not enthusiastically endorse the prophet's message—why they had not "called upon" the Lord (43:22–24). To do so would have meant really believing that God's power was stronger than the Babylonians, a high stakes political gamble if they were wrong!

Cyrus, the Lord's Anointed (Is. 45:1)

In 559 B.C. Cyrus the Great became the ruler and founder of the Achaemenid dynasty of Persia, which expanded quickly in all directions to become a world empire. Arising from the desert fringes of Mesopotamia, Cyrus ultimately conquered the Neo-Babylonian Empire and absorbed it into his realm in 539 B.C. The defeat of Babylon expanded the Persian Empire to include almost the entire ancient Near East. Only Egypt remained independent.

The ancient mind would ask, "What god has empowered this Persian king, Cyrus?" The Judean prophet answered by identifying Cyrus as a world leader chosen by Yahweh, the God of Israel (Is. 45:1–7). Even more amazingly, the prophet uses language reserved for Israelite and Judean kings to describe God's election of Cyrus. Cyrus is Yahweh's "anointed" (Is. 45:1), the agent by which the Babylonian subjection of the Judean exilic community would be ended.

The Servant of the Lord (Is. 49:1—51:23)

A "servant of the Lord" is one who voluntarily serves God, as did Abraham (Ps. 105:42). The phrase "My servant" appears frequently in Is. 41—53. Sometimes the phrase describes the entire nation of Israel, God's chosen Jacob (41:8). This meaning is found most often in chs. 41—48. But the nation Israel proved to be an unproductive servant. Assigned to bring "light to the Gentiles, to open blind eyes" (42:6, 7), she herself became blind (42:18–20).

The most important passages concerning "My servant" are the famous Servant Songs (42:1–4; 49:1–6; 50:4–11; 52:13—53:12). Sometimes in these songs, the servant again is identified with the nation of Israel (49:3), but the words "Behold, My Servant" (Is. 52:13) begin a definitive description of the Servant through whom God would deliver Israel from their sins (Is. 52:13—53:12). From the earliest days of the church, Christians have considered this "Servant" to represent prophetically Jesus Christ, and with good reason. In a very profound sense, the life of Christ reflects and fulfills the life of the Servant.

What is said about the Servant is nothing less than tragic. Like the Servant, Jesus proclaimed good news to the community. Like the Servant, Jesus' good news threatened those who had most accommodated themselves to the foreigners: the prophet's exilic community with the Babylonians; Jesus' Jerusalem priesthood with the Romans. Like the Servant, Jesus did not alter His message, and like the Servant, He paid for it by His life—disgraced, shamed, and held in no account.

Jesus, therefore, relived and fulfilled the theological and social dynamics encountered by the Servant. No one expected that the Messiah would come as a servant: quiet, unassuming, and suffering. This Servant "was wounded for our transgressions"; He was "oppressed" and "afflicted"; yet, by "His stripes we are healed" (53:5, 7). In raising Jesus from the dead, God has allotted Jesus "a portion with the great" (53:12), "exalted and extolled" (52:13). For so many reasons, Christians cannot read Is. 52:13—53:12 without hearing echoes of the life of Christ.

Cyrus Allows the Judeans to Go Home
(2 Chr. 36:22, 23)

When Cyrus II conquered Babylon, he ruled Babylon not as a conquering foreigner, but as a successor to the previous Babylonian kings. This policy meant that the conquered people could maintain their local customs and culture, as well as their deities. Thus Cyrus restored honor and dignity to the Babylonian god Marduk.

Such a tolerant policy of allowing local cultures some autonomy in regard to their traditions had its advantages for Cyrus. This method was in direct contradiction to the harsh policies of deportation employed by the Assyrian and Chaldean kingdoms. Cyrus, though a conquering king, could also appear to be a benevolent king who assisted conquered peoples in preserving their sacred traditions.

Just as Cyrus respected the god Marduk of the Babylonians, so also did he respect the God Yahweh of the Judeans. Cyrus's proclamation (2 Chr. 36:22, 23) allowed the Judeans to return to Judea, to rebuild the Jerusalem temple, and to carry back the sacred objects confiscated by Babylon (Ezra 1:7–11). The Judean understanding of this restoration event placed a high view on Cyrus as the one Yahweh had anointed to overcome all nations (Is. 45:1–7).

WISDOM IN THE ANCIENT NEAR EAST

The teaching tradition that is called "wisdom" appears in the Bible in the books of Proverbs, Ecclesiastes, and Job. The wisdom tradition is associated most of all with the figure of Solomon. Ecclesiastes and the proverbs ascribed to Solomon are often read in light of his reputation for wisdom (see "The Book of Proverbs"). The Book of Job and certain other proverbs, though, can be read in light of the larger world of non-Israelite wisdom.

Wisdom teachings appear to have several underlying assumptions. First, the proverbs of the wisdom teachers, or sages, assume that the world is orderly. Everything on earth happens for a just reason. This fairly optimistic premise is followed by an even more hopeful thought: human beings are able to understand that order. The world and its workings are comprehensible; therefore, the goal of the wise is to search out the underlying order of the world. Finally, the source of this knowledge is very human. The way to uncover the fixed principles by which the world operates is, first, through one's own experience and observation, and second, through tradition, which is the experience of those who came before.

Wisdom, as represented by this general description, is not unique to Israel and the Bible. In fact, the true center of the wisdom tradition in the ancient world seems to have been Egypt. The Egyptian sages were famous throughout the ancient Near East, and enough Egyptian wisdom writings have been discovered to indicate that this fame was deserved. Other wisdom writings have been found in Mesopotamia, especially in Babylon, and the Bible itself testifies to the fame of Edomite sages (Jer. 49:7; Obad. 1:8).

While wisdom teaching was common in many cultures, Israel's version of wisdom teaching is somewhat distinct. The basic assumptions of wisdom were quite secular. They spoke of worldly matters and had little to say about God. Wisdom was sought through human experience, not through prayer or any direct divine revelation. Israel's sages, not quite comfortable with such a focus, sought to incorporate God more fully. As a result, Israel's central theme was "The fear of the LORD is the beginning of wisdom" (Prov. 9:10). Devotion and obedience to God were seen as prior to and more important than the human quest for wisdom.

Some wisdom teachings are attributed to Solomon, and these can be read in the context of his reign. Most wisdom literature, however, is not so easily associated with a particular person or time. Indeed, wisdom seems rather uninterested in questions of chronological time. The sages sought to expound universal and eternal principles and were less concerned with specific historical events.

Wisdom teachings largely ignored the fluctuating fortunes of historical kings and kingdoms, which perhaps explains why wisdom did not change greatly over time. Wisdom resisted new ideas and fads, preferring to pass on ancient and deep-rooted traditions. Indeed, many proverb collections are presented as a parent's instruction to a child (Prov. 1:8; 4:1; 31:1). Wisdom teachings dealt with universal matters that apply just as well in every age, such as family relationships, wealth, hard work, and honesty.

EPOCH SIX
Chronological Reading Guide

- ❑ Proverbs 22:17—24:34; 30:1—31:31
- ❑ Job 1:1—42:17

Words of the Wise (Prov. 22:17—24:34)

The Book of Proverbs is a collection of short, pithy instructions. It is, in fact, a collection of collections of proverbs and wisdom teachings. While these collections appear in the Bible, they also show similarities to non-Israelite wisdom. By placing devotion and obedience to God above the human quest for wisdom, the Israelite sages were distinct from other wisdom teachers. But after giving primary position to God, they proceeded to search for wisdom by the same secular methods as other cultures: they stressed personal experience and tradition. As a result, the Book of Proverbs remains one of the most secular of all biblical books.

Two collections in the Book of Proverbs are identified by introductory attributions ascribing these teachings to "the wise" (Prov. 22:17; 24:23). Many of the proverbs found in these collections (Prov. 22:17—24:22; 24:23–34), as well as the outline by which they are arranged, appear also in a book of Egyptian wisdom, called *The Instruction of Amen-em-hotep*. The relationship is too close to be coincidental. While it is difficult to tell which is oldest, it is clear that both the biblical proverbs and the Egyptian texts are versions of a single wisdom discourse.

The Wisdom of Agur and Lemuel (Prov. 30:1—31:31)

The final two chapters of Proverbs are attributed to men named Agur and Lemuel. Neither of these men is mentioned elsewhere. Appearing in both attributions (Prov. 30:1; 31:1) is the Hebrew word *massa'*, which can be translated as "burden" or "utterance," as it is used by the prophets (Is. 17:1; 19:1). The word might also be the name of a place—Massa (Gen. 25:14; 1 Chr. 1:30). If so, the attributions might associate Agur and Lemuel with a country or city named "Massa." For instance, Prov. 31:1 would begin, "The words of Lemuel, king of Massa, which his mother taught him."

Even if these teachers are not from a place called Massa, they do not appear to be Israelite. There was no King Lemuel in Israel, and the name "Agur" is not formed in a typical Hebrew fashion. Agur's name does appear in Sabean inscriptions, and in light of that foreign source, it is interesting that the teachings of Agur include some of the most religiously oriented of all the proverbs in the book.

Humans in Heaven (Prov. 30:4)

Agur asks in his proverb, "Who has ascended into heaven?" (Prov. 30:1, 4). In the ancient mythology of Mesopotamia and Syria-Palestine, human beings did not enter heaven. The common belief was that the gods had created people for the express purpose of serving on earth.

Myths from Mesopotamia attempt to explain why humans are not in heaven. The story of Adapa is a Mesopotamian myth known from a tablet found at Asshur and at Tell el-Amarna, Egypt, dating from around 1350 B.C. The myth relates how the priest Adapa went to heaven and was offered food that would have made him immortal and allowed him to stay in heaven. He refused and was cast out of heaven.

The story of Etana is credited as the work of Lu-Nanna, an official in the court of Shulgi, king of Ur (2094–2047 B.C.). It tells how Etana tried to reach heaven by flying up on the back of an eagle, but the gods threw him back to earth. Heaven is for gods; earth is for humans.

In contrast to these Mesopotamian myths is the story of Elijah. This prophet of Yahweh was so important that he was taken, while still alive, into heaven by God (2 Kin. 2:1, 11, 12). The story would have been more wondrous in Elijah's time than now, since people then did not think that humans, living or dead, were allowed into the realm of the gods.

THE BOOK OF JOB

The Book of Job is a work of unparalleled magnificence and power. Its depth of thought and feeling, its shining moments of insight, and the transcendent poetry of the central section all give this book a unique place, not only in Scripture but in all of world literature.

This book also stands apart in terms of its historical setting. On the one hand, certain aspects of Job's life sound much like the life of Abraham. His wealth, as was Abraham's, was based on numbers of domestic animals. Similar to Abraham, he offered his own sacrifices to God, without a priestly intermediary. For reasons such as these, many scholars have set the book in Abraham's time during the Middle Bronze Age (2000–1500 B.C.).

Nevertheless, the Book of Job itself offers no historical specificity. We are told only of "a man in the land of Uz, whose name was Job" (Job 1:1). The location of the land of Uz is uncertain, but it was more likely in Edom than in Israel. The name Uz appears several times as an Edomite name (Gen. 36:28; 1 Chr. 1:42). Associating Uz with Edom makes sense. Job's three friends appear as wisdom teachers, and Edom was famous for its wise men. Indeed Job's first friend, Eliphaz the Temanite, also has an Edomite name (see Gen. 36:15, 16). If Job was an Edomite, he would not be a contemporary of Abraham, since the Edomites descended from Abraham's grandson Esau.

Besides a geographical setting that is possibly Edomite and at least non-Israelite, all that the Book of Job provides is the intellectual setting of the wisdom tradition. The wisdom setting is by far the most important context. The book both speaks within and speaks against the teaching of the sages, as represented by Job's three friends Eliphaz, Bildad, and Zophar. As these friends try to "comfort" Job, they present the wisdom worldview in speeches that are little more than strings of proverbs. And when Job opposes the friends, he opposes some of wisdom's basic assumptions.

Most significantly, Job rejects wisdom's view that the world is orderly, that all is arranged according to just principles. His tragedy is not just. Righteousness does not always result in good fortune. Bad things do happen to good people. His friends' argument—that Job must have sinned to deserve such suffering—only indicates the poverty of this particular aspect of wisdom teaching. Job also rejects the idea that wisdom is to be sought from tradition. If his three friends represent the teachings of tradition, he wants nothing to do with it (Job 12:2, 3).

Nevertheless, Job does not give up his search for enlightenment and never completely gives up his hope for justice. Nor does he surrender his faith in knowledge by experience. Indeed, it is experience that he seeks: he demands that he be allowed to see God, to present his complaint before Him. Job's wish is granted in God's majestic appearance and speech (Job 38—41). Not all of Job's questions are answered, but it is enough for Job to have experienced God Himself.

The Book of Job belongs in the context of Israel's wisdom tradition, but at what point in the long history of Israel's wisdom? The story of Job was evidently known to the prophet Ezekiel, preaching in exile in Babylon, who used Job as an example of righteousness (Ezek. 14:14, 20). More certain than when Job's story takes place or when the Book of Job was written is that it came to prominence during and after the Babylonian captivity. It is not hard to imagine why. A people stunned by the destruction of all that they had held dear—their nation, their city, their temple—dealt with the same questions that Job himself confronted.

Since a definite historical setting for the Book of Job is unknown, one can read the book in light of the suffering of the Exile and the questions the exiles faced. The prologue (Job 1; 2) concerns the question of Job's motive for serving God. Satan insinuates that people lead upright lives because of selfishness, not because of love for God. God, however, expresses His complete confidence in His servant Job before the hosts of heaven, citing Job to prove that a person can live a blameless and upright life.

OUTLINE OF JOB

I. The Dilemma of Job	**1:1—2:13**
A. Circumstances of Job	1:1–5
B. First Assault of Satan	1:6–22
C. Second Assault of Satan	2:1–10
D. Arrival of Job's Friends	2:11–13
II. The Debates of Job	**3:1—37:24**
A. First Cycle of Debate	3:1—14:22
B. Second Cycle of Debate	15:1—21:34
C. Third Cycle of Debate	22:1—26:14
D. Final Defense of Job	27:1—31:40
E. Solution of Elihu	32:1—37:24
III. The Deliverance of Job	**38:1—42:17**
A. First Controversy of God with Job	38:1—40:5
B. Second Controversy of God with Job	40:6—42:6
C. Deliverance of Job and His Friends	42:7–17

Enter the Adversary—Satan (Job 1:6–12)

In the scenes of the heavenly assembly (Job 1; 2), only one heavenly being, other than God Himself, is identified. This character is referred to in Hebrew only by his title, which means "the adversary." In English he is called "Satan" (Job 1:6; 2:1). The Adversary is a divine figure, one of the "sons of God," who serves under and reports to Yahweh.

In the human royal courts of the ancient Near East, one officer of the king's court was assigned to seek out and report any behavior contrary to the laws or proclamations of the ruler. The Adversary performed this office for Yahweh in heaven, and so could be considered "the divine prosecuting attorney." It was his responsibility to bring charges and produce proofs. The case being brought against Job is a test, as both God and the Adversary know that Job has been perfect (Job 1:8).

The behavior of the Adversary conforms to the accepted manner of secondary level deities in Canaanite mythology. The Adversary differs in one sense from the deities portrayed in the Ugaritic myths: he accepts orders from his superior and carries them out only within the guidelines established by God, never breaking the rules imposed upon him. The responsibility for Job's ordeal lies with God, who instigated the debate and authorized the activity proposed and carried out by the Adversary (Job 1:12; 2:3).

In the Book of Job the Adversary is a member of the divine court in good standing. The idea for this character could have had its source in almost any human royal court. Later, the idea developed into Satan as the embodiment of all evil, as is found in some New Testament passages (Rom. 16:20). Such a development begins to show in the Chronicler's figure of Satan as a divine being opposing the will of God (1 Chr. 21:1).

Babylonian Job and Other Innocent Sufferers (Job 10:2)

Ancient people believed that gods governed the universe based on some principle of right and wrong. They were confident that pious acts would result in well-being, but aware that wrongdoing would result in misfortune or distress. When misfortune struck, they would consult the gods to discover the cause of their misfortune. If innocent, they would seek divine justice from the gods. So Job, not understanding why he must suffer, calls on God, "Show me why You contend with me" (Job 10:2).

Ancient Near Eastern literary efforts that grapple with the problem of unjust human suffering are not unique to the Scriptures. From Mesopotamia there are at present four known documents that are superficially similar to the Book of Job: *Man and His God*; *I Will Praise the Lord of Wisdom*; *The Babylonian Theodicy*; and *Dialogue Between a Master and His Slave*.

In a copy of the Sumerian *Man and His God* from the early 2nd millennium B.C., an individual complains about his plight to his deity. He accuses his god of becoming angry and leaving him unprotected from unscrupulous human enemies, who know that the worshiper's god will not harm them. Finally, the sufferer forgoes his right to protest divine actions and confesses his own guilt. The relationship between himself and his god is repaired.

Despite being unjustly placed in an unfortunate condition, the sufferer in *I Will Praise the Lord of Wisdom* still extols the virtues of his god. He does complain that his god's face is far from him and concludes that the gods must have a different system of merit that cannot be known by humans. Nonetheless, he encourages humans to continue to perform the proper cultic acts of worship.

The Babylonian Theodicy has often been labeled "The Babylonian Job." The sufferer in this case disputes, like Job, with an educated friend. The sufferer implies that the gods are to be blamed for much of the suffering that occurs. He also maintains that morality is not profitable, as the gods ultimately have no regard for it. The story ends with the sufferer calling upon his god to "pasture his flock."

The *Dialogue Between a Master and His Slave* has only occasional similarities to the Book of Job. Many of the conditions of the master's distress can be compared to that of Job.

Sheol for All the Dead Without Distinction (Job 26:5, 6)

In the world of ancient Judah and Israel people were never expected to enter heaven after death. With the exception of Elijah (2 Kin. 2:11), and possibly of Enoch, who entered heaven alive (Gen. 5:24), humans who died went to a watery domain known as Sheol (Job 26:5, 6).

The understanding of the afterlife in Judah and Israel resembled that current in Mesopotamia and Syria-Palestine. Under the earth, in a dark muddy realm, was Sheol—the netherworld where all the souls of the dead go, whether good or evil. The popular notion in Egypt of an afterlife with a touch of hope for a good eternity did not influence Palestine, despite Egyptian control of Canaan for a millennium. In Palestine, Sheol was understood as a place of darkness, meaninglessness, and hopelessness. Once entering the netherworld, one had to stay there. The prospect of eternity in a most unpleasant place made a long life in this world quite desirable.

The dead retained their individuality in the netherworld, and one could have contact with them. Tubes have been found in the tombs of Palestine from the Bronze Age through the Hellenistic period that allowed food or wine to be dropped into the netherworld. The living sought information from the dead through necromancy, as Saul attempted to consult Samuel's spirit rising from Sheol (1 Sam. 28:11–19).

The cultures surrounding Judah and Israel had deities who ruled the netherworld. In Mesopotamia the divine couple Nergal and Ereshkigal hanged the corpses of the dead on butchers' hooks like slabs of meat. Egypt's afterlife under the rule of Osiris was more appealing, if you survived the journey to the land of the blessed dead. Syria-Palestine had the god Mot (meaning "death") who was hungry to devour the living. The voraciousness of the netherworld and the mercilessness of its ruler, Mot, are reflected in the "devouring" and "king of terrors" of Job 18:11–14.

Were You There at the Beginning? (Job 38:7)

Public building projects in the ancient Near East were begun with religious rituals, including liturgical singing in praise of the major deities. Kings ritually, if not actually, helped set the foundations of temples and symbolically aided the construction workers in laying walls and fastening gates. In Job 38:4–7, the universe is pictured as a great building project by God. All the inhabitants of heaven sing for joy as the foundations of the earth are laid (Job 38:7).

The heavenly beings who sing and shout are "the morning stars" and "the sons of God" (38:7). In the group of languages called Northwest Semitic, which includes Hebrew, "sons of God" is a standard way to describe the pantheon of deities. The specific mention of the morning stars may reflect Egyptian notions that creation begins anew each morning just as light appears along the horizon. Thus creation begins anew when the morning stars are in the sky. God reminds Job that he was not present, and cannot know what happened at creation when the heavenly choir sang (Job 38:4).

Leviathan, the Sea Serpent (Job 41:1)

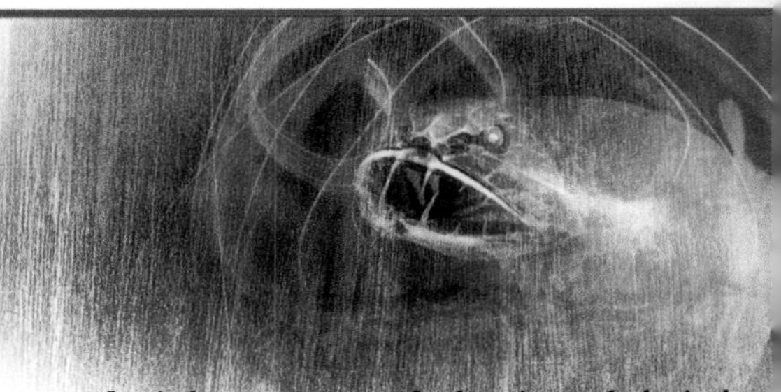

In Job 41 God describes Leviathan, a creature familiar to Job (Job 3:8). This picture of the ultimate sea serpent contrasts the powerlessness of humans against the all-powerful might of God. Although some have supposed that Job 41 speaks of a crocodile or whale, the description of the sea creature is not one that is familiar from nature.

The questions asked of Job stress in minute detail how powerful and how invincible the sea serpent is in the eyes of humans. God Himself, however, created this creature to "play" in the sea (Ps. 104:25, 26). A contrast reveals the unfathomable power of God: Leviathan terrifies humans, but to God, it is simply His "little rubber ducky." Leviathan is greater than any other living thing, save One. God alone has no fear of this creature.

There are a number of myths concerning a huge serpent coming from a variety of African cultures. The serpent is presented as an ally of the highest deity. To keep the world from disintegrating, the snake encircles it and grasps its own tail in its mouth, physically holding the universe together. Earthquakes are understood as the serpent moving. Should the serpent die or cease constricting the land, the world would dissolve back into the sea.

Leviathan appears as Lothan in mythological texts dating around 1400 B.C. In these texts from Ugarit, a Canaanite city-state on the northeast coast of the Mediterranean, the serpent Lothan is associated with the god of the sea, Yam, whom Baal defeats in battle. Possibly a story similar to this Canaanite myth was known in Israel, telling how God defeated Leviathan long ago and placed the serpent in its current status. Imagery from such a story remains in Ps. 74:13, 14, which describes God's victory over Leviathan and the sea serpents.

The original readers of the Book of Job must have recognized in Job 41 the awesome power of God. If at one time in mythological narratives Leviathan was opposed to God, now the sea serpent had become one of God's most impressive servants.

THE PERSIAN EMPIRE

Cyrus the Persian established one of the most successful and enduring of the great ancient empires. Part of his success came from his practice of showing respect for the religious beliefs of his captured peoples. In his first year, according to both Persian records and the biblical account, he proclaimed that all the captive peoples whom the Babylonians had dragged into exile should be allowed to go free (2 Chr. 36:22, 23; Ezra 1:1–4). Unlike the Assyrian and Babylonian rulers, Cyrus did not seek to impose his own religion on his subjects.

When Cyrus died in 530 B.C., he was succeeded by his son Cambyses (530–522 B.C.). There are some indications that Cambyses was mentally unstable and perhaps epileptic, but he evidently inherited some of his father's ability as a general. In 525 B.C. Cambyses captured Egypt. The Persian Empire had now exceeded the geographic boundaries of any of the earlier empires.

While Cambyses was returning from the conquest of Egypt, word reached him that he had been deposed by someone claiming to be his brother. For reasons not completely clear, Cambyses committed suicide. One of his officers, named Darius, took his place. Darius put down that rebellion and several others in the next few years, and in the end it was Darius who reigned as the next Persian emperor (522–486 B.C.). Known as Darius the Great, Darius I was as gifted an administrator as Cyrus was a general, and under his rule the extensive organization of the Persian Empire took place. The resulting system of regional governors, satraps, and official inspectors was bulky but effective.

During Darius's reign, a new player appeared in the political life of the ancient Near East: Greece. Darius expanded the Persian Empire through the region of Asia Minor and sought to go the next step, into the Greek peninsula. Greece at this time consisted of many independent city-states, but faced with such a formidable invader, these states joined together. Under Miltiades, a general from the city of Athens, the Greek alliance turned Darius's armies back at the battle of Marathon (490 B.C.).

Darius's son Xerxes I (486–465 B.C.) invaded Greece again in 480 B.C., but after some initial success was also turned back. His successor, Artaxerxes I (465–424 B.C.), ultimately gave up Persian designs on Greek land and signed the Peace of Callias in 449 B.C. The empire was beginning to face internal problems, such as rebellions in Babylon and Egypt. It no longer had the resources to wage new wars of conquest.

Under Persian rule, the Jews faced their own internal disputes. When Cyrus proclaimed that captive peoples could return to their homeland, some of the exiled Jews discovered that they would rather stay where they were. Many had become quite comfortable living in foreign lands, and the prospect of returning home to start over in the ruined city of Jerusalem was daunting.

Several small groups of Jews did return to Jerusalem, though. The first group was led in 538 or 537 B.C. by one Sheshbazzar (Ezra 1:8–11), who became the first Judean governor after the Exile, but otherwise is totally unknown. A second group, led by a direct descendant of King David, named Zerubbabel, was more successful. Under the leadership of Zerubbabel and a priest named Jeshua, this group arrived in Jerusalem and immediately began rebuilding the temple.

In Palestine, though, the returning exiles were confronted by the people who had not been taken to Babylon, who had been on the land all that time, and the confrontation was not friendly. The returned exiles saw those who had stayed in Palestine as mixed-breed Jews who defiled the true worship of God. This was particularly so for the inhabitants of the region of Samaria, the Samaritans, whom the returned exiles regarded with a dislike and suspicion that would still be evident in the New Testament, 500 years later. Both Jews and Samaritans claimed descent from Abraham and worshiped Abraham's God, but they were deeply separated from each other.

So Judaism was divided. First, Jews were divided between those in Palestine (the returned exiles) and those scattered throughout the Persian Empire (the "Diaspora" or "dispersion"). Second, even those in Palestine were split between the returned exiles, who saw themselves as the ethnically and religiously pure remnant of their nation and faith, and the ones who had stayed behind in the land, like the Samaritans.

EPOCH SIX
Chronological Reading Guide

- ❑ Ezra 1:1—4:5; 4:24—5:1
- ❑ Haggai 1:1—2:23
- ❑ Zechariah 1:1—8:23
- ❑ Ezra 5:2—6:22
- ❑ Daniel 6:1–28
- ❑ 1 Chronicles 1:1—9:34
- ❑ Esther 1:1—10:3
- ❑ Ezra 4:6–23
- ❑ Malachi 1:1—4:6
- ❑ Ezra 7:1—10:44
- ❑ Nehemiah 1:1—10:39
- ❑ Psalms 1, 91, 119
- ❑ Nehemiah 11:1—12:30
- ❑ Psalms 120—132
- ❑ Nehemiah 12:31–47
- ❑ Psalms 133, 134, 104, 107, 111—118, 135, 136, 145—150
- ❑ Nehemiah 13:1–22
- ❑ Psalm 92
- ❑ Nehemiah 13:23–31
- ❑ Joel 1:1—3:21
- ❑ Isaiah 56:1—66:24
- ❑ Zechariah 9:1—14:21

THE BOOK OF EZRA

The story of the Jews' return from exile and the restoration of their ruined temple and city is told in the Book of Ezra and continued in the Book of Nehemiah. The central figure is Ezra, a scribe from a priestly family. But Ezra himself does not appear in the book until ch. 7. The earlier chapters are devoted to the rebuilding of the temple by the returned exiles under the political leader Zerubbabel and the priestly leader Jeshua. To rebuild the temple, they had to overcome opposition from "the people of the land" (Ezra 4:1–5), but in the end they completed the structure.

Tradition holds that the author of the book is Ezra himself. If so, then Ezra may have also been the Chronicler, the author of the priestly history found in 1 and 2 Chronicles, because the Book of Ezra picks up at the precise moment that Chronicles leaves off. Chronicles ends (2 Chr. 36:22, 23), and the Book of Ezra begins (Ezra 1:1–4), with the decree of Cyrus in 538 B.C. that allowed the exiles to return. Other scholars believe that one or more editors compiled the material now known as 1 and 2 Chronicles, Ezra, and Nehemiah.

OUTLINE OF EZRA

I. Restoration of the Temple	**1:1—6:22**
A. Return to Jerusalem Under Zerubbabel	1:1—2:70
B. Construction of the Temple	3:1—6:22
II. Reformation of the People of God	**7:1—10:44**
A. Return to Jerusalem Under Ezra	7:1—8:36
B. Restoration of the People	9:1—10:44

TIME CAPSULE  573 to 500 B.C.

573	The prophet Ezekiel receives visions of the new temple
562–560	Evil-Merodach succeeds Nebuchadnezzar as king of Babylon
559–530	Cyrus the Great of Persia
550	Cyrus successfully unites the Persian and Median tribes
538	Cyrus issues proclamation of freedom for the Jews
537	Zerubbabel and Jeshua begin construction of a new temple
536	Work is stopped on the Jerusalem temple
515	Dedication of the second temple in Jerusalem
500	Rise of democracy in Athens
500	Persians begin a royal mounted messenger service

Cyrus's Religious Propaganda (Ezra 1:2–4)

Cyrus, king of Persia, issued proclamations to specific groups of deported persons. One proclamation, appearing in the Book of Ezra (Ezra 1:2–4), was for the Jews; another for the Babylonians. In the Cyrus Cylinder, the king announced that the "Lord of the gods" (meaning Babylon's god Marduk) chose him (Cyrus) to conquer the world and set the religious situation in Babylonia right after years of abuse. According to the proclamation, all the sanctuaries were in ruins, and Marduk wished for Cyrus to rebuild them for the Babylonian people. For this reason Marduk allowed Cyrus to conquer Babylon.

Cyrus also claimed it was the will of Marduk to return items that were brought to Babylon during the rule of the Neo-Babylonian Empire. Statues of other gods, along with implements used in their worship, would be returned when conquered peoples returned to their homelands. Temples would be rebuilt and worship restored.

Certainly Cyrus believed that his empire was built with the help of the god who ruled over the entire earth. In writing to various peoples, he called that deity by the name of the highest god of the people to whom he wrote. This might be a classic case of political propaganda, or Cyrus may have assumed that there was one god, who was called different names by different peoples. In either case, Cyrus both appealed to the gods to support his kingship and to the peoples of his new empire to accept him as rightful ruler.

Restoring Worship in Jerusalem (Ezra 3:1—4:5)

The exact dates for the returns led by Sheshbazzar (Ezra 1:11) and by Zerubbabel (Ezra 2:2) are unknown. Some have identified Sheshbazzar with Zerubbabel, but such identification is not certain. Sheshbazzar could be considered the earlier leader, whose place was later taken by Zerubbabel.

After arriving in Jerusalem, the returnees reestablished their forms of worship, erecting an altar as the first step in restoring the sacrificial system (Ezra 3:3). The 7th month (3:1), corresponding to September-October, was an appropriate time for the people to assemble in Jerusalem, since three holy days were celebrated at that time. Scholars commonly suggest that this 7th month occurred in either 538 or 537 B.C., thus shortly after Cyrus's proclamation. The 2nd year "of their coming" (3:8), when work began on the temple's foundation, would then be either 537 or 536 B.C.

Laying the Foundation of the Second Temple (Ezra 3:8–13)

Judah's temple, the house of Yahweh, had remained desolate since its destruction by the Babylonians in 586 B.C. In the 2nd year after the exiles returned from Babylon, around 537 or 536 B.C., Zerubbabel, a descendant of David, and Jeshua the high priest broke ground to begin the construction of a new temple (Ezra 3:8). The event was met with great ceremony and joy, but also with sadness (3:9–13). The structure was much smaller than the previous temple of King Solomon, which had been built on the same site.

The joy and grief reveal that laying the foundation of the second temple was an event of great importance. The temple had an indispensable theological function to play. It was the very center of God's presence in Judah. It was the point where sacrifices were made in response to Yahweh's gracious choice of Israel as His people.

Yet the temple had important political and economic roles to play in society as well. It was the institution that held all of Judean society together, past as well as present and future. It gave political identity to the people. Access to its courts identified who was properly a citizen and who was excluded.

Economically, rooms in the temple functioned as a treasury—the society's bank. Because of the temple's demands for tithes and offerings, a large portion of the Judean economy passed through temple personnel and storehouses. Without the temple, the Judean people had little chance of pulling together as a coherent society to face the challenges of the future.

The laying of the foundation for this new temple, therefore, represented the rebirth of the kingdom of Judah. Given their past, Judeans could well appreciate that such an event was worthy of both great joy and sadness.

Opposition to the Temple (Ezra 4:24—5:1)

Ezra 4:5 reports that the rebuilding of the temple was frustrated during the last years of Cyrus's reign (539–530 B.C.) until the time of Darius (522–486 B.C.). Strangely, though, the passage that follows (Ezra 4:6–23) describes events that took place during the reigns of the two kings who succeeded Darius: Ahasuerus (4:6) and Artaxerxes I (4:7, 11, 23). The appearance of Ahasuerus and Artaxerxes at this point in Ezra (4:6, 7) presents a curious chronological problem.

Ahasuerus, also known as Xerxes I (486–465 B.C.), was the son of Darius. Artaxerxes I (465–424 B.C.) was Darius's grandson and Xerxes' son. After describing events during their later reigns (between 486 and 424 B.C.), the narrative returns to the 2nd year of Darius's reign (520 B.C.; Ezra 4:24). Since Xerxes and Artaxerxes reigned after Darius, the events of 4:6–23 are definitely reported out of chronological order. Perhaps this passage was inserted into the middle of Darius's reign to serve as an example of the kind of tactics employed by the "adversaries of Judah and Benjamin" (4:1).

THE BOOK OF HAGGAI

The "adversaries of Judah and Benjamin," whose help in rebuilding the temple Zerubbabel and Jeshua had rejected (Ezra 4:1–3), were successful in stopping the work on the temple. The foundation had been laid before the work stopped (Ezra 3:10, 11), but nothing further was done from that point. The work stoppage lasted from sometime during Cyrus's reign (c. 536 B.C.) until the 2nd year of Darius I (520 B.C.).

At that time two prophets, Haggai and Zechariah, arose to urge the completion of the temple construction. The ministries of these two prophets, who were contemporaries, are dated specifically in 520 B.C. (Ezra 4:24—5:1; Hag. 1:1; Zech. 1:1). The Book of Ezra reports that in that year Haggai and Zechariah prophesied and the Jews "began to build the house of God" (Ezra 5:1, 2). The Book of Haggai consists of the call to complete the temple.

Prophecy in the years after the Exile was different from the great prophecies of such pre-exilic prophets as Isaiah and Jeremiah. To begin with, the earlier prophets tended to speak about, and to, the kings. But in the restored Judah after the Exile there was no king. Prophets very often spoke to the priests and elders instead. Indeed, many of the prophets themselves seemed to have a priestly perspective. This is certainly true of Haggai, who speaks primarily of the temple and of the particularly priestly concern of ritual defilement (Hag. 2:10–14).

OUTLINE OF HAGGAI

I. The Call to Rebuild the Temple	**1:1–15**
A. The People's Indifference	1:1–11
B. The People's Repentance	1:12–15
II. God's Greater Temple and Blessings	**2:1–23**
A. Encouragement from God	2:1–9
B. Holiness and Worship	2:10–19
C. God's Blessing on Zerubbabel	2:20–23

STARTING OVER IN A DIFFICULT LAND (HAG. 1:6)

The Babylonian destruction of Jerusalem left Judean society in shambles (2 Kin. 25:11, 12). Later, power struggles within the Judean community further emptied the society of necessary leadership and institutions (Jer. 41:1–3). Archaeological surveys suggest that Judah lost 90% of its population during these years. Judean society in the land of Judah had collapsed.

So approximately 50 years later, when an enthusiastic group of Judean exiles made the journey with high hopes (Ezra 1:11), the depopulation of the area had taken its toll on the environment. Jerusalem must have been a mess. There is no evidence that anyone attempted to rebuild the city after the destruction of 586 B.C. The returnees to the site of Jerusalem would have been met by wild animals, weeds, dirt, and mounds of debris in the very locations where their ancestors' homes once stood.

The new economy, like the old, depended upon agricultural production. Yet the fields would have suffered from 50 years of neglect. Land would have grown hard and become overgrown with brush. It must have taken intensive manual labor and a lengthy time to get the fields—and thus the economy—to return to productivity again.

Finally, the weather did not cooperate. The prophet Haggai warned of a drought: "the heavens above you withhold the dew, and the earth withholds its fruit" (Hag. 1:10). Difficult circumstances had grown desperate. He aptly describes the dire straits of the community that had returned to Jerusalem: "You have sown much, and bring in little; you eat, but do not have enough" (Hag. 1:6). The task of starting over in the land had proven to be very difficult.

THE BOOK OF ZECHARIAH

Haggai's companion in prophecy was Zechariah, but Zechariah's work is quite different from Haggai's. He is less exclusively concerned with the temple, for instance, and does not sound quite so priestly. Most obviously, though, he presents his message in a very different fashion. Where Haggai had preached prose sermons, Zechariah describes visionary experiences, often in poetry—or at least in very poetic prose.

Zechariah's visions are every bit as historically specific as Haggai's speeches, though. Both the governor Zerubbabel (Zech. 4:6–10) and the high priest Jeshua (spelled "Joshua" in Zech. 3:1–5) are identified. Zechariah calls these two leaders of the returned exiles the "two anointed ones" (4:14).

Zechariah seems to envision not just a rebuilt temple but a restored nation and a glorious new Jerusalem, with a Davidic king at its head. Zerubbabel, like the Messiah, was from the line of David. The possibilities of this connection would not have been missed by Zechariah's original audience. Jeshua the high priest is also described in messianic language. He is called the "Branch" (Zech. 6:12), a word used by the prophets Isaiah (Is. 4:2) and Jeremiah (Jer. 23:5) to refer to the Messiah.

After chs. 1—8, though, the Book of Zechariah changes dramatically. Chapters 9—14 still include visions, but these visions are much more obscure and no longer come with their own interpretation. The clear references to identifiable historical persons are gone. It becomes much more difficult to date these chapters, but they are different enough from chs. 1—8 that many scholars consider them to be speaking of a later time.

Zechariah's ministry began during the 2nd year of Darius I, approximately in November of 520 B.C. (Zech. 1:1). The foundation of the second temple had been sitting abandoned for possibly 16 years by this time, and Zechariah encourages a disheartened postexilic community. In the month of Shebat (probably February, 519 B.C.), Zechariah received his first vision (Zech. 1:7).

OUTLINE OF ZECHARIAH

I. Call to Repentance	**1:1–6**
II. The Eight Visions of Zechariah	**1:7—6:8**
A. Horses	1:7–17
B. Horns	1:18–21
C. The Surveyor	2:1–13
D. Cleansing of the High Priest	3:1–10
E. Lampstand and Olive Trees	4:1–14
F. Flying Scroll	5:1–4
G. Woman in a Basket	5:5–11
H. Four Chariots	6:1–8
III. The Crowning of Joshua	**6:9–15**
IV. The Question of Fasting	**7:1–3**
V. The Four Messages of Zechariah	**7:4—8:23**
A. Rebuke of Hypocrisy	7:4–7
B. Repent of Disobedience	7:8–14
C. Restoration of Israel	8:1–17
D. Rejoice in Israel's Future	8:18–23
VI. The Two Burdens of Zechariah	**9:1—14:21**
A. The Rejection of the Messiah	9:1—11:17
B. The Reign of the Messiah	12:1—14:21

CLOTHING, SYMBOLS OF INNER BEING (ZECH. 3:1–5)

The Satan who accused the high priest Joshua (or Jeshua; Zech. 3:1) was acting as the Adversary, the heavenly officer in charge of finding those who break the laws of God. God intervened on Joshua's behalf.

Joshua, as high priest, represented the people of Jerusalem before Yahweh. In the ancient Near East high priests interceded for their people with the gods. But no high priest was allowed before any deity when in a state of ritual uncleanness or in improper clerical garments. Anyone who approached a god without the proper garments was punished with death. The official cultic clothing was to be worn properly so that the rituals would be pure and properly performed. A clean garment reflected a clean soul.

The Adversary, Satan, correctly opposed the priest in this case on two grounds. The Jerusalem which Joshua represented before Yahweh had defamed itself, causing the Exile in the first place (2 Kin. 23:26, 27), and for this alone the Adversary had cause to oppose Joshua's appearing before Yahweh. Yet in addition, the priest, while approaching God, wore filthy garments in clear violation of priestly rules.

The Adversary's accusation was accurate, but he did not understand the extent of God's forgiveness. Yahweh had delivered the people of Jerusalem from exile, not so much because they deserved to return, but because God granted them grace. The change in Judah's status is symbolized by God's clothing of Joshua in clean garments (Zech. 3:4, 5). The high priest did not do this for himself, but God, through mercy, reinstated Joshua and Jerusalem—they were "a brand plucked from the fire" (3:2).

Tattenai's Opposition (Ezra 5:2—6:22)

When Zerubbabel and Jeshua resumed work on the temple in 520 B.C., Tattenai, one of the Persian Empire's many local officials, tried to halt the work through intimidation (Ezra 5:4, 10). When that failed, he wrote an official letter to King Darius, reporting the Jewish settlers' insubordination. To Tattenai's probable surprise and dismay, Darius discovered that the Jews did indeed have royal permission for their work, and he commanded Tattenai to help the Jews and to pay their expenses from Tattenai's own regional tax collections (6:8–10).

The portion of the Book of Ezra from Ezra 4:8 through 6:18 is not written in Hebrew, but rather in the related language of Aramaic. Since Aramaic evidently served as the trade language of both the Babylonian and Persian empires, it is easy to see why the official letters of chs. 5 and 6 (as well as those of chs. 4 and 7) are in that language. Yet the switch of language may also serve as a reminder that the Jews, while back in their hereditary land, were still under foreign control. When the book describes the Passover celebration, that most Jewish of observances, the language reverts to Hebrew (6:19–22).

The temple was finished and dedicated in the month of Adar of Darius's 6th year, corresponding to March 515 B.C. In the following month of Nisan, the 1st month of the year, the Jews celebrated the Passover (6:19). Apparently the month name "Nisan" was taken from the Babylonian language, for this 1st month had been known by the Canaanite name "Abib" after the Exodus (Deut. 16:1). Though the name of the month had changed, the Jews were again observing Passover at their temple during their 1st month. The "descendants of the captivity" (Ezra 6:19) were really the people of the covenant again.

Darius the Mede (Daniel 6:1–28)

Of all the chronological puzzles in the Book of Daniel, the most perplexing is the mention of "Darius the Mede." According to the apparent chronology of Daniel, this king succeeded Belshazzar, the son of Nabonidus, last of the Babylonian kings (Dan. 5:30, 31). But he apparently ruled before Cyrus (Dan. 6:28).

Identifying "Darius the Mede" is difficult since none of the extensive Babylonian or Persian records mention such a Median king in Babylon or anywhere else in the time between Belshazzar and Cyrus. There was a King Darius, but he was a Persian, not a Mede, and he reigned after, not before, Cyrus and Cyrus's son Cambyses.

Some scholars believe that the stories involving Darius the Mede are highly embroidered accounts from which no genuine historical person will ever be identified. Others have suggested that "Darius" actually refers to Cyrus, who did indeed follow Belshazzar in Babylon, and who took that city at the head of both Median and Persian forces. Yet another solution proposes that Darius was not actually king, but was one of Cyrus's officials, named Gaubaruwa, who had been granted certain royal powers. These suggestions locate the story of Dan. 6 sometime around 539 B.C.

A third possibility is that the person intended by "Darius the Mede" was actually the later king of Persia, Darius I (522–486 B.C.). He might have been called a Mede, since his empire and its laws had roots in both Media and Persia. Darius's decree in Dan. 6 is called "the law of the Medes and Persians" (6:12, 15). Moreover, Darius is described as organizing an official bureaucracy of 120 satraps (Dan. 6:1, 2), which was indeed Darius I's most lasting contribution to the Persian Empire. Reading Dan. 6 in the context of Darius I locates the story around or after 522 B.C.

Darius the Mede may never be identified. Whoever he was, he ruled over the world's greatest empire. But, as Dan. 6 makes clear, neither his worldly power nor his unchangeable laws can stand against the sovereignty of Daniel's God.

TIME CAPSULE	**495 to 450 B.C.**
495–400	The Elephantine Papyri are written in Aramaic
490	Persian King Darius I is defeated by the Athenians at Marathon
486–465	Xerxes I of Persia is also known as Ahasuerus
484–425	Greek historian Herodotus
480	Xerxes is defeated by the Athenians at Salamis
469–399	Socrates, Greek philosopher
465–424	Artaxerxes I of Persia is known as Longimanus
460–404	Conflict between Sparta and Athens
450	Winches in use in Greece

BUILDING AND DEDICATING THE SECOND TEMPLE

Cyrus's Persian army defeats Babylon (Dan. 5:30) 539 B.C.

Cambyses ascends to the throne of Persia 530 B.C.

The temple is dedicated in Jerusalem (Ezra 6:15–18) 515 B.C.

B.C. 540 — 535 — 530 — 525 — 520 — 515

Cyrus allows the Jews to rebuild the temple (Ezra 1:2, 3) 538 B.C.

Zerubbabel lays the foundation of the temple (Ezra 3:8–11) 536 B.C.

Darius I crushes rebellion and becomes king of Persia 522 B.C.

Zerubbabel resumes work of rebuilding the temple (Hag. 1:14, 15) 520 B.C.

Darius issues decree to allow work on the temple (Ezra 6:8–12) 520 B.C.

The Medes and Persians (DAN. 6:8)

The kingdom of Media is first mentioned in Assyrian sources describing the 9th-century campaign of Assyria's Shalmaneser III (858–824 B.C.) into the land of the Medes. Media was apparently situated in the area of modern west-central Iran and flourished for the next two centuries, according to the same Assyrian sources.

In the Assyrian texts the Medes are pictured in these centuries as comprised of a group of small autonomous tribes. The Greek historian Herodotus (484–425 B.C.) gives a legendary account of a unification of Median tribes occurring during the 7th century B.C. By the late 7th century the unified Median tribes, led by Cyaxares (c. 625–585 B.C.), were allied with the Chaldeans against Assyria. The unified Medes thus contributed to the downfall of the Assyrian capital of Nineveh in 612 B.C.

The Median kingdom continued under Astyages (c. 585–550 B.C.), successor of Cyaxares, until the middle of the 6th century B.C. In 550 B.C. Cyrus of Persia successfully united the Persian and Median tribes, though it is uncertain whether the Medes were conquered or were peacefully incorporated into Cyrus's empire.

Cyrus was apparently related to the royal houses of both Media and Persia. Thus the union of the two nations may have been accomplished as the result of Cyrus's legal claim to the throne. Media continued to be geographically distinct even under Persian government, and the Medes were second only to the Persians in importance in the Persian Empire. So even after Persia absorbed Media in 550 B.C., the Medes continued to be recognized as a distinct people. This situation is evident in the recurring phrase "the law of the Medes and Persians" (Dan. 6:8, 12, 15).

Priestly Genealogies (1 Chr. 1:1—9:34)

Among the returned exiles in Jerusalem were probably several factions. The most influential of these was the priestly faction. The high priest Jeshua served as a coruler with Zerubbabel, and the next major Jewish leader to appear in Jerusalem would be the priestly scribe Ezra.

A traditional concern of the Jewish priests was genealogies, the records of who descended from which ancestors. The priests were the ones responsible for maintaining genealogical records, which explains why the genealogies that are preserved tend to be most complete when they describe the priestly families. Perhaps their task to record and preserve the Israelite bloodlines made the priests the ones most concerned about avoiding intermarriage with non-Jews (see Ezra 9; 10).

The priestly history of the kingdom of Israel begins with a series of priestly genealogies (1 Chr. 1—9). These serve as a sort of historical shorthand to bridge the generations from the first man, Adam (1 Chr. 1:1), to the first king, Saul (1 Chr. 9:35–44), after which the historical narrative itself begins in 1 Chr. 10.

That, at least, is the purpose of these genealogies in their current location at the beginning of the Book of 1 Chronicles. But in fact, the genealogies of 1 Chr. 1—9 go much further than just to King Saul. The names in ch. 9 appear to be the names of priests and Levites who lived in Jerusalem after the return from Babylonian exile (see 1 Chr. 9:1, 2). Perhaps the genealogies of 1 Chr. 1—9 were collected originally for the returned exiles and only later were adapted by the priestly writer of Chronicles to serve as a brief historical prologue to his history of the kingdom.

These genealogies, as a priestly summary of Israelite history, served two important purposes for the community of returned exiles. First, they demonstrated to that ragtag group of refugees that they were part of a much larger, much more impressive divine plan, which began with Adam and continued through Abraham (1 Chr. 1:28), Israel or Jacob (2:1), Aaron (6:50), and David (3:1). These lists also stressed that Israel's future hope rested on the priests. Aaron, Moses' priestly brother, receives more space than Moses himself (6:49–53). Moreover, long sections are devoted to the names, duties, and dwellings of the priests and Levites (6:31–81; 9:3–34).

THE BOOK OF ESTHER

The reign of the Persian king Darius I (522–486 B.C.) was as successful as it was long. He established a workable system of government, and he built splendid buildings, extensive roads, and even a canal in Egypt between the Nile River and the Red Sea. He was succeeded by his son Xerxes I (486–465 B.C.), called Ahasuerus in the Bible, who achieved significantly less than his father.

In the Book of Esther, Ahasuerus is caricatured as a weak and foolish king, with no mind of his own. But the book is not really about Ahasuerus. Like the narratives of Dan. 1—6, the Book of Esther was meant to encourage Jews living in a foreign land. Indeed, during the Persian period, most Jews lived outside of Palestine, surrounded by potential enemies. These Jews of the Diaspora (meaning "dispersion") faced different pressures and different problems than those Jews who had returned to Palestine. Thus the Diaspora Jews began to develop a different religious focus.

The most striking difference between the religion of the Diaspora and the religion of the returned exiles had to do with intermarriage. Where Ezra and Nehemiah would rage at the Palestinian Jews who married outside of the faith (Ezra 9; 10; Neh. 13:23–28), the Book of Esther reports calmly and without apology of Esther's marriage to the Persian Ahasuerus.

Moreover, whereas the Palestinian Jews were vocal and very demonstrative about their beliefs, the Jews of the Diaspora had learned to be prudent with their faith. Esther did not tell her husband that she was a Jew. Even more striking, the story of Esther tells very clearly how God protected His people by providing them an advocate in the king's own court, yet the book recounts God's providence without ever actually mentioning the name of God. The Jews of the Diaspora were willing to die for their faith, but they did not court trouble. Until they had to take a stand, they maintained a sort of underground religion.

Some historical problems pertain to the Book of Esther. In all the royal records and histories from the court of Xerxes, there is no mention of a Queen Vashti, a Queen Esther, a prime minister named Mordecai, or a massacre of Jewish enemies. For this reason, some scholars suggest that the book was not intended as a historical narrative but rather as an instructional work of fiction. Others, though, maintain the book's historicity, noting especially the Feast of Purim, which commemorates the events described in the book, and supposedly the Jews would be unlikely to establish such a feast for the plot of a fictional short story.

The narrative begins in the 3rd year of Ahasuerus's reign (Esth. 1:3), which was 483 B.C. The first return of Jews to Jerusalem had already occurred (537 B.C.), but the later returns under Ezra (possibly 458 B.C.) and Nehemiah (445 B.C.) were still in the future. The feast that the king prepared (1:5) should perhaps be identified with the assembly at Shushan that Herodotus, the Greek historian, reports was called by Ahasuerus in 483 B.C. Such magnificence and abundance were undoubtedly calculated to impress the leaders of the empire that the emperor had the power and wealth to rule as he wished.

OUTLINE OF ESTHER

I. The Threat to the Jews	**1:1—4:17**
A. The Selection of Esther as Queen	1:1—2:20
B. The Formulation of Haman's Plot	2:21—4:17
II. The Triumph of the Jews	**5:1—10:3**
A. Triumph of Mordecai over Haman	5:1—8:3
B. Triumph of Israel over Her Enemies	8:4—10:3

The Weak and Temperamental King (Esth. 1:1)

In the Book of Esther, Ahasuerus (Esth. 1:1) is the king of Persia who chose Esther as his queen. He has been identified with the celebrated Xerxes I (486–465 B.C.), the fourth major king of the Persian Achaemenid dynasty (559–331 B.C.). Shortly after the outset of his reign, Xerxes quelled a rebellion in Babylon, destroying the city and carrying away the statue of Marduk, the city's patron deity.

Xerxes is best known from the writings of Herodotus (484–425 B.C.), the Greek historian who wrote the history of the wars between Greece and Persia. The son of Darius I, the Great (522–486 B.C.), Xerxes continued his father's intervention in Greek affairs, preparing a massive invasion of Greece in 480 B.C. Despite winning the first battle at Thermopylae, the venture proved fatal. The Persian navy was decisively defeated at the Bay of Salamis. Dejected, Xerxes fled Greece before the final defeat of his army at Plataea in 479 B.C.

The Persian name for Ahasuerus means "mighty man," which is ironic in view of this king's description in the Book of Esther and in the writings of Herodotus. Herodotus depicts Xerxes as an incompetent and fickle monarch, not unlike the portrayal of Ahasuerus in Esther. His roller-coaster temperament is witnessed in his reaction to Vashti's rejection (Esth. 1:9–12) and to Esther's plea for her people (Esth. 7:1–10).

Mordecai, Esther's Famous Guardian (Esth. 2:5–7)

One of the main characters in the Book of Esther is Mordecai, who is described as Esther's guardian and adoptive father (Esth. 2:5, 7). The name "Mordecai" is a Gentile name, likely derived from the Babylonian name "Marduk," the head of Babylon's pantheon of gods. Mordecai would have also had a Jewish name, just as Esther's Jewish name was Hadassah (Esth. 2:7).

An official named "Marduka" is mentioned in a Babylonian tablet found in modern central Iraq. The tablet is dated to the reign of Xerxes I (486–465 B.C.), a king identified with the "Ahasuerus" of the Book of Esther (Esth. 1:1). Marduka was a scribe of the governor of Babylon. The same name (written with the consonants mrdk) has also been found in Aramaic papyri of the same century, representing an official in northern Mesopotamia.

Some scholars have concluded that either of these Mesopotamian documents could indeed be naming the Mordecai who was Esther's guardian. At least, the existence of officials with the name "Mordecai" in this period supports the picture of Mordecai as a famous person in the Persian Empire (Esth. 9:4).

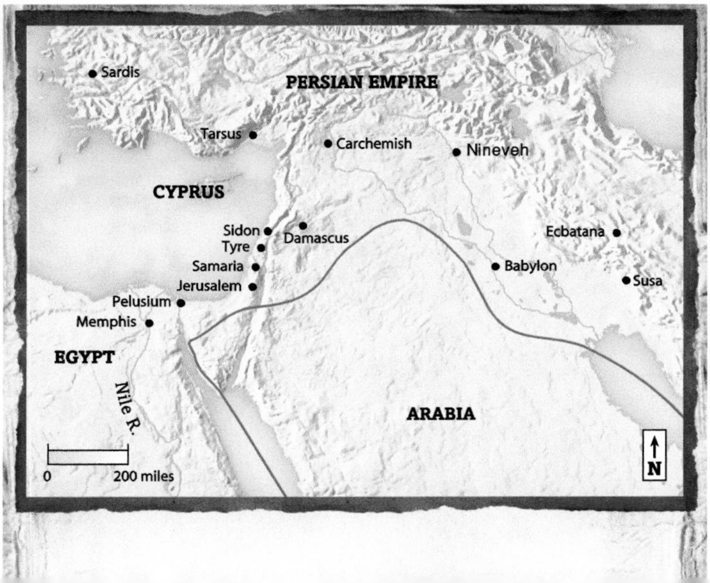

The Persian Empire
The rise of Persia was rapid. In 550 B.C. Cyrus the Persian inherited the kingdom of the Medes. In 547 B.C. he captured the Lydian capital of Sardis. In 539 B.C. he took Babylon without a fight. By 500 B.C. the Persian Empire stretched from India in the east through Asia Minor to Greece in the west, and included Egypt and some of coastal Africa to the south.

THE BOOK OF MALACHI

Much is uncertain about the prophetic Book of Malachi. Nothing is known of the prophet outside of the words in the book. Indeed, it is not even certain that "Malachi" is a name. In Hebrew, the name "Malachi" (Mal. 1:1) simply means "My messenger" (as it is translated in Mal. 3:1), and it could be understood as an anonymous prophet, designated as God's messenger.

Also uncertain is the book's historical context. When did this prophet live? To whom were these words directed? No one can be completely sure, but some guesses are more probable than others. For instance, Malachi's emphasis on the temple and on correct priestly ritual indicates that he spoke at a time when there was a temple standing, either before the temple was destroyed in 586 B.C. or after the second temple was completed in 515 B.C. The later time is suggested by the reference to Judah's political ruler as "your governor" (Mal. 1:8), since it was during the Persian period that Judah no longer had a king.

Malachi's preaching has a very priestly tone. The sins that he condemns are sins of inappropriate worship: offering blemished sacrifices (1:8, 14), carelessness on the part of priests (2:7, 8), and neglecting the temple tithes (3:8–10). Such an emphasis fits well in the priest-dominated community of returned exiles, though Malachi's criticism of unworthy priests would surely not have been popular among the priests themselves. One period in which Malachi's preaching could have occurred would be the generation after the rebuilding of the temple, when the priests and people had grown complacent.

This at least was the situation that was encountered by Ezra and Nehemiah when they arrived in Jerusalem (around 458 and 445 B.C.). Since both leaders instituted reforms to rectify the very problems that are described in Malachi, perhaps the most likely time for the Book of Malachi is early in the reign of Artaxerxes I (465–424 B.C.), just before the arrival of the reformer Ezra in 458 B.C.

OUTLINE OF MALACHI

I. The Privilege of the Nation	**1:1–5**
II. The Pollution of the Nation	**1:6—3:15**
A. Sin of the Priests	1:6—2:9
B. Sin of the People	2:10—3:15
III. The Promises of the Nation	**3:16—4:6**
A. Rewards of the Book of Remembrance	3:16–18
B. Rewards of the Coming of Christ	4:1–3
C. Prophecy of the Coming of Elijah	4:4–6

Sun God or Sun of Righteousness
(Mal. 4:2)

The prophet Malachi borrowed the imagery of sun worship when he mentioned the "wings" of the "Sun of Righteousness" (Mal. 4:2). Another prophet, Ezekiel, saw in his temple vision some two dozen men worshiping the sun (Ezek. 8:16). For Ezekiel, this may have been the worst example of turning away from Yahweh. The prophets knew there was no sun god, but many Judeans still worshiped Shemesh, the Canaanite sun deity.

The sun god was thought to traverse the heavens by day in his chariot drawn by horses. At night the god traveled the length of the underworld. Because this deity was able to see all the living and the dead, the sun god was called upon to witness a person's innocence, and was thus the god of justice.

Worship of the sun in Judah seems to have been a long-standing activity. The horses set up for the god at the temple (2 Kin. 23:11) indicate that worship of the sun was accepted by the priests of Yahweh. Possibly devotees kissed the back of their hands to honor the sun god (Job 31:27). Kissing was a sign of submission, as shown by Assyrian reliefs where dignitaries assume this attitude before the king.

Hymns to the sun god were used in temple worship. Even one of Israel's psalms (Ps. 104:19, 22) appears to be an adapted form of an Egyptian hymn, composed about 1350 B.C. to Egypt's sun god Aten. The psalm was probably taken over from Egyptian or Canaanite sun worship and rewritten to praise Yahweh.

The winged disk was a popular symbol for the sun god in the ancient Near East. Malachi responds that justice or righteousness should not be sought from an Egyptian or Canaanite sun god, but from Yahweh, who "shall arise with healing in His wings" (Mal. 4:2).

Ezra the Scribe (Ezra 7:1—10:44)

Artaxerxes I may have halted work on the walls of Jerusalem (Ezra 4:21), but it was still Persian policy to permit and encourage captive peoples to worship in their own ways. Following this policy, Artaxerxes allowed yet another group of exiled Jews to return to Jerusalem to establish the worship of Israel's God. Under the leadership of a priestly scribe named Ezra, the group arrived in Jerusalem in the king's 7th year (Ezra 7:8), which for Artaxerxes I was 458 B.C. Some scholars locate this return in 428 B.C. (the 37th year of Artaxerxes I) or in 398 B.C. (the 7th year of Artaxerxes II).

In the history of the returned exiles, the figure of Ezra towers above all others. If the return from captivity in Babylon was seen as a new Exodus (and it often was), then Ezra was seen as the new Moses. Like Moses, he led the people through the wilderness with only God for protection (Ezra 8:21–23), settled disputes (Ezra 9; 10), and proclaimed the law (Neh. 8). The picture of Ezra in later Jewish tradition became even more Mosaic. There is even a legend that the Books of Moses were destroyed when the temple fell, but God miraculously restored them to Ezra.

At the same time, Ezra represents a new type of leader, never before seen in Israel. He was a religious reformer without a king. Although he arrived with the permission and approval of Artaxerxes, he did not use royal authority as a basis for his reforms. Furthermore, although much of Ezra's reform was concentrated on the temple, the temple was not the whole focus of his work, as it seemed to be to earlier priestly leaders such as Jeshua.

Ezra's focus and authority was Scripture, which at that time meant the Books of Moses. In the years before the Exile, Scripture had not been treated as particularly significant. Indeed, when a part of the Law of Moses was found and read during King Josiah's reign, the king and people had evidently never heard such a message before (2 Kin. 22:8–13). Israelite worship had been concentrated on the temple, not the law. During the Exile, though, that changed. Without a temple, the Jews had to find a new center for their faith. They became the people of the Book. In this context, a new kind of religious leader arose. The Hebrew word for these leaders, usually translated "scribes," means in a sense "bookmen," learned men who were able to read and write. Ezra represents this new sort of leader. Although he is from the high priestly line of Aaron (Ezra 7:1–5), his true authority comes from his standing as "a skilled scribe in the Law of Moses" (7:6).

In Ezra 7:27—9:15, the Book of Ezra shifts to a first-person memoir format. Ezra tells his own story. While this may not seem unusual to modern readers, it is a striking new development in biblical history. The thoughts and feelings of the human actor are more clear, but the thoughts of God are less accessible, being presented through that human's consciousness.

The arduous journey from Babylon to Jerusalem took 4 months (Ezra 7:9; 8:31). Soon upon arriving, Ezra had to address the practice of mixed marriages among the Jewish community in Judah and Jerusalem. This practice had also been a problem for the Israelites at the time of the Exodus from Egypt (Num. 25:1–9). In that original Exodus, the priest Phinehas put a stop to the practice. In this second Exodus, from Babylon, the priest Ezra took charge. An assembly was convened in the 9th month (Ezra 10:9), and a 3-month investigation of the problem undertaken from the 10th month until the 1st month of the following year (10:16, 17). Ezra had to help the Jews arrive at a new understanding of themselves and of the distinctiveness of their faith in God.

The Levitical Singers (Ezra 7:24)

During the time of Ezra and Nehemiah, various groups were associated with the temple, including priests, Levites, gatekeepers, singers, and Nethinim (Ezra 7:24; Neh. 7:73; 10:28). We should not think that these "singers" of the temple were merely a church choir. The role of Levitical singers went much beyond one of simply making music.

King David appointed Levitical singers to accompany the ark of the covenant as it was brought up to Jerusalem (1 Chr. 15:16–25). They transformed the hard work of a "moving day" into a joyous, holy procession of Yahweh. Levitical singers were also present under King Solomon when the ark of the covenant was placed in the temple and the first temple sacrifices were made (2 Chr. 5:7, 11, 12). Later Judahite kings employed singers on important occasions. In the Passover celebrations led by kings Hezekiah (2 Chr. 30:21, 22) and Josiah (2 Chr. 35:15, 16), Levitical singers accompanied the sacrifices with songs of praise. Before King Jehoshaphat led his army out to battle a coalition of Ammon, Moab, and Mount Seir (Edom), the Levitical singers sang praises in the temple (2 Chr. 20:18, 19).

The Chronicler reports a function of the Levitical singers that is surprising to us today. When Jehoshaphat led his forces into battle, the singers were advancing before the Judahite army (2 Chr. 20:21, 22). It is common for armies to go into battle by marching to the beat of music. In addition, song or music, particularly the sound of horns or trumpets, was often used in antiquity as a way of communicating battle orders above the din of battle (Judg. 7:16–18; Job 39:24, 25). Thus the Levitical singers had been an important group before the Exile, but still were in Ezra's time, as they were granted tax exemption by the Persian king Artaxerxes (Ezra 7:24).

THE BOOK OF NEHEMIAH

Closely associated with the Book of Ezra is the Book of Nehemiah. Where Ezra was the religious leader in Jerusalem, Nehemiah became the secular leader, the official governor of the Persian province of Judah (Neh. 5:14). Nehemiah's great concern was the ruined state of the city, left without walls since Artaxerxes I had earlier halted the repairs (Ezra 4:21). Using his position as a trusted servant in the inner court of Artaxerxes, Nehemiah obtained permission to resume that labor and complete the walls of Jerusalem. He began his work in the 20th year of Artaxerxes' reign (445 B.C.; Neh. 1:1).

The chronology of Ezra and Nehemiah is perplexing. They seem to have been contemporaries in Jerusalem, but neither makes much mention of the other. Although the Book of Nehemiah recounts one incident involving Ezra (Neh. 8) and twice mentions the two leaders together (Neh. 8:9; 12:26), Ezra and Nehemiah appear to have carried on their reforms separately. Also puzzling is that Ezra put an end to the practice of intermarriage between the returned Jews and the people of the land (Ezra 9; 10), yet Nehemiah had to deal with the same problem (Neh. 13:23–28). The priestly laxity that Nehemiah encountered (13:4–9) is especially strange coming so soon after Ezra's reforms.

For these reasons, many scholars believe that Ezra actually came after Nehemiah, perhaps during the reign of Artaxerxes II (404–359 B.C.). If Ezra arrived in the 7th year of this Artaxerxes' reign (Ezra 7:8), thus in about 398 B.C., Ezra's work would have been the final word in the reform efforts. Using this date, however, makes it impossible for Ezra and Nehemiah to have been contemporaries, despite Neh. 8:9; 12:26. Furthermore, Ezra's proclamation of the Law of Moses (Neh. 8) would have occurred long after Nehemiah's time.

Another proposal speculates that the number now reading "7th year" in Ezra 7:7, 8 was damaged, and originally read "37th year." If Ezra arrived in the 37th year of Artaxerxes I (about 428 B.C.), Ezra's reforms would have occurred after those of Nehemiah, but still during Nehemiah's years in Jerusalem. To change Ezra 7:7, 8 hypothetically, though, is a questionable basis for such a conclusion; and the traditional order of Ezra 7—Neh. 13 seems most likely. Ezra's reforms began in 458 B.C., but like all religious revivals, they did not affect everyone nor did they last forever. When Nehemiah arrived 13 years later, there was still much to be done.

As in the Book of Ezra, parts of the Book of Nehemiah are told in the hero's own words. From these portions, called Nehemiah's memoirs, one not only learns the history, but much about Nehemiah himself: an impatient, often difficult, but incorruptible man who sought no human reward but only to serve his God (Neh. 13:14, 22, 31).

OUTLINE OF NEHEMIAH

I. The Reconstruction of the Wall	**1:1—7:73**
A. Preparation to Reconstruct	1:1—2:20
B. Reconstruction of the Wall	3:1—7:73
II. The Restoration of the People	**8:1—13:31**
A. Renewal of the Covenant	8:1—10:39
B. Obedience of the Covenant	11:1—13:31

Geshem the Arab (NEH. 2:19)

Nehemiah names three specific opponents who attempted to thwart his plans for rebuilding the walls of Jerusalem in the mid-5th century B.C. (Neh. 2:19). Sanballat the Horonite is identified as the governor of Samaria in documents from the Jewish colony at Elephantine in southern Egypt. Tobiah, described as an "Ammonite official," was possibly a governor over Ammon. The third opponent, Geshem the Arab, likewise was a governor under Persian rule.

The name "Geshem," which probably means "big man" in Arabic, is often mentioned in Nabatean and northern Arabian inscriptions. Geshem was apparently an important person, since Sanballat threatened to send a letter to the Persian king quoting Geshem. The letter would have contained a false report accusing the Jews of planning to rebel against Persian rule (Neh. 6:5, 6).

Three sources possibly refer to the Geshem who opposed Nehemiah. A 5th-century B.C. Aramaic inscription from Egypt refers to a certain "Qaynu, the son of Gashmu, the king of Kedar." Kedar was one of the main Arab groups in this period. Moreover, both a contemporary account and a king list from Dedan mention Gashmu. If Nehemiah's "Geshem the Arab" was indeed a Kedarite king, his influence would have stretched from northern Arabia to include Judah.

Ezra Reads the Law (Ezra 7:1—10:44)

At Neh. 7:73 the Book of Nehemiah changes. First, the narrative is no longer told in Nehemiah's own words; the governor's memoir is temporarily suspended. Second, the main character in Neh. 7:73—8:18 is not Nehemiah but Ezra the scribe (who is not mentioned at all in Neh. 1—7).

These sudden changes are made much more striking by another curiosity. The apocryphal book of 3 Esdras and the writings of the Jewish historian Josephus both tell the story of Ezra, but in those accounts, the event described in Neh. 8 comes immediately after Ezra 10. In other words, in those ancient texts, Neh. 8 is not a part of the story of Nehemiah at all, but instead a part of the story of Ezra. Many scholars suggest that Neh. 8 was once a part of the Book of Ezra, but was later placed in the middle of the Book of Nehemiah by the editing process that tied these books together.

If Neh. 8 was originally part of the Book of Ezra, then it is uncertain when Ezra read the Law of Moses in the square (Neh. 8:1–3). Nevertheless, it is at least possible to read Neh. 8 following the building of the walls. According to Neh. 8:9, Nehemiah was present at Ezra's reading, and such an event would have been an appropriate way to dedicate the recently completed city walls.

It is also possible to read Neh. 8—10 in the context of the people renewing their covenant with God. The 7th month, Tishri (Neh. 7:73b), corresponding to September-October, was an important time of sacred assemblies. The walls had been completed in the preceding month of Elul (Neh. 6:15), and the timing was now right to gather in Jerusalem for festival celebration and covenant renewal. On the 1st day of the month Ezra read the Law (8:2); for 7 days during the month the people observed the Feast of Tabernacles (8:18); and on the 24th day they made a public confession of sins (9:1–3). Finally, the leaders publicly signed the covenant (10:1–27), and the people, beginning with the priesthood, joined the covenant by taking an oath (10:28, 29).

TITHE AND LOYALTY (NEH. 10:37, 38)

An old Canaanite tribute called the "tenth" or "tithe" was payment of a lesser important king to a more powerful one. Tablets from the ancient city of Ugarit, located on the Mediterranean coast, mention such a payment. A king of a smaller village would pay the 10 percent tax, as a representative for his city. His payment was a sign of loyalty to the regional ruler. In return, the more powerful king was obligated to protect those subjects who had paid their tithe.

In the Bible, the payment of tithes became a sign of loyalty to the Israelite God (Mal. 3:8–10). The tithe was taken from the harvest and the herds, both of which were crucial to Israel's physical existence (Deut. 14:22, 23). Bringing God His just due obligated Him to His duties as Savior and Protector (Mal. 3:11). So it was that Nehemiah led the postexilic Jewish community, much in need of God's protection, in the bringing of the tithes to the Levites and to the temple.

Wisdom Psalms (Ps. 1; 91; 119)

The wisdom tradition was one of the most enduring of all ancient Near Eastern traditions, but as time passed it changed slightly, at least in Israel. Some late books of Jewish wisdom place new stress on reverence toward, and obedience to, the Torah. This new Torah-centered teaching, often called "scribal wisdom," was not typical of earlier wisdom writings like the Book of Proverbs. It does appear, however, in the apocryphal book of Ecclesiasticus, written about 180 B.C. and also known as *The Wisdom of Jesus Son of Sirach*.

A few hints of scribal wisdom do appear in the "wisdom psalms." These few psalms offer calm and measured advice, drawing simple distinctions between the righteous and the wicked in ways reminiscent of the Book of Proverbs. The entire Book of Psalms is introduced by one of these wisdom psalms (Ps. 1), which describes in stark contrast the lifestyle of the righteous (1:1–3) and of the wicked (1:4, 5).

One psalm especially fits the description of scribal wisdom. The longest psalm in the Book of Psalms (Ps. 119) offers an extended meditation on the beauty and usefulness of the Torah. It even uses the literary device of alphabetic acrostic, which is typical of wisdom writings (for instance, Prov. 31:10–31). Each verse within a particular stanza of the Hebrew Ps. 119 begins with the same letter of the Hebrew alphabet.

Many other psalms, while not as clearly wisdom psalms, contain elements of wisdom thought. For instance, Ps. 49 speaks on a favorite wisdom theme, the vanity of worldly wealth, and Ps. 111 uses the wisdom slogan "the fear of the LORD is the beginning of wisdom" (111:10; see Prov. 1:7). The contrast between the righteous and the wicked appears in parts of Ps. 36, 37, 91, and 112.

The three scribal psalms (Ps. 1; 91; 119) are without any superscription or any other indication of their date. Nevertheless, the "scribal wisdom" of Ps. 1 and 119 is likely related to the new emphasis on the Scripture that characterized Judaism after the Exile. Just as a new sort of priestly leader developed in the position of the scribe, so a new Torah-centered type of wisdom developed in the new world that the returned exiles faced.

Zerubbabel the Governor (NEH. 12:1)

The name "Zerubbabel" (Neh. 12:1) is a Babylonian name, most likely meaning "seed of Babylon." Zerubbabel was from a Judean family but had grown up in Babylon. In his adult years, however, he had the opportunity to return to his ancestral home in Jerusalem.

Zerubbabel was descended from royalty (1 Chr. 3:17–19). His grandfather had been Jehoiachin (or Jeconiah), the king of Judah whom the Babylonians had taken out of Jerusalem into captivity in 597 B.C. Since Zerubbabel was thus an heir to the throne of David, and the rightful king of Judah, some Judeans hoped that Judah might regain a degree of national power under his leadership. He was compared to a "signet ring" (Hag. 2:23), an instrument belonging to a king, used to impress a seal of his authority.

The political situation of Judah, however, had changed since Zerubbabel's grandfather had ruled. The Persians now were in control. While a Persian king did appoint Zerubbabel to be the governor of the Persian province of Judah, he would not be given the power of a king. The "governor of Judah" (Hag. 1:1) was given charge of the local political situation in Judah and Jerusalem, but would not rule a kingdom.

During Zerubbabel's oversight, the returnees from the Exile completed rebuilding the temple. With Zerubbabel in Jerusalem and the temple completed, hopes were inspired for a rebirth of the Davidic monarchy. Many hoped that Zerubbabel would become more than governor—to rise as Israel's king. But after the temple rebuilding, Zerubbabel no longer appears in any known records. Regardless, a Davidic messianic hope never again departed from Israel.

THE PERSIAN KINGS

The Persian Empire profoundly altered the course of Judah's history. For the Jews this was a period of restoration and reconstruction. For the Persians it was a period of imperial expansion. Several Persian kings are mentioned in the Bible.

DATE	KING	REFERENCE
559–530 B.C.	Cyrus the Great • conquered Babylon and ordered the temple to be rebuilt, 539 B.C.	Dan. 1:21; Is. 44:28; 2 Chr. 36:22, 23; Ezra 1:1–4
530–522 B.C.	Cambyses II • son of Cyrus • invaded Egypt, 525 B.C.	
522 B.C.	Smerdis • a magi named Gaumata who pretended to be Cambyses' younger brother Bardiya • led a rebellion against Cambyses	
522–486 B.C.	Darius I • defeated by the Athenians at Marathon, 490 B.C.	Ezra 4:5; Hag. 1:1; Zech. 1:1
486–465 B.C.	Xerxes I • also known as Ahasuerus • son of Darius I • defeated by the Athenians at Salamis, 480 B.C.	Ezra 4:6; Esth. 1:1
465–424 B.C.	Artaxerxes I • son of Xerxes I	Ezra 7:7–26; Neh. 2:1–8; 13:6, 7
424 B.C.	Xerxes II • son of Artaxerxes I	
423–404 B.C.	Darius II • son of Artaxerxes I	Neh. 12:22

Songs of Ascents (Ps. 120—134)

After the workers had finished rebuilding the walls of Jerusalem, the Levitical singers and their instruments were summoned, and the city was formally dedicated in ceremonies that included the singing of psalms. It is impossible to know exactly which psalms were sung, of course. Surely many of the old psalms, from the days of Solomon's temple, were used, but others may have been written specifically for use in the second temple.

One group of psalms (Ps. 120—134), all linked by the superscription "A Song of Ascents," has a particularly clear connection to temple worship. The title indicates that these songs were sung by worshipers on their way up the hill toward the gates of Jerusalem and the temple. The psalms speak of the joy of worshiping in the Lord's house (Ps. 122; 134), of the need for purity of heart in the true worshiper (Ps. 125; 128; 131), and call for God's blessing in distress (Ps. 120; 129; 130; 132). All the Songs of Ascents appear together, suggesting that at one time they formed an independent collection, a temple songbook, which was later incorporated as a block into the Book of Psalms.

Some of these psalms may be quite old. Several have the superscription "Of David," and one, "Of Solomon" (Ps. 127). Others, though, obviously were composed after the Babylonian exile: one psalmist praises God for His mighty deliverance of "the captivity of Zion" (Ps. 126:1). Such a clear historical reference makes it likely that the Songs of Ascents were put together in this collection for use in the second temple. If so, then some of these psalms may well have been sung at the dedication of the rebuilt Jerusalem, on Mount Zion "which cannot be moved, but abides forever" (Ps. 125:1).

The Last Word in Praise (Psalms 104; 107; 111—118; 135; 136; 145—150)

Most of the songs of praise that appear near the end of the Book of Psalms lack superscriptions. Because they are not specified as being psalms of David or of another psalmist, and perhaps because they appear at the end of the biblical book, these hymns are often considered the latest of the psalms. Perhaps they were written during the Persian era, to be sung in the rebuilt temple. Such a hymn as Ps. 136 was certainly intended for use in public worship; one can almost hear the Levitical singer chanting a verse and the congregation responding to each line with the refrain, "For His mercy endures forever."

Many of these late hymns follow the same pattern, beginning and often ending with the refrain "Praise the LORD" (Hebrew *hallelujah*; Ps. 111—113; 117; 135; 146—150). Such a frequent pattern seems to indicate that regular and fairly rigid patterns for public songs of praise had developed in the restored temple. Apparently instrumental accompaniment was common: Ps. 150 calls for various instruments to be used in praising God, just as Levitical instruments were used at the dedication of the walls (Neh. 12:27).

It is significant to find so many hymns near the end of the Book of Psalms. Most of the laments—the songs of complaint and petition to God—appear early in the Psalter, whereas the greatest concentration of hymns of praise is at the end. Reading the Book of Psalms from start to finish, then, is a journey from distress and supplication to thanksgiving and praise.

Nehemiah's Religious Reforms (Neh. 13:1–22)

Nehemiah began his term of office in 445 B.C., and his greatest accomplishment was the rebuilding of the city walls. They were completed in only 52 days (Neh. 6:15), but these quickly erected walls may have been just makeshift structures. The Jewish historian Josephus writes that the final walls took over 2 years, being completed in 437 B.C.

Nehemiah remained in Jerusalem until the 32nd year of Artaxerxes (433 B.C.), at which time he returned to Artaxerxes' court (Neh. 13:6). Soon, though, he convinced the Persian king to reappoint him to Judah, and he returned to find matters in an unacceptable state.

Nehemiah, like Ezra, was a purist in religious matters. True worship was only possible by the undefiled, and to Nehemiah that disqualified all of the people who had remained in the land during the Exile. Only the returned exiles, who had kept the faith pure even while in captivity, were acceptable. When Nehemiah found that Tobiah, an Ammonite official (Neh. 2:19), had been given rooms in the temple itself, he was aghast and removed Tobiah with characteristic promptness (Neh. 13:7–9). Nehemiah also restored the official support of the Levitical ministers (13:10–14) and resumed enforcement of Sabbath laws (13:15–22).

Tobiah, the Enemy of Nehemiah (NEH. 13:7)

Sometime after 433 B.C., Nehemiah returned from Persia to Judah only to find that his personal enemy Tobiah had wormed his way into the temple itself (Neh. 13:7). Tobiah was not a Judean, but an Ammonite. The "evil" that Nehemiah discovered was that the high priest had taken an Ammonite into the temple, something forbidden in the Law of Moses (13:1).

There were several conflicts between Nehemiah and Tobiah. First Tobiah opposed Nehemiah's rebuilding of Jerusalem's walls (Neh. 2:10, 19). Accusations that Nehemiah was rebelling against the Persian king who had appointed him Judah's governor failed to stop the work. Tobiah further ridiculed the walls (Neh. 4:3) and then plotted with others to attack Jerusalem before the walls could be completed (4:11, 15). These attempts likewise failed.

Tobiah was nothing if not persistent. He, with others, attempted to lure Nehemiah away from Jerusalem in order to assassinate him (6:1, 2). Later on, Tobiah sent him threatening letters (6:19).

Attempting to infiltrate the temple was possibly Tobiah's new strategy to undermine Nehemiah's authority. Most likely he wished to rule over Jerusalem himself, even though he was an Ammonite, not a Judean. He most likely desired to absorb Judah into his own realm, since, as an "Ammonite official" (2:19), he possibly held a position in Ammon similar to Sanballat's in Samaria and Nehemiah's in Judah.

Tobiah was from a powerful, wealthy Ammonite family who impacted Jewish history later on. Archaeologists have discovered a palace-fortress just to the east of Judah from a century after Nehemiah's time. The fortress has the name "Tobiah" inscribed at the entrance. Unable to gather control of Jerusalem, Tobiah and his family eventually carved out landholdings and political power in Ammon, just east of the Jordan River.

The Sabbath After the Exile (Ps. 92)

When the Jerusalem temple was destroyed in 586 B.C., the Jews in exile had to find and emphasize religious practices that did not require a physical temple. One was Scripture (see "Ezra the Scribe"). Another was the observance of the Sabbath. Although the Sabbath law was one of Israel's most ancient, being the fourth commandment (Ex. 20:8–11), it was not treated as a central truth of the faith until after the temple had been destroyed. To Jews living in foreign lands, the visible distinctive of Sabbath observance became an essential mark of the true believer. It was no less than a public statement of faith.

Even after some exiled Jews returned to Jerusalem and rebuilt the temple, Sabbath observance remained a nonnegotiable element of true worship. When Nehemiah returned to Jerusalem for a second term as governor, one of his first actions was to enforce the Sabbath laws. As always, he was abrupt and severe, even offering threats of physical violence (Neh. 13:21).

For some, the Sabbath day was a reminder and an opportunity to give thanks to God for His great blessings. This, at least, was the perspective of the anonymous psalmist responsible for Ps. 92. Others, though, would simply treat the Sabbath as another law to be followed, and Nehemiah's heavy-handed enforcement of the Sabbath law only added to that legalism. By the time of Christ, legalism had almost obliterated the joy of Sabbath thanksgiving that is so evident in Ps. 92 (see Mark 2:23–28).

THE BOOK OF JOEL

Nothing is known about the prophet Joel except for what the Book of Joel itself offers. All information beyond the name of his father Pethuel (Joel 1:1) must be concluded by examining Joel's prophecies.

Joel prophesied in Jerusalem at a time when there was a temple standing (Joel 2:17), but beyond that no one is certain when Joel was active. Some scholars have suggested that Joel was one of the earliest of prophets, prophesying in the 8th century B.C., even before Amos and Hosea. Others place him later, even as late as the Persian period. The book can be read in a context, such as the time of the Persian Empire, when Jerusalem had no king. Joel calls for a national day of fasting and repentance, to be led by the elders and the priests (1:14; 2:15–17). Had Joel prophesied during the monarchy, the king would surely have had a part in such a solemn assembly.

The Persian era suits Joel's prophecies in other ways. Like Malachi, Joel shows a strong priestly orientation. He sees repentance as an official priestly task instead of an individual responsibility (Joel 2:17). He refers once to the Greeks (3:6), a reference that would make the most sense when the Greek city-states were gaining international recognition for their wars against Persia. Finally, Joel shows an amazing awareness of earlier prophecies, quoting extensively from their works. His most interesting quotation (Joel 3:10) reverses an earlier prophecy found in both Isaiah (Is. 2:4) and Micah (Mic. 4:3). Now plowshares would become swords and pruning hooks, spears.

In whatever era Joel spoke, the immediate concern of his prophecy was a plague of locusts. To an agricultural society, the vast swarms of locusts that occasionally appeared in the ancient Near East spelled famine and death. Joel uses one such disaster to call the people back to true faith in God. The locust swarm was a "day of the LORD," and a still more devastating, universal day of the Lord was still to come (Joel 2:30, 31; 3:14–16). Only if the people truly repented could Jerusalem become the holy and eternal city that it was meant to be (3:17, 20, 21).

OUTLINE OF JOEL

I. The Day of the Lord in the Past	**1:1–20**
A. Past Day of the Locust	1:1–12
B. Past Day of the Drought	1:13–20
II. The Day of the Lord in the Future	**2:1—3:21**
A. The Coming Day of the Lord	2:1–27
B. The Ultimate Day of the Lord	2:28—3:21

THE DAY OF JUDGMENT (JOEL 1:15)

Among the Old Testament prophets the phrase "day of the LORD" (or "day of Yahweh") meant disaster and destruction for Judah and Israel. The prophet Joel could only announce, "Alas for the day!" (Joel 1:15). In the ancient Near East, the "day" of a deity meant a time of celebration in which that particular deity was honored as the most powerful god of the pantheon. In the liturgical calendars of Egypt and Mesopotamia there were holy days set aside all through the year for the worship of the various deities.

In the cultures of both Egypt and Mesopotamia, banquets and celebrations marked each god's day. In Egyptian festivals, the image of the god was brought from the temple and carried through the streets. In Mesopotamia, the statues of many gods might be brought in procession to the temple of the god whose day it was to join the celebration. As supreme ruler for that day, the deity was asked to bring justice to the world. Loyal worshipers were expected to be rewarded and the wicked punished.

The people of Judah similarly considered the day of Yahweh to be one of festivals and good times. Prophets like Joel (Joel 1:15) and Amos (Amos 5:18), however, proclaimed a contrasting view. They agreed that Yahweh would indeed bring judgment and true justice on that day. But, since the people had not lived by the rules of God, the judgment that would come would result in their own destruction.

Isaiah and the Restoration (Is. 56:1—59:21)

The prophet Isaiah lived in Judah during the reigns of Ahaz (735–715 B.C.) and Hezekiah (715–686 B.C.), and most of the early passages in the book refer to those kings and to the Assyrian Empire, which was expanding at that time. Most of these prophecies are dark and pessimistic, speaking of inevitable judgment and destruction, because Judah had refused to hear God's words.

Strikingly different are the oracles of salvation in Is. 40—55, which promise a return from exile and a rebuilding of Jerusalem and the temple (Is. 44:28). These prophecies explicitly name Cyrus the Persian (44:28; 45:1), identifying the approaching salvation as the restoration of Jerusalem after the Babylonian exile, almost 200 years after the prophet Isaiah himself was active.

A third major shift in the Book of Isaiah begins at ch. 56. Where chs. 40—55 spoke of a day when the temple would be restored, chs. 56—66 assume that a temple is standing (56:7; 66:6). Since these final chapters follow immediately after the prophecies of the temple's restoration, it is reasonable to assume that they speak of the second temple, built during the Persian era.

If the prophecies of Is. 56—66 do speak of the second temple period, it is remarkable how much their message is in tension with the actual practices of the second temple. All the leaders of the community of returned exiles were meticulous about avoiding foreigners, but the prophet declares that foreigners will be God's servants (Is. 56:3–8). He promises a time when the temple will be "a house of prayer for all nations" (56:7), and when the sacrifices of foreigners will be acceptable on the temple altar. The theme of the faithful Gentiles is resoundingly repeated in chs. 60—62, where the Gentiles will come to God's light (60:3), will build the city walls (60:10), and will see the righteousness of God's people (62:2). If certain members of the restoration community in Jerusalem opposed the exclusivism of Ezra and Nehemiah, as seems likely, they had powerful support in these prophecies.

Jerusalem, the Future World Center (Is. 60:14)

In Is. 60 is a vision of a new Jerusalem that would become the world imperial center. All the nations would converge upon Jerusalem, bringing their wealth as tribute to the city's king, the Lord God (Is. 60:4–7).

Very similar imagery is found in pictures in the ceremonial hall in Persepolis, the capital of the Persian Empire. On the stairway that leads up to the throne of the Persian king, who was considered the "King of Kings," stand carvings of other kings in various ethnic dress. Each king bears a valuable, unique gift from his own country to offer to the Great King.

The Great King is not directly represented in the pictures—he is there in concept. Yet in the center, accompanying the king, is an image of the Persian god, Ahura Mazda. Ahura Mazda was represented by a winged sun, indicating his rule of light over "all the earth" to fight back the forces of darkness. The Great King, therefore, was considered to be Ahura Mazda's representative.

The prophet uses very similar imagery to articulate God's promise to Jerusalem. The city's gates will be "open continually," allowing kings to approach "in procession," bringing "the wealth of the Gentiles" (60:11). Jerusalem, not Persepolis, will be the imperial center of the world.

Furthermore, the prophet depicts God in solar imagery similar to that found at Persepolis. Yet this imagery represents not Ahura Mazda, the Persian god, but Yahweh, the God of Israel at the center of the city. Yahweh, not Ahura Mazda, will rule in Jerusalem. Yahweh, not Ahura Mazda, will be "an everlasting light" (60:19).

These prophecies offered great hope for the returnees, a hope reechoed for all people in the Book of Revelation (Rev. 21:23). Though a "deep darkness" may cover the earth, Yahweh will arise over Jerusalem as a sunrise, and His glory will attract peoples from afar (Is. 60:1–3).

The Apocalyptic Visions of Zechariah (Zech. 9:1—10:12)

The oracles of Zech. 1—8 are filled with symbolic vision reports, but they are still very specific, and they helped inspire the newly returned exiles in Jerusalem to finish rebuilding the temple. At ch. 9, though, the Book of Zechariah changes. Symbolic visions are no longer interpreted by a helpful angelic guide, as were the visions in the first half of the book. Indeed, the prophecies of Zech. 9—14 are among the most difficult to place in historical context. Some scholars place them in Darius's reign, along with the first half of the book, while others date them much later in the Persian period or even after the Persian Empire had been replaced by the Greek Empire of Alexander the Great.

Reading Zech. 9—14 in the Greek era is suggested by the mention of Greece (Zech. 9:13), and by the list of conquered cities (9:1–8), which supposedly follow the path of Alexander the Great's conquest of Palestine in 332 B.C. The destruction of Tyre (9:2–4) is particularly telling, since Alexander was the only conqueror of the ancient world who succeeded in capturing that island fortress. Still, a list of cities and one mention of Greece does not mean that these chapters were written after Alexander. Greece had been an important international player at least since the Greek alliance defeated Darius I at Marathon in 490 B.C.

The prophecies of Zech. 9—14 do not appear to be speaking of the same historical context as Zech. 1—8. What time they do speak of, however, is uncertain. It was a time when the Persian province of Judah was under bad leadership (10:2, 3), faced economic oppression and distress (11:5), and had turned to idolatry (13:1, 2). Such conditions could have existed either before the arrival of Nehemiah as governor in 445 B.C. or sometime after his tenure had ended.

Alexander's Siege of Tyre (Zech. 9:3, 4)

Tyre's fortunes changed through a dramatic event at the end of the Persian period (559–331 B.C.). The city had furnished troops, ships, and a seemingly impregnable port for Persian naval encounters in the Mediterranean during two centuries. The prophet Zechariah describes Tyre's demise with a prophecy often related to this time period. God would destroy Tyre's "power in the sea" (Zech. 9:3, 4).

Alexander the Great was the first to completely subdue Tyre. His Greco-Macedonian armies laid siege to the island in 332 B.C., successfully storming the city after 7 months. The campaign required the building of a massive causeway, 300 yards wide and about half a mile long, extending from the mainland to the island, using the remains of destroyed buildings. Reputedly, over 30,000 citizens of Tyre were sold into slavery, and 2,000 of that city-state's leaders were crucified. Tyre never again reached the economic and political prominence it had enjoyed in previous centuries.

The Last Battle Won (Zech. 14:1–21)

The vision of Zech. 14, with its picture of a final battle (14:3) and an eternal spring of living waters (14:8) has much in common with both Ezek. 38 and 39 and with Rev. 20—22, two other apocalyptic visions. To struggling Jewish settlers oppressed by wicked and self-serving governors (Zech. 12:5, 6), Zechariah offered a future hope.

Like the prophecies of Is. 56—66, those of Zech. 9—14 speak of the restored Jerusalem, but without the priestly emphasis of such Persian era prophets as Haggai and Malachi. Where the priestly prophets stressed the role of God's holy temple, Zechariah offered a radical vision of a time when no temple will be necessary. Instead, everything in Jerusalem, from the harnesses of the horses to the pots and pans of the kitchen, will be holy to God (14:20, 21). Also like Is. 56—66, Zechariah rejects the exclusivism of such leaders as Ezra and Nehemiah. All nations and families of the earth will be able to worship God and keep the Jewish celebration of the Feast of Tabernacles (14:16–19).

TIME CAPSULE	447 to 332 B.C.
447–438	The Parthenon erected on the Acropolis in Athens
445	Nehemiah's mission to Jerusalem
434–404	Sparta defeats Athens in Peloponnesian War
428–347	Plato, Greek philosopher
400	Invention of the screw
390	Rome is sacked by the Gauls
384–322	Aristotle, Greek philosopher
356	Alexander the Great is born
332–37	Hellenistic period
332	Alexander's armies lay siege to the island of Tyre

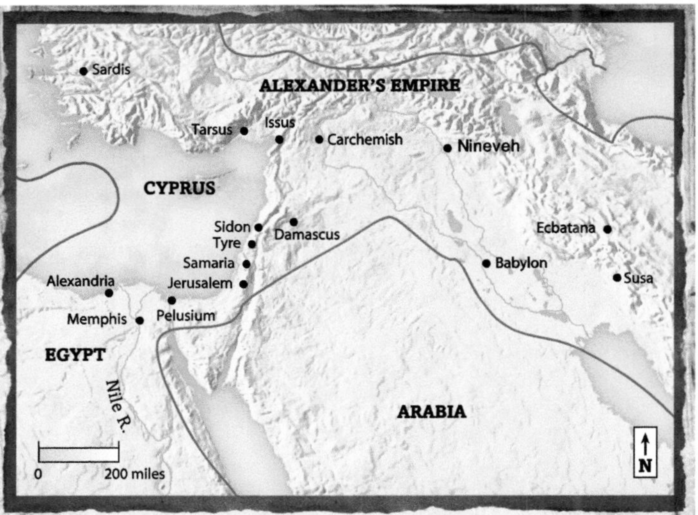

Alexander's Greek Empire

In 334 B.C. a 22-year-old Alexander began a military quest to destroy the Persian Empire. Moving from west to east, he was victorious in battle at Issus in 333 B.C. against the Persian Darius III. Moving south, Alexander defeated the Phoenicians at Tyre in 332 B.C., swept through Palestine, and conquered Egypt in 331 B.C. Darius III was defeated again near Nineveh. Alexander's campaigns secured vast territory for the Greek Empire before he died in 323 B.C.

EPOCH SEVEN

BETWEEN THE TWO TESTAMENTS

332—37 B.C.

The Old Testament provides scant information on events following the end of the Persian period (c. 331 B.C.). One prophecy of Zechariah (Zech. 9) possibly refers to the conquests of Alexander the Great in 332 B.C. At least one interpretation of Daniel's later visions (particularly Dan. 8—11) refers to events after Alexander's Greek kingdom was divided, resulting eventually in the Ptolemies and the Seleucids of the 2nd century B.C. Yet, for the most part, the Old Testament is silent on the approximately 300 years before the birth of Jesus Christ (c. 5 B.C.). This epoch is known appropriately as "the Intertestamental Period" since it is the time between the testaments—between the last writings of the Old Testament and the first writings of the New.

For Judea, the epoch is characterized not only as "between the testaments," but also as between Persian rule and Greek rule, between Greek rule and Judean independence, between independence and Roman rule, with Herod the Great on the throne. It was a time when the faith of the Jewish people was tested, both by oppression and freedom. It is a time little known to the Bible, but fully attested in the Apocrypha.

ARCHAEOLOGY AND THE PAST

Archaeology hints of extensive building and rebuilding during this period. All over Palestine, cities were rebuilt by the Greek Ptolemies from Egypt or by the Greek Seleucids from Syria. Samaria was settled by colonists from Macedonia, and coastal cities in Palestine became Greek. East of the Jordan River, there were many Greek colonies (called the Decapolis in the Gospels). Specific archaeological data is scanty because so much of the building material was reused by later peoples.

The Jewish colony in Egypt continued to thrive. Papyrus documents list Jewish names in Alexandria and all the way up the Nile to present-day Aswan. The Nash Papyrus, a small fragment from this period containing the Ten Commandments in Hebrew, shows that at least some Jews in Egypt could still read Hebrew.

In Palestine itself, one important monument is the painted tombs of Marisa, in southern Judah. These tombs were carved out of the rock and painted elaborately, with the spaces between the paintings being filled with inscriptions and graffiti. The city of Marisa had been the capital of Edomite territory in southern Judah, a region eventually influenced by Greek culture. Names recovered from the tombs are Greek, Phoenician, and Idumean (all of southern Palestine eventually became known as Idumea).

Coins in Palestine show the succession of rulers. Many coins are from the Seleucid rulers of Syria, but coins dated after the Maccabean revolt of 166 B.C. indicate a free Judea. The Judean coins show the Hasmonean rulers becoming more and more secular. ("Hasmonean" derives from the family to which the Maccabees belonged. It was the name applied to the dynasty of Maccabean high priests and kings who ruled Judea between 142 B.C. and 63 B.C.)

One of the most famous archaeological remains from the period is the early occupation at Qumran, south of Jericho on the shores of the Dead Sea. Qumran was apparently settled by a sect of strict Jews who did not approve of the Hasmoneans being both kings and high priests. Josephus, the Jewish historian of the 1st century A.D., tells us that the founders of Qumran were the Essenes, a kind of monastic community. Their settlement was later abandoned and then resettled. It was near Qumran that the famous Dead Sea Scrolls were found in 1947.

THE PEOPLES AND GROUPS

At the beginning of the period the most influential people were the Greeks and their successors. Alexander the Great founded colonies for his soldiers all over his empire. His generals who succeeded him ruled in Syria (the Seleucids) and in Egypt (the Ptolemies) and continued the ancient struggle between Asia and Africa for control of Palestine. While they fought each other over Palestine, both agreed on the importance of establishing Greek culture in the land. The increasing Greek influence would lead ultimately to revolt on the part of the Jews and to defeat of the ruling Seleucids. The incredible struggle of the Jewish people against Greek culture culminated in a Jewish political kingdom independent of Gentile control.

Other peoples figure importantly in this time of Jewish history. The Edomites, who had long been an enemy of Israel, lost their territory in Transjordan and the Sinai to the rising power of the Nabatean Arabs. Many Edomites moved to southern Judah, where they became known as Idumeans. The Idumeans were conquered by the Jews and forced to convert to Judaism, but, ironically, an Idumean would come to rule the Jewish state. Not only was Herod the Great an Idumean, but his brother-in-law was descended from the priests of Koze, an ancient Edomite god.

By 312 B.C. the Nabateans established themselves at Petra, the former capital of Edom, and in this great center they carved homes and temples out of the sandstone. By controlling the desert highways south of the Dead Sea, they became great traders, dominating much of the spice trade in the Middle East.

The Samaritans inhabited the area immediately north of Jerusalem and Judea. Tension between Samaritans and Jews goes back at least to the reconstruction of the Jerusalem temple (538 B.C.). Yet a definite break between these groups occurred around either 388 or 332 B.C. when the Samaritans built a rival temple on Mount Gerizim, claiming Shechem rather than Jerusalem as the location of the true house of God. Both the temple and the city were destroyed by the Jewish ruler John Hyrcanus around 129 B.C.

At the close of the period the most powerful people were the Romans. The first record of Romans in Palestine is the treaty entered into by Judas Maccabeus and the Senate of Rome. Judea and Rome became allies just as Rome was beginning to consolidate its power and expand its territory. The alliance was helpful to the Jews for a few decades, then the Romans moved into Palestine and took control in 63 B.C. Pompey, Julius Caesar, Mark Antony (and Cleopatra), Augustus, and Crassus are Romans associated with Jewish history. Herod the Great was a friend of Caesar, Antony, and Augustus, changing sides with the changes of power in Rome.

THE BIBLICAL LITERATURE

The books associated with this period are found primarily in the Apocrypha. The books of Maccabees exalt Jewish martyrs and encourage the Jews to be strong in their faith. The history of the Jewish revolt that began in 166 B.C. is told in 1 and 2 Maccabees. Stories about the Jews' struggle with Greek culture are found in 3 and 4 Maccabees. The Wisdom of Jesus Son of Sirach (also called Ecclesiasticus) covers ethics in public life, standing in the tradition of Proverbs and Ecclesiastes. The writer wrote in Jerusalem around 180 B.C.

These apocryphal books provide the background for a period almost unknown to the Old Testament, except for the last chapters of the Book of Daniel. The apocalyptic visions of Dan. 7; 8 reveal the kingdoms that came after Babylon, extending at least as far as the Greek Empire established by Alexander and possibly to the Roman Empire. Daniel's vision of 70 weeks (Dan. 9) points toward either Greek or Roman times of the 2nd or 1st century B.C. The Greek kingdoms that controlled Palestine during the 2nd century B.C., particularly the reign of Antiochus IV (175–164 B.C.), come into view in Dan. 10—12.

These visions of Daniel reveal that the trials of God's people would get worse before they got better. Other empires would succeed Babylon, and the later ones would persecute the Jews for their religion, threatening not only their lives, but the continued worship of God. But there is a further message: the pagan kings would not be able to ignore or defy God. Exalt themselves as they might, they would be brought low before the God of Israel. The final outcome would be determined not by earthly armies, but by heavenly ones.

THE GREEK EMPIRE

The Persian Empire continued for another century after the death of Artaxerxes I (424 B.C.). Various kings of varying ability ruled Persia, but no great advances were made by the empire, and no new territories were added. Indeed, some of the empire's conquered territories were lost. Egypt, at the far southwestern end of the empire, rebelled several times, and in 404 B.C. finally won independence from its Persian overlords.

Besides rebellions within its own dominion, Persia's most significant threat continued to be the growing power of the independent city-states of Greece. Both Darius I (522–486 B.C.) and Xerxes I (486–465 B.C.) attempted to invade Greece but were turned back. Later Persian kings gave up plans for conquest, being content simply to keep the Greeks from encroaching on Persian territory. This goal was made easier by wars between the fiercely independent Greek city-states, such as the Peloponnesian War between Athens and Sparta (434–404 B.C.). While the Greeks fought each other, the Persian kings Artaxerxes I (465–424 B.C.), Xerxes II (424 B.C.), and Darius II (423–404 B.C.) were able to concentrate their military forces in Asia Minor, making that area a buffer between Greece and the rest of the Persian Empire.

Despite continuous conflict between the Greek city-states, this century was the golden age in Greece. The city of Athens, which had led the Greek alliance against Darius I and Xerxes I, became the center of Greek politics, literature, and philosophy. In Athenian politics, this was the age of Pericles. In literature, this century saw such Greek dramatists as Aeschylus, Sophocles, and Euripides. Athenian philosophers of this time included Socrates, Plato, and near the end of the century, Aristotle.

Despite great diversity, Greek art and thought shared a few significant presuppositions. Most important of these was a new emphasis on the beauty and value of the human being. Before this time, most cultures saw people as weak creatures, helpless before the more powerful forces of nature and of the gods. In 5th-century Greece, this view changed. Humans came to be perceived as having intrinsic value as well as the strength to overcome (or at least endure) the worst that fate or the gods could offer. The Stoic philosopher Protagoras summarized this humanism with his dictum, "Man is the measure of all things." This philosophical position was to prove much more enduring and influential in world history than any of the military or political achievements of Athens.

No human glory lasts forever, and the glory of Persia and of the Greek city-states began to fail simultaneously. In Persia, the collapse came from within. After Artaxerxes II (404–359 B.C.), Persia was ruled by a series of violent, ambitious men, most of whom gained the throne by assassinating their predecessor and all possible rivals. One of these, Artaxerxes III (359–338 B.C.) seemed to be restoring Persian might—he even recaptured Egypt in 343 B.C.—but that return to glory was illusory. Artaxerxes III was poisoned and replaced by his son Arses (338–336 B.C.).

The threat to Greece came from without, from the land of Macedon to the north. The king of Macedon, Philip II (359–336 B.C.), marched his armies south and by 338 B.C. had captured the whole Greek peninsula. Although not a Greek himself, Philip had his son tutored in Greek thought by none other than the great Greek thinker Aristotle. When Philip was murdered in 336 B.C., his son was ready to expand both the kingdom of Macedon and the culture of Greece into Persian territory. Philip's son was named Alexander (336–323 B.C.).

Alexander the Great's conquests, in their swiftness and effectiveness, are the stuff of military legend. In 334 B.C. Alexander crossed the Hellespont into Asia Minor and overcame all opposition. He met the main Persian force, under Darius III (336–331 B.C.) in 333 B.C. and routed it, sending Darius himself fleeing. Before pressing on into Mesopotamia, the center of Persian power, Alexander marched south and conquered Palestine and Egypt in 332 B.C. Moving north again, he took Mesopotamia in 331 B.C. and everything else he could find to conquer by 327 B.C. The new Greek Empire stretched from Macedon to Egypt, from Greece to India. Alexander himself died of a fever in Babylon in 323 B.C. at the age of 33.

Upon Alexander's death, his generals began fighting over his newly acquired empire. The next few decades were marked by a series of shifting alliances, intrigues, and wars. No one general was strong enough to take control of the whole empire. At first the empire was divided into four parts, but by 280 B.C. three separate dynasties were established: the Antigonids in Macedonia, the Ptolemies in Egypt, and the Seleucids in Persia and Syria.

The land of Palestine, which included Judah and Jerusalem, was at first a part of the Ptolemaic kingdom, centered in Egypt. In about 200 B.C., however, Palestine was captured by the Seleucid king Antiochus III (223–187 B.C.). Now Judah was part of the Seleucid kingdom, based in Syria. The Jews, who had been largely left alone under Ptolemaic rule, now faced danger. The Seleucid king Antiochus IV Epiphanes (175–164 B.C.) sought to establish Greek religion and culture in his realm and to wipe out all rival beliefs. He outlawed the Jewish faith, burned all copies he could find of the Jewish Scripture, and in 167 B.C. sacrificed pigs to Zeus on the altar of the Jerusalem temple. Faithful Jews rebelled and in 164 B.C. were able to cleanse and rededicate the temple, a rededication still celebrated today in the Feast of Dedication, or Hanukkah.

For 300 years after the death of Alexander, the ancient world was controlled by the descendants of his Greek generals. Greek became the official language of trade, and Greek culture found its way into every land. As early as 215 B.C., however, a rival to Greek power began to appear to the west—Rome. In 30 B.C. the last of the Hellenistic (Greek) kingdoms, the Ptolemaic dynasty in Egypt, was absorbed into the new Roman Empire.

EPOCH SEVEN
Chronological Reading Guide

- ❑ Daniel 7:1—12:13

The Apocalyptic Visions of Daniel (Dan. 7:1–28)

The young Jewish exile Daniel interpreted a dream for the king of Babylon, Nebuchadnezzar (Dan. 2). That interpretation was a foretelling of future kingdoms and empires, starting with the Babylonians and moving through the Persian and Greek empires. Since Daniel's dream interpretation was part of a narrative from the time of Nebuchadnezzar (Dan. 2), it could be read in that context.

Several of Daniel's own visions appear to parallel Nebuchadnezzar's dream narrated in Dan. 2. Like that dream, the visions of Dan. 7; 8 describe the kingdoms that will follow the kingdom of Babylon and extend at least as far as the Greek Empire established by Alexander.

Daniel's visions are the best examples of apocalyptic literature in all the Old Testament. Apocalyptic literature was a particularly Jewish form of writing, fairly common in the centuries after the destruction of Jerusalem in 586 B.C. Apocalyptic texts usually presented symbolic visions, with every detail appearing to have a specific hidden meaning, though not always explaining it. The primary purpose of apocalyptic writing was to comfort those who were persecuted for their faith. Such comfort was found in knowing that all the kingdoms of earth, however powerful they might appear, would one day be crushed and replaced by God's eternal kingdom, in which the faithful would be vindicated (Dan. 2:44, 45; 7:27; 8:25).

Apocalyptic visions thus refer to two or even three separate time frames. First, there is the time of the visionary, which in Dan. 7; 8 is the reign of Nabonidus and Belshazzar. Second, there is the time of persecution to which the comfort is offered. That time, for Dan. 7; 8, may be the time of Daniel, or it may be a much later persecution, the time of the future events described in the visions. Finally, there is the final time—an ultimate day of the Lord, when all will be set right, a time sometime after the persecutions.

The visions of Dan. 7; 8 speak of a series of kingdoms, beginning with the Babylonian Empire; however, exactly which kingdom is not completely clear. The four beasts (Dan. 7:3–7), for instance, might refer to (1) Babylon (the lion), (2) Media (the bear), (3) Persia (the leopard), and (4) Greece (the dreadful beast). Alternately, the last three kingdoms could be Persia, Greece, and Rome. Thus the last beast, in which Daniel is most interested, could be either the Greek Empire or the Roman Empire.

The "little horn" of Dan. 7:8, then, would be a proud king of this last kingdom, who would greatly persecute God's people. Should that kingdom be Greece, the little horn might refer to Antiochus IV, the Seleucid ruler who defiled the Jerusalem temple in 167 B.C. References to Greece in Daniel give this interpretation some support: the vision of Dan. 8 specifically identifies the final kingdom as Greece (Dan. 8:21), and Dan. 10; 11 include some clear references to the time of Antiochus. Other scholars, interpreting the fourth kingdom as Rome, have identified the little horn as Nero Caesar, or as some other figure who persecuted Christians.

ALEXANDER THE GREAT CONQUERS PERSIA

B.C. 360 — 350 — 340 — 330 — 320

- Alexander is born to Philip II of Macedon 356 B.C.
- Alexander serves as coregent with his father 340 B.C.
- Philip II is assassinated and Alexander becomes king 336 B.C.
- Alexander defeats Tyre after 7-month siege (Zech. 9:3, 4) 332 B.C.
- The city of Alexandria is founded in Egypt 331 B.C.
- The Macedonian army defeats Darius III at Gaugamela (Dan. 8:6, 7) 331 B.C.
- Persian governor surrenders Persepolis to Alexander 330 B.C.
- Alexander dies in Babylon at age 33 (Dan. 8:8) 323 B.C.

TIME CAPSULE	327 to 215 B.C.
327	Alexander conquers all of Persia before age 30
323	Alexander dies and his empire is divided among four of his generals
301	Seleucus conquers Syria; Ptolemy controls Palestine
264–241	First Punic Wars (Rome vs. Carthage)
215	Rome begins to rival Greek power in the West

TIME CAPSULE	200 to 164 B.C.
200	Ptolemies lose control of Palestine to the Seleucids
175–164	Antiochus IV is one of the cruelest rulers of the Seleucid dynasty
167	Antiochus offers sacrifices to Zeus on the altar of the Jerusalem temple
164	Judas Maccabeus frees Jerusalem from the Seleucids

ALEXANDER THE GREAT (DAN. 8:21)

Alexander the Great, born to Philip II of Macedon and Olympias of Epirus in 356 B.C., is depicted in Daniel's vision (Dan. 8:5, 21) and prophecy (Dan. 11:3). After the assassination of his father in 336 B.C., Alexander inherited the rising kingdom of Macedon, the Greek-speaking state north of modern Greece. He was able to sustain his father's recent conquests in Greece and then manipulate the Greek city-states to join him in the conquest of the great Persian Empire.

Before the age of thirty (327 B.C.), Alexander had conquered all of Persia, from Lycia to the Indus River. He then returned to Babylon and prepared to make the city his new capital. He may also have contemplated the conquest of the western Mediterranean world, but if so, that ambition was cut off by his premature death in 323 B.C.

Following the decease of Alexander, the empire broke up and was divided among four of his generals, symbolized by the four horns (Dan. 8:8, 22) and the four winds (Dan. 11:4). One of these generals, Ptolemy I, founded the Ptolemaic dynasty of Egypt, which he ruled himself from 305 to 282 B.C. The Ptolemies initially controlled Palestine until being defeated by the Seleucids in 200 B.C.

Alexander's conquests had far-reaching effects on the Near East. Greek language and culture were introduced to this area, considerably reshaping Near Eastern civilization. This mixture of Greek and Near Eastern civilizations became known as Hellenism.

Hellenism greatly influenced Israel's culture, especially through the Septuagint, a Greek translation of the Hebrew Old Testament. The Septuagint became the Scripture of the early Christians. New Testament writers frequently quoted the Septuagint (as does Paul in Rom. 15:12) as a source of inspired teaching (see Rom. 15:4). Other Jewish writers, such as Philo and Josephus, interpreted the Septuagint allegorically and quoted it often.

Daniel and the Greeks (Dan. 10:1—12:13)

The final vision of the Book of Daniel (Dan. 10—12) is the clearest in terms of its historical context. Although it certainly may be reinterpreted to apply to other and later times, it also certainly speaks of events in the 2nd century B.C., when the Greek kingdoms controlled Palestine.

The vision begins with a description of the heavenly messenger who brought the vision to Daniel (Dan. 10:4–9). This messenger is clad in radiant gold and his eyes are fiery. Daniel is frightened, but the messenger gives him courage to face the vision (10:10, 18). The apocalyptic visions of the New Testament writer John described in the Book of Revelation begin in almost exactly the same way (Rev. 1:12–20).

As the vision itself is revealed (Dan. 11:2—12:3), its relation to the historical events of the Greek Empire becomes apparent. As the last kings of Persia are ruling, a great king shall arise in Greece who will "rule with great dominion" (11:2, 3). This king must be Alexander (336–323 B.C.). After the great king dies, though, his kingdom will be divided among those who are not his heirs (11:4), the Greek generals who divided Alexander's empire. After this, the vision is only interested in two of those kingdoms, the ones most closely concerned with the land of Judah and Jerusalem. These are the kings of the South (the Ptolemies, based in Egypt) and the kings of the North (the Seleucids, based in Syria).

The vision describes the relations between the Ptolemies and the Seleucids in amazing detail. For instance, the attempted marriage alliance between the two kingdoms (11:6) probably refers to an event of 250 B.C. The Ptolemies and Seleucids were briefly united in the troubled marriage of Berenice, daughter of Ptolemy II (285–246 B.C.), to the Seleucid king Antiochus II (261–246 B.C.).

Various Seleucid kings are alluded to in Dan. 11. Antiochus III (223–187 B.C.) was the king who finally captured Judah and Jerusalem from the Ptolemies (11:11–19). His immediate successor, Seleucus IV (187–175 B.C.), had a mostly peaceful reign, though in the end he was murdered (11:20). The hated Antiochus IV (175–164 B.C.) attempted to stamp out all religions except those of Greece and showed a particular hatred for the religion of the Jews (11:21–45). The vision first describes his military campaigns against Egypt (11:25–28), then his persecutions of the Jews (11:30–39). Antiochus IV outlawed Jewish religion, forced Jews to eat pork or die, burned the Jewish Scriptures, and in the worst act of all, set up an altar to the Greek god Zeus in the Jerusalem temple (the "abomination of desolation," 11:31).

The rest of the vision is somewhat less specific. The distant future seems to be the focus of ch. 12, which offers the general prediction that all such evil worldly kingdoms will fall at the last day before the eternal victory of Israel's God (12:1–3). Although it is easy to be diverted by the specifics of the historical visions, this is the heart of all apocalyptic writing: the promise that God will one day right all wrongs and His faithful will dwell with Him "like the stars forever and ever" (12:3).

Historical specificity such as appears in Dan. 11 is rare in biblical prophecy. It is especially remarkable since Daniel's exile is placed more than 400 years before the events so minutely described in the vision (Dan. 1:1–7). Because of this, many scholars suggest that the visions of Dan. 7—12 were actually written in Palestine during the persecutions of Antiochus IV (167 B.C.) and attributed after the fact to the famous exile Daniel. Such late attributions are fairly common in other apocalyptic writings of Greek and Roman times and would have been a familiar literary device to the original readers.

Other scholars emphasize that accurate foretelling of the future is possible for God, even down to minute details, and accept Daniel's authorship. Whether these visions were written during the Babylonian exile (597–538 B.C.) or during the reign of Antiochus IV (175–164 B.C.), the message is the same: the faithful ones who are persecuted, particularly those persecuted by Antiochus, can take heart. God will overcome His enemies at last.

THE MACCABEAN REVOLT

Year (B.C.)	Event
167 B.C.	Antiochus Epiphanes desecrates the temple (Dan. 8:11)
166 B.C.	Mattathias begins the Maccabean revolt
166 B.C.	Mattathias dies and is succeeded by his son Judas Maccabeus
164 B.C.	Judas Maccabeus rededicates the temple in Jerusalem
161 B.C.	Judas defeats Seleucid army of Nicanor
160 B.C.	Judas is killed in battle at Elasa
160 B.C.	Jonathan Maccabeus becomes leader of the Jews
153 B.C.	Jonathan is appointed high priest of the Jews

B.C. 170 165 160 155 150

Antiochus IV—Epiphanes or Epimanes? (DAN. 11:21–31)

Thirteen kings of the Greek Seleucid dynasty from Syria bore the name of Antiochus. Antiochus III (223–187 B.C.), the great conqueror, was eventually defeated by the Romans at Magnesia in 190 B.C. and forced to send his son as a hostage to Rome. That son, Antiochus IV (175–164 B.C.), would return from Rome to become one of the cruelest rulers of the Seleucid dynasty. He is likely the "king of the North" alluded to in Daniel's prophecy (11:21–45).

Ancient historians describe the character of Antiochus as volatile and unstable. The Greek historian Polybius (who published about 145 B.C.) gave him the nickname Epimanes, meaning "mad." Like his father, Antiochus sought to create a united Seleucid empire from a variety of diverse elements, not only politically, but culturally and religiously. Those who refused to be fully assimilated, such as the Jews, were considered a threat and forced into a policy of Hellenization.

In 169 B.C. Antiochus attacked the city of Jerusalem and looted the temple (2 Macc. 5:11–21). Two years later he again attacked that Jewish city on a Sabbath, killing the male children and enslaving other inhabitants. The city walls were demolished and a military garrison was established. After prohibiting any Jewish religious rituals and forbidding the reading of the Scriptures, Antiochus performed a pagan sacrifice to Zeus in the temple, erecting an altar to Zeus over the altar of burnt offering. This desecration is alluded to as the "abomination of desolation" (Dan. 11:31).

Soon thereafter violent resistance came from the Jews. By 164 B.C. Judas Maccabeus had freed Jerusalem from Seleucid hands. Antiochus died in October of that year, during a campaign against Persia. The nickname Epimanes ("mad") was possibly more relevant than his surname Epiphanes (meaning "the manifest god"). The Seleucid ruler had insanely persecuted the Jews, but his persecutions did not last. In December, 164 B.C., exactly 3 years after he defiled the temple and just 2 months after his death, Judas dedicated a new altar of burnt offering.

TIME CAPSULE 129 to 37 B.C.

129	John Hyrancus I destroys the Samaritan temple on Mount Gerizim
63	Pompey captures Jerusalem, and Rome takes control of Palestine
44	Julius Caesar is assassinated
37	The Romans conquer Jerusalem
37	Herod the Great rules as king of Judea

THE ROMAN EMPIRE

The cruelty of Antiochus IV Epiphanes (175–164 B.C.) soon caused a revolt led by a Jewish family known as the Maccabees (166–160 B.C.). The Maccabean revolt ultimately secured Jewish independence from Syria, and the Maccabees (or Hasmoneans) governed Judea for almost a century, starting in 142 B.C.

Hasmonean is the name given to the dynasty of Jewish rulers who held power following the Maccabean revolt. Under Judas Maccabeus the Jews gained independence from their Syrian rulers. Jewish leadership passed from Judas to his brother Maccabens and then to another brother Simon. Simon Maccabeus became high priest of the Jews and further established the family in power. When Simon's son, John Hyrcanus I (135–104 B.C.), succeeded his father, this signaled the beginning of the Hasmonean dynasty. Their rule continued under Aristobulus (104–103 B.C.), Alexander Jannaeus (103–76 B.C.), Salome Alexandra (76–67 B.C.), and Aristobulus II (67–63 B.C.).

The Hasmonean rulers were recognized by Rome, but their period of rule was troubled by constant war with their neighbors, political infighting, murder, terrorism, and conflict between the Pharisees and the Sadducees. Although Judea was nominally still a province of Syria, in practical terms the country was independent and remained so until 63 B.C., when Rome invaded. The Romans sent the famous general Pompey the Great to end Hasmonean rule and to establish Roman authority in Jerusalem.

According to tradition, Rome was founded in 753 B.C. by Romulus, who became its first king. The little kingdom grew in size and importance, absorbing its immediate neighbors through the reign of seven kings, until the tyranny of Tarquinius Superbus drove the people to revolt and to take the government into their own hands. A republic was established, and Roman citizens had a voice in governmental affairs.

During the period of the republic, Rome extended her borders throughout all of Italy and much of the known world. The Roman occupation of Syria under Pompey in 63 B.C. marks the beginning of the Roman period in Palestine, and for the next century Roman soldiers were stationed in Jerusalem. Under the watchful eye of Rome, Herod the Great (37–4 B.C.) became governor of Galilee (47 B.C.) and later ruler of Judea (37 B.C.). As king, Herod controlled not only the political life in Judea, but also the important office of high priest, although the religious affairs of the nation were led by the Pharisees and Sadducees.

By defeating Antony and Cleopatra in 31 B.C., Octavian became the head of the Roman Empire. He ruled under the title of Augustus, bringing a period of peace and prosperity to the empire until his death in A.D. 14. It was during the reign of Augustus, and just before the death of Herod the Great, that Jesus Christ was born (about 5 B.C.). With this event the chronology of the Old Testament era formally comes to an end.

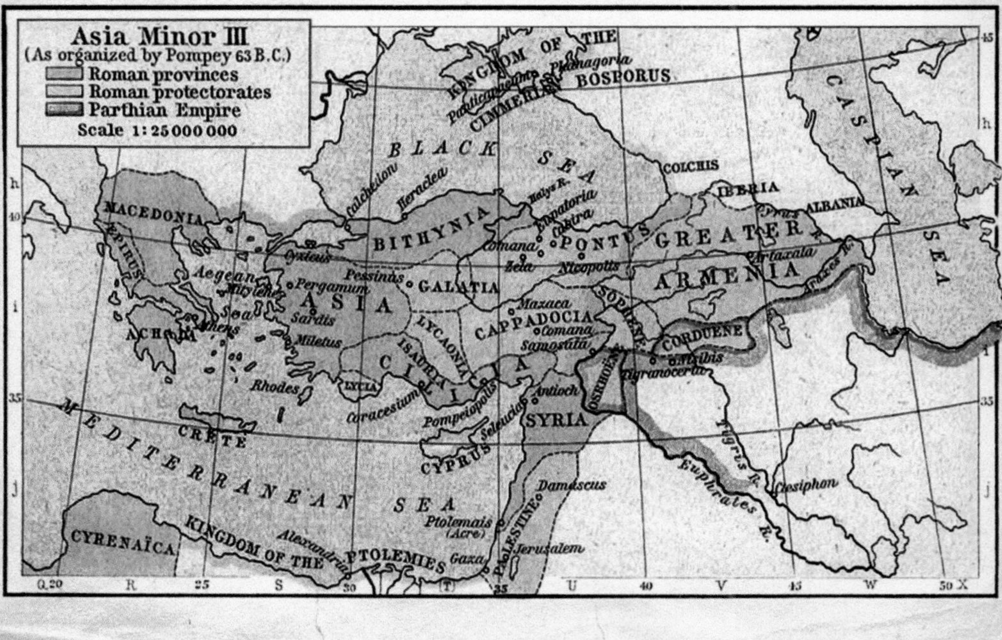

THE COMING OF THE MESSIAH

37 B.C.—A.D. 30

The epoch that witnessed the Messiah's coming actually began with the rise to power of King Herod the Great. The lives of Herod and his sons were closely connected with the earthly life of the Messiah, Jesus of Nazareth. According to the Gospel of Matthew, Herod the Great ordered the deaths of all male children in Bethlehem who were under the age of two (Matt. 2), an order that forced Joseph to flee, taking his wife and young Child to Egypt.

After Herod's death, his sons continued to impact the life of the Messiah. One of Herod's sons was partly responsible for the Messiah becoming known as "Jesus of Nazareth." When Joseph returned from Egypt with Mary and Jesus, he chose to avoid Judea. Herod's son, Archelaus, ruled over Judea and was worse than his father, so Joseph (with Jesus) settled in Nazareth of Galilee. Herod Antipas, another son of Herod the Great, ordered the death of John the Baptist and held a mock "hearing" of Jesus after His arrest. Despite having positions of power, the Herodian family was overshadowed by the great events that occurred during their time: the ministry, crucifixion, and resurrection of the Messiah, bringing victory over sin, death, and the devil.

ARCHAEOLOGY AND THE PAST

Archaeological discoveries in the Holy Land from the Roman period (37 B.C.–A.D. 325) fall into two categories: those that shed light on the Roman world, and those that shed light on the life of Jesus. Sometimes the same archaeological find fits into both categories.

The Roman period, archaeologically, is the world of Herod the Great. Among his many building accomplishments is the great seaport Caesarea Maritima. Excavations have uncovered the theater, the harbor, vast warehouses, temples, and one important inscription. A stone bearing the name of Pontius Pilate, the governor, reminds us that Caesarea was also the headquarters of Roman forces occupying the land. Military installations were placed all over Judea, since it was a border province. Roman Jericho, built on a site different from both Old Testament Jericho and the modern city, was also the work of Herod. The ruins of a magnificent palace and baths have been uncovered in Jericho's excavations.

In Jerusalem are more remains of Herod's building programs. The Wailing Wall is actually part of the great retaining wall Herod built around the Temple Mount to make a surface large enough for the temple rebuilding project. On the western side of the Old City, at a site called the Tower of David, are the remains of one of the towers Herod built to defend the

city. It is probably the tower called Phasael, as described by Josephus. Either in one of these towers, or in his great palace nearby, Herod and his soldiers mocked Jesus.

The ministry of Jesus is illumined by archaeology. In Galilee, the famous "Jesus boat" was discovered in a lake during a drought. One can picture Jesus, Peter, and the others setting out across the lake in such a boat, since it is much like the ones used by fishermen of the 1st century. In Capernaum, the center of Jesus' Galilean ministry, are at least two possible links to Jesus. The synagogue that visitors see is dated to the 4th century, but more recent excavations have shown the foundations of a 1st-century building underneath it. Since synagogues were always built on the same site, the 1st-century synagogue may have been where Jesus preached. Nearby are the ruins of an octagonal church. Archaeologists believe that this ancient church is on the site of Peter's house, and that the foundations discovered underneath the church are literally the remains of the building where Jesus stayed while in Capernaum.

Around Jerusalem are many reminders of Jesus' ministry. Just over the Mount of Olives is the village of Bethany, where we find a 1st-century tomb belonging to a wealthy family. This is the traditional tomb of Lazarus, having a vestibule chamber and a small inner chamber. Somewhere on the Mount of Olives is the Garden of Gethsemane. Whether it was located at the Church of All Nations or nearby at the "Tomb of Mary" is debated. But beyond debate is the reality that Jesus prayed in this vicinity.

Excavations at the southern end of the Temple Mount have uncovered the steps that led up to the temple. Several steps remain in an unrestored condition and represent the way 1st-century persons, including Jesus, usually entered the temple. The steps are also identified as the "rabbis' teaching steps," meaning that Jesus likely sat on them, teaching His disciples and the crowds.

On the north end of the Old City are twin pools that possibly represent the Pool of Bethesda, where Jesus healed a lame man. The porches mentioned in John's Gospel (John 5:2) stood along the sides of the pools and on the causeway between them. Back on the south end of the city are the remains of the Essene Gate, a 1st-century gate that led into Jerusalem. Nearby the gate are the remains of the house of Caiaphas, who was high priest at the time of Jesus' trial. A dank, cold basement cell reminds us that Jesus may have been imprisoned there for at least a few hours. A paved courtyard above reminds us of Peter's denial by the high priest's house.

One of the most powerful archaeological remains is the discovery of a man who had been crucified. Johanan, the name inscribed in the stone box that held his bones, had nail marks in his wrists, and one nail driven through the heel bones. The wood of the cross had been cut apart and buried with him. Johanan's bones illustrate crucifixion, a common method of execution for the Romans, and possibly suggest the way Jesus Himself was executed.

Archaeologists almost universally agree that the site of Jesus' tomb is located inside the Church of the Holy Sepulchre. At two points in the church, one can actually see what is left of the hill of Calvary. The traditional site of Jesus' burial is found very near other 1st-century tombs.

THE PEOPLES AND GROUPS

Peoples outside Judea and Galilee were also prominent in this period. The Nabateans were an Arabic people, with their capital at Petra to the south. The daughter of the Nabatean king Aretas IV married Herod Antipas. When Antipas threw her over for his own sister-in-law Herodias, war broke out between Herod Antipas and the Nabateans. This was the same Herod who beheaded John the Baptist and held a hearing for Jesus at the request of Pilate.

Southeast of the Sea of Galilee were the cities of the Decapolis. Founded by Greeks and Macedonians, the Decapolis was united not by political organization, but by Hellenistic culture and institutions. Gerasa has been excavated, and one can see the city walls, temples, the marketplace, and paved streets with colonnades. The only remains of 1st-century Philadelphia are the ruins of a Roman theater, near the downtown heart of a bustling, modern city.

The Gospels mention such groups as the Samaritans, Pharisees, Sadducees, and Zealots. The Samaritans and Jews suffered a long history of hatred for each other, going back to the fall of Israel in 722 B.C. But out of this background of hatred, Jesus identified a Samaritan as one who was truly a neighbor to a Jewish person in need. The Sadducees were the priestly aristocracy in Jerusalem, the leaders of the people. They walked a fine line between Jewish nationalism and keeping the peace with their Roman overlords. The Pharisees were a group of laymen dedicated to the keeping of the Law (Torah). They had a saying: if all Israel would keep Torah perfectly for just one day, the Messiah would come.

Some Pharisees opposed Jesus; others befriended Him—warning Him of trouble, speaking for Him at His trial, providing a place for His burial. The Zealots were the revolutionary underground. Jesus' disciple Simon "the Zealot" probably belonged to one of the 1st-century groups that actively opposed Roman rule.

THE BIBLICAL LITERATURE

The biblical books relating the time of the Messiah are the Gospels—Matthew, Mark, Luke, and John. Although they tell us almost everything we know about the life and teachings of Jesus, they are not true biographies. Rather, they are theological documents telling who Jesus is and why He is important. They say little about Jesus' family background and youth, and nothing about His physical appearance. They concentrate almost totally on Jesus' ministry, but even here they do not give enough information to reconstruct the history of those years with absolute certainty. Rather, they focus on Jesus' person and His teachings and give considerable attention to His death and resurrection and the surrounding events.

Matthew, Mark, and Luke are called the Synoptic Gospels. The name "Synoptic" means that they view the life of Jesus from a common perspective. After introducing Jesus in different ways depending on their purpose, they relate the ministry of John the Baptist, the baptism and temptation of Jesus, His ministry in Galilee, His journey to Judea and ministry there, His final week in Jerusalem, His death, and His resurrection.

The Gospel of John differs from the Synoptics in a number of ways. It tells us more about Jesus' early ministry in Judea. John also records long thematic discourses by Jesus instead of the usual shorter sayings of the Synoptics. More than the Synoptics, John includes theological reflection on the meaning of Jesus' life and death. The four Gospels together give us a more complete picture of Jesus than any one of them would by itself.

INTRODUCTIONS TO JESUS CHRIST

Each of the four Gospels uniquely introduces the story of Jesus Christ as marking a new beginning in God's dealings with His people. The Gospel of Mark uses a brief superscription (Mark 1:1) and prophetic announcement (1:2, 3) to make it clear that Jesus Christ is the Son of God, a truth previously declared by the prophets. Matthew begins his Gospel with a genealogy (Matt. 1:1–17), showing his Jewish readers that Jesus is truly the Messiah by tracing His ancestors back to David. That Jesus' ancestry goes back also to Abraham evidences Jesus' fulfillment of God's promises to Israel.

Two Gospel writers, John and Luke, alert their readers concerning their purpose for writing a Gospel. Luke provides a brief preface (Luke 1:1–4) in which he sets out his intention. In a prologue, John begins with a clear statement about Jesus' preexistence and divinity. He wanted his readers to know and believe that "Jesus is the Christ, the Son of God" (John 20:30, 31).

EPOCH EIGHT
Chronological Reading Guide

- ❑ John 1:1–18
- ❑ Luke 1:1–4

THE BOOK OF JOHN

While the first three Gospels portray mainly what Jesus did and how He taught, John's Gospel is topical, not primarily chronological. His purpose in writing is to set forth Christ in His deity as the Son of God in order to spark believing faith in his readers. It moves beyond the obvious facts of Jesus' life to deeper, more profound meanings. It revolves around seven miracles and seven "I am" statements of Christ that are springboards for lengthy discussions that reveal important truths about Christ and how we may know God.

The author of this Gospel is identified only as the disciple "whom Jesus loved (13:23; 19:26; 20:2; 21:7, 20), which appears as a title or nickname for John the apostle. His knowledge of Palestinian geography and Jewish customs makes it clear that he was a Palestinian Jew, and his meticulous attention to numbers and names indicates that he was an eyewitness, which matches his claim (1:14; 19:35; 21:24, 25). That the author was John is also consistent with the external testimony of the early church. Irenaeus, Clement of Alexandria, Theophilus of Antioch, Origen, and other church fathers bore witness to the Johannine authorship.

John was evidently among the Galileans who followed John the Baptist until they were called to follow Jesus at the outset of His public ministry (1:19–51) and later called to become full-time disciples (Luke 5:1–11). John was among the twelve men who were selected as apostles (Luke 6:12–16) and became one of the "pillars" of the church in Jerusalem along with James and Peter (Gal. 2:9). Tradition says that John later went to Ephesus (perhaps just before the destruction of Jerusalem). He was eventually exiled by the Romans to the island of Patmos (Rev. 1:9).

Until recently it was popular to propose a second-century date for this book. The discovery in 1935 of the John Rylands papyrus 52, a fragment from John written around A.D. 125, overthrew that conjecture. Conservative scholars typically date the book between A.D. 85 and 90.

OUTLINE OF JOHN

I. The Incarnation of the Son of God	**1:1–18**
II. The Presentation of the Son of God	**1:19—4:54**
A. By John the Baptist	1:19–51
B. In Galilee	2:1–12
C. In Judea	2:13—3:36
D. In Samaria	4:1–42
E. In Galilee	4:43–54
III. The Opposition to the Son of God	**5:1—12:50**
A. At the Feast in Jerusalem	5:1–47
B. During Passover in Galilee	6:1–71
C. At the Feast of Tabernacles	7:1—10:21
D. At the Feast of Dedication	10:22–42
E. At Bethany	11:1—12:11
F. At Jerusalem	12:12–50
IV. The Preparation of the Disciples	**13:1—17:26**
A. In the Upper Room	13:1—14:31
B. On the Way to the Garden	15:1—17:26
V. The Crucifixion and Resurrection	**18:1—21:25**
A. The Rejection of Christ	18:1—19:16
B. The Crucifixion of Christ	19:17–37
C. The Burial of Christ	19:38–42
D. The Resurrection of Christ	20:1–10
E. Appearances of Christ	20:11—21:25

THE WORD BECOMES FLESH (JOHN 1:14)

John's Gospel describes Jesus' preexistence by identifying Him as the divine "Word" (John 1:1), or, as expressed in the Greek language, the *Logos.* Many Greek philosophers spoke of the *Logos* as universal Reason. People familiar with Greek thought could have understood John to be proclaiming Jesus as the organizing principle or "Reason" behind the universe.

Some Jewish people adapted the Greek idea of *Logos* to fit the traditional Jewish idea of the Word, but more people thought of the Word in traditionally Jewish categories. They identified God's creative Word with divine Wisdom, which they also identified with God's Law (the Torah). They brought various ideas together: that God created all things through the Law or Wisdom (John 1:3), that the Word was life and light (1:4), and that Wisdom had been with God from the beginning (1:2).

In the prologue of his Gospel, John declares something that neither the Greek philosophers nor the Jewish teachers conceived: the Word became flesh and dwelt among His people. To the Greeks *Logos* was invisible reason, not part of the material world. To the Jewish teachers Wisdom was a divine attribute of Yahweh. But to John the Word was the divine Christ who became a human being. The Word's glory was "full of grace and truth," revealing to us the full character of God (John 1:14, 17, 18).

EARLY LIVES OF JOHN THE BAPTIST AND JESUS

Elizabeth and Mary, the mothers of John and Jesus, were either blood relatives or close kinswomen (Luke 1:36). The angel Gabriel appeared to both families—to Elizabeth's husband and to Mary herself—and announced their future sons John and Jesus. Even before birth, these babies were named (Luke 1:13, 31) and set apart for unique missions (1:16, 17, 32, 33).

Practically nothing is known of John's boyhood, except that he "grew and became strong in spirit" (Luke 1:80). Only slightly more is known of Jesus' upbringing. Early in His life Jesus was taken to Nazareth, a town of Galilee, and there raised by His mother, Mary, and her husband, Joseph, a carpenter by trade. Hence the Child was known as "Jesus of Nazareth" (Mark 1:24).

Jesus was His mother's firstborn child; he had four brothers (James, Joses, Judas, and Simon) and an unspecified number of sisters (Mark 6:3). The only incident preserved from His first 30 years (after His infancy) was His trip to Jerusalem with Joseph and Mary when He was 12 years old (Luke 2:41–50). Occurring in the year that, as a Jewish boy, He attained the age of religious responsibility, the trip was at a crucial juncture of His development.

EPOCH EIGHT
Chronological Reading Guide

- ❑ Luke 1:5–80
- ❑ Matthew 1:1–25
- ❑ Luke 2:1–38
- ❑ Matthew 2:1–23
- ❑ Luke 2:39–52

THE BOOK OF LUKE

Luke is the first of a two-part work that traces the history of the life of Jesus (the Gospel of Luke) to the founding of the early church (the Acts of the Apostles). The writer carefully documents the perfect humanity of the Son of Man, Jesus Christ, and places Jesus within the context of world history. Luke emphasizes Jesus' ancestry, birth, and early life before moving carefully and chronologically through His earthly ministry. He presents Jesus as the fulfillment of the history of salvation.

The author does not identify himself by name. Although not an eyewitness of the events he reports, he has followed them closely enough to write an orderly, reliable narrative (1:1–4). He is an educated man with the best command of Greek of any New Testament writer. As a Gentile, the author is interested in Gentiles; he is equally disinterested in matters purely Jewish. At some point in his life he joined the apostle Paul. The few glimpses we get of Luke from Paul's epistles—a beloved and compassionate physician (Col. 4:16), who was with Paul during his Roman imprisonment (Philem. 24; 2 Tim. 4:11)—parallels what we gather from Luke and Acts. Early Christian writers, including Irenaeus, Tertullian, Clement of Alexandria, Origen, Eusebius, and Jerome, strongly support Luke as the author of Luke and Acts.

The date of Luke's writing can only be guessed from inferences. Luke tells us that he drew upon earlier accounts, some of which were written (1:2). The Gospel of Luke probably was written sometime shortly after A.D. 70.

OUTLINE OF LUKE

I. Introduction to the Son of Man	**1:1—4:13**
A. Preface	1:1–4
B. Events Preceding Christ's Birth	1:5–56
C. Events Accompanying Christ's Birth	1:57—2:38
D. Events During Christ's Childhood	2:39–52
E. Events Preceding Christ's Presentation	3:1—4:13
II. The Ministry of the Son of Man	**4:14—9:50**
A. Presentation of Christ	4:14–30
B. Demonstration of Christ's Power	4:31—5:28
C. Explanation of Christ's Program	5:29—6:49
D. Expansion of Christ's Program	7:1—9:50
III. The Rejection of the Son of Man	**9:51—19:27**
A. Increasing Opposition to Christ	9:51—11:54
B. Instruction in View of Christ's Rejection	12:1—19:27
IV. The Crucifixion and Resurrection of Christ	**19:28—24:53**
A. Last Week of Christ	19:28—23:56
B. Victory of Christ	24:1–53

The Birth of John the Baptist (Luke 1:5–80)

Luke gives an extraordinary glimpse of ordinary, pious Jews at the time. We should not imagine that everyone was as spiritually bankrupt as the Jewish leaders who later opposed Jesus. The lives of the barren, old Elizabeth and the young, Virgin Mary intersect at the point of God's unexpected favor to His humble servants. Elizabeth was from the tribe of Levi (Luke 1:5) and was also related to Mary (1:36). Because Elizabeth was barren and elderly, the birth of John the Baptist is presented by Luke as a special work of God.

Luke implies that John was born 6 months before Jesus (Luke 1:26) and that the two were relatives (1:36). No other Gospel mentions their kinship, and John's Gospel raises a question: If Jesus and John the Baptist were related, why did John not recognize Jesus at the time of His baptism (John 1:31)? Some think that the Baptist knew Jesus, but did not recognize Him as the Messiah. Geography allows for another possibility: Luke indicates that John was raised in the wilderness of Judea (Luke 1:80), whereas Jesus was raised in Nazareth of Galilee (2:39). During their early years they were separated by quite a distance by ancient standards, possibly distant enough to be unfamiliar with each other as adults.

The Birth of Jesus (Matt. 1:18–25; Luke 2:1–20)

No one knows precisely when Jesus was born. Even His year of birth is only an educated guess based on the information available. The intention of the medieval creators of our calendar was to set the date of Jesus' birth at A.D. 1. They simply miscalculated. The Jewish historian Josephus places the death of Herod the Great in 4 B.C., and both Matthew (Matt. 2:1) and Luke (Luke 1:5) presume that Herod was king at the time of Jesus' birth. But it is not clear how much before Herod's death Jesus was born.

We know that Herod became king of the Jews in 37 B.C. Outside of Matthew (Matt. 2:16), no historical record mentions Herod's slaughter of the infants in Bethlehem. Josephus does write that Herod ordered the murders of members of his own family to protect his throne. So it is not surprising that a few peasant children in Bethlehem went unnoticed among Herod's many atrocities, leaving us no help with dating. Since Herod's calculations led him to target children under two years old, Jesus' birth likely occurred one or two years before Herod's death—in either 6 or 5 B.C.

A date of about 5 B.C. would fit with Luke's note that Augustus, who reigned from 27 B.C. to A.D. 14, was the Roman emperor when Jesus was born (Luke 2:1). Luke's mention of Quirinius (2:2), however, creates a problem. After Herod died, Rome divided his territory among his surviving sons. Archelaus ruled in Judea (see Matt. 2:22) until he was deposed by the Romans in A.D. 6. Only then was Quirinius appointed governor, after serving for more than a decade as commander of the Roman troops in the area. Perhaps Luke simply identified him by his later office.

Some have tried to specify Jesus' birth date by appeal to astronomical phenomena that might explain the star of Bethlehem (Matt. 2:2, 7, 9, 10). Halley's Comet appeared in 12 or 11 B.C. and another comet in 5 B.C. But in antiquity comets were thought to forecast evil, not blessed, events. In 7 B.C. a rare (once every 794 years) conjunction of the planets Jupiter, Venus, and Saturn occurred in the constellation Pisces. Whether Matthew's star was any of these is pure speculation. For ancient people the star confirmed again that Jesus was the Messiah who fulfilled Balaam's star prophecy (Num. 24:17).

THE BOOK OF MATTHEW

The opening book of the New Testament, Matthew is the Gospel written by a Jew to Jews about Jesus, the King of the Jews, the long-awaited Messiah. Through a carefully selected series of Old Testament quotations, Matthew documents Jesus' claim to be Messiah. His genealogy, baptism, messages, miracles, death, and resurrection all point to the same inescapable conclusion: Christ is the King.

While the Gospel does not name its author, the author knew the geography of Palestine well, was familiar with Jewish history, customs, ideas, and classes of people, was well acquainted with the Old Testment, and the terminology of the books suggests the author was a Palestinian Jew. Other details point specifically to Jesus' disciple Matthew as the writer of this Gospel. As a tax collector (Mark 2:14), he would have been literate and familiar with record keeping. The early church uniformly attributed this Gospel to Matthew, and no tradition to the contrary ever emerged.

Matthew wrote the Gospel before the destruction of Jerusalem in A.D. 70. He describes Jerusalem as the "holy city" and as though it was still standing (4:5; 17:53), and he speaks of the custom of the Jews as continuing until "this day" (27:8; 28:15). Furthermore, Jesus' prophecy (recorded in 24:2) of Jerusalem's destruction includes no indication that it had already occurred when Matthew wrote Jesus' words. In light of this, it is reasonable to conclude that the book was written sometime between A.D. 50 and 60.

OUTLINE OF MATTHEW

I. The Birth and Preparation of the King	**1:1—4:11**
A. Jesus' Birth and Childhood	1:1—2:23
B. Jesus' Preparation	3:1—4:11
II. The Declaration of the King's Principles	**4:12—7:29**
A. The Beginning of Jesus' Ministry	4:12–25
B. Kingdom Principles	5:1—7:29
III. The Manifestation of the King	**8:1—11:1**
A. Demonstration of Jesus' Power	8:1—9:34
B. Declaration of Jesus' Presence	9:35—11:1
IV. Opposition to the King	**11:2—13:53**
A. Evidence of the Rejection	11:2–30
B. Illustrations of Opposition	12:1–50
C. Jesus' Adaptation to Opposition	13:1–53
V. The King's Reaction to Opposition	**13:54—19:2**
A. Jesus' Withdrawal	13:54—16:12
B. Jesus' Instruction to His Disciples	16:13—19:2
VI. Formal Rejection of the King	**19:3—25:46**
A. Continued Instruction to His Disciples	19:3—20:34
B. Formal Presentation of the King	21:1–17
C. The Nation's Rejection of the King	21:18—22:46
D. The King's Rejection of the Nation	23:1–39
E. Predictions of the Rejected King	24:1—25:46
VII. Crucifixion and Resurrection	**26:1—28:20**

Betrayal and Betrothal (MATT. 1:18)

The betrothal of Mary and Joseph (Matt. 1:18) involved much more than engagement does today. Even though a young Jewish man was considered an adult around age 13, he would work for a few years to save up for his marriage, around the age of 18 or 20. After the making of a legal contract between the two families, the young man and the woman (who was normally between the ages of 12 and 16) were "betrothed."

The fact that Mary became pregnant after their betrothal but before their wedding prompted Joseph "to put her away" (Matt. 1:19). A betrothed couple could not sleep together before the wedding. In fact, Galilean parents normally kept the man and woman from spending time together privately until the wedding (normally a year after betrothal).

The commitment of a betrothal was so legally binding that a divorce was required to break it off (1:19). Joseph had little choice. If a man's betrothed wife became pregnant, people would assume that she had regarded him as an inadequate man and this would publicly humiliate him. Worse yet, should he not divorce her most people would assume that he was the one who had gotten her pregnant, and he would bear great shame in a culture that was obsessed with shame and honor.

Jewish law required a man to divorce a wife who had been unfaithful. Joseph could have divorced Mary publicly in a court. The court would not only establish his innocence, but also profit him financially: he would get to keep Mary's dowry (the money her father gave her for her marriage). By planning to divorce her privately (writing out a certificate of divorce for her in front of two witnesses), Joseph elected to forfeit profit rather than shame her any further.

Augustus, the First Roman Emperor (Luke 2:1)

Luke refers to "Caesar Augustus" as the Roman emperor who ruled the Mediterranean world during the birth and youth of Jesus (Luke 2:1). The Roman Senate gave the title "Augustus" to this ruler in 27 B.C. He was born Gaius Octavius in 63 B.C., the great-nephew of the famous Julius Caesar.

In his will Julius Caesar made Octavius his adopted son. The untimely death of the dictator in 44 B.C. by assassination was the beginning of Octavius's path to the emperorship. He changed his name to Gaius Julius Caesar Octavian.

Octavian, as he was now called, sided with Mark Antony against the assassins of his adopted father. He initiated a coalition of three dictators—himself, Antony, and Marcus Lepidus—known as "the Triumvirate." The three not only gained victory over Caesar's murderers by 42 B.C., but also carried out the bloodiest purge in Rome's history. From 36 to 33 B.C. there was a break in relations between Octavian and Antony, culminating in Octavian's dominion over the empire by 31 B.C.

After 27 B.C. Octavian became known as "Augustus," the name bestowed on him by the Senate. He was the first Roman emperor, reigning solely as ruler of the Roman realm for more than 40 years (27 B.C.–A.D. 14). In essence, Augustus was the second founder of Rome, reorganizing it as an empire, and presiding over the Silver Age of Latin literature, dominated by names such as Virgil, Livy, and Ovid.

Augustus did not change foreign policy in Palestine much from that of his predecessors. He continued the employment of client kingdoms in the remote parts of the Roman Empire and in 30 B.C. confirmed Herod the Great as ruler of Judea.

Jesus' Childhood in Nazareth of Galilee (Matt. 2:22, 23; Luke 2:39, 40)

Matthew's Gospel does not specify Joseph's hometown, but indicates that he decided not to return to Bethlehem of Judea to avoid living in the territory of Archelaus. The choice to settle instead in Nazareth of Galilee fulfilled a messianic prophecy (Matt. 2:23), for which no corresponding verse is found in the Old Testament.

Luke's Gospel, however, presumes that Joseph and Mary were residents of Nazareth (Luke 1:26; 2:4, 39). Jesus' birth in Bethlehem occurred because of a census that required His parents to return to their ancestral home (2:1–4). Not mentioning the family's flight to Egypt, Luke reports only that from Bethlehem they traveled to Jerusalem (2:21–38) before returning home to Nazareth where Jesus was raised.

Obviously, the details of Jesus' childhood were buried in obscurity. Such things did not matter when He was thought to be only the son of simple peasants. After His death and resurrection, these differing accounts of His childhood did agree on two central points: He was born in Bethlehem in fulfillment of popular messianic expectations, but He was better known as "Jesus of Nazareth" (Matt. 26:71; Mark 1:24; 16:6; Luke 18:37). The so-called "Infancy Gospels" among the New Testament apocrypha offer wild speculation about events surrounding the youth of their wonder-child hero.

TIME CAPSULE	30 to 4 B.C.
30	Octavian confirms Herod the Great as king of Judea
27–A.D. 14	Augustus Caesar is founder and emperor of the Roman Empire
20–A.D. 50	Historian Philo is part of wealthy Jewish family of Alexandria
20–19	Herod begins rebuilding the temple in Jerusalem
12	Quirinius elected counsel of Rome
10	Birth of Herod Agrippa I
7	Herod the Great executes his sons Alexander and Aristobulus
7	Census of Judea under Quirinius
5	Birth of Jesus Christ
4	Death of Herod the Great
4–A.D. 6	Archelaus rules as ethnarch of Judea and Samaria
4– A.D. 39	Herod Antipas rules as tetrarch of Galilee and Perea
4–A.D. 6	Philip rules as tetrarch of Gaulanitis

THE YOUNG JESUS

Herod the Great executes his oldest son, Antipater 4 B.C.

Herod the Great dies (Matt. 2:19) 4 B.C.

Jesus astonishes teachers in the temple (Luke 2:46, 47) A.D. 7

B.C. 10 — 5 — A.D. 1 — 6 — 11

Census of Judea under Quirinius (?; Luke 2:2) 7 B.C.

Jesus Christ is born (Matt 1:24, 25) 5 B.C.

Augustus makes Judea a Roman province A.D. 6

Quirinius takes a tax census of Judea A.D. 6

Jesus Visits the Temple (Luke 2:41–52)

The date of Jesus' visit to the temple depends on the year of His birth. If He were born in 5 B.C., this temple event could have occurred about A.D. 7. However, the date also depends on how exact we understand the age 12 (Luke 2:42).

The circumstances described in this event do not present Jesus as a child-prodigy. A Jewish boy was considered a man, accountable to the Law's demands, following his bar mitzvah at age 13. (Bar mitzvah, meaning "son of the commandment," is a religious rite of passage comparable to catechism and confirmation in some Christian traditions.) It was customary for Jewish parents to take their son to the temple one or two years before he turned 13. Thus Jesus' visit to the temple at this age and His questions of and by the teachers of the Law are consistent with normal Jewish practice. He took His relationship with God seriously. What was exceptional was His level of understanding (Luke 2:47).

BEGINNING OF JESUS' MINISTRY

John the Baptist prepared the way for Jesus' ministry. The silence of John's early years was broken by his thundering call to repentance sometime around A.D. 26 or 27, shortly before Jesus began His ministry. Matthew's Gospel pictures John preaching in the wilderness of Judea (Matt. 3:1), calling people to repentance and baptism (3:3–10), announcing Jesus as the Coming One (3:11, 12), and baptizing Him (3:13–17).

According to the Synoptic Gospels, the main phase of Jesus' ministry began in Galilee after John's imprisonment by Herod Antipas. Possibly John's arrest was a signal for Jesus to proclaim His message in Galilee: "The time is fulfilled, and the kingdom of God is at hand" (Mark 1:14, 15). In the Gospel of John, however, there is indication that Jesus ministered for a short time in Judea, while John the Baptist was still preaching (John 3:22—4:3). Some of John's disciples even became concerned because Jesus "baptized more disciples than John" (John 3:36; 4:1). John reassured his followers: Jesus' ministry was given to Him by God; John himself was only a forerunner (3:27, 28).

EPOCH EIGHT
Chronological Reading Guide

- ❑ Matthew 3:1–12
- ❑ Mark 1:1–8
- ❑ Luke 3:1–18
- ❑ Matthew 3:13–17
- ❑ Mark 1:9–11
- ❑ Luke 3:21, 22
- ❑ John 1:19–28
- ❑ Luke 3:23–38
- ❑ John 1:29–34
- ❑ Matthew 4:1–11
- ❑ Mark 1:12, 13
- ❑ Luke 4:1–13

THE BOOK OF MARK

Unlike Matthew or Luke, Mark does not dwell on Jesus' family history or career. Instead, this Gospel is a record of Jesus' actions and achievements. It presents Jesus as Savior-King, who conquers demons, disease, and death. Its emphasis on Jesus' mighty works makes this Gospel action-packed, fresh, and vivid. Mark constantly uses the present tense to create the impression of an eyewitness account and provides considerable detail. Yet his Gospel is the most concise of all the Gospels, because he omits Jesus' longer discourses.

The Gospel of Mark nowhere mentions the name of its author. The earliest witness to identify the author was Papias (A.D. 60–130), a bishop of Hierapolis. Papias called him Mark, an interpreter of Peter. Papias then added that Mark had not followed Jesus during His lifetime, but later had written down Peter's recollections accurately, although not always in their proper order. Subsequent tradition unanimously agrees with Mark's authorship.

John Mark was a native of Jerusalem (Acts 12:12), and later he became an associate of both Peter (1 Pet. 5:13) and Paul (2 Tim. 4:11). Eusebius wrote that Mark composed his Gospel in Rome while in the services of Peter. If Peter died in Rome between A.D. 64 and 68, the Gospel would have been written in Italy between A.D. 55 and 65. There are good reasons to believe that Mark recorded Peter's eyewitness account. Morever, it is unlikely that the early church would have assigned a Gospel to a minor figure without this connection, since the books of the New Testament normally required authorship by an apostle to qualify for acceptance in the canon.

OUTLINE OF MARK

I. The Identity of the Servant Son of God	**1:1–13**
II. The Servant Son's Initial Ministry	**1:14—8:30**
A. Fame and Popularity	1:14–45
B. Opposition and Conflict	2:1—3:55
C. Explanation of Opposition	4:1–41
D. Belief and Unbelief	5:1—8:30
III. The Servant Son's Approach to the Cross	**8:31—10:52**
A. Announcement of His Coming Death	8:31—10:34
B. Teaching and Practice of Servanthood	10:35–52
IV. The Servant Son's Ministry and Death	**11:1—15:47**
A. Jesus' Initial Ministry in Jerusalem	11:1–33
B. Rising Opposition	12:1–44
C. The Olivet Discourse	13:1–37
D. Jesus' Preparation for His Death	14:1–42
E. Jesus' Rejection	14:43—15:47
V. The Living and Victorious Servant Son	**16:1–20**

John the Baptist (Matt. 3:1–12; Mark 1:1–8; Luke 3:1–18; John 1:19–28)

The description of John the Baptist in Matthew and Mark (Matt. 3:4; Mark 1:6) resembles that of Elijah in 2 Kin. 1:8. There were popular expectations of an Elijah-like figure who would prepare for the coming of the Messiah, and both Gospels explicitly report that Jesus identified John as the fulfillment (Matt. 11:14; 17:10–13; Mark 9:11–13). But according to the Fourth Gospel, John himself denied this identification (John 1:21, 25). Possibly the Baptist did not realize the true significance of his role. He could only describe himself as a herald preparing the way for the Lord's coming (John 1:23).

Luke dates the beginning of John's ministry as the 15th year of the Roman emperor Tiberius (Luke 3:1). Tiberius had a 2-year coregency with Augustus, his adoptive father, before Augustus died. Depending on whether Luke refers to the beginning of the coregency or of Tiberius's independent rule, the 15th year would be A.D. 26 or 28.

John's Baptism of Repentance (Mark 1:4)

Some people who claimed to be especially holy lived in the wilderness. Also, Jewish people anticipated a new exodus through the wilderness (Is. 40:3), so many who claimed to be prophets or messiahs gathered followings in wilderness areas. Only there were they usually safe from interference by the established Jewish and Roman authorities. Thus John the Baptist began his ministry "in the wilderness" (Mark 1:4).

Like other ancient peoples, Jewish people had many symbolic rituals involving water. They washed themselves before festivals and after contact with anything they considered impure. A washing ritual was also performed when a person was initiated into a wilderness sect such as the Essenes (who wrote the Dead Sea Scrolls). But John's baptism was different from these ritual washings; it was a once-for-all baptism, like the kind Gentiles experienced when they converted to Judaism.

John had a message for those who came for baptism: water alone could not change them; they needed genuine repentance. This was also true for baptisms of Gentiles into Judaism and baptisms of Jews becoming Essenes; both required a pure heart as well as water. Yet while Jewish people often spoke of "repentance" as a regular act each time one sinned, John preached a special repentance, a turning from sin to God. John thus expected from his own people the kind of repentance they expected of Gentiles who converted to Judaism (Matt. 3:8, 9).

The Baptism of Jesus (Matt. 3:13–17; Mark 1:9–11; Luke 3:21, 22; John 1:29–34)

In the Synoptic Gospels Jesus' baptism marks His inauguration as the servant Messiah and the dawning of the new age of the Spirit. The Spirit is the agent of a new beginning. The open heaven, the descending dove, and the confirming heavenly voice highlight the ultimate revelatory significance of the baptism. Jesus was anointed by the Spirit of God as the Messiah and the Servant of the Lord described centuries earlier by the prophet Isaiah (Is. 11:2; 42:1; 61:1).

Mark's account of Jesus' baptism was open to several possible false interpretations. Readers of his Gospel might conclude (1) that Jesus was a repentant sinner (Mark 1:4, 9), or (2) that He was inferior to John who baptized Him (1:9), or (3) that He became the Son of God at His baptism (1:10, 11).

The other evangelists denied such speculations early in their Gospels. The birth narratives in Matthew and Luke emphasize that Jesus was conceived of the Holy Spirit (Matt. 1:20), and even as a baby was the Christ (Luke 2:11). He was neither sinful nor inferior prior to His baptism. John's prologue makes it clear that Jesus did not become the Son of God through baptism, but had been such from eternity (John 1:1–18).

Each evangelist further reformulates the baptism story to preclude any confusion Mark's account might allow. Matthew introduces a dialogue between John and Jesus in which Jesus explained His true motive for receiving baptism ("to fulfill all righteousness"; Matt. 3:15) and John acknowledged his inferiority to Jesus (3:14). Luke reports the imprisonment of John (Luke 3:19, 20) before describing Jesus' baptism. In his baptism narrative Luke nowhere refers to John and describes the Spirit as coming upon Jesus in response to His own prayer (3:21).

The Fourth Gospel stresses John's inferiority to Jesus (John 1:6–8, 19–37) and never mentions Jesus' baptism by John nor John's preaching of repentance. John served only as a witness to Jesus: (1) that Jesus received the abiding Spirit; (2) that He is the One who baptizes with the Spirit; and (3) that He is the Son of God (John 1:32–34).

The Temptation of Jesus (Matt. 4:1–11; Mark 1:12, 13; Luke 4:1–13)

In all three Synoptics Jesus' temptation is not that of any ordinary individual, but of the Messiah, the Spirit-anointed Servant and Son of God (Ps. 2:7; Is. 42:1), as the heavenly voice affirmed at His baptism (Matt. 3:17). The Spirit led Jesus to face the question of what kind of Messiah He would be.

During the Intertestamental Period many Jews had come to believe that somehow Satan had wrested from God control of this earth. Thus, when Jesus emerged victorious from His test by Satan, He could announce the good news of the nearness of the kingdom of God (Mark 1:15; Matt. 4:17), the messianic age (Luke 4:14–22), or the age of the Spirit (John 4:23, 24; 7:37–39).

The order of the three temptations is different in Matthew and Luke. Matthew's order moves toward a more logical climax: "turn stones to bread" (Matt. 4:3); "throw Yourself from the temple" (4:6); "give You all things" (4:9). Luke's order, making the temple the last temptation, moves Jesus once again toward His destiny in Jerusalem: "turn stone to bread" (Luke 4:3); "give You all things" (4:6, 7); "throw Yourself from the temple" (4:9).

TIME CAPSULE	A.D. 6 to 27
6–15	Annas is high priest in Jerusalem
6	Augustus deposes Archelaus and exiles him to Gaul
6	Augustus makes Judea a Roman province
7	Jesus questions the teachers in the temple
14	Augustus dies and Tiberius becomes emperor
18–36	Caiaphas is high priest in Jerusalem
26–36	Pontius Pilate is prefect of Judea
27	John the Baptist baptizes Jesus
27	Rebuilding of the temple still in progress after 46 years

THE GALILEAN MINISTRY

Jesus' ministry is traditionally divided into segments: a Galilean ministry, a journey toward Jerusalem, a Judean ministry, and the Passion Week in Jerusalem. Whereas Matthew, Mark, and Luke narrate only one visit to Jerusalem as the climax of Jesus' ministry, John recounts that Jesus regularly followed the practice of Palestinian Jews by observing the pilgrimage feasts. The three feasts of Passover (Unleavened Bread), Pentecost (Weeks), and Tabernacles involved pilgrimages to Jerusalem (Deut. 16:16; see John 5:1; 7:2–10). As a consequence of this attention to feasts, John's Gospel includes several trips back and forth between Galilee and Judea that are not mentioned by the Synoptic Gospels. What emerges from a comparison of the four Gospels is a complementary view of Jesus' public ministry: Matthew, Mark, and Luke emphasize His activities in His native Galilee; John gives most of his attention to Jesus' work in Jerusalem and surrounding Judea.

EPOCH EIGHT
Chronological Reading Guide

- ❑ John 1:35—4:45
- ❑ Matthew 4:12–22
- ❑ Mark 1:14–28
- ❑ Luke 4:14–37
- ❑ Matthew 8:14–17
- ❑ Mark 1:29–34
- ❑ Luke 4:38–41
- ❑ Matthew 4:23–25
- ❑ Mark 1:35–39
- ❑ Luke 4:42—5:11
- ❑ Matthew 8:1–4
- ❑ Mark 1:40–45
- ❑ Luke 5:12–16
- ❑ Matthew 9:1–17
- ❑ Mark 2:1–22
- ❑ Luke 5:17–39
- ❑ Matthew 12:1–14
- ❑ Mark 2:23—3:6
- ❑ Luke 6:1–11
- ❑ Matthew 12:15–21
- ❑ Mark 3:7–19
- ❑ Luke 6:12–19
- ❑ Matthew 5:1–48
- ❑ Luke 6:20–36
- ❑ Matthew 6:1–34
- ❑ Luke 11:1–4
- ❑ Luke 12:22–34
- ❑ Matthew 7:1–29
- ❑ Luke 6:37–49
- ❑ Luke 11:5–13
- ❑ Matthew 8:5–13
- ❑ Luke 7:1–17
- ❑ John 4:46–54
- ❑ Matthew 11:2–19
- ❑ Luke 7:18–50
- ❑ Matthew 12:22–50
- ❑ Mark 3:20–35
- ❑ Luke 11:14–36
- ❑ Luke 8:19–21
- ❑ Matthew 13:1–52
- ❑ Mark 4:1–34
- ❑ Luke 8:1–18; 13:18–21
- ❑ Matthew 8:23–34
- ❑ Mark 4:35—5:20
- ❑ Luke 8:22–39
- ❑ Matthew 9:18–34
- ❑ Mark 5:21–43
- ❑ Luke 8:40–56
- ❑ Matthew 13:53–58
- ❑ Mark 6:1–6
- ❑ John 5:1–47
- ❑ Matthew 9:35—11:1
- ❑ Mark 6:7–13
- ❑ Luke 9:1–6
- ❑ Matthew 14:1–12
- ❑ Mark 6:14–29
- ❑ Luke 3:19, 20; 9:7–9
- ❑ Matthew 14:13–21
- ❑ Mark 6:30–44
- ❑ Luke 9:10–17
- ❑ John 6:1–15
- ❑ Matthew 14:22–33
- ❑ Mark 6:45–52
- ❑ John 6:16–21
- ❑ Matthew 14:34–36
- ❑ Mark 6:53–56
- ❑ John 6:22–71
- ❑ Matthew 15:1–20
- ❑ Mark 7:1–23
- ❑ Matthew 15:21–31
- ❑ Mark 7:24–37
- ❑ Matthew 15:32–39
- ❑ Mark 8:1–10
- ❑ Matthew 16:1–12
- ❑ Mark 8:11–26
- ❑ Matthew 16:13–28
- ❑ Mark 8:27—9:1
- ❑ Luke 9:18–27
- ❑ Matthew 17:1–13
- ❑ Mark 9:2–13
- ❑ Luke 9:28–36
- ❑ Matthew 17:14–23
- ❑ Mark 9:14–32
- ❑ Luke 9:37–45
- ❑ Matthew 17:24—18:9
- ❑ Mark 9:33–50
- ❑ Luke 9:46–50

The First of Seven Signs (John 2:1–12)

In Cana of Galilee Jesus performed the first of several signs. John's account of Jesus' public ministry (John 1:19—12:50) is often called "the Book of Signs," because John had a special interest in the role that signs played in revealing Jesus' relationship with the Father (see John 20:30, 31). Traditionally, seven miracles have been isolated as being particular "signs" for John: transformation of water into wine (2:1–11), healing of a nobleman's son (4:46–54), curing of a paralytic (5:1–15), feeding of the 5,000 (6:1–15), walking on the sea (6:16–21), healing a blind man (ch. 9), and raising Lazarus (ch. 11).

Jesus' First Visit to Jerusalem (John 2:13–25)

Jesus' "cleansing of the temple" raises a chronological question regarding when this incident in Jerusalem may have occurred. All four evangelists report Jesus' prophetic demonstration, which provoked direct challenges to His authority from the religious leadership in Jerusalem (Matt. 21:23–27; Mark 11:27–33; Luke 20:1–8; John 2:18–22).

Comparing John with the Synoptics leads us to ask whether the temple cleansing occurred once or twice, and whether it happened at the beginning or end of Jesus' ministry. John reports the incident early in his Gospel account. The other evangelists, though, associate it with the events of Jesus' Passion. Some suggest that Jesus "cleansed" the temple both at the outset and at the conclusion of His ministry. Others believe that John and the Synoptics report a single event at different points in their Gospels for theological or literary reasons.

The Jewish leaders misunderstood Jesus' saying regarding the temple (John 2:19). Jesus' body was the temple that would be destroyed in His crucifixion, but raised up in His resurrection (2:21, 22). He was not speaking of the building that Herod had begun to reconstruct 46 years previously. The task of rebuilding the temple began in Herod's 18th year (c. 20–19 B.C.) and continued beyond his lifetime. A passage of 46 years would date this Jerusalem visit of Jesus in about A.D. 27, at the spring Passover celebration.

Nicodemus, the Pharisee (John 3:1–36)

John's mention of the Passover (John 2:13, 23) gives the impression that Nicodemus came to Jesus during this feast, immediately following the temple cleansing. This Pharisee, who was a member of Judea's ruling class (3:1), asserted that Jesus' signs revealed Him to be "a teacher come from God" (3:2; see 2:18, 23). Such a statement from one who himself was a prominent "teacher of Israel" (3:10) emphasizes John's view that the conflict between Jesus and the Jewish religious leaders would focus on authority, or more particularly the origin of authority.

John is clear about the origin of Jesus' own authority and that of His followers: it comes "from above." As the "Son of Man" who "came down from heaven" (3:13), Jesus could reveal "heavenly things" (3:12). Likewise, His followers knew about these heavenly things, for they had been "born again" or "from above" (3:3, 5–7). After Jesus had left Jerusalem, John the Baptist emphasized this same point during a controversy with Jewish leaders (3:22–36).

Marveling over Jesus with a Woman (John 4:27)

Jesus' encounter with a woman at Jacob's well could look very ambiguous (John 4:6–8). In fact, 1st-century cultural norms gave Jesus' disciples reason to be troubled. Jesus had crossed ethnic, moral, and gender barriers that most of His contemporaries felt should not be crossed.

A history of ethnic conflict had left little chance of positive interaction between Jewish people and the Samaritans (4:9). They ridiculed each other's holy places, and once the Samaritans had even defiled the Jerusalem temple. The Judeans for their part had completely destroyed the Samaritan temple on Mount Gerizim nearly two centuries before. By Jewish standards, Samaritan drinking vessels were technically unclean, so Jesus' request for water probably led the woman to think that He was not very religious (4:7).

Jesus also crossed a moral barrier. This woman's personal life was probably considered loose by Samaritan standards, since she had been married five times and was not married to the man with whom she was living. Talking with this woman at a well was an ambiguous situation. Even the Samaritan woman, telling Jesus that she was unmarried, may have misread His motives, though He quickly set the matter straight (4:17, 18).

Finally, Jesus crossed a gender barrier in force among His fellow Jews. Many sages, such as Jesus son of Sirach, warned against being seen speaking with women, offering two reasons. First, one could easily fall prey to temptation; second, one could get a bad reputation because of what people might think, even if the woman turned out to be one's sister.

That the disciples were astonished to find Jesus talking with this woman fits their culture. That they said nothing shows their respect for and trust in Jesus (4:27).

Early Ministry in Galilee (Matt. 4:12–22; Mark 1:14–20; Luke 4:14–30)

Matthew and Mark begin their accounts of Jesus' Galilean ministry by summarizing the content of His preaching in a virtual slogan: "Repent, for the kingdom of heaven is at hand" (Matt. 4:17; see Mark 1:15). Simon Peter, Andrew, James, and John immediately accepted Jesus' call. Matthew is particularly interested in the events of Jesus' life that fulfill Old Testament prophecies (Matt. 1:22, 23; 2:5, 6). Both the inception of the ministry in Galilee and its positive reception are for Matthew yet further fulfillments of prophecy (Matt. 4:13–16).

Luke, however, begins his account with Jesus' rejection in the synagogue of His hometown of Nazareth (Luke 4:14–30). This choice may seem a strange illustration that Jesus "taught in their synagogues, being glorified by all" (4:15). Nevertheless, Jesus' reading of Isaiah. 61:1, 2 provides a more extensive summary of His ministry. Although Jesus was met by opposition from the beginning, Luke insists that "Joseph's son" ministered "in the power of the Spirit" (Luke 4:14, 18, 22).

Healing the Sick (Matt. 8:14–17; Mark 1:29–34; Luke 4:38–41)

The brief accounts of the healings of Peter's mother-in-law and of others in the village highlight particular interests of the evangelists. Matthew once again links the details of Jesus' life with Israel's prophetic tradition (Matt. 8:17 cites Is. 53:4).

Mark uses this episode to introduce his theme of the "messianic secret" (Mark 1:43, 44; 3:11, 12). For Mark, only Jesus' death on the cross can reveal what it really means for Jesus to be the Messiah and "Son of God" (Mark 15:39). So in Mark's presentation, Jesus is careful to keep His identity secret so as to avoid the popular misconceptions about what the work of the Messiah would be. For that reason, Jesus "did not allow the demons to speak, because they knew Him" (Mark 1:34).

Cleansing the Leper (Matt. 8:1–4; Mark 1:40–45; Luke 5:12–16)

The cleansing and healing of a leper, an outcast from society, is a second instance of Mark's "messianic secret" theme. Mark highlights two dynamics of Jesus' secret identity. First, those who did not completely understand Jesus' messiahship, supposing Him to be only a miracle worker or healer, could in fact hinder His ability to accomplish His ministry. Because of their reactions, Jesus "could no longer openly enter the city" (Mark 1:45). Second, Mark shows that those whose lives had genuinely been changed by the gospel were not able to contain their excitement and enthusiasm about what God had done for them (see Mark 5:18–20).

Luke's narrative does not mention the leper spreading the news of his cleansing. Perhaps Luke wished to downplay any appearance of the leper disobeying Jesus' instructions. It is enough for Luke to note simply that a report concerning Jesus did spread as a result of this healing (Luke 5:15).

Events in Capernaum (Matt. 9:1–17; Mark 2:1–22; Luke 5:17–39)

Each of the Synoptic Gospels recounts a cluster of exchanges in Capernaum between Jesus and certain Jewish religious teachers. The encounters emphasize the importance of forgiveness in Jesus' ministry, a focus that is established in the opening report of the healing of a paralytic. Jesus used His ability to perform miraculous healings as proof "that the Son of Man has power on earth to forgive sins" (Mark 2:10). Traditional religion believed that God alone forgave sins (Luke 5:21). So Jesus' new offer of forgiveness marked a radical change in God's dealings with humanity.

Eating a meal in a tax collector's house was the occasion to show that God's forgiveness was now readily available to all. Jesus could now fellowship with "sinners" without being tainted by the ritual impurity that concerned the scribes and Pharisees (Luke 5:30). Although Jesus came to call sinners to repentance (Mark 2:17), His ministry was a time to celebrate this forgiveness rather than to fast or mourn (Matt. 9:14, 15).

Jesus' Followers (Matt. 12:15–21; Mark 3:7–19; Luke 6:12–19)

Mark presents the continuing growth of Jesus' ministry by contrasting two groups of His followers: a "great multitude" (Mark 3:7) and the "twelve" (3:14). These groups differ not only in their size, but also in their relationship to Jesus. The exuberance of the multitude remained a potential hazard to Jesus' ministry (3:9), so Jesus continued to silence the unclean spirits that exclaimed His identity (3:11, 12). In contrast to the hindering multitude, Jesus selected twelve men who would "be with Him" and extend His preaching and healing ministry (Mark 3:14, 15).

Luke likewise mentions both the multitude and the twelve, although in the opposite order. He may have placed the multitude last as a transition to his "Sermon on the Plain." The sermon is so-named because it was preached in a "level place" (Luke 6:17). The multitude, along with "a crowd of His disciples," thus became the extended audience for that sermon (6:17, 20).

Matthew mentions only the multitude in this account, having already listed the twelve apostles earlier (Matt. 10:2–4). In keeping with his interest in prophetic fulfillment, Matthew compares Jesus' efforts to limit the spread of His fame to the unassuming attitude of the Servant in the prophecies of Isaiah (Matt. 12:18–21; Is. 42:1–4). Jesus came in humility and gentleness as the prophesied Servant.

Sermon on the Mount or Plain (Matt. 5:1–48; Luke 6:20–36)

The presentations of Jesus' teachings in Matthew's "Sermon on the Mount" (Matt. 5—7) and Luke's "Sermon on the Plain" (Luke 6:20–49) illustrate the so-called "Synoptic problem." There are tremendous similarities between their presentations, but also differences. The name "Synoptic" means that the Gospels view the life of Jesus from a common perspective. Yet the three Synoptic Gospels vary in what material they include and in how they arrange specific events, and such differences are apparent between Matthew's and Luke's record of Jesus' sermons.

Some believe these differences resulted because Jesus repeated His teachings on various occasions and each evangelist provided only a summary of Jesus' teaching in each episode. Thus, Luke's "Sermon" is about a third the length of Matthew's. Others think these differences show that both Matthew and Luke used an earlier collection of Jesus' teachings that did not reveal the original setting in which the teachings were given. Thus, Matthew gathers a number of sayings from this collection or source for his "Sermon on the Mount," whereas Luke independently uses the source in forming his "Sermon on the Plain" and later treatment of prayer (Matt. 6:1). The source is usually called the "Q" source, apparently from the German word *Quelle*, meaning "source."

Matthew had a theological interest in presenting Jesus as a "new Moses" who calls into being the church as a "new Israel." Comparisons with Moses develop this theme. Matthew presents five major sermons by Jesus (Matt. 5—7; 10; 13:1–52; 18; 24; 25), possibly alluding to the traditional "Five Books of Moses." The first of Matthew's sermons is set "on a mountain" (Matt. 5:1) and discusses fulfilling the law (5:17–48), recalling Moses receiving the law on Mount Sinai.

Praying to Our Father (Matt. 6:7, 9)

Jesus cautioned His disciples not to pray "as the heathen do," using "vain repetitions" and "many words" (Matt. 6:7). When Greeks and Romans prayed, they often called deities by as many different names and titles as possible. Also, their prayers frequently reminded the deity of any favors he or she owed the worshiper because of sacrifices the worshiper had offered.

Jewish people, however, were not supposed to barter with God or try to impress Him with titles. They were to approach God with confidence that He was their Father, as the Old Testament taught them (see Ex. 4:22; Is. 63:16). Most children in the ancient world saw their father as a strong provider and protector (with whom they did not need to bargain). Jewish prayers therefore regularly invoked God as "Our Father in heaven" and trusted Him to provide (Matt. 6:8, 9; 7:7–11).

Teaching His disciples to pray (Matt. 6:9, 10), Jesus adapted a fairly common Jewish prayer called the Kaddish that came to be prayed regularly in the synagogues: "Exalted and hallowed be His great name . . . and may He cause His kingdom to rule . . ." This was a prayer for the future kingdom. The Jewish people longed for the ultimate coming of God's reign when He would rule the earth unchallenged and restore justice and mercy in all the world. At that time God's name would be "hallowed," shown to be holy (Ezek. 39:7, 27); people would no longer "profane" it by swearing oaths by it lightly or living in such a way as to dishonor it.

"Hallowing God's name" was a central principle of Jewish ethics: Live even among the Gentiles in such a manner that people will honor God. The reverse of such honorable behavior, "profaning God's name," was considered so odious that some teachers insisted those plotting to do evil should disguise themselves as Gentiles first! Those who would utter this prayer in sincerity—yearning for God's name to be shown holy in the age to come—must live in the present in such a way so as to honor that name now.

How to Understand a Parable (Mark 4:2)

Ancient Jewish teachers often told stories to illustrate whatever moral principle they were trying to communicate. Sometimes these parables had one central point. In other cases, such as Jesus' parable of the sower and the four soils (Mark 4:2–8), parables included several points of comparison.

Sometimes sages would tell a parable or a riddle that hearers would understand only if they had the key to interpretation. Usually only disciples of that teacher who spent enough time with him to learn his teachings would understand his point. This might happen with Jewish teachers who felt that some subjects in particular were best discussed only in private or in very small gatherings.

With some parables, then, the details had symbolic significance. This teaching device was a way of encouraging students to consider deeply the teacher's words and to weed out the uncommitted. The stories conveyed truth to attentive hearers who were eager to understand. At the same time the figurative language sometimes veiled truth from persons who did not want to believe it. While the multitude heard Jesus' parable (Mark 4:1, 2), only His disciples sought its meaning in private (Mark 4:10; Luke 8:9).

Rejection at Nazareth (Matt. 13:53–58; Mark 6:1–6)

Even at the midpoint of His Galilean ministry, Jesus continued to be met with resistance and unbelief in His hometown of Nazareth (see Luke 4:16–30). Mark once again closely connects Jesus' miracles and His teachings: the people wondered "what wisdom" Jesus possessed to be able to perform "such mighty works" (Mark 6:2).

Matthew characteristically maintains more of a distinction between teaching and miracles, speaking of them individually: "this wisdom and these mighty works" (Matt. 13:54). Being attracted to Jesus' miraculous works is not sufficient to make one a true disciple of His. Faith, for Matthew, is crucial, and the limited miracles performed in Nazareth are directly attributed to the people's "unbelief" (Matt. 13:58).

Jesus' Second Visit to Jerusalem (John 5:1–47)

According to John's Gospel, Jesus returned to Jerusalem to attend a pilgrimage feast. It is impossible to identify the "feast of the Jews" (5:1), which forms the setting for this healing account. It could have been Pentecost. John explicitly identified Passover as the occasion for Jesus' previous pilgrimage (John 2:13, 23), and Pentecost is the next feast after the combined festival of Passover and Unleavened Bread. Furthermore, the Feast of Pentecost was traditionally associated with the giving of the law to Moses at Mount Sinai. Thus Jesus' allusions to the writings of Moses (5:39, 45–47) were possibly prompted by the occasion of Pentecost.

Jesus' first Jerusalem pilgrimage might be dated to the spring Passover celebration of A.D. 27 (John 2:13). This second pilgrimage could represent the Pentecost occurring only several weeks later, or be understood as Pentecost of the following year, early summer of A.D. 28. On the other hand, it could have been Passover of spring, A.D. 28 or the Feast of Tabernacles in fall, A.D. 28.

IMMORALITY AND HEROD'S POLITICS (MARK 6:17)

Herod Antipas was the tetrarch of Galilee and Perea (4 B.C.–A.D. 39). Reports of Jesus' works made Herod's guilty conscience remember his crime against John the Baptist (Mark 6:14). John had boldly denounced Herod's immorality in marrying his brother's wife (6:18). The law prohibited adultery and incest; sleeping with one's brother's wife was considered incestuous as well as adulterous (Lev. 18:16). But given his political problems in 1st-century Galilee, Antipas may have viewed John's moral criticisms as a political threat that could stir unrest.

While Antipas was planning to marry his brother's wife, his first wife realized that he was also planning to divorce her. She fled home to her father, Aretas IV, ruler of the Nabatean Arabs, reporting Antipas's intentions. This created friction between the two kingdoms, and Aretas invaded Antipas's kingdom in A.D. 36. He would have destroyed it had not the Romans intervened. Many Galileans felt this defeat was God's judgment on Antipas for executing the Baptist.

This political embarrassment was not the last problem Antipas's liaison with Herodias caused him. When in A.D. 37 her brother Agrippa I was appointed "king" of Gaulanitis, Herodias persuaded her husband Herod Antipas to request the same title. So enraged was the emperor at Antipas for making such a request, however, that he banished him to Gaul in A.D. 39, and Herodias went off into exile with him. The Gospel of Mark ironically refers to Antipas as "King Herod" (Mark 6:14), even though he was technically only a "tetrarch" (Matt. 14:1). Possibly under Herodias's influence Antipas thought of himself as a king.

Controversy over Traditions (Matt. 15:1–20; Mark 7:1–23)

The "tradition of the elders" (Matt. 15:2) contained hundreds of rules, which Jewish teachers had developed over the centuries to ensure that the people properly kept God's law. Jesus called these teachers "hypocrites" because they emphasized the many commandments of their human tradition, being concerned only with outward conduct while they ignored the inner dynamic and moral demands of the law. This is the only episode in which Mark reports Jesus referring to His Pharisaic opponents as "hypocrites" (Mark 7:6). Matthew, by contrast, recounts several such instances (especially in Matt. 23).

The details of this particular controversy show that "hypocrisy" for Jesus was not "saying one thing and doing another." The Pharisees did observe the ritual washings that Jesus' disciples had occasionally neglected (Mark 7:2, 3). In the Jewish literature of this period written in Greek, a "hypocrite" was a godless person who substituted human standards and desires for God's commandments. Thus, when people scrupulously observed traditions that had the effect of countering God's command (Matt. 15:3–6; Mark 7:9–13), they became "hypocrites" not because their actions were inconsistent but because they consistently ignored God's will. Ritual purity cannot cleanse a person defiled by his or her own evil actions (Matt. 15:17–20; Mark 7:15, 18–23).

The Christ and His Disciples (Matt. 16:13–28; Mark 8:27—9:1; Luke 9:18–27)

Peter's confession at Caesarea Philippi, identifying Jesus as "the Christ of God" (Luke 9:20), marked an important milestone in Jesus' ministry. Nevertheless, the disciples still needed to learn much about the nature of Jesus' messiahship, as was demonstrated when Peter rejected Jesus' first prediction of His eventual death and resurrection in Jerusalem (Matt. 16:21–23). They were still focused not on "the things of God, but the things of men" (Mark 8:33).

Jesus' disciples still held the popular conception that the Messiah would bring political and economic success to God's people. Their misconception was exposed by the call for a true disciple to "deny himself, and take up his cross" (Matt. 16:24; Mark 8:34). Thus, Jesus emphasized placing spiritual life ahead of physical life (Mark 8:36). The Son of Man Himself was willing to lose His life to bring spiritual benefit to all.

The Transfiguration (Matt. 17:1–13; Mark 9:2–13; Luke 9:28–36)

Jesus' transfiguration was a visionary revelation (Matt. 17:9) of the divine glory that the Son (Mark 9:7) possessed from His incarnation (see John 1:14). A brief scene in Luke's Gospel clarifies what was at stake, not only in the vision, but in Jesus' ministry: Jesus discussed His "decease" with Moses and Elijah (Luke 9:31). The Greek word translated "decease" (*exodos*) refers in literary Greek to the process of "death." It recalls the "Exodus" from Egypt as an earlier process of divine redemption. Thus, Jesus' impending death and resurrection, also an "Exodus," would further extend God's redemption to humanity.

The Transfiguration by Rafael Sanzio de Urbino, 1518-1520 located in Florence, Italy

JESUS MINISTERS IN GALILEE

A.D. 19 21 23 25 27 29

Tiberius expels all the Jews from Rome
A.D. 19

Pontius Pilate becomes governor of Judea
A.D. 26

John the Baptist baptizes Jesus (Matt. 3:13–17)
A.D. 26

During Passover, Jesus cleanses the temple (John 2:13–15)
A.D. 27

Jesus heals crippled man at Jerusalem feast (John 5:1, 8)
A.D. 28

Jesus teaches at the Feast of Tabernacles (John 7:2, 14)
A.D. 29

FROM GALILEE TO JERUSALEM

The second traditional segment of Jesus' ministry is His journey from His native Galilee toward Jerusalem during the final year of His life. The Synoptic Gospels relate only one visit to Jerusalem by Jesus during His ministry (Matt. 19:1), a visit that ended with His crucifixion. The Gospel of John, however, reports a series of visits corresponding to the traditional Jewish pilgrimage feasts.

Only Luke gives extended attention to Jesus' specific journey from Galilee to Judea. Much of the information about Jesus' ministry that is unique to the Gospel of Luke is found in a large section (Luke 9:51—18:14) in which Luke emphasizes Jesus' ultimate destination (see Luke 9:53; 13:22, 33). Teachings on the meaning of discipleship are given by a Teacher who was moving steadfastly toward the climax of His earthly ministry.

EPOCH EIGHT
Chronological Reading Guide

- ❑ John 7:1—10:21

Attending the Feast of Tabernacles (John 7:1–52)

One of Jesus' several visits to Jerusalem recorded in the Gospel of John was to attend the Feast of Tabernacles. If the unidentified feast of John 5:1 refers to either Passover or Tabernacles of A.D. 28, this Feast of Tabernacles would have occurred during the fall of A.D. 29.

At the time of this celebration of the Feast of Tabernacles opposition to Jesus' ministry continued to mount (John 7:1, 2). Yet John's Gospel shows that Jesus remained firmly in control of the events: His "time" was not governed by the world's schedule, but by the Father (7:6, 8). Jesus refused to be manipulated by His family into revealing Himself before this divinely ordained time (7:3–8), and His opponents failed in their attempt to seize Him "because His hour had not yet come" (7:30).

Jesus used the traditional practices of the Jewish religious festival to set the stage for His message. The Feast of Tabernacles had come to be closely associated with prayers for the fall rains that were necessary to assure a bountiful springtime harvest. On the final day of the festival, the priest would present a special offering of water, along with the daily drink offering of wine, in thanksgiving and prayer to the God who supplies the life-giving rains. It may have been at the very moment of that ritual that Jesus announced, "If anyone thirsts, let him come to Me and drink" (7:37).

Worshipers at the Feast of Tabernacles may have also made associations between the feast and the ancient Israelites' wanderings in the wilderness. In such a case, Jesus could have suggested a connection with the rock that miraculously provided the Israelites with water in the wilderness (Ex. 17:1–6). His promise of "rivers of living water" (John 7:38) is identified by John as referring to the Holy Spirit (7:39).

Discussions with the Pharisees (John 8:12–59)

Another debate with the Pharisees continues Jesus' teaching on the occasion of the Feast of Tabernacles. Given associations between the feast and the Israelites' wilderness wanderings, Jesus' statement, "I am the light of the world" (John 8:12) possibly recalled the presence of God as a pillar of fire leading the Israelites in the wilderness (Ex. 13:21).

The recurring theme of Jesus' discussions was His relationship with God the Father. His use of the phrase "I AM" as a type of personal address (John 8:58) indicates His unique relationship with the Father. Among Jesus' Jewish contemporaries this phrase was understood as an expression of God's personal name (see Ex. 3:14), so for Jesus to claim it for Himself was to claim unity with God.

Put Out of the Synagogue (John 9:22)

In Jesus' day various groups competed for power in Jerusalem. The Sadducees held the most formal power, since they were backed by the Romans. The Pharisees, however, were more popular with the people and often held prominent roles in the Jerusalem synagogues. Ironically, the Pharisees used their control of the synagogues to wield authority over the very people whom they were supposed to be serving.

When Jesus miraculously helped a blind man receive his sight, the people brought the healed man to the Pharisees (John 9:8–13). Because the healing occurred on a Sabbath, the Pharisees were much concerned about Jesus violating their interpretation of Sabbath laws. In their view, a Sabbath-breaker could not have healed anyone by God's power (9:16).

The blind man's parents, being questioned concerning their son's healing, dared not counter the Pharisees' view (9:20–22). John's Gospel makes it clear that the parents feared being "put out of the synagogue" (9:22). This could mean excommunication, exclusion from the synagogue community. Severely erring members of synagogues were sometimes disciplined by beatings or by temporary or long-term exclusion from their synagogues.

By the time John wrote his Gospel, more than 60 years after Jesus' death, Jewish Christians were being threatened with excommunication from their synagogues because of their belief in Jesus as the Messiah. John warns of this conflict (John 16:2). By retelling the time that Jesus healed the blind man and defended him against those who persecuted him for his faith, John encouraged his own readers in their situation: Jesus would be with them as well.

JESUS' FINAL JOURNEY

The Galilean portion of His ministry now completed, Jesus began a journey to Jerusalem to meet His destiny, a destiny of which He was well aware and which He faced willingly (Mark 8:31; 9:30, 31). In the Synoptic Gospels, this journey is Jesus' only visit to Jerusalem, while in John it is simply the last of several journeys. Though the Gospels differ concerning the number of journeys, they necessarily agree that Jesus made a final such journey shortly before His death. About this final journey the Gospels differ only in the amount of information they provide concerning its various events.

By far the greatest amount of information on Jesus' teachings and deeds while on this journey is in the Gospel of Luke. Luke's unique account of the journey from Galilee to Jerusalem (Luke 9:51—18:14) is called his "travel narrative." There are only a few places in the narrative where the other Gospels offer parallels to Luke's version of events, and these occur mostly toward the end of the journey when Jesus is in Judea but has not yet arrived at Jerusalem.

Matthew and Luke report some of Jesus' same teachings, but do so in different settings. While in Luke's Gospel these teachings were spoken on the road to Jerusalem (Luke 9:57), Matthew places most of them earlier in Jesus' ministry (Matt. 8:18, 19). Many scholars believe that most of Luke's information for the travel narrative came from two written sources, one which was apparently available only to him (called the "L" source for "Luke"), and one which was also employed by Matthew (called the "Q" source).

EPOCH EIGHT
Chronological Reading Guide

- ❑ Matthew 8:18–22
- ❑ Luke 9:51–62
- ❑ Matthew 11:20–30
- ❑ Luke 10:1–42
- ❑ Luke 11:37—12:21
- ❑ Luke 12:35—13:17
- ❑ Luke 13:22—14:24
- ❑ Matthew 18:10–14
- ❑ Luke 14:25—16:31
- ❑ Matthew 18:15–35
- ❑ Luke 17:1—18:14

Through Samaria Toward Jerusalem (Matt. 8:18–22; Luke 9:51–62)

Luke begins his account of the journey to Jerusalem with Jesus traveling to Judea through Samaria, the region directly between Galilee and Judea (Luke 9:52). Mark and Matthew do not mention this direct route through Samaria, but rather a route around Samaria through Perea, called "the region of Judea beyond the Jordan" (Matt. 19:1; Mark 10:1).

Luke's report of Jesus' rejection by a Samaritan village (Luke 9:53) reflects the hostility between Jews and Samaritans. Jesus knew that He would face opposition in Samaria and wished to encounter it head-on, demonstrating His courage and His determination to fulfill His destiny in spite of all opposition. The Samaritan encounter also allowed Him to teach His disciples how to handle such opposition, a lesson they surely needed (Luke 9:55).

Since following Jesus would involve rejection and suffering, His followers could not be halfhearted. Both Luke and Matthew record Jesus' teachings that disciples must be completely committed (Matt. 8:20–22; Luke 9:58–62).

Mission of the 70 Disciples (Matt. 11:20–30; Luke 10:1–24)

Jesus sent out a large group of disciples to prepare the way for Him (Luke 10:1). Just as harvest workers must labor with great haste to bring in their crops before it is too late, so too did Jesus instruct these disciples to hurry and not to concern themselves with insignificant matters such as what they would eat or where they would stay (10:7, 8). They would face great opposition along the way, and Jesus instructed them on how to handle being rejected by a town.

Only Luke suggests that Jesus sent out such a large group of disciples. All three Synoptic Gospels agree that Jesus sent out the twelve disciples to preach and to heal (Luke 9:1–6). Luke, however, mentions this second mission with a much larger group of 70 disciples. The other evangelists do not give the impression that Jesus had such a large and devoted group of followers, while Luke presents the "workers" as more plentiful and the "harvest" as more abundant.

Most of the material in Luke's story of the mission of 70 disciples is also found in Matthew. The different sayings of Jesus in Luke 10:1–24 are sprinkled throughout Matt. 9—11 (Matt. 9:37; 10:7–16, 40; 11:20–27). Possibly both evangelists found these sayings in a common source, each choosing to fit them into his account in a different way.

Hypocrisy of the Lawyers and Pharisees (Luke 11:37—12:12)

Jesus' invitation to dine with a Pharisee results in a wide-ranging series of curses directed against His opponents, the scribes (lawyers) and Pharisees (Luke 11:37–52). Jesus condemned the Pharisees for being excessively concerned with trivial matters, such as ritual purity and tithing, while failing to pursue important matters such as social justice and ethical behavior. The lawyers also are denounced for sharing in the perpetuation of injustice, but they are singled out for criticism for their fathers' part in killing the prophets (Luke 11:47).

On this occasion Jesus' opponents began laying a trap in order to accuse Him of some crime (Luke 11:53, 54). By noting this, Luke anticipates Jesus' arrest, trials, and crucifixion, which all the evangelists do in different ways.

Luke presents these sayings of Jesus as a single speech, given while a guest in the house of a Pharisee. While for Luke this event occurred during the journey from Galilee to Jerusalem, Matthew shows Jesus giving these sayings on several occasions, in a different order, and at times both before and after the journey, but not during it.

FINAL MINISTRY IN JUDEA

Luke presents the teachings of his long travel narrative (Luke 9:51—18:14) as taking place while Jesus was on the way from Galilee to Jerusalem. In contrast, Matthew and Mark indicate very briefly that Jesus departed from Galilee and arrived in Judea (Matt. 19:1; Mark 10:1). No direct announcement of Jesus' entry into Judea appears in Luke's Gospel, but Jesus' location "near Jericho" (Luke 18:35), which is in Judea, is a clear sign that Luke's much longer account of Jesus' journey is nearing its conclusion.

The narration of Jesus' ministry in John's Gospel indicates several trips between Galilee and Judea, while Jesus attended the feasts in Jerusalem. Thus much more of John's story takes place in Judea than does that of the Synoptics. Some events of John's account occur in Judea shortly before the last week of Jesus' life, and these can be considered in connection with His final ministry there. Judea was a very dangerous place for Jesus, yet in spite of this danger He continued to preach and heal right up until the time of His arrival in Jerusalem.

EPOCH EIGHT
Chronological Reading Guide

- ❏ Matthew 19:1–15
- ❏ Mark 10:1–16
- ❏ Luke 18:15–17
- ❏ Matthew 19:16–30
- ❏ Mark 10:17–31
- ❏ Luke 18:18–30
- ❏ Matthew 20:1–16
- ❏ John 10:22—11:57
- ❏ Matthew 20:17–28
- ❏ Mark 10:32–45
- ❏ Luke 18:31–34
- ❏ Matthew 20:29–34
- ❏ Mark 10:46–52
- ❏ Luke 18:35—19:27
- ❏ John 12:1–11

No Divorce—Except for Immorality (Matt. 19:3–9)

Two leading schools of Pharisees debated over what constituted appropriate grounds for divorce. The school of Hillel said that divorce was unfortunate, but that a man could divorce his wife for simply burning his toast. By contrast, the school of Shammai declared that a man could divorce his wife only if she had been sexually unfaithful in some manner, either by adultery or some other form of promiscuity.

Jesus entered the debate over grounds for divorce when the Pharisees questioned Him whether a man could divorce his wife "for just any reason" (Matt. 19:3). While the Shammaites objected to divorces based on weak grounds, they never went so far as Jesus. He replied by allowing divorce in only one situation: when the wife had committed "sexual immorality" (19:9). To divorce and remarry for any other reason was, to Jesus, adultery.

Scholars debate what exactly Jesus had in mind by "sexual immorality." Many think that He was referring to incest or other specific forms of immorality. Normally, though, when the term "sexual immorality" appears without explanation it refers to sexual misconduct of any sort. It would be natural in Jesus' culture for Him to comment on marital unfaithfulness in general while speaking of divorce. When ancient divorces went to court, a charge of immorality could determine who got the wife's dowry.

In Mark's and Luke's Gospels, Jesus' prohibition of divorce offers no exceptions—not even that of sexual immorality (Mark 10:11, 12; Luke 16:18). Some scholars understand these sayings to be rhetorical overstatements, a common Jewish teaching technique. Jesus used the technique when commenting on the seriousness of sin (Matt. 5:29) and on loving riches more than God (Matt. 19:24). This would not weaken Jesus' opposition to divorce, but would recognize that He considered the innocent party in a divorce and allowed exceptions for those divorced or betrayed against their will (Matt. 5:32; see 1 Cor. 7:15).

At the Feast of Dedication (John 10:22–42)

John reports that Jesus was in Jerusalem during the Feast of Dedication (Hanukkah). This feast was celebrated in winter (John 10:22), and the particular feast visited by Jesus was probably in December of A.D. 29. It is not clear whether Jesus had remained in Jerusalem during the 2 months since the Feast of Tabernacles or had recently returned to the city.

Jesus disputed with His opponents over two issues concerning His identity. First, they challenged Him to state "plainly" whether He was "the Christ" (that is, the Messiah; John 10:24). The nationalist character of the Feast of Dedication would have encouraged questions about Israel's Messiah. The festival commemorated the rededication of the temple in 165 B.C. by Judas Maccabeus, who had led Judea's war of independence against the Seleucid ruler Antiochus Epiphanes.

Jesus' opponents raised a second issue, charging that Jesus had committed "blasphemy" by making Himself God (10:33). He performed messianic "works" and claimed that these works bore witness to Him (10:25). Jewish leaders would not have considered that claim in itself blasphemous, for they did not believe that the Messiah would be a divine figure. Rather, it was Jesus' claim of a unique relationship with God that sparked their charge: He actually said, "I and My Father are one" (10:30).

JESUS' FINAL WEEK IN JERUSALEM

All four Gospels stress the importance of Jesus' final week in Jerusalem. The account of this week occupies fully the last half of the Fourth Gospel (John 12—21) and roughly the last one-third of both Matthew (Matt. 21—28) and Mark (Mark 11—16). Early in his own Gospel, Luke announces that Jesus "set His face to go to Jerusalem" (Luke 9:51).

As Jesus determined to move steadfastly toward Jerusalem, He thus moved toward His own death. The final week of His life is often called "Passion Week," an appropriate name since the word "passion" is derived from the Latin word for "suffering." Each of the Gospels reveals that Jerusalem was the place where Jesus fulfilled His mission by being handed over to the rulers, dying for the sins of the world, and being raised from the dead on the 3rd day.

EPOCH EIGHT
Chronological Reading Guide

- ❑ Matthew 21:1–11
- ❑ Mark 11:1–11
- ❑ Luke 19:28–44
- ❑ John 12:12–19
- ❑ Matthew 21:12–17
- ❑ Mark 11:12–19
- ❑ Luke 19:45–48
- ❑ Matthew 21:18–22
- ❑ Mark 11:20–26
- ❑ Matthew 21:23–32
- ❑ Mark 11:27–33
- ❑ Luke 20:1–8
- ❑ Matthew 21:33–22:14
- ❑ Mark 12:1–12
- ❑ Luke 20:9–19
- ❑ Matthew 22:15–22
- ❑ Mark 12:13–17
- ❑ Luke 20:20–26
- ❑ Matthew 22:23–33
- ❑ Mark 12:18–27
- ❑ Luke 20:27–40
- ❑ Matthew 22:34–46
- ❑ Mark 12:28–37
- ❑ Luke 20:41–44
- ❑ Matthew 23:1–39
- ❑ Mark 12:38–44
- ❑ Luke 20:45—21:4
- ❑ Matthew 24:1–35
- ❑ Mark 13:1–31
- ❑ Luke 21:5–33
- ❑ Matthew 24:36—25:46
- ❑ Mark 13:32–37
- ❑ Luke 21:34–38
- ❑ John 12:20–50
- ❑ Matthew 26:1–16
- ❑ Mark 14:1–11
- ❑ Luke 22:1–6
- ❑ Matthew 26:17–29
- ❑ Mark 14:12–25
- ❑ Luke 22:7–30
- ❑ John 13:1–30
- ❑ Matthew 26:30–35
- ❑ John 13:31–35
- ❑ Mark 14:26–31
- ❑ Luke 22:31–38
- ❑ John 13:36—17:26
- ❑ Matthew 26:36–56
- ❑ Mark 14:32–52
- ❑ Luke 22:39–53
- ❑ Matthew 26:57–75
- ❑ John 18:1–11
- ❑ Mark 14:53–72
- ❑ Luke 22:54–71
- ❑ John 18:12–27
- ❑ Matthew 27:1–26
- ❑ Mark 15:1–15
- ❑ Luke 23:1–25
- ❑ John 18:28–40
- ❑ Matthew 27:27–31
- ❑ Mark 15:16–20
- ❑ John 19:1–16
- ❑ Matthew 27:32–56
- ❑ Mark 15:21–41
- ❑ Luke 23:26–49
- ❑ John 19:17–37
- ❑ Matthew 27:57–66
- ❑ Mark 15:42–47
- ❑ Luke 23:50–56
- ❑ John 19:38–42
- ❑ Matthew 28:1–8
- ❑ Mark 16:1–8
- ❑ Luke 24:1–12
- ❑ Matthew 28:9–15
- ❑ John 20:1–13
- ❑ Mark 16:9–13
- ❑ Luke 24:13–49
- ❑ John 20:14–31
- ❑ Matthew 28:16–20
- ❑ Mark 16:14–18
- ❑ John 21:1–25
- ❑ Mark 16:19, 20
- ❑ Luke 24:50–53

Sunday: The Triumphal Entry (Matt. 21:1–11; Mark 11:1–11; Luke 19:28–44; John 12:12–19)

Jesus' entry into Jerusalem was hailed by the populace as a decisive event. His foreknowledge of where to find a colt on which He was to ride (Matt. 21:2) indicates that this event played a predetermined role in His mission. Large crowds welcomed Him along the approach down the Mount of Olives to the Kidron Valley and up the hill to the Temple Mount. They chanted a refrain from the Psalms, "Hosanna! 'Blessed is He who comes in the name of the LORD!'" (Mark 11:9; Ps. 118:25, 26).

The Gospel writers capture the full significance of Jesus' climactic arrival in Jerusalem. Both Matthew (Matt. 21:5) and John (John 12:15) interpret the Triumphal Entry according to the prophecy of Zech. 9:9—Jesus is the messianic King coming to His bride, Zion (Jerusalem). He was greeted by the hailing of the multitudes, and the response, John reports, like the raising of Lazarus before, aroused fears of a popular uprising in the minds of the religious leaders who opposed Jesus (John 12:19).

In spite of such acclamation, Jesus wept over the city. Only Luke's Gospel presents Jesus as aware that He would be rejected by the people, and that destruction lay ahead for them (Luke 19:41–44). Such destruction tragically occurred during the Roman occupation of A.D. 70.

Monday: Cleansing the Temple (Matt. 21:12–17; Mark 11:12–19; Luke 19:45–48)

Due to overcrowding in the city, perhaps, Jesus and the disciples stayed with friends in Bethany, a small village over the crest of the Mount of Olives, two miles to the east of Jerusalem (Mark 11:11). In Mark's account, they reentered the city on "the next day" (11:12), thus on Monday, and on this day Jesus cursed the fig tree (11:14) and cleansed the temple (11:15). Matthew's account, however, presents a different sequence: Jesus cleansed the temple while it was still the 1st day (Sunday), and only then retreated to Bethany (Matt. 21:17).

Israel's most solemn festival, Passover, was a pilgrim festival, drawing 100,000 or more pilgrims to Jerusalem each spring. Like other observant Jews, Jesus and His followers arrived early in order to purchase a lamb for slaughter, to procure a place to celebrate the feast, and to undergo the necessary rites of purification.

The commercial ventures of the temple were overseen by the Sadducees and were very lucrative. The commercialization of the temple took place in the Court of the Gentiles, depriving Gentiles of their only place to worship. Jesus justified His attack on the animal dealers and currency exchangers by quoting the prophet Isaiah, "My house shall be called a house of prayer for all nations" (Is. 56:7). Matthew, who writes his Gospel for a primarily Jewish audience, omits the phrase "for all nations," being irrelevant for his audience. Mark possibly includes the phrase to show that Jesus is also Savior of the Gentiles.

Tuesday: Faith and Forgiveness (Matt. 21:18–22; Mark 11:20–26)

As He did after the 1st day (Mark 11:11), Jesus withdrew from the city at the close of the 2nd day also (11:19). Mark's account now indicates the beginning of the 3rd day, "in the morning" (11:20), thus Tuesday. On this day Mark describes the withering of the fig tree (11:21), which Jesus had cursed the previous day. Like Mark, Matthew notes the beginning of a new day "in the morning" (Matt. 21:18). For Matthew, though, this is only the 2nd day (Monday), and the fig tree is cursed and withers on this same day (21:19–22).

Both Matthew and Mark relate the cleansing of the temple to the cursing of the fig tree. The activity in the temple, like the fig tree, had the appearance of life but could be as fruitless as was the greed of the moneychangers. Mark links the two events by recording the cursing of the tree before the temple episode and the withering of the tree after (Mark 11:14, 21). The fig tree was often a symbol of judgment upon Israel in the Old Testament (Jer. 8:13), and Mark uses this symbolism to represent judgment upon the religious observances in the temple.

Discourse While on the Mount of Olives (Matt. 24:1–35; Mark 13:1–31; Luke 21:5–33)

The Kidron Valley falls away beneath the Mount of Olives, leaving a spectacular panorama of Jerusalem and the Temple Mount to the west. The vista from the Mount of Olives provides the setting for a final discourse of Jesus on future events.

The discourse warns of approaching tribulation. The first focus is the near future and the destruction of Jerusalem by the Roman army. All three Synoptics warn of this impending catastrophe, but Luke provides an explicit allusion to the sack of Jerusalem under Titus in A.D. 70, crushing the Jewish revolt.

The second focus of the Mount of Olives discourse is the distant future. "Eschatology" is the technical term in Judaism that refers to events attending the end of time. The destruction of Jerusalem was seen by Jesus and the Gospel writers as a symbol or anticipation of the catastrophes of the end time, before which the Son of Man will return in glory. Jesus' instruction to the disciples on what to say when they are hailed before the authorities is included by Mark and Luke in this eschatological discourse (Mark 13:9–13; Luke 12:12–19). Matthew's Gospel reports these words earlier as part of Jesus' mission instructions to the twelve disciples (Matt. 10:17–22).

The Abomination of Desolation (Mark 13:14)

Matthew and Mark refer to the "abomination of desolation," assuming that their readers will know what it is (Matt. 24:15; Mark 13:14). Modern scholars differ among themselves as to whether this "abomination" will be repeated in the future, but most agree that at least part of it has already occurred. The prophecies of Daniel speak of an abomination that would lead to desolation (Dan. 9:27; 11:31; 12:11). Later writings, such as 1 Maccabees and the Psalms of Solomon, use Daniel's terms to describe the repeated attacks on Jerusalem's temple.

One Jewish historian who lived in the 1st century A.D., Josephus, describes the war of A.D. 66–70 similarly as a desolating sacrilege. Josephus believed that when Jewish patriots slaughtered the priests in the Jerusalem temple, they defiled the temple, hence inviting destruction (see Matt. 23:38—24:2). Early Christian writers tell us that before the Romans closed in on Jerusalem, the Jewish patriots began to seize control of the city, forcing the Christians to flee.

In A.D. 70, just 3½ years after the desecrating slaughter in the temple, the Romans finally took Jerusalem. They slaughtered or enslaved most of the Jerusalemites, but according to Josephus self-proclaimed prophets promised those who were taking refuge in the temple that God would protect the sacred building. But God did not, and after the Romans burned the temple they placed on it their standards, bearing the insignia of the emperor who was worshiped as a god.

Most Jewish people, including the Essenes who wrote the Dead Sea Scrolls, considered the Roman standards to be idolatrous. Some preferred to die rather than allow the standards into Jerusalem. Tragically, the Romans offered sacrifices to their standards on the site of the temple. Judean Jews revolted again in A.D. 132 and were again brutally suppressed by the Romans around 135. After that, the Romans built a pagan temple on the site once reserved for the worship of Israel's God. These acts were truly "abominations."

Plot, Anointing, Betrayal (Matt. 26:1–16; Mark 14:1–11; Luke 22:1–6)

Judas Iscariot, one of the twelve disciples, entered into conspiracy with the chief priests to betray Jesus into their hands. The motive for Judas's betrayal is obscure. As treasurer of the twelve disciples, his person or office may have inclined him to opportunism and even greed (John 12:4–6). Luke (Luke 22:3) and John (John 13:2, 27) ascribe his betrayal of Jesus as the work of Satan. Only Matthew records the betrayal price of thirty silver pieces, recalling perhaps Zech. 11:12 and assuring his readers that this monstrous deed was foreseen by God.

Between the plotting of the Jewish leaders and Judas's betrayal, Matthew and Mark include a story of Jesus' anointing by an unnamed woman of Bethany. A similar though not identical story appears in John's Gospel (John 12:1–8), where the woman is identified as Mary, the sister of Lazarus, from Bethany (12:3). A third anointing of Jesus by a contrite woman who washed His feet with her tears and wiped them with her hair in the house of Simon the Pharisee appears early in Luke's Gospel (Luke 7:36–50).

The exact relation of these stories to each other is uncertain. Luke's story is the most remote from the others. John's story is possibly a different version of Matthew's and Mark's record of the anointing at Bethany, and may even preserve the anointing's more historical placement before the Triumphal Entry. Mark frequently sandwiches two different stories together to achieve a single theological purpose, and the placement of the anointing could have been followed by Matthew.

Mark indicates the timing of the chief priests' plotting: the Passover and Feast of Unleavened Bread were only two days away (Mark 14:1; see Matt. 26:2). Because Mark and John disagree on whether the Last Supper was a Passover meal, it is impossible to know certainly that the Passover was on Friday, and whether "two days before Passover" was thus a Wednesday.

Thursday: Preparation for the Last Supper (Matt. 26:17–29; Mark 14:12–25; Luke 22:7–30; John 13:18–30)

The four Gospels record that Jesus shared a farewell meal with His disciples on the eve of His crucifixion. All of the Gospels agree that Jesus was placed in the tomb on late Friday, immediately before the Sabbath began at sundown. Friday was known as the Preparation Day—the day before the Sabbath (Mark 15:42; Luke 23:54; John 19:31). So the last supper of Jesus with His disciples was eaten on Thursday, the previous night.

The Synoptics present the Last Supper as being the Passover meal. Passover began at sunset with the meal ushering in the new day, the 15th of Nisan. The celebration was the focal point of a week-long festival in Jerusalem commemorating the Exodus from Egypt. Each of the Synoptics relates that Jesus knew where He and His disciples would "eat the Passover," and sent them to prepare (Mark 14:12–16).

In John's Gospel, the Last Supper was not the Passover meal. John does not report Jesus sending the disciples ahead into Jerusalem to prepare the Passover room, nor does he record Jesus' familiar words of institution during the course of the meal (Mark 14:22–25). Rather he suggests that Jesus was crucified on the day before Passover began—"the Preparation Day of the Passover" (John 19:14, 16). In John's sequence, the Last Supper was celebrated on Passover eve, and Jesus was tried the next day while the Jewish authorities themselves were preparing to eat the Passover meal (18:28).

Various suggestions attempt to account for the discrepancy between John and the Synoptics. One possibility is that John's account follows a different calendar. More probably, however, John makes Jesus' death coincide with the sacrifice of the Passover lamb in the temple. This powerfully signifies that Jesus is "the Lamb of God" (John 1:29) who is killed at the same time the lambs are being prepared for the evening Passover meal (19:14).

All four Gospels set the Last Supper in the context of Judas's betrayal of Jesus. In each account, Jesus announces that the betrayer is present among them at the meal. Matthew (Matt. 26:25) and John (John 13:26) specifically identify the betrayer to be Judas. In ancient Judaism, table fellowship was the supreme act of intimacy and trust. Judas's betrayal at a meal—and in the Synoptics, a Passover meal—thus heightens its treachery.

His Body, His Blood, and Passover
(Mark 14:22, 24)

The Synoptic Gospels present Jesus sharing the Passover meal as His last supper with the disciples. He reinterpreted the common elements of the celebration in the light of a new covenant. The unleavened bread became His body (Mark 14:22) and the wine became His blood (14:26).

Customarily, the head of a Jewish household would explain what the elements of the Passover meal meant. When explaining the bread, he would announce, "This is the bread of affliction which our ancestors ate when they came from the land of Egypt." This was one way Jewish people could identify with their ancestors whom God had first redeemed from captivity.

The head of the household normally blessed the bread and wine at other meals as well, but at Passover, when four cups of red wine were drunk, he would lift the cup a handbreadth above the table and recite a special blessing. Jewish men normally sat in chairs for meals, but they reclined on couches in typical Greek fashion when eating at banquets such as the Passover. With their feet pointed away from the center of the room (see Luke 7:38) and their heads more toward the center (see John 13:23), they generally reclined on one elbow, using the other arm to reach the food on the table beside them.

Jesus' remark about the "blood of the new covenant" (14:24) looked back to when God redeemed Israel from Egypt (Ex. 24:8). By His blood being "shed for many," Jesus possibly alluded to the suffering Servant pouring out His life (Is. 53:12). He saw Himself as redeeming His people by His own death.

Jewish people customarily finished their meal by singing more psalms from the Hallel (Ps. 113—118). Likewise, Jesus' disciples sang "a hymn" (Mark 14:26) before departing for Gethsemane, where they would, in the end, desert Jesus.

Jesus' Prayer and Arrest in Gethsemane (Matt. 26:36–56; Mark 14:32–52; Luke 22:39–53; John 18:1–11)

After the Last Supper, Jesus retired to an olive grove in the Kidron Valley. Matthew and Mark call the place "Gethsemane," a Hebrew word meaning "olive press" (Matt. 26:36; Mark 14:32), whereas John simply designates it a garden (John 18:1). There, according to the Synoptic Gospels, Jesus prayed in great anguish and sorrow to be spared the ordeal of crucifixion. But the Father remained silent and the disciples succumbed to sleep.

The Gospel of John omits the account of Jesus' prayerful agony and records only His arrest in Gethsemane. The presence of a "detachment of troops" in the garden (John 18:3) indicates that Roman as well as Jewish authorities were responsible for the arrest. John underscores Jesus' royal authority by recording a hesitancy and trepidation on the part of the soldiers at the moment of encounter (18:4–9).

According to the Synoptic Gospels, the arrest occurred on the heels of Jesus' prayer. Matthew reminds his readers that Jesus was not powerless to prevent His seizure, but allows it in fulfillment of God's will (Matt. 26:52–54; see John 18:11). Mark includes a singular and curious note about a young man fleeing naked in the wake of Jesus' arrest (Mark 14:51, 52). As some have supposed, the Gospel writer is possibly making a disguised reference to himself.

JESUS' PASSION WEEK IN JERUSALEM (A.D. 30)

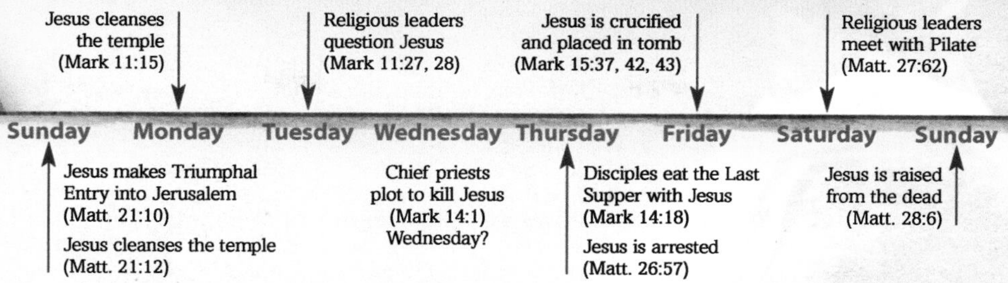

Annas and Caiaphas the High Priests (Matt. 26:57)

Caiaphas was the Jewish high priest at the time of Jesus' crucifixion, exercising an active role in His trial proceedings (Matt. 26:3, 57, 62). However, another high priest, Annas, seems to have been influential at the same time as Caiaphas. Since the office of high priest was usually occupied by only one person, the situation of these two high priests is somewhat perplexing.

The Jewish historian Josephus writes that Annas was appointed high priest by the Romans in A.D. 6 and deposed in A.D. 15. Caiaphas was high priest at a later time, being appointed in A.D. 18 and not deposed until A.D. 36. Caiaphas's approximately 18-year tenure as high priest was a relatively long time compared to most Roman appointees. At any rate, he had a very close relationship with the Roman authorities, which likely explains his long tenure in office.

Luke's writings, both his Gospel and Acts, place Annas's influence as high priest much later than A.D. 15, the date when Josephus states Annas was deposed. Luke names Annas and Caiaphas together as co-high priests in about A.D. 26 (the 15th year of Tiberius; Luke 3:2). Furthermore, Acts 4:6 lists Annas as high priest and Caiaphas as belonging to the family of the high priest, not long after Jesus' death, about A.D. 30 or 31.

Apparently, Annas's influence continued long beyond A.D. 15, the date when he last served officially as high priest. According to Josephus, five of Annas's sons were also appointed high priest at various times. Moreover, John's Gospel informs us that Annas was a relative (father-in-law) of Caiaphas (John 18:13). Possibly Annas retained a position of leadership within the high priestly family, while his son-in-law, Caiaphas, served as the appointed high priest.

Friday: Before Pilate the Governor (Matt. 27:1–26; Mark 15:1–15; Luke 23:1–25; John 18:28–40)

On the morning of the next day, Friday, Jesus faced the second of two trials: a hearing before Pontius Pilate. Pilate was procurator or governor of Judea from A.D. 26 to 36. As might be expected, the charges before Pilate changed from Jewish legal allegations to political allegations, especially that Jesus claimed to be "King of the Jews" (Mark 15:2).

The Synoptic Gospels report that Jesus remained silent during the interrogation, responding only briefly and vaguely to Pilate's questions (Matt. 27:14). John's Gospel, however, relates how Pilate engaged Jesus in reluctant conversation, with Jesus explaining that His kingdom is not of this world (John 18:36).

The hearing before Pilate is augmented by three incidents. Judas's remorse at betraying Jesus resulted in an attempt to return the ransom money, and in Judas's suicide by hanging (see Acts 1:18). Only Matthew includes this story (Matt. 27:3–10), likely to show his Jewish readers a fulfillment of Old Testament prophecy. The Old Testament quotation in Matt. 27:9, 10 is largely from Zech. 11:12, 13, but Matthew may have ascribed it to the better-known prophet Jeremiah because he refers to the buying of a field (Jer. 32:6–9).

A second incident is the warning about Jesus' innocence that Pilate received from his wife (Matt. 27:19). Although Matthew's source for this information is unknown, it effectively heightens Pilate's guilt in the sentencing of Jesus.

Only Luke's Gospel reports the third incident: an additional hearing of Jesus before Herod Antipas (Luke 23:6–12). That Pilate would refer Jesus to Antipas is understandable, since Roman rulers were customarily in Jerusalem during Jewish festivals, and since Jesus came from Galilee, over which Antipas had jurisdiction. Luke may have included this incident because it supported the prophecy of Ps. 2:1, 2, wherein kings and rulers plotted against God's anointed (see Acts 4:25–28).

Pilate deserves no sympathy for his dilemma in sentencing Jesus. As governor, he was authorized with plenary power by Rome, so his weakness and vacillation should not be mistaken for virtue. Josephus recounts Pilate's effective and indeed ruthless use of that power on a number of occasions. By choosing the path of least resistance in Jesus' case, Pilate was responsible for a monstrous evil: the release of a convicted assassin and the condemning of the righteous Son of God to torture and death.

TIME CAPSULE	A.D. 29 to 30
29	Herod Antipas orders the death of John the Baptist
29	Pontius Pilate strikes coins in Jerusalem and Caesarea
29	Jesus attends the winter Feast of Dedication (John 10:22)
30	Jesus makes His Triumphal Entry into Jerusalem
30	Jesus is arrested, tried, crucified, buried, and resurrected
30	Jesus ascends to heaven

Sentenced to Crucifixion (Matt. 27:27–31; Mark 15:16–20; John 19:1–16)

Jesus was delivered by Pilate to be scourged before execution. Commonly practiced before crucifixion, the scourge consisted of a leather whip with bone, rock, or metal in the ends that ripped the flesh from a prisoner's back. Scourging severely weakened a prisoner, thereby hastening death on the cross, or sometimes was fatal itself. In addition to the scourge, Jesus was subjected to the soldiers' mockery about Him being "King of the Jews."

The scourging and mocking took place in the Praetorium. This area, which John identifies as "the Pavement" (John 19:13), functioned as the Roman governor's headquarters. It was often also the governor's residence, and Mark describes it as a "hall" (Mark 15:16). Some think that the Praetorium was located at Herod the Great's palace in the western part of Jerusalem. One archaeologist identified the Praetorium with the square in front of the palace, which Herod built in 23 B.C.

The accounts of Matthew and Mark report Jesus being crucified following the flagellation, but John's Gospel relates a continuation of the hearing (John 19:8–11). The effect of this long hearing before the governor reinforces Jesus' innocence. Pilate appealed for Jesus' release, but ceased such efforts when faced with a new political threat. The governor would not risk accusations of disloyalty to Caesar (John 19:12, 15). In the end, the blame for Jesus' death falls on the religious leaders and the crowd, as well as Pilate.

Crucifixion at Golgotha (Matt. 27:32–56; Mark 15:21–41; Luke 23:26–49; John 19:17–37)

The crucifixion of Jesus is related in all the Gospels with reserve and brevity and without sentimentality. The dominant theme lies on the mockery rather than on the physical suffering of Jesus.

The details of the crucifixion, however, vary in the Gospel accounts more than usual, doubtlessly due to the different theological emphases of the Gospel writers. Only Luke, from his interest in outsiders and the outcast, reports Jesus' compassion on the women of Jerusalem (Luke 23:27–32) and on the repentant thief on the cross (23:39–43). Only Matthew reports the opening of the tombs at the death of Jesus and the entry of the saints into the Holy City. This unusual story (Matt. 27:51–53) may reflect Matthew's purpose of showing that the Old Covenant leads to and is fulfilled by Jesus Christ.

Significant variations are found in the Fourth Gospel. Only John records the argument between Pilate and the chief priests about the sign on the cross reading "The King of the Jews" (John 19:19–22). Only John mentions that Jesus' tunic was not divided (19:24; see Ps. 22:18). Only John tells how Jesus entrusted His mother to the beloved disciple at the cross (19:25–27), an episode that heightens the authority of that disciple in John's Gospel.

Another account unique to John provides a final reminder that Jesus is the true Passover lamb (19:31–37). The soldiers forego the breaking of Jesus' legs, fulfilling the words of Psalm 34:20: "He guards all his bones; not one of them is broken" (John 19:36). The piercing of Jesus' side, at which blood and water flow forth (symbolizing Holy Communion and baptism), further emphasizes that the Christian sacraments originate from and supersede the Jewish Passover celebration.

The Burial of Jesus (Matt. 27:57–66; Mark 15:42–47; Luke 23:50–56; John 19:38–42)

After the crucifixion, Joseph of Arimathea asked Pilate for the body of Jesus. Joseph is presented as a righteous seeker of the kingdom of God (Mark 15:43) and a secret follower of Jesus (John 19:38). Though he was a member of the Sanhedrin, the council that delivered Jesus to the Roman authorities, he did not consent to the council's actions (Luke 23:50, 51). Upon receiving permission from Pilate, Joseph took Jesus' body down from the cross and placed it in a rock tomb near the site of the crucifixion before the onset of the Sabbath. A group of women (Luke 23:55), including Mary Magdalene (Matt. 27:61), observed the burial.

Nicodemus, a Pharisee, came to Joseph of Arimathea to assist in the burial of Jesus (John 19:39). Earlier he had come to Jesus "by night" (John 3:1, 2), possibly because he wished their meeting to be secret. When the Pharisees pushed for Jesus' arrest, Nicodemus argued a legitimate point of law that Jesus deserved a hearing (7:50–52). The plea fell on deaf ears. Appearing only in John's Gospel, Nicodemus is an example of one whose regard for Jesus as a teacher from God was based primarily on Jesus' miraculous signs. He seems to have been sincere in his approach to Jesus, but lacked understanding of the salvation He offered.

Friday was the "Day of Preparation" for the Sabbath (Matt. 27:62). The conference of the priests and Pharisees with Pilate occurred on Saturday, the Sabbath day itself. Only Matthew's Gospel records this incident, revealing the insincere piety of the Jewish leaders: they were so concerned about Jesus' claim to rise "after three days" (27:63) that they were willing to violate the Jewish Sabbath.

Sunday: Morning at the Tomb (Matt. 28:1–8; Mark 16:1–8; Luke 24:1–12; John 20:1–13)

The Gospels agree that Jesus was raised bodily from the dead on Sunday, the first day of the week. They also agree that Mary Magdalene was the first witness of the empty tomb, and most probably of the resurrected Lord. This is an important piece of historical evidence, since the testimony of a woman was of no legal value in ancient Jewish society. Had some early church writers invented a story of the resurrection, they would not have emphasized Mary's witness in the narrative.

Like the crucifixion accounts, the resurrection accounts diverge in a number of particulars. Only Matthew reports an earthquake and the rolling away of the stone from the tomb (Matt. 28:2). Since Matthew also reported an earthquake at the crucifixion (27:51), the second earthquake may show the equal significance of the resurrection. Matthew and Mark speak of one angel at the tomb (Matt. 28:5; Mark 16:5), whereas Luke and John speak of two (Luke 24:4; John 20:12). Matthew and Mark report only the women visiting the empty tomb, while Luke and John tell of a visit by Peter (Luke 24:12), with John relating a footrace between Peter and the beloved disciple to the tomb (John 20:3–8).

The Ascension of Christ (MARK 16:19)

Since His birth in Bethlehem by the miracle of the Incarnation, Christ had lived physically on earth. But 40 days after the resurrection, His earthly ministry ceased with His ascension into heaven (Mark 16:19; Luke 24:50, 51). To a large extent the ascension was for the benefit of Jesus' followers. They could no longer expect His physical presence. They must now wait for the promised Holy Spirit through whom the work of Jesus would continue.

The ascension marked the beginning of Christ's intercession for His followers at the right hand of God. There He makes continual intercession for all believers (Rom. 8:34; Heb. 4:14; 6:20; 7:25). Although Christ is not physically present with His people today, He is no less concerned for them or less active on their behalf. Christians enjoy peace, hope, and security because Christ is their advocate with the Father (1 John 2:1).

The ascension set in motion the coming of the Holy Spirit with His gifts for believers (John 14:16–18, 26; 16:7–15; Acts 2:23; Eph. 4:11, 12). God determined that the presence of Jesus would be replaced by the presence of the Holy Spirit, who could be everywhere at the same time. Jesus' followers now enjoy the presence of the Spirit and the operation of the Spirit's gifts through them.

One additional result of the ascension is that Jesus began His heavenly reign at the right hand of the Father (1 Cor. 15:20–28). This reign will last until His Second Coming, when He will return to the earth as the reigning Messiah (Acts 3:20, 21).

Finally, the ascension of Christ is the pledge of His Second Coming: "This same Jesus, who was taken up from you into heaven, will so come in like manner as you saw Him go into heaven" (Acts 1:11). Jesus will return to earth in bodily form just as He ascended into heaven.

THE CHURCH AGE

A.D. 30—100

The beginning of the church is a fascinating story of the Holy Spirit at work, leading the followers of Jesus into new ways and new worlds. The period from roughly A.D. 30 to 100 saw the glory of the first Pentecost, the struggle of the church to organize for mission, the conversion of Saul (Paul), the mission to the Gentiles, and the spread of the faith to Rome, Alexandria, and Antioch (the three greatest cities of the Roman Empire). Dozens of other cities and villages in Asia Minor, Greece, and Egypt would hear the Good News concerning the Man of Nazareth: "This Jesus God has raised up" (Acts 2:32).

As the gospel spread beyond Judea to Samaria and the Gentile world, many converted to the belief that "Jesus Christ is the Son of God" (Acts 8:37). The new believers met with opposition. Gentiles called these disciples of Christ by the name "Christians" (Acts 26:28; 1 Pet. 4:16), but did so with an element of scorn. Another scornful label for the early Christian movement was "the Way" (Acts 19:9). The term was appropriate, though, for Christ had made a "new and living way" for people to enter into the presence of God (Heb. 10:20).

ARCHAEOLOGY AND THE PAST

Archaeological finds from this period are a rich treasure, even when narrowly restricted to those directly connected with the church. The most significant of the riches are those associated with Jerusalem and the journeys of Paul.

In Jerusalem are two inscriptions that possibly reflect this period. The Theodotus Inscription, discovered on the hill known as the Ophel, describes a synagogue built specifically for visitors and immigrants from abroad. This Ophel synagogue has been identified with the Synagogue of the Freedmen, some of whose members opposed Stephen (Acts 6:9). A second inscription once stood in the temple, marking the boundaries beyond which Gentiles were not permitted to go, on pain of death. A crowd accused Paul of bringing a Gentile into the temple, in direct violation of this ban (Acts 21:28).

The destruction of Jerusalem by the Romans in A.D. 70 left ruins, some of which have remained. The most famous of these is a restored room from the lowest floors of the home of a member of one of the high priestly families, the house of Kathros. The Christians left Jerusalem at the outbreak of the Jewish revolt in A.D. 66 and went to Pella (modern Jordan), escaping the destruction of the city. They returned after the war and built a church under the leadership of Simeon, a cousin of Jesus. Many archaeologists believe that a small part of that church can still be seen today, behind what is called "David's Tomb."

Archaeological treasures abound in the cities of Paul's journeys. In Antioch of Pisidia, for example, is the *Monumentum Ancyranum*, on which is carved the deeds of Augustus Caesar and the hope for universal peace. Christianity was able to spread quickly in a Roman world because of the Roman peace. The excavated city square in Antioch featured a temple of the Anatolian god Men, showing that Christianity existed also in a cosmopolitan world, steeped in ancient cultures and religions, all under the aegis of Rome.

The ancient city of Ephesus has remains that reflect Paul's long ministry there. The temple and the statues of the Greek goddess Artemis, who became identified with the Roman goddess Diana, help explain why the Ephesians might riot when the worship of Artemis was threatened by Christianity. In Asia, Artemis assumed characteristics of the mother goddess, and her temple was one of the Seven Wonders of the ancient world, still magnificent in ruins. Also among the excavations in Ephesus were a collection of papyri with magical formulas written on them. The ancient world was much taken with magic, used both as a blessing and a curse, and the papyri recall the magic books that were burned during Paul's time (Acts 19:19).

The accounts of Paul's travels mention his experiences in the agora, or marketplace, of two cities. Philippi was a trading city; and Lydia, one of Paul's converts, likely operated her business (she bought and sold expensive purple cloth) near what is now the ruins of the agora (Acts 16:14, 19). The ruins of another agora still exist in Athens, where Paul first encountered the Athenian philosophers (Acts 17:17).

Archaeological finds are rich in Corinth, in the city that existed in Paul's day. Corinthian ruins include the marketplace and a stone bench identified as the bema, the judgment seat where Paul was brought before the proconsul Gallio. Also from Corinth is an inscription mentioning Gallio. Everywhere he went, Paul was in touch with Roman authorities, either because he was in trouble with them, or because they were protecting him, or both. Inscriptions from Corinth identify the meat market, and also name "Lucian the butcher." Butchers and meat markets recall Paul's writing to the Corinthian church over the issue of eating meat from the market that had been sacrificed to idols (1 Cor. 10:25).

The ruins of Rome, Paul's final destination, are overwhelming, and remind us of the persecution that the church endured. The Colosseum was the site of athletic events, chariot races, and gladiatorial combats. It is quite likely that Christians lost their lives there, thrown to the lions or other forms of torture. The magnificent arch of Titus is a monument to the Roman victory over the Jews and the destruction of Jerusalem. On it are carved Roman soldiers carrying the menorah (the golden lampstand) and table from the temple. The catacombs, or underground cemeteries, of Rome remind us that Christians were an illegal organization, and they often met in secret in the cemeteries.

THE PEOPLES AND GROUPS

The whole New Testament story unfolds under the reign of emperors of the Roman Empire, which reached the height of its power from about A.D. 100 to 175. Of the various emperors who ruled during the New Testament period, Claudius was responsible for expelling the Jews from Rome (Acts 18:2), and Nero was the emperor to whom Paul appealed his case (Acts 25:11). The destruction of Jerusalem was accomplished in the year A.D. 70 by the Roman general Titus, who later became emperor himself.

Christianity developed amongst a rich mixture of religious cults represented in the Roman world. The most striking feature of Roman religion was its ability to merge the best features of several religions. As the empire expanded, it imported and assimilated many religious ideas and pagan gods from Greece and the Orient. Roman gods were fused and identified with the gods of the Greeks. Buildings, temples, and monuments to these gods were erected. Astrological beliefs and magical practices flourished.

An "imperial ruler cult" developed in the 1st century B.C. when the Roman Senate voted to deify Julius Caesar and to dedicate a temple to his honor. Among all the emperors, only Julius Caesar, Augustus, and Claudius were deified. This phenomenon apparently had more political than religious meaning.

THE BIBLICAL LITERATURE

The beginnings of the Christian church are related in the Book of Acts, the letters of Paul, and the general letters that make up the rest of the New Testament. Acts might more accurately be called the "Acts of the Holy Spirit," for Luke shows the role of the Spirit in guiding and strengthening the church. The Spirit's activity is prominent in the founding of the church through the work of Stephen, Philip, Peter, and especially Paul.

Paul's letters are the oldest Christian documents we have and make up the bulk of the New Testament. Galatians was possibly the earliest letter. Shortly thereafter are 1 and 2 Thessalonians, written on Paul's second missionary journey, and 1 and 2 Corinthians and Romans, written on the third journey. The letters of Ephesians, Philippians, Colossians, and Philemon all give indication of being written in prison. The letters of 1 and 2 Timothy and Titus are called the Pastoral Epistles, addressing not churches, but pastors. Paul's letters tell us a great deal about the problems the churches faced as a result of their faith; opposition came from outside (pagan and public hostility) and from inside (heresies and persons struggling for position and power).

The General Epistles and the Book of Revelation tell us most of what we know about the early church beyond Paul. Hebrews was written to Jewish Christians. It emphasizes the humanity of Jesus, His perfect sacrifice, and His bringing forgiveness to all. The letter of James reminds Christians that real faith leads to faithful living, affecting the little acts of daily life.

The key to 1 Peter is hope in Christ, even in times of persecution. It was written for the church in Asia Minor, and may originally have been a treatise on the meaning of baptism for daily life. The letters of Jude and 2 Peter were written to counter false teachers. The early church expected Jesus to return at any minute, and 2 Peter calls on the church to live faithfully in anticipation of that return. Jude reminds its readers that God's grace is not an excuse for immoral living.

Of the three letters associated with John, 1 John is a sermon, calling for a return to the fundamental of the faith: Jesus came in the flesh for our salvation. Of the two letters written by "the Elder," 2 John emphasizes the commandment to love, while 3 John is a warning against a false teacher (already appearing in the church!).

The Book of Revelation calls the church to be faithful and stand firm. In the great cosmic struggle between good and evil, a struggle in which Christ will prevail, faithful Christians will share in His final triumph.

THE GOSPEL TO THE JEWS

Under Roman rule the Jews were given a special status with certain legal rights. They were permitted to practice their own religion and to build their synagogues. They also were exempt from military service and were not required to appear in court on the Sabbath. Relationships between the Jews and the Romans were mostly positive. The birth and development of Christianity took place among the Jews and within the borders of the Roman Empire. In its early years, Christianity was regarded by Rome as a sect of Judaism and was thus ignored.

The Gospels ended with an emphasis on the ascension of the risen Christ (Mark 16:19, 20; Luke 24:50–53). The Book of Acts opens with special attention to this important event in Christian history (Acts 1:1–11). The eleven apostles, and many other Jewish believers, were joyous after witnessing the Ascension. Yet they were at a loss to know what to do next, other than selecting a successor to Judas. All this mingling of hope and uncertainty vanished at Pentecost.

Henceforth, with courage and power, they gave witness to their conviction that Jesus was alive. Their claim was confirmed by undeniable miracles performed in His name (Acts 4:14). The witness of these Christians brought consternation to persons responsible for Jesus' death. Those who killed Him thought they had disposed of Him. Now His authority and power were stirring Jerusalem more than ever. There was intense opposition led by Saul of Tarsus and the rulers in Jerusalem. Yet the gospel spread rapidly to Judea, Samaria, and the entire Mediterranean world.

EPOCH NINE
Chronological Reading Guide

- ❑ Acts 1:1—8:3

THE BOOK OF ACTS

The Book of Acts is the second of a two-volume set, the first volume being the Gospel of Luke. Both books are addressed to Theophilus and written by one of Paul's associates named Luke "the beloved physician" (Col. 4:14). The author of Acts was a companion of Paul in many of his journeys, as implied by his use of the pronoun "we" to indicate he was traveling with Paul (see Acts 16:10). He was also with Paul during his imprisonment in Rome (2 Tim. 4:11).

Luke shows the link between what he reported in his Gospel and what he now reports in this book: the events of Jesus' ministry are the foundation for the results obtained by the message of His Spirit-inspired witnesses. Since the risen Christ was not seen in public, the burden of proof for the resurrection event lay with those who had firsthand experience of His post-resurrection appearances (see 1 Cor. 15:4–8). The Gospels, Acts, and Paul's letters go to great lengths to convince the reader that Jesus' appearances were not fantasy or the result of wishful thinking, but rather "hard evidence" that calls for faith.

The date of Luke's writing is not easily determined. The author possibly concluded his account 2 years after Paul's imprisonment in Rome, about A.D. 62 (Acts 28:30). Luke writes to Theophilus (meaning "lover of God"), who was probably a prominent Gentile believer.

OUTLINE OF ACTS

I. The Witness in Jerusalem	**1:1—8:3**
A. The Power of the Church	1:1—2:47
B. The Progress of the Church	3:1—8:3
II. The Witness in Judea and Samaria	**8:4—12:24**
A. The Witness of Philip	8:4–40
B. The Conversion of Saul	9:1–31
C. The Witness of Peter	9:32—11:18
D. The Witness of the Early Church	11:19—12:24
III. The Witness to the Ends of the Earth	**12:25—28:31**
A. The First Missionary Journey	12:25—14:28
B. The Jerusalem Council	15:1–35
C. The Second Missionary Journey	15:36—18:22
D. The Third Missionary Journey	18:23—21:14
E. The Trip to Rome	21:15—28:31

The Day of Pentecost (Acts 2:1–47)

The Day of Pentecost came 50 days after the offering of the firstfruits (Lev. 23:10, 15, 16) at the Passover observances. It was a celebration of the wheat harvest, with pilgrims gathering from various nations of the Roman world. The crowd included Jews living outside of Palestine, as well as proselytes (Gentiles who had accepted the Jewish faith). Luke lists their homelands beginning in the East (Acts 2:9), then in Asia Minor (2:9, 10), and on to other Mediterranean areas—North Africa, Rome, and Crete (2:11).

Less than 2 months had passed since Jesus had been executed. In a sermon to the crowd on this occasion, Peter solemnly charged the Jewish leaders with crucifying the "Man attested by God," their Messiah. Yet while they were responsible, Jesus' death was no accident: He was "delivered by the determined purpose and foreknowledge of God" (Acts 2:22, 23).

The Early Christians in Jerusalem (Acts 3:1—5:42)

The healing of the lame man (Acts 3:1—4:31) and the miraculous deliverance of Peter and John from prison (5:12–42) are examples of the witness of the early Christians in Jerusalem. This witness brought them into conflict with the Jewish authorities, for the "notable miracle" performed by the disciples (4:16) was done publicly and therefore placed the religious leaders in an embarrassing position. The people had accepted the explanation given by the disciples—God had healed the lame man.

While the early Christians lacked temporal resources, they were not short on spiritual power. Some people supposed that these followers of Jesus were just another sect of Judaism or were trying to start a new mystery religion around Jesus of Nazareth. But miracles were convincing others that the disciples were truly serving God, so the temple officials moved to suppress the people's interest in the new religion. One Pharisee, the highly respected Gamaliel, suggested that this movement might fail, as had the movement led in A.D. 6 or 7 by the insurrectionist Judas the Galilean (Acts 5:37–39).

Food for the Hellenist Widows (ACTS 6:1)

Tensions developed in the Jerusalem church over alleged discrimination on the basis of language and culture. Scholars differ in their descriptions of the two opposing groups: the "Hebrews" and the "Hellenists." The Hebrews are often described as Aramaic-speaking Jews native to Palestine. The Hellenists were possibly Greek-speaking Jews from outside of Palestine. Most Jews in Jerusalem, however, would have spoken Greek as at least one language, so more likely the Hellenists were Diaspora (foreign) Jews who had settled in Jerusalem.

Widows were a disadvantaged segment of ancient society, invariably poor and easily oppressed. Jewish people traditionally cared for the widows and other poor through the charity collections of local synagogues. The Hellenist synagogues, however, probably had more widows to care for than other synagogues, and were stretched to the limit in their capacity to help. Since it was considered pious to spend one's last days in Jerusalem, many foreign Jewish men moved to Jerusalem when they retired, eventually leaving an inordinate number of foreign Jewish widows needing support.

This broader societal problem spilled over into the church: how would they care for the foreign Jewish widows among them? And how could they be sure to keep this minority group within the church from feeling second-class? Most people in antiquity simply told offended minorities to be quiet, but the apostles had a different solution: they selected members of the Hellenist minority to run the food distribution program. All seven of those selected have Greek names (6:5), suggesting that all or most were foreign Jews. These seven Hellenists were commissioned for the office of charity distributor, a highly respected position in Jerusalem (6:6).

Stephen, the First Martyr (Acts 6:1—8:3)

The synagogue was a local assembly of Jews who met for prayer and scripture exposition. In cities throughout the Roman world, synagogues became the focal point of Jewish life. The Synagogue of the Freedmen included Greek-speaking (Hellenist) Jews whose ancestors had been slaves of the Romans, later set free. Thus Stephen, a Hellenist himself, was accused of blasphemy by those of his own cultural group.

Stephen was ultimately brought before the Sanhedrin ("the council," 6:12), which consisted of religious leaders from the various Jewish sects in Jerusalem. There he spoke on a theme that was not well received by his audience: Israel's rejection of God's leaders had now climaxed in the Jewish authorities' rejection of Jesus. Further, he used the history of Israel to show that God does not dwell in the temple (7:44–50). Stephen's execution sometime around A.D. 32 marked the beginning of "a great persecution" against the early Christians (7:57—8:3). A young Pharisee named Saul, who served as custodian for Stephen's executioners (7:58), would lead that persecution.

Stoning of Saint Stephen
Kölner Dam
Cologne, Germany

THE GOSPEL TO THE GENTILES

Following Jesus' ascension in rapid succession was Pentecost and the birth of the church, as distinct from a mere Jewish sect. Thousands of Jews became believers. This new church met in the temple courts and the Jewish synagogues, as well as in private homes of believers (Acts 5:42). Yet the Good News would not be contained in Jerusalem; soon it was taken to the Samaritans and to the "God-fearers" in Caesarea and Antioch (10:2; 11:19, 20).

God Himself made it clear that Gentiles should be included in His church. Philip was sent and directed by an angel (8:26) and by the Spirit (8:29) to the desert region near Gaza where he made the first Gentile convert, a court official who served Candace, the queen of the Ethiopians. An angel also directed the Roman officer Cornelius to send for Peter (10:3, 5). By a vision (10:9–16) and by the Spirit (10:19) Peter was instructed to go.

As Peter preached on Jesus' resurrection, the Holy Spirit fell upon the Gentiles. This miracle of divine grace was God's gift to the Gentile believers and His answer to those who questioned sharing the gospel with non-Jews. Eventually, the Jerusalem church acknowledged acceptance of Gentiles (11:18), and Antioch became a center of the Gentile church (11:26). Nevertheless, the first non-Jews to be evangelized by the early church were the Samaritans.

EPOCH NINE
Chronological Reading Guide

❑ Acts 8:4—12:25

Philip and the Samaritan Pentecost (Acts 8:4–40)

Philip "preached Christ" to the Samaritans (Acts 8:5) in fulfillment of his Master's mandate (Acts 1:8). Their reception of Philip's message about the kingdom of God and about Jesus Christ was a significant step in the spread of the gospel. Samaritans, who were considered heretics by orthodox Jews, had received Christ. Perhaps the Samaritans accepted the gospel more readily than Jews because they did not have to unlearn previous misconceptions about the coming Messiah. As the apostles continued to preach in many villages of Samaria, Samaritans became an accepted part of the church (8:25).

TIME CAPSULE	A.D. 30 to 36
30	Jesus ascends to heaven
30	The Day of Pentecost
32	Philip the evangelist preaches to an Ethiopian official
34	Saul is converted
35	Saul preaches Christ in Damascus
36	Pontius Pilate recalled to Rome for misconduct
36	Caiaphas is deposed from the high priesthood

CANDACE'S EUNUCH BELIEVES (ACTS 8:27)

This Ethiopian eunuch represents a significant conversion to Christianity. With him, the Christian faith reached out to a distant land south of Egypt, to someone who exercised "great authority" as the treasurer "under Candace." Candace is not a personal name, but a title, like pharaoh. As the pharaoh was king of Egypt, so the candace was queen of Meroe, a kingdom on the Nile River south of Egypt. It was common in Eastern countries for eunuchs to hold positions of high authority in a queen's court.

More importantly, the gospel reached out to one who previously was an "outsider" to Israel's religion. Eunuchs were excluded from religious service in Israel (Deut. 23:1). The law prohibited them from serving as priests, who were required to have a whole body, free from blemishes (Lev. 21:17–20). The eunuch could worship in Jerusalem and read the sacred Scriptures (Acts 8:28), but could not be a full member of the Jewish religion.

Who Was the God-Fearing Cornelius?
(Acts 10:1, 2)

Caesarea Maritima, the coastal city and home of Cornelius, served as the capital for the province of Judea. As such, the city contained the residence for the Roman governor of Judea, as well as a regular Roman garrison (Acts 10:1). A legion of the Roman army was comprised of ten cohorts; five cohorts of about 600 soldiers each were stationed at Caesarea, while another cohort remained garrisoned on the Temple Mount in Jerusalem.

Centurions, such as Cornelius, commanded units that generally averaged 80 men. In contrast to high-class Romans who aspired to higher offices, centurions usually began as regular soldiers and worked their way up through the ranks. Army service for males usually began around age 17, and roughly half of the enlisters who survived the required 20 years of service were highly rewarded.

The devout Cornelius (10:2) was a member of the "God-fearers," a class of religious people named in many ancient Jewish sources. God-fearers, while not full converts to Judaism, did respect Israel's God and His teachings. Inscriptions reveal that many soldiers were interested in foreign religions such as Judaism.

"Christians" in Antioch (Acts 11:26)

When Barnabas came to Antioch, he found a group of people who were already disciples of Jesus Christ as Lord (Acts 11:22–24). Soon Saul joined Barnabas, teaching many disciples in the city. It is here in Antioch that these disciples were identified with the term "Christian," a term appearing only here and twice elsewhere in Scripture (Acts 26:28; 1 Pet. 4:16).

The word "Christian" is commonly assumed to be of Latin derivation, being found in the 2nd-century A.D. writings of such Latin authors as Tacitus, Suetonius, and Pliny the Younger. Pliny, the Roman governor of Bithynia and Pontus, writes around A.D. 111 to the emperor Trajan that those who admitted to being "Christians" were thus persecuted.

But the Romans were probably not the first to refer to certain people as "Christians." In the 1st century, followers of a certain leader were identified by attaching the ending "-ians" to the leader's name. Thus the followers of Herod were called "Herod*ians*" (Mark 3:6).

There is no evidence that the followers of Jesus used the term to describe themselves. In fact, the other two occurrences of the term "Christian" in Scripture seem to imply an element of scorn. In Acts 26:28 Agrippa does not really intend to become a "Christian" himself, and in 1 Pet. 4:16, Peter possibly speaks of those who were suffering precisely because they claimed to be "Christians."

THE GOSPEL TO THE GENTILE WORLD

The entire Book of Acts is an expansion and fulfillment of the promise "you shall be witnesses...in Jerusalem...Judea and Samaria, and to the end of the earth" (Acts 1:8). The gospel had already spread beyond Judea to the Samaritans (8:5), to an Ethiopian (8:27), to God-fearing Gentiles in the household of Cornelius (10:44, 45), and to Hellenists at Antioch (11:20). In the remainder of the account of Acts, Luke describes how the gospel was carried into the Gentile world. This new initiative was begun by the church at Antioch sending out Barnabas and Saul (13:2, 3).

The change of thrust toward pagan non-Jews rather than to skeptical Jews is made clear by Paul's announcement in Antioch of Pisidia: "we turn to the Gentiles" (13:46). Paul (Saul's Roman name) now focused his strategy on Gentile evangelism. His sermons, as recorded in Acts, indicate the way the Good News was presented to Gentiles (13:16–41) and to a sophisticated audience (17:22–31), emphasizing the activity of the Holy Spirit and the power of Jesus' resurrection.

The great increase of Gentile converts caused alarm among many of the Jewish Christians in Judea. They feared that too many Gentiles would hurt the character of the church. Militant Jewish nationalists were already beginning a movement to require Gentile converts to become circumcised and follow the Jewish law. The stage was set for a Jerusalem conference of church leaders (Acts 15); the problem was how to reconcile the new communities of believers with the customs of Jewish law.

EPOCH NINE
Chronological Reading Guide

- ❑ Acts 13:1—15:35
- ❑ Galatians 1:1—6:18
- ❑ James 1:1—5:20
- ❑ Acts 15:36—18:11
- ❑ 1 Thessalonians 1:1—5:28
- ❑ 2 Thessalonians 1:1—3:18
- ❑ Acts 18:12—19:22
- ❑ 1 Corinthians 1:1—16:24
- ❑ Acts 19:23—20:1
- ❑ 2 Corinthians 1:1—13:14
- ❑ Acts 20:2, 3a
- ❑ Romans 1:1—16:27
- ❑ Acts 20:3b—21:16

PAUL BECOMES A MISSIONARY

A.D. 30 — 35 — 40 — 45 — 50

- Saul is converted on road to Damascus (Acts 9:1–9) A.D. 34
- Saul, called Paul, visits Arabia (Gal. 1:17) A.D. 35
- Saul escapes from Damascus (Acts 9:23–25) A.D. 37
- Riots break out between Jews and Gentiles in Alexandria A.D. 38
- Barnabas and Saul carry relief to Jerusalem (Acts 11:27–30) A.D. 44
- Paul, Barnabas, Judas, and Silas are sent to Antioch (Acts 15:22–31) A.D. 49
- Paul and Barnabas attend the Jerusalem Council (Acts 15) A.D. 49

Multicultural Prophets at Antioch (Acts 13:1)

Five leaders are named as prophets and teachers in the church at Antioch of Syria: Barnabas, Simeon, Lucius, Manaen, and Saul (Acts 13:1).

Simeon and Manaen are common Jewish names. Simeon's surname "Niger" was a frequent Roman name, making it possible that he, like Saul (Paul), was a Roman citizen. On the other hand, "Niger" seems to be a nickname rather than his birth name, and its Latin meaning ("black") could suggest that Simeon was descended from North African converts to Judaism.

Manaen had been "brought up" (13:1) with Herod Antipas, the tetrarch of Galilee. This phrase sometimes described those who shared the same wet nurse, meaning that Manaen possibly had been a high-status servant in the royal household. When slaves grew up with a master's son, the two often became close, and the son often freed the slave after inheriting him. In this case, Herod Antipas had already lost his position when the emperor banished him to Gaul in A.D. 39.

Lucius was a common Greek name, but that does not determine his ethnic background. Many Jews had Greek names, especially outside Palestine. Cyrene, his place of origin, had a very large Jewish population, so Lucius was possibly a Hellenistic Jew.

The other named Antioch prophets were Barnabas, a Levite who originated from Cyprus (Acts 4:36), and Saul, the Pharisee from Cilicia (Acts 22:3; 23:6). The combined cultural backgrounds of these five individuals brought to the church a diversified staff of prophetic leaders.

Conference in Jerusalem (Acts 15:1–35)

The many Gentiles won to Christ precipitated the Jerusalem Council, where it was decided that circumcision would not be required of Gentile Christians. Attempts to place this conference chronologically are complicated by apparent differences between Luke's description of the event and Paul's account in Gal. 2:1–10. The most notable difference in the accounts is the issue of circumcision itself. In Luke's account, circumcision is the central concern. In Paul's account, circumcision was at best incidental to the conference. If the issue had been decisively settled there, he could have simply appealed to the "apostolic decree" (Acts 15:23–29) when he was disputing with the Judaizers in Galatia.

Several suggestions have been offered for relating Luke's and Paul's accounts. A first proposal holds that, despite the differences, the similarities between Acts 15 and Gal. 2 suggest that these accounts are two reports of the same event. A second proposal, though, identifies the events described in Gal. 2 with Paul's second visit to Jerusalem, correlating that visit with the famine-relief trip mentioned in Acts 11:27–30. (Paul's first visit to Jerusalem is mentioned in Gal. 1:18.) In both of these views, the Jerusalem Council is usually dated around A.D. 49.

A third proposal arises because during Paul's final visit to Jerusalem, James appeared to inform him for the first time about the ruling of the conference (see Acts 21:17–25). So, it is supposed, Paul was not at the meeting during which the decision regarding circumcision of Gentiles was reached. In this view, the events described by Paul in Gal. 2 are usually associated with the visit to Jerusalem mentioned in Acts 18:22, and dated about A.D. 52.

THE LETTER TO THE GALATIANS

The most crucial factor in dating the letter to the Galatians is the relationship between the journey of Paul to Jerusalem mentioned in Gal. 2:1 and the Jerusalem Council mentioned in Acts 15. If the decision of the council in Acts 15 had been common knowledge when the letter was written, Paul would surely have used the council's decision in defense of Gentile freedom and especially in his rebuke of Peter (Gal. 2:11–13). It is therefore possible that Galatians is Paul's earliest letter and was written by A.D. 49 just prior to the Jerusalem Council of Acts 15. Those who associate Paul's account in Gal. 2:1–10 with the Jerusalem visit mentioned in Acts 18:22 date this letter to about A.D. 53, and thus after the Thessalonian letters.

The destination of this letter to Galatia was a group of churches that Paul himself had founded (Gal. 1:2, 8, 9; 4:19). His close relationship with them is reflected in 4:11–14. Until the 18th century most readers understood "Galatia" to be the territory in the heart of Asia Minor whose boundaries included Bithynia and Pontus on the north, Phrygia on the southwest, and Cappadocia on the east. However, the Book of Acts offers no record of Paul evangelizing in this "North Galatian" area, apart from brief hints (Acts 16:6; 18:23).

The "South Galatian" theory understands Galatia to refer to the Roman province of Paul's day, which included Pisidia, Lycaonia, and parts of Phrygia and Cappadocia. Also included were the cities of Antioch, Lystra, Derbe, and Iconium that Paul visited on both his first (Acts 13; 14) and second (Acts 16) missionary journeys.

OUTLINE OF GALATIANS

I. Defense of the Gospel of Grace	**1:1—2:21**
A. Introduction	1:1–9
B. Divine Source of Paul's Gospel	1:10–16
C. Apostolic Confirmation	1:17—2:21
II. Gospel of Grace Explained	**3:1—4:31**
A. Holy Spirit Is Given by Faith	3:1–5
B. Abraham Was Justified by Faith	3:6–9
C. Justification Is by Faith	3:10—4:11
D. Blessings Come by Faith	4:12–20
E. Law and Grace Cannot Co-exist	4:21–31
III. Gospel of Grace Applied	**5:1—6:18**
A. Position of Liberty	5:1–12
B. Practice of Liberty	5:13–15
C. Power of Liberty	5:16–26
D. Performance of Liberty	6:1–10
E. Conclusion	6:11–18

Christians of Antioch in Syria (Gal. 2:11)

The city of Antioch in Syria was founded by the first Seleucid king, Seleucus I (c. 300 B.C.). Situated on the Orontes River, its size varies from an estimated 200,000 to 600,000 inhabitants. According to the Jewish historian Josephus (A.D. 37–100), the city also had a substantial Jewish population (*Antiquities of the Jews*, 12.119).

The Roman general Pompey took Antioch in 64 B.C. and declared it a free city. It then became the capital of the Roman province of Syria and the third largest city in the empire. The extant buildings, temples, aqueduct, masonry works, hippodrome, and gridlike street plan of Antioch attest to its great importance.

This great city became a center for Christianity. Many believers fled there after the stoning of Stephen and preached to Antioch's Jewish population (Acts 11:19). The Antioch Christian community prospered and soon faced the task of unifying its Jewish and Gentile members. For a year Barnabas and Paul taught these believers, who were the first to be called "Christians" (Acts 11:25, 26). That this church had ample resources can be seen by their sending relief to the Jerusalem church (Acts 11:27–30).

Abba, Father (Gal. 4:6)

Following some Old Testament models, Jewish prayers often addressed God as "Father," "our Father," or "our Father in heaven." They normally avoided, however, the more familiar title "Abba." Children called their fathers "Abba," a title of endearment, intimacy, and respect. Adults continued the practice, though apparently less frequently, again emphasizing the intimacy of the father-child relationship. Jesus' use of this title in prayer (Mark 14:36) demonstrated His distinctive intimacy with the heavenly Father, an intimacy that provided the model for those who followed Him by the Spirit (Rom. 8:15).

Jesus' native language was Aramaic (a Semitic language related to Hebrew), and *abba* is an Aramaic word. The Gospels, however, were written in Greek rather than in Aramaic, "Abba" being one of the few original Aramaic words preserved in a Gospel. What is most surprising is that Paul's Greek-speaking readers in Galatia already knew what "Abba" meant (Gal. 4:6). The Roman readers especially (Rom. 8:15) could not have learned this from Paul since he had not visited Rome before writing his letter there. Possibly the early Christians picked up Jesus' use of "Abba" to represent the intimacy with God which Jesus had provided for them as well.

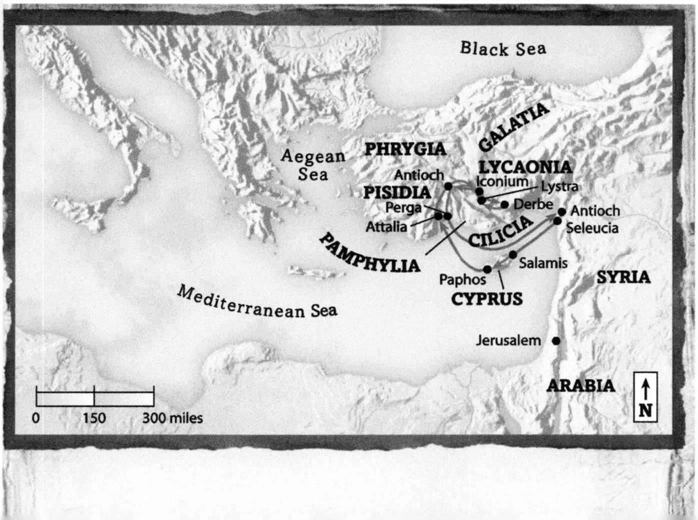

Paul Goes to Galatia

Paul and Barnabas were sent out from the church at Antioch to the cities of Galatia in Asia Minor. This first missionary journey (Acts 13; 14), setting out around A.D. 46, took them to Cyprus, and then to Pisidian Antioch, Iconium, Lystra, and Derbe. The Jewish synagogues in these cities provided Paul a platform for preaching the gospel. Only when rejected by the Jews did Paul and Barnabas turn to the Gentiles with the gospel (Acts 13:46).

THE LETTER OF JAMES

The writer of this letter identifies himself only as "James, a bondservant of God and of the Lord Jesus Christ" (1:1). The name "James" has usually been identified with the James who led the church in Jerusalem (Acts 15:13). Paul referred to this James as "the Lord's brother" (see Mark 6:3) and included him among the "apostles" (Gal. 1:19). He also characterized him as one of the "pillars" of the church (Gal. 2:9). When Peter left Palestine (Acts 12:17), James seems to have become the leader of the Jerusalem church.

Since the early centuries, however, there has been disagreement about whether James, the Lord's brother, actually wrote this letter. There are no allusions to a personal relationship with Jesus, and indeed Jesus is only mentioned twice (James 1:1; 2:1). Both the quality of the letter's Greek and the structure of its arguments have suggested to some that the author was a Hellenistic Jew rather than a Jew from Palestine. If so, then the letter is pseudonymous, and the actual author associated the work with James the Just (as he was later known) by using his name. It is also possible the letter was written by a Hellenistic Jew actually named "James," who is otherwise unknown to us.

No evidence determines exactly when the letter was written. Scholars who believe the letter to be an authentic work of James the Just necessarily date it before his martyrdom in A.D. 62. Since the letter does not hint at any controversy over the issue of circumcision, some would date it around A.D. 45, before the Jerusalem Council. Others, however, would place it late in James's life after the controversy had diminished. Those who view the letter as pseudonymous usually date it in the last quarter of the 1st century (c. 75–100).

OUTLINE OF JAMES

I. The Test of Faith	**1:1–18**
A. The Purpose of Tests	1:1–12
B. The Source of Temptations	1:13–18
II. The Characteristics of Faith	**1:19—5:6**
A. Faith Obeys the Word	1:19–27
B. Faith Removes Discriminations	2:1–13
C. Faith Proves Itself by Works	2:14–26
D. Faith Controls the Tongue	3:1–12
E. Faith Produces Wisdom	3:13–18
F. Faith Produces Humility	4:1–12
G. Faith Is Dependent upon God	4:13—5:6
III. The Triumph of Faith	**5:7–20**
A. Faith Endures	5:7–12
B. Faith Prays for the Afflicted	5:13–18
C. Faith Confronts the Erring	5:19–20

Various Trials of the Poor (James 1:2)

The letter of James seems especially to address the trials of the poor (James 1:2), suggesting a right response to poverty and suffering. In Judea at this time, wealthy Sadducean priests were seizing the tithes that rightfully belonged to the poorer priests. In Galilee, rich landlords were repressing the poor peasants who worked on their estates. Similar situations existed throughout much of the Roman Empire, where poverty, repression, and violence were the standard fare of the day.

The letter of James was written to encourage Christians who were suffering. The opening prologue summarizes the appropriate responses to their trials, responses that the rest of the letter discusses: wisdom (1:5), faith (1:6–8), and endurance (1:9–11). The letter also describes tensions between the rich and the poor: The wealthy are arrogant against the poor (2:1–4), and even repress them (2:6, 7) and withhold their wages (5:4). Yet the poor are advised not to retaliate with violence in deed (4:1, 2) or, perhaps more tempting, in words (4:11; 5:9).

TIME CAPSULE	A.D. 37 to 44
37–41	Caligula is emperor of Rome
37–44	Herod Agrippa I
37–100	Life of Jewish historian Josephus
37	Saul visits Jerusalem, then goes to Syria
39	Herod Antipas is deposed and sent into exile
41	The Roman army declares Claudius emperor
44	Herod Agrippa I dies suddenly in Caesarea

PAUL BEFORE THE AREOPAGUS (ACTS 17:19)

In A.D. 50 Paul visited Athens and began preaching in the agora, the marketplace that served as the center of public life in ancient Greece (Acts 17:17). Paul was summoned by the Athenians to the Areopagus, where he preached his sermon about the "unknown God" (Acts 17:19–23). The purpose of his visit to the Areopagus and its council is not certain, but he may have been on trial to defend his beliefs. We know of one individual from the Areopagus council, Dionysius, who became convinced of the truthfulness of Paul's message (Acts 17:34).

The Areopagus was a prominent hill in Athens (nearly 400 feet high) that was associated with the Greek god of war, Ares. Although ancient references to the council of the Areopagus are few, it is evident that it was an aristocratic body that advised the king. It then assumed royal functions after the Athenians deposed their monarchy (sometime before 800 B.C.). With the rise of democracy in 500 B.C. the council lost some of its power and became largely an esteemed group with religious functions.

By the 1st century A.D. the council of the Areopagus had regained much of its former authority. The assembly to which Paul preached was again the chief governing body in Athens, a position it would keep until the advent of Christian domination in the 4th century A.D.

THE FIRST LETTER TO THE THESSALONIANS

Paul, Silas, and Timothy came to Thessalonica on Paul's second missionary journey (Acts 17:1–9). Paul's stay at Thessalonica was brief, at most only a few months. From there he went to Berea (17:10), on to Athens (17:15), and then to Corinth (18:1). From Athens Paul sent Timothy to encourage the Thessalonians, and when Timothy returned to him at Corinth, the apostle was overjoyed at the news of the strong faith of the Thessalonians. From Corinth he wrote the first Thessalonian letter in late A.D. 50 or early 51. First Thessalonians is one of the earliest of Paul's letters, and thus it is also one of the first books in the New Testament to be written.

Thessalonica, now called Salonika, was an ancient Greek city, the capital of the Roman province of Macedonia. Paul began his ministry there in the Jewish synagogue; however, the church that resulted included not only Jews, but also a number of devout Greeks and many leading women. Many Jews of Thessalonica did not become believers, and the synagogue rulers eventually rejected Paul and drove him from the town (Acts 17:10).

Paul did not have the time in Thessalonica to instruct his converts as thoroughly as he would have liked. Thus, in this letter he wanted to express his joy at their steadfastness, encourage them in the midst of suffering, and correct misconceptions about the Lord's return.

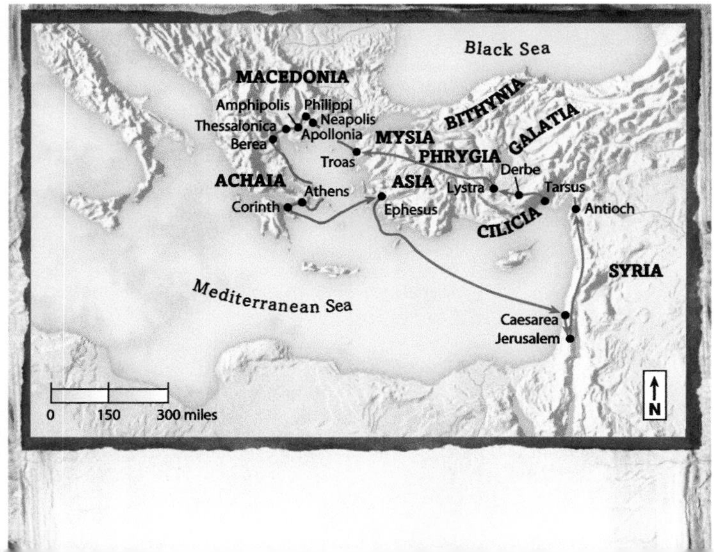

Paul's Second Missionary Journey

Paul's second missionary journey took him back to Asia Minor, then over to Europe to the cities of Philippi (Acts 16:11–40), Thessalonica (17:1–9), Berea (17:10–15), Athens (17:16–34), and Corinth (18:1–17). Most scholars agree that this trip ended about A.D. 52 when Paul returned to Antioch (18:22), but the beginning of the trip is variously dated between 46 and 50.

A disagreement between Paul and Barnabas over whether John Mark should accompany them on the new mission resulted in two missions instead of only one (15:37–40). Barnabas and Mark went one direction, while Paul ministered with Silas throughout this journey (15:40), with Timothy joining them at Lystra (16:1–3). The gospel spread further as Paul came into contact with Roman authorities and Greek philosophers.

OUTLINE OF 1 THESSALONIANS

I. Paul's Personal Reflections	**1:1—3:13**
A. Praise of Their Growth	1:1–10
B. Founding of the Church	2:1–16
C. Strengthening of the Church	2:17—3:13
II. Instructions to the Thessalonians	**4:1—5:28**
A. Directions for Growth	4:1–12
B. Concerning the Dead in Christ	4:13–18
C. The Day of the Lord	5:1–11
D. Holy Living	5:12–22
E. Conclusion	5:23–28

Pictures of the End Time (1 THESS. 4:16)

The "voice of an archangel" and the "trumpet of God" (1 Thess. 4:16) emphasize the divine authority behind Paul's description of Jesus' return. The images and pictures Paul uses for the end time overlap with those of other Jews of his time, though he omits most elements found in contemporary Jewish descriptions. What Paul does describe especially matches Jesus' picture of the end time (trumpet, clouds, angels, times and seasons, sudden destruction).

Jewish readers familiar with the Old Testament recognized the importance of trumpets for gathering the assembly, sometimes to battle. Gentile readers probably knew the Roman use of trumpets to gather troops or to send signals in battle. Most relevant, Jewish tradition, as emphasized in a daily synagogue prayer, portrayed the gathering of Israel in the end time as accompanied by the sounding of a trumpet.

The highest archangel, according to Jewish tradition, was Michael (Dan. 10:13), who was also the special patron for Israel. Each nation had a guardian angel, but Michael was especially powerful, as the guardian of God's chosen people. Jewish traditions sometimes gave Michael special prominence in the final battle; though, for Paul, Jesus fulfilled this function Himself (1 Thess. 4:16).

The "shout," conjoined with the trumpet, may picture the battle cry offered by a commander. The Old Testament sometimes portrays God as a divine warrior, occasionally mentioning His battle cry (Is. 42:13).

Jesus' teaching about the end time (Matt. 24) is probably the background for Paul's own teaching, which he claimed was by "the word of the Lord" (1 Thess. 4:15). As Jesus described the coming Son of Man, He applied to Himself a variety of end-time descriptions that the Old Testament and Judaism normally reserved only for God (Matt. 24:30, 31). Similarly, Paul applies these same descriptions to the coming Christ.

THE SECOND LETTER TO THE THESSALONIANS

It appears that several issues Paul addressed in 1 Thessalonians were still very much alive when the second Thessalonian letter was written: the suffering of Christians, idleness, and the Lord's return. Thus, Paul could have written this letter from Corinth a few months after writing 1 Thessalonians, probably late in A.D. 51.

While both letters are very concerned with the Second Coming of Christ, some scholars question whether Paul is the author of both. In 1 Thessalonians, Paul was so certain of the nearness of Christ's return that he anticipated both himself and some of the Thessalonians being alive to see it (1 Thess. 4:15). A somewhat different view is expressed in 2 Thessalonians. Several specific events, some involving "the man of sin," must transpire before the Lord's coming (2 Thess. 2:1–12). Those who are convinced that Paul's theology about the end of time could not have changed to this degree in only a few months conclude that 2 Thessalonians is a pseudonymous letter. Some later writer, writing sometime after Paul's death (A.D. 80–100), but using his name (2 Thess. 3:17), addressed mounting concerns about the delay in Christ's return.

OUTLINE OF 2 THESSALONIANS

I. Paul's Encouragement in Persecution	**1:1–12**
A. Thanksgiving for Their Growth	1:1–4
B. Encouragement in Affliction	1:5–10
C. Prayer for God's Blessing	1:11-12
II. Paul's Explanation of the Day of the Lord	**2:1–17**
A. Events Preceding	2:1–12
B. Comfort of the Believer	2:13–17
III. Paul's Exhortation to the Church	**3:1–18**
A. Wait Patiently for the Lord	3:1–5
B. Withdraw from the Disorderly	3:6–15
C. Conclusion	3:16–18

Paul Before Gallio (Acts 18:12–22)

The emperor Claudius Caesar (A.D. 41–54), while favorable toward the Jews early in his reign, later forbade their assembly. Suetonius, a Roman historian, indicates that Claudius "expelled from Rome the Jews, who were constantly rioting under the leadership of Chrestus." Two Jewish refugees affected by this expulsion (which is dated in A.D. 49 by Orosius, a church historian) were Aquila and Priscilla. Luke records that when Paul stayed with them in Corinth, they "had recently come from Italy" because of Claudius's edict (Acts 18:2, 3).

During a period of 18 months Paul established a flourishing Christian congregation (18:11). In A.D. 51 he was brought before Gallio, the Roman proconsul of Achaia (southern Greece). The archaeological remains of Gallio's judgment hall have now been discovered. Perhaps more important, however, is an inscription found at Delphi that mentions Gallio and fixes his brief proconsulship over Achaia (about one year) in A.D. 51–52. The likelihood, then, that Paul founded the church in Corinth in A.D. 51 is one of the most certain points for establishing the chronology of Paul's ministry.

TIME CAPSULE	A.D. 46 to 52
46–120	Life of Plutarch, Greek philosopher
46	Beginning of Paul's first missionary journey
49	Paul and Barnabas attend the Jerusalem Council
49	Claudius expels Jews from Rome
50	Beginning of Paul's second missionary journey
51	Paul appears before Gallio
52	Paul preaches in the school of Tyrannus in Ephesus

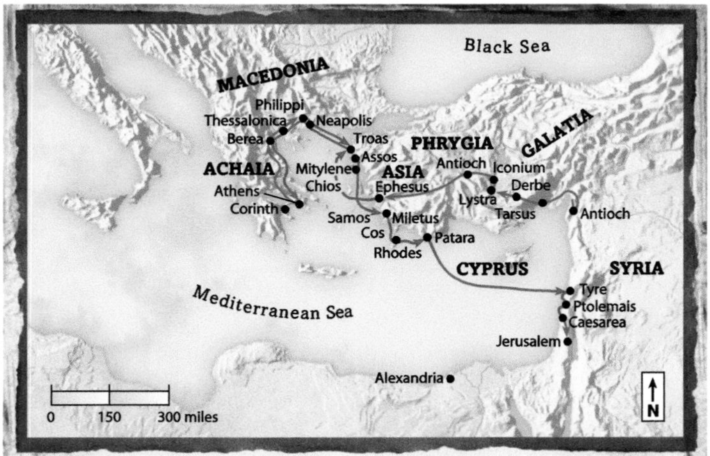

Asia and Greece Revisited

On Paul's third missionary journey (Acts 18:23—19:22) he visited the places in Galatia and Phrygia (Acts 18:23) that he had evangelized on his first journey. He also revisited Macedonia and Greece (20:1–3), evangelized on his second journey. But the focus of the third journey was Ephesus in western Asia Minor (19:1—20:1). Here the gospel dramatically overturned paganism and its magic (Acts 19:23). This journey concluded with Paul's fateful trip to Jerusalem (21:1–14).

Paul taught daily in Ephesus as he had done in Corinth. Ephesus was the political and religious center of the province of Asia, so visitors, as well as residents, heard and shared the gospel. After teaching for 3 months in the Jewish synagogue, Paul retreated to the school of Tyrannus (19:8, 9). Luke indicates a long ministry for Paul over a 2-year period (19:10), while his total stay in Ephesus lasted approximately 3 years (20:31), usually dated from A.D. 52 to 55. One result of this Asian ministry was the planting of the church at Colosse by Epaphras (see Col. 4:12).

THE FIRST LETTER TO THE CORINTHIANS

The apostle Paul is almost universally recognized as the author of 1 Corinthians. In the letter, probably written about A.D. 55 during the third missionary journey, he remarked, "I will tarry in Ephesus until Pentecost" (1 Cor. 16:8). Since he was planning his departure, he probably wrote 1 Corinthians during the last of his 3 years in Ephesus (Acts 20:31).

Corinth had been founded as a Roman colony during the century before Christ. It was strategically located in the Roman province of Achaia on a narrow strip of land between the Aegean Sea and the Adriatic, with two adjoining ports. Corinth's location made it a center of the trade routes passing from east to west. Prosperity brought luxury and immorality. The expression "To live like a Corinthian" to one Athenian writer meant living in gross immorality.

The church that Paul had established in Corinth during his second missionary journey (Acts 18:1–17) was very diverse, including men and women, rich and poor. The report from Chloe's household informed Paul of divisions in the church; they were developing conflicting loyalties to different human teachers (1 Cor. 1:10–13). He wanted them to understand that salvation is not based on human wisdom or personalities, but on Christ crucified and the work of God in building His church.

OUTLINE OF 1 CORINTHIANS

I. In Answer to Chloe's Report of Divisions	**1:1—4:21**
A. Introduction	1:1–9
B. Report of Divisions	1:10–17
C. Reasons for Divisions	1:18—4:21
II. In Answer to Reports of Immorality	**5:1—6:20**
A. On Incest	5:1–13
B. Concerning Litigation	6:1–11
C. Warning Against Sexual Immorality	6:12–20
III. In Answer to the Letter of Questions	**7:1—16:24**
A. Counsel Concerning Marriage	7:1–40
B. Counsel Concerning Spiritual Liberty	8:1—11:1
C. Counsel Concerning Public Worship	11:2—14:40
D. Counsel Concerning the Resurrection	15:1–58
E. Counsel Concerning Giving	16:1–4
F. Conclusion	16:5–24

PATRONS, CLIENTS, AND PUFFED-UP CHRISTIANS (1 COR. 4:6)

In a patronage system, social power and status was not so much based on wealth, but on friendships. The greater the number and status of those friends who owed you honor, the more your influence increased in the society. Having friends in high places helped "broker" situations into results that were desired. Of course, this led to great social competition between clients of different patrons and between the patrons themselves. To whomever a person "belonged" could determine how much access that person had to what the Greco-Roman world offered.

This seems to be the background for the divisions in the church at Corinth. Rather than one church, the body of Christ, the Corinthians seemed to think of themselves as clients of specific Christian leaders. Perhaps they even saw these leaders as special "brokers" to God.

Apparently, inner-church patronage systems led to competition, even jealousy and quarreling within the church. By allowing their conduct to mirror the surrounding social world, these puffed-up Corinthian Christians were in danger of fragmenting their fragile unity (1 Cor. 4:6). Paul saw these divisions as a sign of the spiritual immaturity of these believers. Ultimately, for Paul, not patronage, but cooperation mattered in the church, for it was neither the planter nor the waterer, but God who provided "the increase" (1 Cor. 3:8).

Paul's Authority and Epistle (1 Cor. 5:1—6:20)

Paul addressed three specific areas in which the Corinthians had rejected his authority: They had condoned incest by one of their members (1 Cor. 5:1–13), compromised their Christian witness by suing one another in the secular courts (6:1–11), and allowed some of their members to visit prostitutes (6:12–20). In an earlier letter (5:9), he had already written to the Corinthians dealing with some of these matters.

This "earlier letter" would necessarily have predated what is now known to us as 1 Corinthians. Some scholars believe it may be preserved in what is now known as 2 Corinthians (supposing that 2 Corinthians itself is made up of parts of several letters). Others, though, point out that sexual immorality—the topic of the earlier letter (1 Cor. 5:9)—is addressed only in 2 Cor. 12:21. They conclude that this "earlier letter" was simply not preserved, perhaps being lost by the early church.

DIVORCE AND REMARRIAGE AT CORINTH (1 COR. 7:15)

Jewish law permitted only the husband to initiate a divorce. Only under extreme circumstances could the wife request a court to compel a husband to divorce her. By contrast, Roman law viewed marriage as a matter of mutual consent and so dissolved a marriage if either party requested it. Under Roman divorce, the children went to the father. Rapid remarriage was customary and society encouraged it (especially for young women), so the church congregation in Corinth probably included some new converts who had been remarried one or more times before their conversion.

Paul addressed the Christians who wanted to divorce spiritually incompatible spouses. Offering his own judgment, he contended that spiritual incompatibility did not provide adequate grounds for a divorce (1 Cor. 7:12–14). In addition, by giving the command of "the Lord" (1 Cor. 7:10, 11), he seemed to cite Jesus' general prohibition of divorce (Mark 10:11, 12).

Ancient interpreters commonly qualified general principles, modifying or interpreting them to account for specific situations. In this manner Paul interprets Jesus' general principle as needing to be qualified for those who are divorced against their will. In cases in which an unbelieving mate deserted the marriage, Paul declared, the believer was "not under bondage" (7:15).

In using the phrase "not under bondage," Paul was echoing the exact language of ancient divorce contracts, which spoke of marriage as "binding" a woman to her husband and divorce as "loosing" or "freeing" a woman for remarriage. Such divorce terminology appears in Jewish texts, such as the Mishnah, and in actual 1st-century Jewish divorce contracts that have been recovered. Ancient readers would have understood "not under bondage" as Paul's permission for an abandoned person to remarry.

Covering a Woman's Head (1 Cor. 11:5, 6)

Proper conduct in worship is expressed in different ways in different times and places. Paul was concerned that the conduct of women at the church in Corinth was not following the then current customs for public worship (1 Cor. 11:5, 6). Accepted social custom called for Jewish and Christian women to cover their hair.

Customs varied somewhat. Lower-class women in much of the Mediterranean world covered their heads, especially in the eastern Mediterranean. Far to the east, conservative women veiled even their faces; in most other places, they simply wore a shawl that covered their hair. Many ancient texts inform us why married women needed to cover their heads: hair was the crown of the woman's beauty, and for a wife to expose this to the public gaze was to act promiscuous.

Not all women in Corinth were this conservative, however. Upper-class women were especially prone to showing off their hairstyles. Because the Corinthian churches met in well-to-do members' homes, affluent and poorer women came into contact with one another, producing a clash of different views concerning covering their heads. To one group, uncovered heads represented progressive freedom; to the other, ostentation and seduction.

Paul thus faced a serious conflict in the church that had to be addressed gently. Arraying a variety of arguments—some traditionally Jewish, some more in keeping with Greco-Roman moralists' tastes—he acknowledged the Corinthian women's freedom but called on them to use it responsibly for the sake of others who might stumble. Those who might still be contentious about this issue should bow to custom: other Christian churches did not allow women to worship with uncovered heads; neither should the Corinthians (11:16).

Ask at Home, Not at Church (1 Cor. 14:34, 35)

Although specific conditions varied from one part of the ancient Mediterranean to another, the Roman world valued the quietness and subordination of wives. Some writers even longed for earlier days when Roman matrons had been even more quiet and submissive. Paul appears to be respecting the culture of his time when he says, "Let your women keep silent in the churches" (1 Cor. 14:34).

The specific sort of quietness Paul intends is debated. It is doubtful that he calls for *absolute* silence of women in church, because he permitted prayer and prophecy under appropriate conditions (1 Cor. 11:4, 5). Suggestions as to what Paul was prohibiting women from doing include teaching Scripture or judging prophecy (14:29). But the only clue in his letter points to the asking of questions (14:35). Possibly Paul exhorted the women to ask their questions privately rather than publicly.

In ancient lecture settings, including Jewish teachers who expounded Torah, the Law, hearers learned more by asking questions than by simply listening. Yet, as Plutarch wrote in *On Lectures*, it was considered rude for the unlearned to ask questions because their questioning slowed everyone else down. Women were on the whole far less educated than men (although exceptions existed) and prone to ask less educated questions. An additional problem for a place such as Corinth may have been the cultural impropriety of women asking questions in what was normally a male-dominated lecture setting.

What is striking in view of 1st-century culture is not Paul's limitation of the Corinthian women but his concern for their learning. Only rarely did ancient writers exhort husbands to take an interest in their wives' education. When writers did suggest instructing wives, they sometimes added words like, "For if left to themselves, women produce only base passion and folly." Paul's concern that husbands take an interest in their wives' learning was among the more progressive voices of his day.

Roman road through ancient Corinth

Paul Versus the Goddess Diana
(Acts 19:24–28)

The Ephesian silversmith Demetrius incited a riot against Paul for preaching in Ephesus that gods "made with hands" are not really gods (Acts 19:26). Ephesus had as many as a quarter million inhabitants, making it the largest city in the province of Asia. Its size was reason enough for Paul to found a church in Ephesus, but another significant factor was religion: Ephesus was the cult center for the worship of Artemis or Diana.

Artemis was a very popular Greek goddess. In Greek religion she was the virgin goddess of the hunt and the moon, and the daughter of the Greek god Zeus. In Roman religion she was identified as the goddess Diana.

Part of what made Artemis important to Ephesus was her temple. It was the largest temple in Asia Minor (modern Turkey). The top of the platform it was built on (that would be the floor of the temple) was 168 feet, 9 inches wide by 365 feet, 9 inches long. The columns were 6 feet in diameter and almost 58 feet tall. By comparison, the floor of the Parthenon at Athens was only about two-thirds the size of the temple at Ephesus, and the Parthenon's columns were only a little more than 34 feet high.

The temple of Artemis was one of the Seven Wonders of the ancient world. Its size and magnificence made it an attraction for tourists and pilgrims. For Ephesus, it was a place for worship, but also a treasury and a storehouse.

Paul took on a sizable opponent in Diana or Artemis. She had become the guardian deity of Ephesus. She influenced the politics, culture, and economy of the city. The people of Ephesus were prepared to defend Artemis against any who would threaten her, and Paul's gospel threatened to destroy the profit of the craftsmen who made silver shrines of the goddess.

THE SECOND LETTER TO THE CORINTHIANS

The letter of 2 Corinthians was written perhaps 6 months to a year after Paul wrote 1 Corinthians, possibly in A.D. 55 at the end of his long ministry in Ephesus (Acts 20:31). The Corinthian church required Paul's continual care. Shortly after his founding mission in Corinth, he sent a letter instructing the church "not to keep company with sexually immoral people" (1 Cor. 5:9). Later, a delegation from Corinth came to Ephesus asking for Paul's guidance; they returned, possibly carrying the letter of 1 Corinthians with them (1 Cor. 16:17–19). Timothy visited Corinth (1 Cor. 4:17; 16:10, 11) and probably returned to Paul in Ephesus with news of opposition to Paul and continued division in the church.

Such unchristian practices in Corinth required correction. Paul made a "sorrowful" visit (2 Cor. 1:23—2:1), which did not resolve these problems. He then sent a "severe" letter delivered to the Corinthians by Titus (2 Cor. 2:3–5). When finally Paul was reconciled to the church, he wrote to them both to celebrate their restored relationship and to have them prepare for yet another visit (2 Cor. 1:13–16).

Scholars disagree over whether 2 Corinthians is a single letter or it was compiled from several shorter letters. Some think there were four letters: Paul's "earlier" letter (1 Cor. 5:9); 1 Corinthians; the "severe" letter (2 Cor. 2:3); and 2 Corinthians. In this case, 1 Corinthians would have been the second letter Paul wrote to the Corinthian church; and 2 Corinthians, at least the fourth. Thus, one option is to accept that 2 Corinthians was originally written as it now appears in the New Testament, and suppose that the "earlier" letter against sexual immorality and the "severe" letter have been lost.

An alternative is to suppose that the "earlier" letter, warning against sexual immorality, is part of 2 Corinthians. Similarly, the four final chapters (2 Cor. 10—13) are considered to be the so-called "severe" letter, the letter written "out of much affliction and anguish" (2 Cor. 2:4). Those favoring this option point to a marked contrast: the positive relationship between Paul and the Corinthians evidenced in the early chapters of 2 Corinthians versus Paul's harsh attacks on some in Corinth in 2 Cor. 10—13.

OUTLINE OF 2 CORINTHIANS

I. Paul's Explanation of His Ministry	**1:1—7:16**
A. Introduction	1:1–11
B. Explanation of His Change of Plans	1:12—2:13
C. Paul's Philosophy of Ministry	2:14—6:10
D. Paul's Exhortation to the Corinthians	6:11—7:16
II. Paul's Collection for the Saints	**8:1—9:15**
A. Example of the Macedonians	8:1–6
B. Exhortation to the Corinthians	8:7—9:15
III. Paul's Vindication of His Apostleship	**10:1—13:14**
A. Paul Answers His Accusers	10:1–18
B. Paul Defends His Apostleship	11:1—12:13
C. Paul Announces His Coming Visit	12:14—13:10
D. Conclusion	13:11–14

LETTERS OF COMMENDATION (2 COR. 3:1–3)

Western culture has a long history of personal references. Without phones or faxes, the typical recommendations in the Greco-Roman world took the form of letters. The writer of the letter often requested, on the basis of his or her previous relationship with the recipient, that the recipient welcome, provide hospitality for, and cooperate with the person being commended.

Usually the commended person also delivered the letter. The writer, who was well known to and respected by the letter's recipient, would thus presuppose a face-to-face encounter between the one he was commending and the recipient. Someone who lacked a letter of commendation could appear to be a vagrant out to take advantage of the hospitality of others.

Early Christians wrote these letters to form a support network among the widely dispersed churches. One group of "brethren" wrote a letter of commendation for the Alexandrian Jewish Christian named Apollos, "exhorting the disciples to receive him" (Acts 18:27). The apostle Paul recommended Epaphroditus to the Philippian church, including a commendation within his broader letter (Phil. 2:25–30).

Paul's Third Visit to Corinth (2 Cor. 10:1—13:14)

In the final chapters of 2 Corinthians Paul defends himself against false teachers who had come to Corinth and claimed authority greater than his. He wrote this defense of his apostolic authority in advance of his third visit to Corinth (12:14; 13:1), and thus after his "sorrowful" visit (see 1:23—2:1). Paul's uncharacteristic personal boasts (12:1) and his harsh condemnations of his opponents are in stark contrast to his warm regard for the Corinthians in other parts of 2 Corinthians (see 7:8–11, 16). Possibly these chapters were written soon after the "sorrowful" visit while emotions were still high on both sides, whereas the earlier chapters were written later once Paul and the Corinthians had been reconciled.

Still, 2 Corinthians could have been written by Paul as it now appears in the New Testament. The apostle could have made reconciliation with some of the Corinthians while yet dealing with other opponents in the church.

THE LETTER TO THE ROMANS

From the earliest time, no one has questioned that the author of this epistle was Paul. Paul probably wrote Romans from Corinth. Gaius, who was Paul's host at the time of the writing (Rom. 16:23), had been one of the prominent converts of his ministry in Corinth (1 Cor. 1:14). Phoebe, who delivered the epistle, was a member of the church in Cenchrea, a harbor town near Corinth (16:1, 2).

The letter is to be dated toward the latter part of Paul's missionary work when he was engaged in the collection of a fund for the church in Jerusalem. When Paul wrote to the Corinthians while traveling from Ephesus to Corinth, the collection was still incomplete (2 Cor. 8:1–7). At the time he wrote to the Romans, this collection seems to have been completed (15:26–28). Therefore, it is likely that Paul wrote the epistle to the Romans from Corinth when he stayed there for 3 months in A.D. 56 at the end of his third missionary journey, before he traveled to Jerusalem (15:25; Acts 20:2, 3).

OUTLINE OF ROMANS

I. Revelation of the Righteousness of God	**1:1—8:39**
A. Introduction	1:1–17
B. Condemnation for Sin	1:18—3:20
C. Justification: God's Righteousness	3:21—5:21
D. Righteousness Accomplished	6:1—8:39
II. Vindication of the Righteousness of God	**9:1—11:36**
A. Israel's Past: Election	9:1–29
B. Israel's Present: Rejection	9:30—10:21
C. Israel's Future: Restoration	11:1–36
III. Application of the Righteousness of God	**12:1—16:27**
A. Christian Duties	12:1—13:14
B. Christian Liberties	14:1—15:13
C. Conclusion	15:14—16:27

VILE PASSIONS AND UNNATURAL LUSTS (ROM. 1:27)

Greek culture rarely frowned upon, and indeed frequently promoted, male homosexual intercourse. Because most males did not marry much before age 30, younger men had three primary opportunities for sex: with slaves, with prostitutes, or with each other. Close male bonds in many parts of Greek society made sex with other males a frequent option.

By the 1st century, many upper-class Roman males had adopted Greek values toward homosexual behavior, exhibiting such conduct at fashionable parties. At the same time, Roman society as a whole was far less disposed to such practices than Greek society had been (especially that of Athens). Some Roman philosophers, such as Seneca, spoke against homosexual practice. Some philosophers regarded sex with members of a person's own gender as "against nature."

Jewish society opposed homosexual behavior even more. Literature from early Jewish sources gives indication of Jewish adulterers, Jewish fornicators, and Jewish males committing sexual sins, but homosexual behavior is treated in Jewish writings as a distinctively *Gentile* sin. Jewish writers also viewed homosexual behavior as "against nature," and as a sin that warranted God's judgment.

As Paul discussed how God judges Jews and Gentiles, he made a point that Jewish Christian readers who looked down on Gentiles would quickly grasp. First he addressed sins that his readers would agree are sinful as a prelude to mentioning other sins that they themselves possibly did not condemn. If they agreed that homosexual practices were "vile passions" (Rom. 1:26, 27), how could they approve of other "such things" (Rom. 1:29–32)? Thus he prepared his readers for the realization that "*all* have sinned" (Rom. 3:23).

PAUL IS ARRESTED AND SENT TO ROME

Year	Event
A.D. 56	Paul writes letter to the Romans from Corinth
A.D. 57	Nero compels senators to fight in the stadium
A.D. 57	Agabus warns Paul not to go to Jerusalem (Acts 21:10–14)
A.D. 57	Paul visits the Jerusalem temple and is arrested (Acts 21:30)
A.D. 59	Nero orders the death of his own mother, Agrippina
A.D. 59	Paul appeals to Nero Caesar (Acts 25:10–12)
A.D. 59	Festus sends Paul to Rome (Acts 26:32)

A.D. 56 57 58 59 60

WARRING WITH THE EVIL IMPULSE WITHIN (ROM. 7:21–23)

When Paul wrote about living life under the law of God (Rom. 7), perhaps he was describing, from his new Christian perspective, his own genuine experience under the law. The Church Fathers were divided on whether Paul wrote of his present experience or of his preconversion experience. Whichever, he agonized over the battle to do God's will, saying, "Evil is present with me" (Rom. 7:21).

Jewish people commonly believed that a child was born with a *yetzer hara*, an evil impulse. When a Jewish boy entered adulthood, he would accept responsibility for the commandments (a custom which later evolved into bar mitzvah, the religious rite of passage). According to Jewish belief, once a boy accepted the commandments, he found in God's law strength to overcome his evil impulse. After this, two impulses—good and evil—would battle within him, in a struggle similar to Paul's description.

Philosophers also discussed a struggle, one between human reason and human passion. In the philosophers' view, a person overcame passions by depending on reason. For Paul, however, the battle appeared futile, because mere knowledge without transformation of character could not bring victory. Any solution to the struggle that depended on human effort, whether on a person's reason or on knowledge of Torah, was inadequate.

Victory was possible, Paul realized, through God's Spirit (8:2–4). Interestingly, one strand of Jewish tradition emphasized that in the end time, when the Messiah came, God would publicly slay the evil impulse. For Paul, the Messiah's work of delivering from sin was an accomplished act of history (Rom. 6:5, 11), and the gift of the Spirit was the foretaste of future glory (8:23).

En Route to Jerusalem (Acts 20:3b—21:16)

The account of Paul's travels to Jerusalem at the end of his third missionary journey (Acts 20:3b—21:16) is one of three segments in the Book of Acts known as the "we" passages (also 16:10–18; 27:1—28:16). These accounts appear to relate firsthand reports of events at which the author of Acts was personally present.

Scholars differ over the significance the "we" passages have concerning the authorship of Acts as a whole. Since Paul was known to have had an associate named Luke (Philem. 1:24; Col. 4:14; 2 Tim. 4:11), these firsthand accounts might support the traditional view that Luke wrote Acts. Other scholars suggest that the "we" passages may represent a source used by the author of Acts. In this case, the author of the source for the "we" passages need not have been the author of the entire book.

At Tyre Paul heard the first Spirit-inspired prediction of trouble facing him at Jerusalem (Acts 21:4). But Paul was undeterred. His destination was Jerusalem, hoping to be there by the Day of Pentecost in A.D. 57. After that, he planned to visit Rome (see 19:21).

THE GOSPEL FROM JERUSALEM TO ROME

Acts presents Rome as the guardian of law and order, a situation that often worked to the advantage of Paul and the gospel. Christians were expected to observe Roman law and not to get involved in disorderly, suspicious, or treasonous activity. The Romans, for their part, recognized Christianity as a legal and valid religion with the right to exist.

Paul's Roman citizenship granted him certain privileges as well as protection from Jewish fanaticism. His defense before the Roman governors Felix and Festus, as well as his specific appeal to plead his case before Caesar (Acts 25:10–12) are examples of Roman civil and legal law protecting Christianity.

The final chapters of Acts portray Paul as a witness for Jesus Christ on trial for the gospel. He defends himself before a Jerusalem crowd (Acts 22:1–21), before Felix (24:10–21), and before King Agrippa (26:1–32). He was not found guilty of any crime by the Romans, but they kept him in prison to satisfy the Jews. In the view of the author of Acts, God used Paul's imprisonment to bring him to Rome, the heart of the world, and to make him a witness there.

Paul's appearance in Rome was ironic, because he came as a prisoner and not as a missionary (Acts 28:19, 20). In a Roman house he was held in confinement awaiting a trial that apparently never took place.

EPOCH NINE
Chronological Reading Guide

- ❑ Acts 21:17—24:27
- ❑ Philippians 1:1—4:23
- ❑ Acts 25:1—28:31
- ❑ Philemon 1:1–25
- ❑ Colossians 1:1—4:18
- ❑ Ephesians 1:1—6:24
- ❑ 1 Timothy 1:1—6:21
- ❑ Titus 1:1—3:15
- ❑ 2 Timothy 1:1—4:22
- ❑ 1 Peter 1:1—5:14
- ❑ Jude 1:1–25
- ❑ 2 Peter 1:1—3:18
- ❑ Hebrews 1:1—13:25
- ❑ 1 John 1:1—5:21
- ❑ 2 John 1:1–13
- ❑ 3 John 1:1–14

Paul Arrested in the Temple (Acts 21:17—23:22)

After arriving in Jerusalem, Paul went to James, the brother of Jesus, and to the elders telling them about his work among the Gentiles. The leaders of the church rejoiced over the conversion of Gentiles, but they were worried about Jewish hostility. Rumors were circulating that Paul had taught Jews living outside of Palestine not to keep the Jewish law. To avoid a dispute, Paul was urged to join with four men who had taken a Nazirite vow. By accompanying them to the temple and paying the expenses of the sacrificial offerings, Paul would demonstrate that as a Jew he was keeping the law, despite his witnessing to Gentiles.

Paul was also accused of profaning the temple by bringing a Gentile into its inner courts. Gentiles were allowed in the outer court, called appropriately the Court of the Gentiles, but they were forbidden to come into the Court of Women or the Court of Israel. Signs warned that Gentiles entering these courts would be put to death.

Though Paul had not brought Gentiles into the temple, accusations of such led to an attack against him. The mob stopped beating Paul only because the Roman soldiers intervened to save his life.

Before the Governor at Caesarea (Acts 23:23, 24)

The seaport of Caesarea on the Mediterranean coast was first founded as a trading station by the Sidonian king Strato in the 4th century B.C. But it is Herod the Great (37–4 B.C.) who is known as the builder of the city. Caesarea was in a ruined state when Herod began building operations in 22 B.C. His dream was to have an international port built in a Roman provincial style that would challenge Egypt's Alexandria as the leading trading center in the eastern Mediterranean. The city—an engineering wonder, with many unique features—was completed in about a dozen years according to the Jewish historian Josephus. The builders used a siltation system and made use of hydraulic concrete (poured into the sea as liquid but hardened underwater). The harbor complex was the most elaborate of its day.

After Herod's time, the Roman procurators made Caesarea the official seat of rule. During Jesus' time Pontius Pilate governed Judea from Caesarea, and archaeologists have discovered a fragment of an inscription bearing Pilate's name at the theater there. Antonius Felix was the procurator (or governor) ruling at Caesarea between A.D. 52 and 59, which explains why Paul the prisoner was taken there to stand before him (Acts 23:23, 24).

The Letter to the Philippians

Paul's immediate purpose for writing a letter to the Philippians was to thank them for a gift they had sent him (Phil. 4:14–18). Their messenger, Epaphroditus, had recovered from a serious illness and could carry this letter as he returned to Philippi (2:25–30). Paul's authorship of the letter to the Philippians has never been seriously questioned. There has been frequent and vigorous debate, however, over the date as well as the place of writing.

One view is that Paul wrote Philippians from Rome between A.D. 61 and 63. Paul was in prison (Phil. 1:12–14), and references to the "palace guard" (1:13) and "Caesar's household" (4:22) might suggest imprisonment in Rome. If so, this letter would have been written sometime after Paul was first placed under Roman guard (Acts 28:16).

Other scholars believe that Philippians was written earlier, either around A.D. 54 or 55 during Paul's ministry in Ephesus (Acts 19), or about A.D. 57–59 during his imprisonment at Caesarea (Acts 24—26). The terms "Caesar's household" and "palace guard" could instead refer to Roman authorities in provincial cities like Ephesus or Caesarea. The location of Ephesus is favored because of hints that frequent travels were made between the prison and Philippi (Phil. 1:26; 2:19, 23–26; 4:18), suggesting that Paul was nearer to Philippi than imprisonment in Rome would allow.

That Paul wrote this letter from either Ephesus or Caesarea can be questioned. The Book of Acts does not mention Paul ever being in prison in Ephesus; although he did write from Ephesus about some threat that he faced in Asia, the Roman province of which Ephesus was the chief city (2 Cor. 1:8–11). The Book of Acts does refer to a Caesarean imprisonment, but Caesarea was much farther from Philippi than was either Ephesus or Rome.

Wherever Paul was imprisoned, the Philippians supported him (Phil. 1:7). In one of his most personal letters, Paul is concerned, yet confident, that God will bring the Philippians' faith to maturity (2:15).

Outline of Philippians

I. Paul's Present Circumstance	**1:1–30**
A. Prayer of Thanksgiving	1:1–11
B. Afflictions Promote the Gospel	1:12–18
C. Afflictions Exalt the Lord	1:19–26
D. Exhortation to the Afflicted	1:27–30
II. Appeal to Have the Mind of Christ	**2:1–30**
A. Exhortation to Humility	2:1–4
B. Christ's Example of Humility	2:5–16
C. Paul's Example of Humility	2:17–18
D. Timothy's Example of Humility	2:19–24
E. Epaphroditus' Humility	2:25–30
III. Appeal to Have the Knowledge of Christ	**3:1–21**
A. Warning Against Confidence in the Flesh	3:1–9
B. Exhortation to Know Christ	3:10–16
C. Warning Against Living for the Flesh	3:17–21
IV. Appeal to Have the Peace of Christ	**4:1–23**
A. Peace with the Brethren	4:1–3
B. Peace with the Lord	4:4–9
C. Peace in All Circumstances	4:10–19
D. Conclusion	4:20–23

Paul's Pedigree as a Pharisee
(Phil. 3:4–6)

Much has been written about the Pharisees in the time of Jesus, yet remarkably little was written by them. Firsthand writings exist from only two persons who identified themselves with the Pharisees: Josephus, the first-century Jewish historian and apologist, and Saul of Tarsus, also known as the apostle Paul. Neither Josephus nor Paul resembles the Pharisees written about elsewhere!

Paul recognized that his time as a Pharisee established for him a pedigree within Judaism that was quite impressive. His own summary of his pre-Christian life (Phil. 3:4–6), therefore, gives us insight into the convictions of at least some Pharisees. For one thing, to be a Pharisee meant for Paul that he interpreted the Law, the Jewish Torah in a certain way (3:5). Josephus also writes that Pharisees had their own interpretation of the Law.

Another conviction that Paul links to his pedigree as a Pharisee is zeal. "Zeal" characterizes those within Judaism who used violence against other Jews for violating the Torah. These Pharisees lived by their particular interpretations, and they were zealous to preserve the traditions of the fathers (Gal. 1:14) and Israel's integrity. The Pharisee Saul demonstrated his own zeal for Judaism by "persecuting the church" (Phil. 3:6).

Another example of such zeal appeared during the Maccabean war (166–160 B.C.), 200 years before Paul's time. The war broke out when the priest Mattathias "burned with zeal" and killed a fellow Jew who was sacrificing to Greek gods in violation of the Torah (1 Macc. 2:23–26). Mattathias cried out, "Let every one who is zealous for the law and supports the covenant come out with me!" (1 Macc. 2:27).

Reflecting on his time as a Pharisee, Paul counted himself amongst the most intense followers of the Law, zealous to the point of using violence to protect Israel from Torah desecration. No wonder he persecuted the church. In the view of the Pharisees, the first Christians, as a Jewish group that was lax in the observance of the Law, represented the defilement of Israel! Saul the Pharisee had lived out his commitment to Israel through the Law; Paul the apostle would live it out through Jesus Christ (Phil. 3:7–9).

Women Leaders in the Philippian Church (Phil. 4:2, 3)

Paul's letters provide insight into the social makeup of the small early Christian communities in the Greco-Roman world. In his letter to the Philippian church, the first two persons he mentions by name are women: Euodia and Syntyche (Phil. 4:2). When Paul describes them as "these women who labored with me in the gospel" and includes them in the category of "fellow workers" (4:3), he indicates that they joined with him as equal partners in his missionary and teaching activity.

The exact nature of their leadership roles in the church at Philippi is not certain. The authority of both women in the church was sufficient, however, for Paul to encourage them to "be of the same mind in the Lord" (4:2). His concern for any dispute they may have had could not have run too deep, though. Along with Clement, he believed that both Euodia's and Syntyche's names were "in the Book of Life" (4:3).

Women played important leadership roles in Paul's churches, two examples being Phoebe in the church at Cenchrea (Rom. 16:1) and Priscilla in Ephesus (1 Cor. 16:19). Particularly in Macedonia, where women often assumed prominent roles in religious cults, it would be natural to find female leaders in a church. Paul supported women's roles in the Christian communities and instructed believers: "there is neither male nor female; for you are all one in Christ Jesus" (Gal. 3:28).

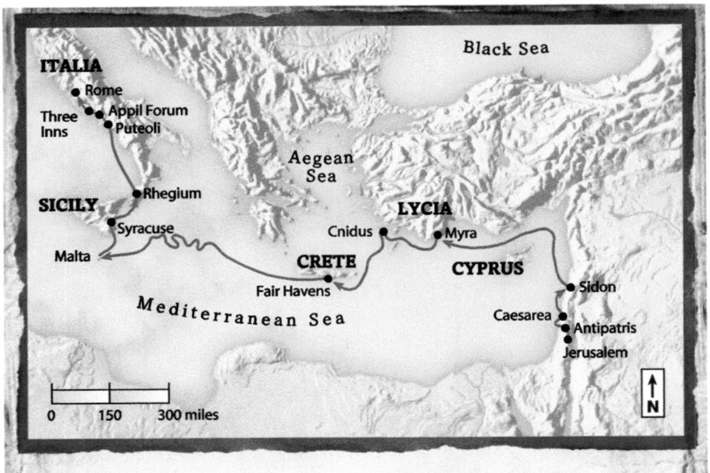

On to Rome

In Jerusalem following his third missionary journey, Paul struggled with Jews who accused him of profaning the temple (Acts 21:26–34). He was placed in Roman custody in Caesarea for two years, but, after appealing to the emperor, was sent by ship to Rome. During this fourth journey (Acts 27:1—28:16), Paul's party departed from the island of Crete only to be shipwrecked on Malta by a great storm. Three months later he finally arrived at the imperial city.

Agrippa, Paul's Judge (Acts 25:23)

Marcus Julius Agrippa was the Roman name of Agrippa II, the last of the Herodian dynasty of five Roman-appointed kings in Palestine. He and his father, Agrippa I, were descended from the Jewish-born Herod the Great, ruler of Judea at the time of Christ's birth (Matt. 2:1).

The writings of the Jewish historian Josephus (A.D. 37–100) provide the most information about Agrippa. Since he was too young to receive the throne of Judea in A.D. 44 when his father died, the Romans appointed a governor. Agrippa himself was given other territories to rule, notably in Galilee.

At the beginning of the Jewish revolt in A.D. 66 Agrippa came to Jerusalem to quell the disorder. Unsuccessful in this venture, he became an ardent Roman sympathizer. Josephus (*The Wars of the Jews* 2:345) attributes a speech to Agrippa in which he warned that the Romans were much too strong for the Jews to resist, and thus they should side with them. After the revolt in A.D. 70 the Romans gave Agrippa additional territory in reward for his loyalty.

In A.D. 59 the apostle Paul stood trial before Agrippa, who was considered an expert on Jewish affairs and was interested in Paul's case (Acts 25:13—26:32). The king was accompanied at the trial by his sister Bernice (25:13, 23). Rumors about Agrippa, who apparently never married, having an incestuous relationship with Bernice were denied by Josephus while supported by the Roman writer Juvenal. Paul's judge was a Jewish king, a Roman sympathizer, and a man of questionable moral reputation. As Paul defended his Christian faith, he appealed to Agrippa's Jewish background, challenging even him to become a believing Jew (26:2, 3, 26, 27).

The Voyage to Rome (Acts 27:1—28:15)

All the participants in the trial at Caesarea, even Agrippa, agreed that Paul was innocent. Christianity was not a crime before a Roman court, and Paul should rightfully have been set free (Acts 26:32). Instead, after having spent approximately 2 years in Roman custody in Caesarea, Paul was sent by ship to Rome (c. A.D. 59 or 60).

The voyage to Rome did not turn out to be a pleasure cruise. Contrary winds delayed the grain ship until fall weather made sailing dangerous (Acts 27:7, 8). It was already late September or early October, the time when the fast on the Day of Atonement was observed (27:9). This late season, plus Paul's God-given foresight, led to his bold prediction: "this voyage will end with disaster" (27:10). After departing the island of Crete late in the fall, his party was shipwrecked on Malta during a storm.

Paul spent the 3 winter months ministering on the island of Malta. According to Pliny the Elder, the seas could open up for safe sailing as early as February, though weather conditions could delay a voyage until sometime in March. So it was possibly in the spring of A.D. 60 that Paul's journey finally reached Italy. Appii Forum, 43 miles from Rome, and Three Inns, 33 miles from Rome (Acts 28:15), were well-known stopping places on the main highway from southern Italy to Rome.

Ruins at Caesarea

Imprisonment in Rome (Acts 28:16–31)

According to the Book of Acts, Paul spent 2 years under house arrest in Rome (Acts 28:16, 30). Acts is silent, however, regarding what happened to him at the end of that time, in late A.D. 62 or early 63. Some scholars argue that Luke intended the prophecy of Paul's martyrdom (Acts 20:24, 38) to inform the reader about his fate. Paul's execution under Nero sometime between the summers of A.D. 62 and 64 would also fit with two developments in Roman history of this period. First, Nero reinstated laws against treason in early 62, and Paul's execution may have been ordered based on such a charge (though Paul claims innocence of such; see Acts 25:8). Second, Nero married Poppaea in the spring of A.D. 62. Her strong support of the Jews may have negatively influenced the disposition of Paul's case.

Other scholars have suggested that Paul, after 2 years of imprisonment, was released about A.D. 63. He then carried on further missionary work in Macedonia (see 1 Tim. 1:3) and, according to some early Christian traditions, possibly also in Spain (see Rom. 15:28). Details of the end of Paul's life are unknown. Apparently he was subsequently rearrested and imprisoned, and Tertullian describes Paul's execution by beheading. Eusebius, the church historian, dates Paul's death in A.D. 67.

THE LETTER TO PHILEMON

Philemon probably lived in the Lycus Valley where Colosse and Laodicea were located (see Col. 4:15). He was a close friend of Paul, indebted to him spiritually, and a helper in his ministry (Philem. 1:1, 19). Onesimus, Philemon's slave, had run away and been converted by Paul. Paul offers two reasons for writing this letter to Philemon: (1) an appeal for him to receive Onesimus as a brother in Christ (1:10–17), and (2) a request for him to prepare a guest room for Paul's coming visit (1:22).

The letters to Philemon and to the Colossians were possibly written by Paul at the same time, about A.D. 62, during his imprisonment at Rome (Acts 28:16–31). Paul described himself both as a prisoner (Philem. 1:1, 9, 23) and as being aged (1:9). Many of the people mentioned in Philemon are also mentioned in Colossians: Archippus (Col. 4:17), Onesimus (Col. 4:9), Epaphras (Col. 1:7; 4:12), Mark, Aristarchus (Col. 4:10), Demas, and Luke (Col. 4:14). Onesimus and Tychicus (Col. 4:7–9) were the bearers of these letters.

An earlier imprisonment, either in Ephesus around A.D. 54 or 55 or in Caesarea, has also been suggested as the time of Paul's writing (see "The Letter to the Philippians"). Ephesus is closer to Colosse than is Rome, thus the close proximity of Ephesus would make more likely both the capture of the runaway slave Onesimus, as well as Paul's own hopes to visit Philemon in the near future (Philem. 1:22).

OUTLINE OF PHILEMON

I. The Prayer of Thanksgiving	1–7
II. The Petition for Onesimus	8–16
III. The Promise of Paul	17–25

More Than a Slave (Philem. 1:16)

Roman law in some respects treated slaves as persons but also viewed them economically as property. While slaves could hold property and buy their freedom, they also could be beaten and interrogated under torture. In the rare case where a head of a household was murdered by one of his slaves, all of his slaves would be executed. Thus, the term "beloved brother" (Philem. 1:16), as Paul calls Onesimus, indicated something more than a slave.

Onesimus was probably a household slave, who had greater opportunities for social advancement than did free peasants, and, in prominent households, often became powerful. Indeed, some noble women even married slaves of Caesar, thereby becoming slaves, to increase their social status! By saving money on the side, household slaves often purchased their freedom, and, with help from their former slaveholders, sometimes attained social prominence and wealth.

Slaveholders would send their trusted slaves on errands, often with money. Occasionally a slave chose to escape rather than return home. Such may be the situation faced by Onesimus.

Roman law required Paul to return Onesimus to his master Philemon or else face severe punishment. Escaped slaves, once recaptured, normally received severe punishment. One option for the slave was to seek out an advocate who would beseech the slaveowner on the slave's behalf. In one situation, a close parallel to Paul's letter, a Roman writer requested clemency for an escaped slave.

THE LETTER TO THE COLOSSIANS

The Book of Colossians is closely related to the books of Ephesians and Philemon. Colossians was probably written before Ephesians, with which it shares main ideas and a general outline. Ephesians seems to expand some of the key ideas of Colossians.

Paul wrote this epistle from prison, as he did Philippians and Philemon. Some scholars believe this was during a first imprisonment in Rome. Colossians could then have been written about A.D. 62, not long before Paul's release. Yet others would place the writing of this letter during an Ephesian imprisonment around A.D. 54 or 55.

The significant difference of the Greek vocabulary and style in Colossians from that of other Pauline letters raises a question whether Paul actually wrote Colossians. Some scholars argue that the theology of the letter and the understanding and organization of the church are more developed than in letters Paul himself wrote. This may indicate that Colossians was written by one of Paul's associates in the decade following his death (perhaps between A.D. 70–75).

Colosse was located on the south bank of the Lycus River near Laodicea and Hierapolis in western Asia Minor, about 100 miles east of Ephesus on the important trade route between Ephesus and the Euphrates Valley. Paul had never visited Colosse, but the gospel had been preached there, as well as in Laodicea and Hierapolis, while he was in Ephesus.

Among the most popular religions of the ancient world were the so-called mystery religions. Details of the initiations, rituals, and doctrines of these religions were kept secret from outsiders. Standard elements were purification, fasting, sacrifice, and ceremonial banquets. Early Christianity showed similarities to the mystery religions, including the idea of "mystery" (Col. 1:25–27).

This letter deals primarily with doctrinal heresy that possibly mixed Judaism with some early form of Gnosticism—that Jesus was super-human, but not truly God. He was greater than human beings, but not great enough to be the Savior. Those who believe in Christ must go through angels to get to the deeper levels of spirituality. Paul built a positive case for the Christian truth in order to show the Colossians the futility of ideas such as these.

OUTLINE OF COLOSSIANS

I. Supremacy of Christ in the Church	**1:1—2:23**
A. Introduction	1:1–14
B. Preeminence of Christ	1:15—2:3
C. Freedom in Christ	2:4–23
II. Submission to Christ in the Church	**3:1—4:18**
A. Position of the Believer	3:1–4
B. Practice of the Believer	3:5—4:6
C. Conclusion	4:7–18

FAMILY VALUES IN THE HOUSEHOLD (COL. 3:18, 19)

Romans in the 1st century felt that religions from the East, such as Judaism, Christianity, and the worship of Isis, undermined traditional Roman family values. Because religious groups were sometimes expelled from Rome, members of persecuted minority religions often adopted traditional "household codes" to prove that they would uphold traditional Roman values. Philosophers from the time of Aristotle onward detailed these "household codes," which showed the male head of the household how to rule his wife, children, and slaves.

The structure of these traditional codes was adopted in Christian letters, including wives, husbands (and fathers), children, slaves, and slaveholders (Col. 3:18—4:1). The Christian adaptation balanced commands for those who were socially inferior (wives, children, bond-servants) with responsibilities for the socially superior (husbands, fathers, masters).

The Christian codes, such as one in Eph. 5, differ considerably from traditional household codes. They address wives, children, and slaves themselves, and not just the male head of the household. They do not tell the husband how to "rule" his wife, but how to love her (Eph. 5:25). Although traditional Greek and Roman values demanded the wife's quiet obedience, the Christian code defines "submission" primarily in terms of respect (Eph. 5:33). The wife's submission was based on the broader Christian virtue of servanthood, which applied to all Christians—husbands as well as wives (Eph. 5:21).

THE LETTER TO THE EPHESIANS

Although the first verse in most manuscripts of this letter reads "To the saints who are in Ephesus," other early copies lack the words "in Ephesus." The letter also does not follow Paul's usual practice of including personal greetings to many friends in the city to which he wrote. One 2nd-century writer even cites this letter by the title "To the Laodiceans." It may be that Paul sent copies of this letter to a number of churches in the region, either supplying the name of each city in the opening greeting or leaving the destination out if the copy was to circulate to several churches.

Ephesians is closely related to Colossians. No other two letters are as similar as these, either in outline and outlook, or in general theme. Half of the verses in Ephesians contain expressions identical to those in Colossians. It is as though Paul wrote Colossians first to meet some special needs of the church there, and then felt that a letter to be circulated among all the churches in Asia Minor ought to elaborate on some of the Colossian themes. The similarities could suggest that both letters were written at about the same time, being composed during Paul's Caesarean or Roman imprisonments.

As is the case with Colossians, there are doubts whether Paul actually wrote the letter to the Ephesians. Like Colossians, the language and theological development in Ephesians is more elaborate than that found in Paul's earlier letters. The tremendous similarities between these two letters lead some to conclude that Ephesians was actually based on Colossians. Some have even suggested that Ephesians may have been written as a kind of introduction to Paul's theology by an associate who was collecting Paul's letters in the years after his death.

Ephesus was a chief city of the west coast of Asia Minor, situated at the mouth of the Cayster River. Paul visited the city on the return part of his second missionary journey, staying only briefly (Acts 18:19–21). He returned on his third journey to spend more than two years strengthening the church (Acts 19). The letter to the Ephesians was also intended to strengthen them, making them more conscious of their oneness in Christ.

OUTLINE OF EPHESIANS

I. The Position of the Christian	**1:1—3:21**
A. Praise for Redemption	1:1–14
B. Prayer for Revelation	1:15–23
C. Position of the Christian	2:1—3:13
D. Prayer for Realization	3:14–21
II. The Practice of the Christian	**4:1—6:24**
A. Unity of the Church	4:1–16
B. Holiness in Life	4:17—5:21
C. Home and Work Life	5:22—6:9
D. Conduct in the Conflict	6:10–24

WIVES SUBMITTING TO HUSBANDS (EPH. 5:22)

The nature of marriage in Asia Minor was very different from marriage today. In the Greek culture that was dominant in and around Ephesus, husbands were on average 12 or more years older than their wives, were usually more educated, and held much higher social status. In one traditional Greek formulation, men used prostitutes for pleasure and wives only to bear them legitimate children.

In most of the Greco-Roman world, marital practices placed women at a disadvantage. Marriage contracts forbade a woman to leave the marital home without her husband's permission. In parts of the eastern Mediterranean a wife not wearing a shawl over her hair in public could be divorced for unfaithfulness, and a woman not divorced or widowed was under the legal control of her husband or father.

Paul's command "Wives, submit to your own husbands" (Eph. 5:22) is at least partly related to concern for Christian witness within the surrounding culture, and is quite mild in comparison to the rest of his culture. What is significant is that Paul modified the culture's values, calling on all believers to submit (5:21), and allowing the husband-wife relationship to be affected by the God-human relationship. Wives were to submit "as to the Lord" (Eph. 5:22), and husbands were to love their wives "as Christ also loved the church" (5:25). While Romans and Greeks supposed that husbands would love their wives, Paul listed such as a command.

THE FIRST LETTER TO TIMOTHY

The letters of 1 and 2 Timothy and Titus constitute a subgroup among the letters of Paul. They are addressed not to churches, but to pastors, Paul's younger colleagues in ministry. Therefore, since the 18th century, these three letters, sharing similar characteristics and contents, have been called the Pastoral Epistles. They presume a time after the close of the Book of Acts and near the end of Paul's life.

The first verse of each letter identifies Paul as the author. Some scholars, however, dispute this claim, since the differences in language and style between these letters and Paul's other letters seem very great. These three short books contain more than 300 words found in no other book that names Paul as its author. Moreover, if Paul was martyred around A.D. 64 at the end of his Roman imprisonment, he would not have had opportunity to write these letters. In that case, an editor or compiler could have produced these letters in the last quarter of the 1st century or first quarter of the 2nd century.

Yet Paul's authorship of the Pastoral Epistles is accepted by those who argue that Paul was released from his Roman imprisonment in late A.D. 62 or early A.D. 63. The only specific historical reference (1 Tim. 1:3) hints at a period of further travel and ministry, during which Paul had stationed Timothy at Ephesus. The letter known as 1 Timothy could then have been written about A.D. 65, in order to provide pastoral care and guidance to a young church leader.

Timothy, a native of Lystra in Asia Minor, was the son of a Jewish mother and Gentile father (Acts 16:1, 2). He was a convert of the apostle Paul, who had evangelized Lystra on his first missionary journey. Timothy joined Paul and Silas on the second missionary journey and traveled with them to Greece. Paul sent him to visit the Thessalonian and Corinthian churches (see 1 Cor. 4:17; 1 Thess. 3:2). In the letter, Timothy is warned against false teaching and given guidance on how to handle it.

OUTLINE OF 1 TIMOTHY

I. Reminders in Ministry	**1:1–20**
A. Warnings Concerning False Doctrine	1:1–17
B. Warnings Concerning Good Warfare	1:18–20
II. Regulations in Ministry	**2:1—3:16**
A. Women in Worship	2:1–15
B. Leadership in the House of God	3:1–16
III. Responsibilities in Ministry	**4:1—6:21**
A. Personal Responsibility	4:1–16
B. Responsibilities in the Church	5:1–25
C. Final Responsibilities of Timothy	6:1–21

Widows in the Household
(1 Tim. 5:8)

The fundamental social institution of the Greco-Roman world was the household. The ancient household included far more people than the modern nuclear family. Everyone involved in the "family business" under the rule of a male administrator, called the "father," was part of the household. Thus the Greco-Roman household consisted of relatives plus various dependents: the father's wife, his slaves, children, as well as clients—those who gave the father honor and influence in exchange for material favors.

One household member who especially needed protection was the widow. In New Testament times, widows had virtually no means of supporting themselves. The early church felt responsible to care for Christian widows, but problems arose in ministering to their needs. As new structures and guidelines had to be developed, the church eventually distinguished between widows who really needed support and those who should be commended to the care of their household (1 Tim. 5:3–5, 8). A Christian father who did not provide for a widow of his household was deemed "worse than an unbeliever" (5:8). Even in non-Christian households of the Greco-Roman world, the head of the household supported poor widows.

THE END OF PAUL'S LIFE

- A.D. 59 — Festus sends Paul to Rome (Acts 26:32) A.D. 59
- A.D. 60 — Paul and Luke arrive at Rome (Acts 28:11–16) A.D. 60
- A.D. 63 — Paul writes from Rome to Philemon A.D. 63
- A.D. 64 — Nero persecutes Christians after the Great Fire A.D. 64
- A.D. 64 — Peter and Paul are executed under Nero (?) A.D. 64
- A.D. 64 — Paul is released and visits Spain (?) A.D. 64
- A.D. 66 — Jewish revolt breaks out against Rome A.D. 66
- A.D. 67 — Paul is executed in Rome (?; 2 Tim. 4:6) A.D. 67

A.D. 59 · 61 · 63 · 65 · 67

THE LETTER TO TITUS

Considerable doubts have been raised about whether Paul actually wrote this letter to Titus (see "The First Letter to Timothy"). Those who accept Paul's authorship believe the letter to Titus was probably written shortly after 1 Timothy, but before the apostle's rearrest and imprisonment in A.D. 66. Paul had left Titus in Crete to oversee the work on that island (Titus 1:5).

Little is known about Titus (he is never mentioned in Acts). He was an uncircumcised Greek who was apparently converted to Christianity under Paul's ministry (Gal. 2:1). He played an important role in Paul's relationship with the Corinthian church (2 Cor. 7:6, 7; 8:16; 12:18).

The letter was written to encourage Titus in his task of organizing, instructing, and appointing leaders for the churches of Crete (Titus 1:5). It was also intended to help him stop the false teachers who threatened church authority, unity, and morality (1:10–16; 3:9–11).

OUTLINE OF TITUS

I. Appoint Elders	**1:1–16**
A. Introduction	1:1–4
B. Ordain Qualified Elders	1:5–9
C. Rebuke False Teachers	1:10–16
II. Set Things in Order	**2:1—3:15**
A. Speak Sound Doctrine	2:1–15
B. Maintain Good Works	3:1–11
C. Conclusion	3:12–15

TIME CAPSULE	A.D. 54 to 62
54	Nero becomes emperor
55–56	Paul travels through Macedonia to Greece
57	Paul is arrested in Jerusalem and appears before Felix
57–59	Paul imprisoned in Caesarea
59–62	Porcius Festus is procurator or governor of Judea
59	Paul appears before Agrippa II and Bernice and Festus
60	Paul and Luke arrive in Rome
62	The apostle James is stoned to death

TIME CAPSULE	A.D. 64 to 79
64–141	Life of the Greek writer Philo of Byblos
66	Outbreak of the Jewish revolt against Rome
67	Roman forces kill 11,000 Samaritans
67	Paul is arrested and executed in Rome
68	Nero, age 30, is forced to commit suicide
70	Titus defeats Jerusalem and burns down the temple
74	Masada falls to the Romans and its defenders commit suicide
79	The volcano Vesuvius erupts, burying Pompeii and Herculaneum

THE SECOND LETTER TO TIMOTHY

As with the other Pastoral Epistles, the letter of 2 Timothy is often not considered to be an original letter of Paul's. Those who do accept Paul's authorship believe that 2 Timothy was probably written in A.D. 67, after Paul had been rearrested. Companions who were recently with him had departed (2 Tim. 4:10), leaving him alone—"Only Luke is with me" (4:11). Presumably, Timothy was still in Ephesus (4:19), where Paul had left Priscilla and Aquila at the end of his second journey (Acts 18:18, 19), and where he had stationed Timothy to oversee the work in Asia Minor (see 1 Tim. 1:3).

The letter of 2 Timothy describes Paul as a prisoner in Rome at the time of the writing (2 Tim. 1:16, 17). The apostle had already endured a "first defense" (4:16) and had been delivered (4:17). Presumably that was a preliminary hearing; he now faced formal trial. Paul expected a negative verdict and the death sentence. He had reached the end of his course in this life; death was imminent (4:6).

The primary object of this letter was to strengthen Timothy so that he would endure in the face of opposition from false teachers. He is encouraged to carry on the gospel ministry and to train others who will take up that ministry after he is gone.

OUTLINE OF 2 TIMOTHY

I. Encouragement in Ministry	**1:1–18**
A. Using Spiritual Gifts	1:1–7
B. Suffering for the Gospel	1:8–18
II. Examples in Ministry	**2:1–26**
A. Characteristics of Faithfulness	2:1–13
B. Handle God's Word Accurately	2:14–26
III. Exhortations in Ministry	**3:1–17**
A. Warnings of Apostasy	3:1–9
B. Ways to Face Apostasy	3:10–17
IV. Encouragements in Ministry	**4:1–22**
A. Preach the Word	4:1–5
B. Final Exhortations	4:6–22

THE WHO'S WHO OF BANQUETING (2 TIM. 2:20, 21)

The Greco-Roman society developed intricate social customs and rituals in order to rank people as honorable or shameful, socially superior or inferior. One of these rituals was the banquet. As a formal dinner party, the banquet helped mark people in their proper "rank" within the society.

As the host, the head of the household, called the "father," occupied the social pinnacle at the banquet. People would not usually attend the banquet given by someone of lesser social standing than themselves. Various arrangements of the banquet ranked the participants socially, such as the seating or reclining assignments. The closer an attendee was to the host, the more status or honor that one possessed at the banquet.

In a spacious "great house" (2 Tim. 2:20) of an extremely wealthy household, a banquet could involve many, many people, all indebted to the father or head of household. Not only access to the host, but also food and serving dishes would mark "who's who" at the banquet. Those possessing sufficient honor or status would eat from platters of precious metals; the common freemen would eat from earthenware with wooden utensils.

The banquet and its social code possibly provide the background for the imagery of vessels in the letter of 2 Timothy (2 Tim. 2:20, 21). Within the "great house" of God the Father, moral purity is the distinguishing mark of a vessel "for honor"; implied, though not stated, is that impurity marks a vessel "for dishonor." Thus in the visible church are people of various kinds—some for good, others regrettably unworthy.

THE FIRST LETTER OF PETER

If Simon Peter was the author of the letter of 1 Peter, he probably wrote it around A.D. 63 or 64, shortly before the beginning of Nero's persecution of Christians at Rome. The name "Babylon" (1 Pet. 5:13), then, is likely a figurative description of Rome. According to early church tradition, Peter was martyred during the reign of Nero in about A.D. 64. Peter's scribe, Sylvanus (5:12), may have been responsible for much of the letter's style and vocabulary.

Some scholars reject Peter's authorship: the good style and extensive literary vocabulary of the author could not have come from a Galilean fisherman. Moreover, the letter shows the influence of Paul's theology and vocabulary, such as the expression "in Christ."

If Peter was not the author, the letter could have been written sometime after A.D. 70. The symbolic reference to Rome as "Babylon," found in several early Christian writings (see Rev. 17:5), probably resulted from Rome's destruction of Jerusalem in A.D. 70, a tragic event that repeated the conquest by Babylon in 586 B.C. The link between being "a Christian" and criminal offenses (4:14–16) might suggest a date around A.D. 90–95, well after Peter's death. The earliest evidence for an official governmental persecution being enforced on more than a local basis is found during the reign of the emperor Domitian (A.D. 81–96).

The Christians who received this letter lived in Pontus, Galatia, Cappadocia, Asia, and Bithynia (1 Pet. 1:1), regions located in Asia Minor. Many of them seem to have been Gentiles (2:10) who were facing persecution from non-Christians around them and perhaps also from government officials. This letter was written primarily to bring them a message of hope and encouragement.

OUTLINE OF FIRST PETER

I. The Salvation of the Believer	**1:1—2:12**
A. Salutation	1:1–2
B. Salvation of the Believer	1:3–12
C. Sanctification of the Believer	1:13—2:12
II. The Submission of the Believer	**2:13—3:12**
A. Submission to the Government	2:13–17
B. Submission in Business	2:18–25
C. Submission in Marriage	3:1–8
D. Submission in All of Life	3:9–12
III. The Suffering of the Believer	**3:13—5:14**
A. Conduct in Suffering	3:13–17
B. Christ's Example of Suffering	3:18—4:6
C. Commands in Suffering	4:7–19
D. Ministry in Suffering	5:1–9
E. Benediction	5:10–14

Persecuted in Bithynia (1 Pet. 1:1)

Bithynia, combined with the nearby territory of Pontus, formed a Roman province in northwest Anatolia. It had been an important kingdom during the Hellenistic period (332–37 B.C.), and a center of Greek language and culture. Although Paul did not evangelize in the region (Acts 16:7), the salutation in 1 Pet. 1:1, addressing Christians in Pontus and Bithynia, shows that Christianity had reached there by other means.

One of the earliest evidences of the Roman awareness of Christianity comes from Bithynia. The letters to the emperor Trajan from Pliny the Younger describe various reasons for the persecution of Christians (*Epistulae* 10.95–96). Pliny was the provincial governor of Bithynia and Pontus in A.D. 111–113. In his official correspondence he expresses to Trajan his alarm regarding the spread of Christianity.

The correspondence between this governor and his emperor offers one look at how the Romans dealt with the Christian religion in Bithynia and Pontus. According to Pliny, it appears that persecution had trimmed the ranks of Christians in the area. Trajan responds to Pliny that Christians should not actively be sought out. However, he allows that those who refused to perform certain Roman orders were to be punished. The letter of 1 Peter to Christians in Bithynia, Pontus, and other regions, offers encouragement during similar persecutions (1 Pet. 1:6, 7).

WIVES, HUSBANDS, AND RELIGION (1 PET. 3:1)

In the Roman world, wives were expected to follow their husband's religion. Many women, however, were drawn to other religious groups, such as Judaism and Christianity, often provoking their husbands' anger. This marital conflict over religion often caused religious groups to face hostility, and the groups frequently responded by upholding Greek and Roman traditional family values, insofar as they could accommodate them.

The letter of 1 Peter advocates submission to all the authority figures of that day, including kings, governors, slave masters, and husbands (1 Pet. 2:13, 14, 18; 3:1). Similarly, ancient writers who delineated proper societal roles usually included sections on how the male head of the household should rule both wife and slaves.

An emphasis on the adornment of the heart rather than on outward appearance (3:3) was common in ancient speeches and writings. Greek and Roman ideals for wifely behavior included submission, meekness, and quietness. Greek and Roman moralists exhorted wives to a meekness that included avoiding all ostentation, dressing simply rather than drawing attention to oneself. These moralists typically pointed out that women could "adorn" themselves with meekness rather than costly garments.

Moralists often drew on examples from the past, because people generally thought that past matrons had been more obedient than were those of their own day. Jewish readers, as well as Gentiles who had begun learning the Old Testament, would recognize Sarah as an ultimate example of proper behavior. Sarah's address of Abraham as "lord" (3:6) probably reflects the standard Hebrew title of respect for husbands.

The letter of 1 Peter exhorts wives whose husbands may have already been distrustful of Christian teaching, suspecting it would subvert their wives' obedience. The model for how to best win over these husbands to Christianity involves adopting the societal norms of a wife's submissiveness and loyalty to her husband.

THE LETTER OF JUDE

The Jude (or Judas) named as the author of this letter (1) is most probably the half brother of Jesus (see Matt. 13:55). He is identified as the "brother of James" (Jude 1), another half brother of Jesus. Some scholars have doubted whether Jude actually wrote this letter, raising questions similar to those raised about James's authorship of the letter bearing his name (see "The Letter of James"). As with the letter of James, however, others accept the book as an authentic letter by Jude himself.

Exactly when Jude wrote the letter depends to some extent on its relationship with the letter of 2 Peter. The marked similarity of wording between Jude 4–19 and 2 Peter 2:1—3:3 indicates direct literary dependence. Yet it cannot be proven whether the 2 Peter passage was borrowed from Jude, or Jude borrowed from 2 Peter, or both letters used ideas from a common source that no longer exists. The apparent literary relationship between the two letters might mean that Jude was written at roughly the same time as 2 Peter.

Jude wrote this letter to a group of Christians who were being led astray by false teachers. He urges them to fight for the truth (Jude 3).

OUTLINE OF JUDE

I. Purpose of Jude	1–4
II. Description of False Teachers	5–16
A. Past Judgment	5–7
B. Present Characteristics	8–13
C. Future Judgment	14–16
III. Defense Against False Teachers	17–23
IV. Doxology	24–25

THE SECOND LETTER OF PETER

Two New Testament letters bear the name of Simon Peter (1 Pet. 1:1; 2 Pet. 1:1). The two have little in common with each other, and the differences in style, vocabulary, and theology between 1 and 2 Peter have led some scholars to doubt whether Peter was the author of 2 Peter. Other scholars recognize these differences, but still accept Peter's authorship of the second letter. Differences in style and vocabulary are explained as the result of Peter using a different secretary to write the second letter, and by treating differing subject matter.

The author of the letter refers to "our beloved brother Paul" and to "all his epistles" (2 Pet. 3:15, 16). Some suppose that if Peter wrote the letter he would never have implied that Paul's writings were equal to "the rest of the Scriptures" (3:16). Moreover, it seems unlikely that Paul's letters would have been gathered into a formal collection prior to Peter's and Paul's martyrdoms under Nero. Nevertheless, others point out that the apostles wrote and taught with a consciousness of having divine authority, as Paul did in his earliest letters (1 Cor. 2:13; Gal. 1:1).

Those who accept Peter's authorship believe he probably wrote in the early 60s, not long before his death. Since the letter of 2 Peter apparently acknowledges the existence of 1 Peter (2 Pet. 3:1), it would necessarily have been written after 1 Peter. If an unknown author wrote the letter, its composition might date to the late 1st century or early 2nd century.

The letter is written out of pastoral concern to counter false teachings and their influence on the lives of early Christians. Certain teachers, for their own personal gain, were promising that people could be Christians and still live immoral lives. The writer of this letter is concerned that there be a check against this false teaching and immoral living even after he is gone (1:12–15).

OUTLINE OF 2 PETER

I. Cultivation of Christian Character	**1:1–21**
A. Salutation	1:1–2
B. Growth in Christ	1:3–14
C. Grounds of Belief	1:15–21
II. Condemnation of False Teachers	**2:1–22**
A. Danger of False Teachers	2:1–3
B. Destruction of False Teachers	2:4–9
C. Description of False Teachers	2:10–22
III. Confidence in Christ's Return	**3:1–18**
A. Mockery in the Last Days	3:1–7
B. The Day of the Lord	3:8–10
C. Christian Maturity	3:11–18

THE LETTER TO THE HEBREWS

Unlike the letters recognized as written by Paul, the letter to the Hebrews is not signed by its author, nor is an addressee named. It is not a circular letter to be read in several churches. The many exhortations remind us of a sermon. Hebrews deals with Christ's priesthood and sacrifice much more thoroughly than any other New Testament book.

Even the early church fathers were uncertain who wrote this letter. The mention of Timothy (Heb. 13:23) has led some to think that Paul or one of his associates wrote the letter. Apollos has been suggested because the style and content of Hebrews reflect a Jew versed in Greek learning and literary style (see Acts 18:24–28). Other suggestions include Barnabas, Luke, Silas, Aquila, or Priscilla as possible authors. But after considering all the evidence, many scholars agree that the authorship of this letter remains unknown.

Hebrews was certainly written during the last half of the 1st century. It is quoted at length in a letter written around A.D. 95 to the church at Corinth by Clement, a leader in the church at Rome. If not written during the lifetime of Paul, Hebrews was most likely written during the lifetime of Paul's younger associate, Timothy (13:23).

Almost all of Hebrews is exposition of Old Testament passages. The author uses Jewish methods of interpretation common in the synagogues of his day. He differs from Jewish interpreters, however, in that he sees Christ as the fulfillment of the Old Testament. The letter is a masterful description of the salvation obtained by Christ's priesthood and sacrifice interwoven with exhortation for Christians to persevere in the benefits of this salvation.

THE FALL OF JERUSALEM

- A.D. 66 — Jewish revolt breaks out against Rome
- A.D. 67 — Josephus is captured, but spared by Vespasian
- A.D. 67 — Paul is executed in Rome (?)
- A.D. 70 — Daily sacrifices in the Jerusalem temple are ended (Heb. 7:27)
- A.D. 70 — Titus defeats Jerusalem and burns down the temple (Luke 21:20)
- A.D. 74 — Masada falls to the Romans and its defenders commit suicide
- A.D. 75 — Josephus publishes *The Jewish War*

A.D. 65 68 71 74 77

OUTLINE OF HEBREWS

I. Christ's Superiority	**1:1—4:13**
A. Over the Prophets	1:1-3
B. Over the Angels	1:4—2:18
C. Over Moses	3:1—4:13
II. Christ's Superior Work	**4:14—10:18**
A. Christ's Priesthood	4:14—7:28
B. Christ's Covenant	8:1-13
C. Christ's Sacrifice	9:1—10:18
III. The Christian's Walk of Faith	**10:19—13:25**
A. Full Assurance of Faith	10:19—11:40
B. Endurance of Faith	12:1-29
C. Call to Love	13:1-17
D. Conclusion	13:18-25

TIME CAPSULE  **A.D. 81 to 135**

81	Domitian becomes emperor
93	Josephus publishes *Antiquities of the Jews*
95	John is imprisoned on the island of Patmos
96	Clement, bishop of Rome, dies
98	Trajan becomes emperor
107	Ignatius, early Christian writer, is executed in Rome
107	Trajan sponsors 123 days of games with 10,000 gladiators
111–113	Pliny is procurator or governor in Bithynia
117	Hadrian becomes emperor
132	The Jews in Palestine revolt under Bar Kochba
135	The Jews are sold into slavery and Jerusalem is destroyed

MELCHIZEDEK IN JEWISH TRADITION
(HEB. 5:8–10)

The author of Hebrews uses the figure of Melchizedek to clarify the nature of the priesthood of Christ. Melchizedek, whose name means "king of righteousness" (Heb. 7:2), appears briefly in Genesis as the king of Salem (Gen. 14:18–20). Despite being mentioned only in Genesis and one psalm (Ps. 110:4), the mystery of Melchizedek's figure inspired much interpretive activity in Judaism during the second temple period.

Such intrigue was not lost on serious interpreters of the Old Testament in antiquity. Melchizedek emerges as the central figure in a fragmentary document found at Qumran. This document, entitled "11QMelchizedek," consists largely of interpretive comments on Old Testament passages, and presents Melchizedek as an important figure in God's judgment upon the earth in the end times.

Another fragmentary text, called "Melchizedek," was found at Nag Hammadi in Egypt. It seemingly contains much older traditions from a group of Jews who found the origins of their theology in the person of Seth, the son of Adam born after Cain killed Abel (Gen. 4:25). In this tradition Melchizedek, "priest of God Most High," receives special revelations concerning Jesus from heavenly messengers. In a second group of revelations Melchizedek himself becomes Jesus, and is both crucified and raised as savior! Such ideas make Jesus the new appearance of Melchizedek.

The author of Hebrews reads the Melchizedek tradition in a restrained manner compared to the speculations current at that time. Ultimately, he is not so much interested in Melchizedek as in Christ, who was the High Priest "according to the order of Melchizedek" (Heb. 5:8–10). Christ's heavenly priesthood surpasses any earthly priesthood, even the priesthood of the king of Salem (Heb. 7:15–17).

Holding Fast the Confession
(Heb. 10:23–25)

The writer of Hebrews addresses Christians faced with persecution from a Roman society that threatened the church's morale. To prevent the church from disintegrating from within, the writer encourages these Christians: "hold fast the confession of our hope" (Heb. 10:23–25). A series of letters between the Roman governor Pliny and the emperor Trajan offers the Roman perspective on the process whereby Christians were examined in times of persecution.

Pliny writes the emperor for advice on how to treat Christians. It seems that local merchants were upset because Christians refused to participate in the civic religious rites, thus cutting down the meat sales at festivals. Pliny states, "I have never been present at an examination of Christians. Consequently, I do not know the nature or the extent of the punishments usually meted out to them, nor the grounds for starting an investigation and how far it should be pressed" (*Epistulae* 96).

Trajan's reply provides some insight into the nature of a Christian's examination. The emperor made the practice of Christianity illegal, responding that when Christians "are brought before you and the charge against them is proved, they must be punished, but in the case of anyone who denies that he is a Christian, and makes it clear that he is not by offering prayers to our gods, he is to be pardoned" (*Epistulae* 10.97).

Apparently, a person accused of being a Christian was brought into court before the governor. Asked if he or she was a Christian, the accused could offer a quick public prayer to the Roman gods, quite possibly to the emperor himself. Refusal to do so meant execution. For Christians to "hold fast the confession," publicly confessing Jesus Christ as Lord, was tantamount to signing their own death warrant.

THE FIRST LETTER OF JOHN

The writer of 1 John does not mention his own name or his position in the church, as does the author of 2 and 3 John who identifies himself as "the Elder" (2 John 1:1; 3 John 1:1). Early church tradition held that 1 John, like the Gospel of John, was written by the apostle John, son of Zebedee. Irenaeus, a 2nd-century church father, quoted John's disciple, Polycarp, to confirm John's authorship of this letter.

There have been debates about the authorship of the Johannine letters going back to the 2nd century. One view is that John the apostle wrote all the New Testament books that bear his name. Another view is that the Gospel and 1 John were written by the same author (who may or may not have been John the apostle), while 2 and 3 John were written by another "Elder" of the churches around Ephesus. Such was the view already of Jerome and possibly also Origen. Finally, some believe all three letters (1, 2, and 3 John) to be by the same author, but not the author who wrote the Gospel.

Many scholars suppose that the Johannine letters were written in the general sequence indicated by their arrangement in the New Testament. Thus, after the Gospel of John, 1 John was the first letter written and was followed later by the roughly contemporaneous letters 2 and 3 John. Those who accept authorship by John, the son of Zebedee, for the Gospel, letters, and Revelation place the letters before his exile to Patmos, where he wrote the Book of the Revelation. John lived until about A.D. 100, and the letter of 1 John is often dated between A.D. 85 and 95.

OUTLINE OF 1 JOHN

I. The Basis of Fellowship	**1:1—2:27**
A. Introduction	1:1–4
B. The Conditions of Fellowship	1:5—2:14
C. The Cautions of Fellowship	2:15–27
II. The Behavior of Fellowship	**2:28—5:21**
A. Characteristics of Fellowship	2:28—5:3
B. Consequences of Fellowship	5:4–21

THE SECOND LETTER OF JOHN

According to early church tradition, the letter of 2 John was written by the apostle John, the same person who wrote 1 John. Yet the author does not refer to himself as an apostle, but rather as "the Elder" (2 John 1). "Elder" was a term of respect used by both Jews and Christians for venerated religious teachers and could have been used of John later in his life (see 1 Pet. 5:1). Some scholars suppose that the elder John who wrote this letter may have been a disciple of the apostle John.

The letter of 2 John was probably written in the final decade of the 1st century. It has the form and size of a normal personal letter of the 1st century. The address—"To the elect lady and her children" (2 John 1)—may well have been a figurative way of referring to a local church and its members, probably in Asia Minor.

OUTLINE OF 2 JOHN

I. Abide in God's Commandments	**1–6**
A. Salutation	1–3
B. Walk in Truth	4
C. Walk in Love	5–6
II. Abide Not with False Teachers	**7–13**
A. Doctrine of the False Teachers	7–9
B. Avoid the False Teachers	10–11
C. Benediction	12–13

THE THIRD LETTER OF JOHN

The letter of 3 John was probably written by the author of 1 and 2 John sometime in the last decade of the first century. The subjects discussed are less doctrinal and more administrative than in 1 and 2 John, applying Christian principles to church life. The letter addresses an individual named Gaius, who probably attended a church in a city of Asia Minor, and reflects a time when Christian evangelists traveled from town to town preaching the gospel. These missionaries depended on the hospitality of local Christians.

OUTLINE OF 3 JOHN

I. The Commendation of Gaius	**1–8**
A. Salutation	1
B. Godliness of Gaius	2–4
C. Generosity of Gaius	5–8
II. The Condemnation of Diotrephes	**9–14**
A. Pride of Diotrephes	9–11
B. Praise of Demetrius	12
C. Benediction	13–14

APOCALYPTIC WRITINGS AND THE END TIME

Several of the later prophets, especially Ezekiel, Daniel, and Zechariah, share certain literary characteristics that are also found in the Olivet Discourse (Mark 13) and the Book of Revelation. Some of these characteristics are the use of fantastic imagery, vivid colors, and numbers with symbolic significance. In the view of some interpreters, these writings also seem to give more attention to explaining the upheavals that will attend the end of time than to contemporary events. Because they explain these otherwise mysterious events, the writings are often called "apocalyptic" from the Greek word *apokalypto*, meaning "to disclose, uncover."

There is also a body of nonbiblical Jewish literature that falls into the category known as apocalyptic. These writings share several common themes: (1) a pessimism over the present; (2) a belief that God will miraculously intervene at the end of time to save His own; (3) the belief that God has secretly disclosed to a chosen few the secrets of the end time; (4) the conviction that these secrets are hidden from the common people in special visions which include secret numbers, strange images, and key phrases. The biblical writings classified as apocalyptic share in the literary features of this noncanonical apocalyptic literature.

Throughout history apocalyptic literature has been most popular when current conditions have turned chaotic. At such times there has been a tendency to find remarkable similarities between one's own situation and the biblical prophecies. This tendency should be resisted. Biblical prophecy was not given in order that we might create a timetable for future events. Rather its authors intended to stimulate obedience to and confidence in God, who remained firmly in control of both contemporary events and the future.

EPOCH NINE
Chronological Reading Guide

❑ Revelation 1:1—22:21

THE BOOK OF REVELATION

The tradition that John the apostle wrote Revelation was widely held during the 2nd century. While the author often names himself as "John," the term "apostle" is never added, although he appears to be a man of stature in the churches (Rev. 1:1,4,9). He never claims to have been an eyewitness of Jesus.

There are significant differences between the Greek style of the Revelation and that of the Gospel and letters of John. In the 3rd century these variations of the original language prompted scholars to question the apostle John's authorship of the Revelation. A debate still continues over whether the John who wrote this book is to be identified with John the apostle, John the Elder, or an otherwise unknown John.

Dating the composition of Revelation is complicated, but Nero (A.D. 54–68) and Domitian (A.D. 81–96) are the Roman emperors whose reigns correspond most closely with the persecutions reflected in the book. The intensity of these persecutions fits better in Domitian's reign than in Nero's.

Four broad schools of interpretation have been applied to the visions and symbolism of Rev. 4—22. (1) "Preterists" view these chapters as referring only to the period of the Roman Empire during John's lifetime and immediately after. (2) "Historicists" view them as describing events that would occur throughout the church age from the ascension of Jesus to His Second Coming. (3) "Futurists" maintain that chs. 4—22 deal chiefly with events of the end times that surround Christ's Second Coming. (4) "Idealists" maintain that these chapters do not prophesy actual events, but paint a symbolic picture of the cosmic conflict between the kingdom of God and the forces of evil.

Elements from all of these views are helpful in understanding the Revelation. This book certainly had relevance to the situation that surrounded its first readers. Yet its primary focus seems to be on events associated with the return of Christ. Also the conflict between God and Satan is often reflected by different symbolic pictures throughout the book. The differing interpretations come closer to each other when we remember that the events of the end time are often an intensification of what Christians have faced throughout the church age.

OUTLINE OF REVELATION

I. "The Things Which You Have Seen"	**1:1–20**
A. Introduction	1:1–8
B. Revelation of Christ	1:9–20
II. "The Things Which Are"	**2:1—3:22**
A. Message to Ephesus	2:1–7
B. Message to Smyrna	2:8–11
C. Message to Pergamos	2:12–17
D. Message to Thyatira	2:18–29
E. Message to Sardis	3:1–6
F. Message to Philadelphia	3:7–13
G. Message to Laodicea	3:14–22
III. "The Things Which Will Take Place"	**4:1—22:21**
A. Person of the Judge	4:1—5:14
B. Prophecies of Tribulation	6:1—19:6
C. Prophecies of the Second Coming	19:7–21
D. Prophecies of the Millennium	20:1–15
E. Prophecies of the Eternal State	21:1—22:5
F. Conclusion	22:6–21

The Heavenly Scroll (Rev. 5:1–5)

The "throne" is an important theological image in the Book of Revelation. The throne is the seat of God, from whence He rules both heaven and earth. God rules not merely over souls, but over all aspects of His creation. In this royal setting appears the image of the heavenly scroll containing God's plan for His creation. Seven seals prevent any created being from opening the scroll (Rev. 5:1–5).

In the ancient Near East, sealed scrolls were the means by which royal authority was exercised over a king's domain. A royal official would inscribe the king's will onto a scroll. The king would seal the scroll with a ring pressed into a wax seal. The scroll would remain bound until it was unsealed and read by the properly designated royal official. Then the king's will could be carried out in the kingdom.

In the ancient Near East this administrative method was transferred to the divine realm. The high god was imaged as possessing heavenly books, sealed shut. It was believed that the future of the world was inscribed on these books, and, at the proper time, the designated heavenly figure would unseal a book, releasing the events recorded in it to take place upon the earth.

The vision of John utilizes the scroll metaphor to depict the unfolding of the will of God on earth. Yet without any properly authorized person to open the scroll, God's will remained merely inscribed in the scroll and not actualized on earth. Unchecked by the divine will, injustice could continue to reign upon the earth. Thus John wept, for no one was found worthy to unseal the scroll (Rev. 5:4).

Yet One was found who is worthy—the "Lion of the tribe of Judah" appearing as a Lamb standing "as though it had been slain" (5:5, 6). The Lion-Lamb, the one who conquers through death, was worthy to open the seals. Through Him the will of God could unfold upon the earth. As the seals are opened, God's judgment springs forth that ultimately leads to the new, purified, just creation. "Worthy is the Lamb who was slain!" (5:12).

The Sevenfold Plagues (Rev. 6:1—16:21)

Three series of sevenfold plagues (seven seals, seven trumpets, seven bowls) form the center of John's vision. Some believe the seven seals (Rev. 6:1—8:5) represent the suffering of the world throughout church history, leading up to the end time. The seven trumpets (8:6—9:21; 11:15–19) and the seven bowls (15:1—16:21) would represent the intensified sufferings that immediately precede the return of Christ. Others think the seals, trumpets, and bowls all describe with increasing intensity the suffering immediately before Christ returns. For still others, the seals, trumpets, and bowls do not form a chronological sequence, but rather symbolize the intensity of evil and chaos experienced by John and his readers. In any case, the sufferings described differ more in degree than in kind from those some Christians have always experienced.

The plagues are interrupted by two interludes. Following trumpets one through six is an interlude (10:1—11:14) before the seventh trumpet sounds (11:15–19). The angel assures Christians that there will be no further delay; the time of the seventh trumpet is the time of the end (10:5–7). Another interlude (12:1—14:20) separates the seven trumpets and the seven bowls. The purpose of this series of visions (14:1–20) is to give Christians courage and to assure them of their ultimate triumph. This will be especially needed as they face intense persecution (ch. 13).

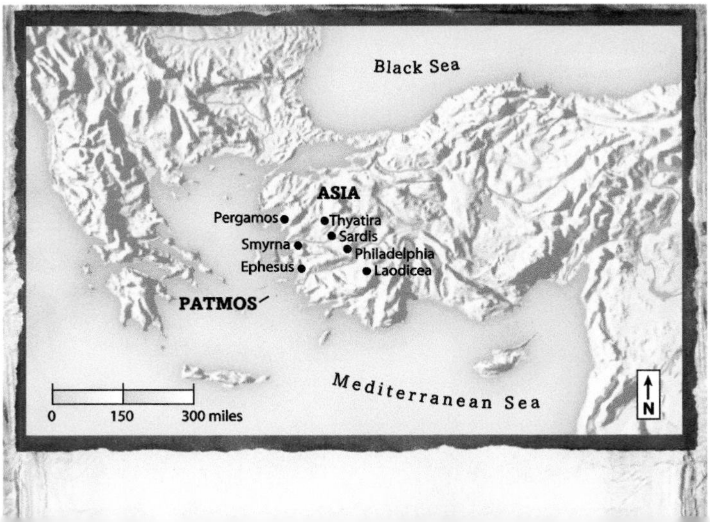

The Seven Churches of Revelation
The churches of seven cities (Rev. 1:11) were recipients of an apocalyptic letter from God, which John was called to write while exiled on the island of Patmos. By commendation, rebuke, and warning, the people of God were exhorted to remain faithful in adversity. These churches held significant roles in the Christian experience of Asia Minor as a result of their location within a transportation network linking different parts of the region.

Symbolic Pictures of Heavenly Conflict (Rev. 12:1)

The Book of Revelation frequently uses visions, symbols, and images that the first readers would have understood. The vision of the woman clothed with the sun, moon, and stars (Rev. 12) portrays the salvation struggle between good and evil.

Throughout the Greco-Roman world people told stories of divine deliverers destined to defeat evil dragons. The dragon tried to slay the newborn deliverer, but the deliverer miraculously survived, grew up, and returned to slay the dragon. In one version of the story, the emperor seems to have claimed to be the dragon-slayer. In Revelation, the wicked emperor is himself a pawn of the dragon, and the true ruler, the Child Jesus, is the One who will triumph over all the world's kingdoms (Rev. 12:5).

The writer of Revelation has interwoven echoes from the Old Testament. The woman with sun, moon, and twelve stars can be interpreted as Israel (see Gen. 37:9), as in some later Jewish traditions about twelve stars. The Old Testament portrays the faithful remnant of Israel as God's virgin bride, in contrast to a portrayal of unfaithful Israel as a prostitute. The Old Testament and the Dead Sea Scrolls portray the righteous remnant of Israel laboring and giving birth to a child, symbolizing the future restoration of God's people (Is. 66:7–10; Mic. 5:3).

In Revelation, the woman's first Child (Rev. 12:2–5) is often interpreted as Jesus and her other "offspring" as Christian believers (12:17). As John wrote to 1st-century churches in Asia (Rev. 1:4, 11), his imagery of a woman birthing her Child and of conflict with the dragon would have been familiar to his readers.

Seven Kings and Seven Mountains (Rev. 17:9–11)

John is shown a vision of a woman on a scarlet beast, a beast described as "having seven heads" (Rev. 17:3). The first interpretation, which identifies the seven heads as seven mountains (17:9), is obvious enough: ancients called Rome the "city on seven hills." Rome annually celebrated a festival recalling its origin on "seven mountains," and this was the city that was currently reigning over the nations (17:18). Without question, in John's day the epitome of the world system was Rome.

The second interpretation, identifying the seven heads with seven kings (17:10, 11), is more complicated. The sixth king is announced as reigning at that time ("one is," 17:10). If the Book of Revelation was written during the reign of the emperor Domitian, it would be possible to count back from Domitian and determine which ruler might qualify to be the one that was to return and "continue a short time" (17:10). One such calculation points to Nero.

Once Vespasian's dynasty (which included his sons Titus and Domitian) had been established, few people would have considered the three brief usurpers who followed Nero (Galba, Otho, Vitellius) as true kings. Some calculations skip these three emperors, thus allowing the six kings to include both Nero and Domitian. Many people anticipated Nero's return even well into Domitian's reign. Indeed, shortly before the Book of Revelation was written, a Nero impostor even tricked the Parthian armies into following him into the Roman Empire (though he was quickly proved an impostor).

Many scholars do not identify the seven kings precisely with seven specific Roman emperors. More importantly, John's interpretation of seven kings does not imply that in writing Revelation he supposed that Nero would literally return from the dead. Rather, he probably uses the popular image of a new "Nero" to communicate a message: "If you thought Nero was bad, wait till you see the final evil ruler." Besides claiming to be a god, Nero was the first emperor to actively martyr Christians. He is a fitting model for other evil rulers of history, especially the final one often known as the Antichrist (1 John 2:18).

The Millennium (Rev. 20:1–15)

The term "millennium," coming from the Latin *mille*, "one thousand," is used to identify the 1,000-year rule of Christ with His saints (Rev. 20:4–7). This is the only place in the New Testament where such a period is described. Christians are divided over how to interpret the 1,000-year reign and the events surrounding it.

Some believe that the binding of Satan represents Christ's victory on the cross. The 1,000 years is, then, symbolic of the church age during which the saints will rule spiritually with Christ. Satan's rebellion at the end of the 1,000 years is his final desperate attempt to challenge God before the return of Christ to judge the world. This view is called amillennialism because it does not believe in a millennial period separate from the church age.

Others believe that the victories of Christ (19:1–21) and the binding of Satan (20:1–3) represent the gradual triumph of the gospel throughout the church age. The millennium is, then, symbolic of an indeterminate time of earthly harmony after the progress of the gospel has resulted in the kingdom of God on earth. Only after this time will Christ return to finally defeat Satan (20:7–10) and judge the world (20:11–15). This view is known as postmillennialism because it teaches that Christ will not return until after the millennium.

Other Christians believe that 19:1–21 depicts Christ's Second Coming, which will culminate in the binding of Satan (20:1–3), after which the saints will be raised and rule with Christ on earth for a period symbolized by 1,000 years (20:4–6). At the end of this period Satan will be released for one last rebellion and will be destroyed (20:7–10). Then the unrighteous will be raised and all will be judged (20:11–15). This position is called premillennialism since it teaches the return of Christ before the millennium.

A New Heaven and a New Earth (Rev. 21:1–22:21)

The dominant theme of Rev. 6—20 is tribulation and death. A new mood is set in chs. 21; 22 that moves from time into eternity and provides a description of the eternal blessedness of God's people in the renewed creation. John's first vision depicts this blessedness in general (21:1–8). When God dwells with humanity, He Himself will tenderly remove every "sorrow" and "pain" just as He promised (21:4, 5; see 7:17).

The second vision describes the New Jerusalem (21:9–21) and life in it (21:22—22:5). The description of this city as made of shining "precious stones" and translucent "gold" suggests a glory and beauty that surpass human experience and imagination—realities for which there are no human words (21:18–21). God's splendor will be fully revealed. It will be the source of joy and light. Life in the New Jerusalem will surpass the blessings of the Garden of Eden.

In all this, John's message is that God's victory has already been won. The Lamb is "King of kings and Lord of lords."

The Great Last Judgment
by Pieter Paul Rubens
c.1617
Kunstareal Art Museum
in Munich, Germany

INDEX
TO THE CHRONOLOGICAL GUIDE TO THE BIBLE

Book Introductions and Outlines
Genesis 3
Exodus 18
Leviticus 23, 24
Numbers 26
Deuteronomy 30, 31
Joshua 35
Judges 41, 42
Ruth 45
1 & 2 Samuel 46
1 & 2 Kings 57, 58
1 & 2 Chronicles 52
Ezra 116
Nehemiah 126, 127
Esther 122
Job 112, 113
Psalms 53
Proverbs 60, 61
Ecclesiastes 62, 63
The Song of Solomon 63
Isaiah 80, 81
Jeremiah 88, 89
Lamentations 99
Ezekiel 97
Daniel 94, 95
Hosea 79
Joel 131, 132
Amos 78
Obadiah 101
Jonah 77
Micah 82
Nahum 90
Habakkuk 91
Zephaniah 86
Haggai 118
Zechariah 119
Malachi 124
Matthew 149
Mark 152
Luke 147
John 146
Acts 181
Romans 196
1 Corinthians 192
2 Corinthians 195
Galatians 186
Ephesians 204
Philippians 199
Colossians 203
1 Thessalonians 189, 190
2 Thessalonians 190
1 Timothy 205
2 Timothy 207
Titus 206
Philemon 202
Hebrews 210, 211
James 188
1 Peter 208
2 Peter 210
1 John 212
2 John 213
3 John 213
Jude 209
Revelation 214

Aaron 18, 22, 26, 35, 69, 122
Abba, Father 187
Abdi-Hepa 26
Abel 5, 211
Abiathar 88
Abijah 69, 70
Abijam 70
Abimelech 43, 44, 45
Abner 51, 52
Abomination of Desolation 140, 141, 170
Abraham 2, 3, 7, 8, 9, 11, 12, 13, 15, 27, 38, 109, 112, 115, 122, 145
Abraham, journeys of 10
Abram 10, 11, 12, 13
Absalom 51, 52
Accad 2, 4, 6, 11
Accadians 2
Achaemenid Dynasty 58
Achaia 191, 192
Achan 36
Acropolis 134
Adad 85
Adad-nirari III 75
Adam 5, 52, 121, 211
Adapa 111
Adonijah 51, 57
advent of writing 1
Adversary 113, 119
Aegean 16
Aeschylus 137
afterlife 114
Agabus 197
Agade 2, 6
Against Apion 61
Agrippa 198
Agrippa I 161, 201
Agrippa II 201, 206
Agrippina 197
Agur 61, 111
Ahab 54, 58, 66, 71, 72, 73, 75
Ahasuerus 118, 122, 123
Ahaz 74, 79, 80, 81, 82, 84, 98, 132
Ahaziah 58, 73, 74, 77
Ahikam 100
Ahmose 8
Ahmose I 19
Ahriman 58
Ahura Mazda 58, 133
Ai 36, 44
Akhenaten 16, 17, 18, 44
Alalakh 54
Alexander 133, 134, 135, 136, 137, 138, 139, 140
Alexander Jannaeus 142
Alexandria 135, 139, 178, 185, 199
alphabet 11
Altars 22
Amalekites 39, 40
Amarna 13, 17
Amarna letters 16, 17, 44
Amaziah 73, 78
Amel-Marduk 104
Amen 19
Amenemhet I 8, 11
Amenhotep I 19
Amenhotep IV 17, 26
amillennialism 217
Ammon 41, 43, 44, 47, 48, 127
Ammonites 44, 49, 56, 98
Amnon 51

Amon 19, 71, 75, 86
Amon-Re 3, 19, 60
Amorite(s) 7, 8, 9, 11, 27, 36
Amos 44, 67, 78, 82, 86, 131
Amram 7
Amurru 8, 16
Anath 32, 42, 43
Anathoth 88, 92
Anatolia 24, 208
Ancestor worship 55
ancient Middle East 26, 39
ancient Near East 1, 2, 3, 4, 5, 8, 11, 22, 23, 28, 30, 33, 35, 44, 47, 54, 59, 64, 73, 75, 85, 89, 107, 108, 114, 119, 132, 215
Andrew 157
Angels 51
Angra Mainyu 58
Annas 154, 173
Antichrist 216
Antigonids 137
Antioch 178, 179, 183, 184, 185, 186, 187
Antioch in Syria 187
Antioch of Pisidia 178, 184
Antiochus Epiphanes 141, 167
Antiochus II 140
Antiochus III 137, 140, 141
Antiochus IV 138, 139, 141
Antiochus IV Epiphanes 137, 142
Antipater 151
Antiquities of the Jews, 187, 211
Antonius Felix 199
Antony 142
apocalyptic 138
Apocalyptic literature 105
Apocalyptic Writings 213
Apocrypha 136
Apollos 195, 210
Aquila 191, 207, 210
Arabia 4, 17, 65, 185
Arabian Desert 107
Arabian Peninsula 65
Arachne 101
Arad 1, 42
Aram 40, 54, 73
Aramaic 13, 120, 187
Aram-Damascus 54, 70, 74, 75
Aramean(s) 31, 40, 56, 58, 70, 71, 84, 91
Aram-naharaim 13
Ararat 81
archangel 190
Archelaus 143, 148, 150, 154
Archippus 202
Areopagus 189
Ares 189
Aretas IV 161
Aristarchus 202
Aristobulus 142
Aristotle 134, 137, 203
ark of the covenant 55
Artaxerxes 6, 118, 130, 137
Artaxerxes I 115, 124, 125, 129
Artaxerxes II 125, 126, 137
Artaxerxes III 137
Artemis 179, 194
Asa 32, 69, 70, 71, 72, 73, 75
Asaph 54
Ascension 180
Ashdod 37, 47, 48, 54
Asher 41

Asherah 22, 34, 42, 43, 71, 72, 79, 86
Asherim 22, 34
Ashes of Sorrow 56
Ashkelon 37, 92
Ashurbanipal 5, 73, 87, 90
Ashur-dan 64
Ashurnasirpal II 75
Ashur-uballit 26
Ashur-uballit I 80, 90
Asia 13, 208
Asia Minor 16, 17, 40, 47, 178, 186, 187, 189, 194, 203, 204, 208, 213, 215
Asshur 8, 64, 80, 83, 111
Asshur-dan III 75
Assyria 7, 8, 16, 24, 47, 64, 67, 75, 76, 77, 79, 80, 81, 82, 83, 84, 86, 87, 89, 91, 92, 97, 98
Assyrian Empire 75, 86, 87, 89, 90, 96, 132
Assyrian pantheon 33
Assyrians 13, 64, 67, 90
Astarte 75
astrology 93
astronomy 93
Astyages 104, 121
Aten 17, 124
Athaliah 71, 73, 75
Athena 101
Athens 115, 116, 134, 137, 189, 194
Athtar 101, 107
Aton 3
Atrahasis 5
Augustus 136, 142, 148, 151, 154, 179
Avaris 8, 14, 17, 19
avenger of blood 46
Azariah (Uzziah) 73, 74, 76
Azariah 67, 78
Baal 17, 22, 34, 42, 43, 52, 55, 71, 72, 74, 79, 86, 98, 101, 107, 114
Baal-Zebub 74
Baasha 69, 70, 72
Babel 6
Babylon 6, 8, 11, 12, 22, 25, 67, 68, 76, 80, 85, 87, 91, 94, 95, 96, 97, 98, 100, 103, 104, 105, 106, 107, 108, 110, 112, 115, 117, 120, 123, 125, 128, 136, 138, 139, 208
Babylonia 1, 2, 6, 7, 11, 24, 83, 91
Babylonian captivity 106, 112
Babylonian Chronicle 81, 90, 95, 96, 102
Babylonian Empire 138
Babylonian exile 25, 52, 57, 80, 94, 102, 105, 109, 115, 117
Babylonians 67, 68, 90, 97
Balaam 29
Balaam's star prophecy 148
Balak 29
Baptism of Repentance 153
Bar Kochba 211
bar mitzvah 151, 197
Barnabas 184, 185, 187, 189, 191, 210
Barnea 22
Baruch 61, 67, 92, 93, 97, 100
Bathsheba 56
battle of Marathon 115
Bay of Salamis 123
bedouins 8
Beelzebub 74
Beelzebul 74
Belshazzar 104, 107, 120, 138
Bene-yamina 7
Ben-Hadad 54, 70, 73, 75
Benjamin 7, 38, 48, 49, 68
Berea 189
Berechiah 93
Berenice 140
Bernice 201, 206
Beth Shemesh 3, 39
Bethany 144
Bethel 22, 36, 39, 69, 78, 86
Bethlehem 143, 148, 150, 177
betrothal 149
between the testaments 135
Bildad 112
Bithynia 184, 186, 208
Black Obelisk 66, 74, 75
blood redeemer 46
Boaz 45, 46
Book of Acts 179, 180, 184, 186, 197, 199, 205
Book of Colossians 204
Book of Daniel 68, 95, 104, 136, 140
Book of Ephesians 203
Book of Esther 104, 123
Book of Exodus 17
Book of Ezekiel 105
Book of Ezra 103, 117, 118, 120, 127
Book of Genesis 2, 8
Book of Haggai 103
Book of Isaiah 107, 132
Book of Jeremiah 93, 95
Book of Job 110, 113
Book of Joel 103
Book of Joshua 17
Book of Judges 41, 43
Book of Lamentations 68, 100
Book of Leviticus 17, 105
Book of Malachi 103
Book of Nehemiah 104, 127
Book of Numbers 17
Book of Philemon 203
Book of Proverbs 111, 128
Book of Psalms 56, 130
Book of Revelation 105, 133, 140, 180, 213, 216
Book of Signs 156
Book of the Law 33
Book of the Revelation 212
Book of Zechariah 103, 133
books of Maccabees 136
Branch 119
Broad Wall 67
Bronze Age 114
bronze serpent 28
Byblos 71
Caesar 136
Caesar Augustus 150
Caesar's household 199
Caesarea 174, 183, 199, 200, 201, 202, 206
Caesarea Maritima 143, 184
Caiaphas 144, 154, 173, 183
Cain 5, 211
Caleb 14, 22, 30
Caligula 188
Calvary 144
Cambyses 103, 115, 120, 121
Cambyses II 129
Cana 156
Canaan 8, 9, 10, 11, 12, 13, 14, 15, 16, 25, 26, 27, 28, 30, 32, 34, 37, 38, 40, 41, 43, 44, 45, 49, 72, 84, 88, 92, 114
Canaanite(s) 17, 21, 27, 34, 37, 40, 49
Candace 183
Capernaum 144, 158
Caphtor 78
Cappadocia 186, 208
Carchemish 91, 96, 104
Carthage 59, 61, 98, 139
catacombs 179
Cayster River 204
Cenchrea 196, 200
census 26
Centurions 184
Chalcolithic period 1
Chaldeans 84, 90, 91
chariots 64
Chemosh 44
cherubim 55
child sacrifice 9, 34, 98
Chloe's household 192
Christian(s) 178, 184
Christian sacraments 175
Church Fathers 197, 210
Church of All Nations 144
Church of the Holy Sepulchre 144
Cilicia 185
circumcision 11, 186
cisterns 88
city gates 57
city-states 1, 4
Claudius 179, 188
Claudius Caesar 191
Clement 200, 210, 211
Clement of Alexandria 146, 147
Cleopatra 136, 142
Code of Hammurabi 21, 33
Code of Lipit-Ishtar 33
Code of Ur-Nammu 33
Colosse 191, 202, 203
Colosseum 179
Colossians 179, 202
Commander of God's army 35
concubine 52
Conquest of Canaan 34
conquest of Canaan 39
Copper-Stone Age 1
Corinth 179, 189, 191, 196, 197, 210
Corinthian church(es) 193, 206
Corinthian women 194
Cornelius 183, 184
Court of Israel 198
Court of the Gentiles 169
Court of Women 198
court prophets 29
Covenant 10, 31
Covenant Code 21, 33
covering a woman's head 193
creation 1, 2
Creation of Man 3
Creation of the World 3
Crete 37, 200, 206
crucifixion 144, 175
cult prostitutes 34
cuneiform 91
curses of disobedience 33
Cush 4
Cushan-Rishathaim 40
Cyaxares 104, 121
Cyprus 37, 40, 185, 187
Cyrus 57, 80, 103, 104, 107, 108, 109, 115, 116, 117, 120, 121, 123, 129, 132
Cyrus Cylinder 103, 117
Dagon 47, 82
Damascus 40, 54, 70, 71, 74, 75, 80, 81, 183, 185
Dan 22, 41, 69
Daniel 94, 95, 120, 138, 140, 170, 213
Daniel's vision of 70 weeks 136
Darius 104, 115, 118, 120
Darius I 58, 103, 119, 121, 122, 123, 129, 137
Darius II 103, 129, 137
Darius III 134, 137, 139
David 39, 40, 45, 46, 47, 48, 49, 50, 51, 52, 53, 56, 57, 58, 59, 62, 64, 68, 69, 85, 100, 103, 117, 122, 128, 145
Davidic Kingdom 58
Day of Atonement 23, 24, 25, 201
Day of Judgment 132
Day of Pentecost 181, 183, 197
day of the Lord 132
day of Yahweh 132

Day Star 107
Dead Sea 136
Dead Sea Psalms 56
Dead Sea Scrolls 50, 136, 153, 170
Death 59
Debir 36
Deborah 41, 43, 45
Decapolis 135, 144
Dedication 30
Delphi 74, 191
Demetrius 194
demons 58
deportations to Babylon 95, 101
Derbe 186, 187
destruction of Jerusalem 178
Dialogue Between a Master and His Slave 113
Diana 179, 194
Diaspora 115, 122, 182
dispersion 115, 122
Dius 64
divided monarchy 66, 70, 71
divination 24
divorce 167
divorce and remarriage 193
Djoser 10
Domitian 211, 214, 216
Dor 98
dragon 216
Ea 5
Early Bronze Age 1, 2, 8, 42, 49
Early Christians in Jerusalem 181
Ebla 54
Ecbatana 107
Ecclesiastes 110
Ecclesiasticus 61, 128, 136
Eden 4
Edict of Horemhab 33
Edom 26, 41, 47, 56, 68, 90, 101, 105, 112, 136
Edomites 58, 136
Egypt 1, 2, 3, 4, 8, 10, 11, 13, 14, 15, 16, 17, 18, 19, 20, 22, 24, 26, 28, 29, 31, 32, 33, 34, 37, 38, 39, 40, 41, 42, 43, 44, 47, 54, 60, 66, 71, 75, 78, 79, 83, 84, 92, 93, 100, 103, 108, 114, 115, 127, 132, 134, 135, 137, 140, 143, 171, 178, 183, 211
Egyptian execration texts 38
Egyptians 64
Ekron 37, 74
El 21, 22, 28, 34, 42, 43, 71, 73
Elah 72
Elam 45, 91
Elamites 8, 9, 84
Elasa 141
Elephantine 103, 127
Eli 43, 45, 47
Elijah 21, 72, 74, 111, 114, 162
Eliphaz 112
Elizabeth 147, 148
Elkanah 47
empty tomb 176
end times 190, 213
Enkidu 59
Enoch 114
Enuma Anu Enlil 93
Enuma Elish 35
Epaphras 191, 202
Epaphroditus 195, 199
Ephesians 179
Ephesus 90, 179, 191, 192, 194, 199, 200, 202, 203, 204, 205, 207, 212
Ephraim 14, 98
Epimanes 141
Epiphanes 141
Epistulae 208
Erech 6
Ereshkigal 114
Eridu 4
Esarhaddon 33, 73, 85
Esau 9, 101, 112
Eschatology 170
Essene Gate 144
Essenes 136, 153, 170
Esther 122, 123
Etana 111
Ethbaal I 54, 71, 72, 75
Ethiopian eunuch 183
Ethiopians 78
Euodia 200
Euphrates River 2, 4, 6, 12, 13, 17, 26, 47, 89, 91
Euphrates Valley 203
Euripides 137
Eusebius 147, 152, 202
Evil-Merodach 104, 116
Exile 125, 130
Exile in Babylon 104
Exodus 14, 16, 20, 108, 125, 171
exodus 18
Exodus, route of 20
Exodus, two dates for 20
Ezekiel 68, 77, 95, 97, 98, 99, 101, 103, 105, 106, 112, 116, 124, 213
Ezion Geber 40, 77
Ezra 102, 103, 116, 122, 124, 125, 126, 127, 130, 132, 134
Fall of Jerusalem 96, 211
Fall of Man 3
Fall of Samaria 82
false teachers 207
fasting 24
Feast of Dedication 138, 167, 174
Feast of Purim 122
Feast of Tabernacles 25, 134, 161, 163, 167
Feast of Trumpets 25
Feast of Unleavened Bread 25, 171
Feast of Weeks 25
Felix 198, 206
fertility rites 34
Festus 197, 198, 206
fig tree 170
First Kings of Israel 53
first missionary journey 205
First Punic Wars 139
First World Empire 6
Firstfruits 25
flagellation 175
Flood 2, 3, 5, 53
Forbidden Religious Objects 22
Fortified Cities 57
funeral songs 99
Gaal 44
Gabriel 147
Gad 41
Gaius 196, 213
Gaius Octavius 150
Galatia 179, 186, 187, 191, 208
Galilee 142, 150, 161, 165, 185, 201
Gallio 179, 191
Gallio's judgment hall 191
Gamaliel 181
Garden of Eden 2, 55, 217
Garden of Gethsemane 144
Gashmu 127
Gath 37
Gaubaruwa 120
Gaugamela 139
Gaul(s) 134, 154
Gaza 37, 47, 84, 92, 183
Gedaliah 67, 95, 100, 101
Gehenna 83
General Epistles 180
Gerasa 144
Geshem 103
Geshem the Arab 127
Gethsemane 172
Gezer 40, 44, 62
Gibbethon 70
Gibeah 39
Gibeon 36, 37
Gibeonites 34
Gideon 40, 51
Gihon 4
Gilead 98
Gilgal 36, 41, 49
Gilgamesh Epic 5, 59
Giza 4, 10
Gnosticism 203
God-fearers 183, 184
goel 46
Gog 105, 106
golden age in Greece 137
golden calf 22
golden calves 69
Golgotha 175
Goliath 50
Goshen 9
Gospel of John 145, 151
Gospel of Mark 145
Gospel to the Gentiles 183
Great Fire 206
Great King 133
Great Pyramid of Giza 4, 10
Greco-Roman society 207
Greco-Roman world 47, 204, 205
Greece 11, 37, 40, 42, 64, 138, 178, 191
Greek 135
Greek alphabet 64
Greek city-states 137
Greek Empire 94, 133, 134, 136, 140
Greek society 196
Greeks 42, 140
Gudea 47
Gulf of Aqaba 17, 20, 40, 65
Gulf of Suez 20
Gutians 8
Gyges 105
Habakkuk 68, 90, 91
Habiru 7, 16, 44
Habor River 47
Hadad 22, 73
Hadad-ezer 54, 73
Hadassah 123
Hadrian 211
Hagar 11
Haggai 102, 103, 118, 119, 134
Hall of Judgment 61
Hall of Pillars 61
Hallel 172
Halley's Comet 148
Hammurabi 6, 7, 8, 11, 19, 21
hanging gardens 67
Hannah 44, 47
Hanukkah 30, 138, 167
Haran 7, 8, 9, 10, 11, 12, 75, 90, 91
harlotry 79
Hasmonean 135, 136, 142
Hathor 22
Hattusilis III 49
Havilah 4
Hazael 54, 74, 75
Hazor 36, 40, 44, 62, 64, 66, 78
heavenly scroll 215
Hebrew alphabet 64
Hebrew Bible 5
Hebrews 180, 182
Hebron 12, 13, 15, 22, 44, 48, 53, 54
Hellenism 139
Hellenistic Jew 188
Hellenistic period 114, 134
Hellenists 182, 184

Heman 54, 59
Hera 64
Herculaneum 206
Herod Agrippa I 150, 184, 188
Herod Antipas 143, 144, 150, 151, 161, 174, 185, 188
Herod the Great 135, 136, 141, 142, 143, 148, 150, 151, 199, 201
Herodian dynasty 201
Herodias 144
Herodotus 77, 121, 122, 123
Heshbon 43, 45
Hezekiah 28, 42, 49, 54, 61, 67, 74, 79, 80, 82, 83, 84, 85, 132
Hezekiah's Tunnel 84
Hiddekel 4
Hierapolis 72, 203
hieroglyphic script 4
High places 49
High Priests 173
Hilkiah 86
Hillel 167
Hiram I 54, 59, 61, 64
Historicists 214
History of Phoenicia 81
Hittite Empire 16, 35, 37
Hittite laws 33
Hittite(s) 17, 18, 19, 30, 31, 42, 49
Holiness Code 33
Holy Communion 175
Holy Spirit 177, 178, 183
homosexual behavior 196
Hophra 96, 100
Horemhab 31, 33
Horus 2, 32
Hosea 67, 69, 79, 88, 131
Hoshea 74, 79, 82, 84
house arrest 202
House of Ahiel 67
House of the Forest of Lebanon 61
household 205
household codes 203
Huldah 85
Hurrian 17
Hurrians 16
husbands 209
Hyksos 8, 13, 14, 17, 19
Hyksos dynasty 19
Hymns 54
hypocrites 161
Iconium 186, 187
Idealists 214
idols 31
Idrimi 54
Ignatius 211
Igris-Halam 54
India 4, 13
Indus 4
Indus River 139
Infancy Gospels 150
intermarriage 126
Intertestamental Period 154
Iran 2
Iraq 2, 4
Irenaeus 146, 147, 212
Irkab-Damu 54
Iron Age 42, 66
Isaac 7, 8, 9, 11, 12, 14, 15
Isaiah 67, 80, 82, 83, 85, 88, 94, 103, 107, 131, 132, 153
Ishbosheth 51, 52, 53, 56
Ishmael 11, 12, 13
Ishtar 7, 73
Ishtar Gate 67
Isin 8
Isis 203
Israel 69
Israel's Feasts 25
Israel's Sacred Times 30
Jacob 7, 8, 9, 11, 12, 14, 15, 109, 122
Jacob's well 157
James 146, 157
James, the brother of Jesus 188, 198
Jebus 38, 40
Jebusites 38
Jeconiah 128
Jeduthun 54
Jehoahaz 73, 75
Jehoash 73, 75, 76
Jehoiachin 89, 94, 95, 96, 97, 101, 102, 128
Jehoiada 75
Jehoiakim 75, 92, 94, 95, 97
Jehoram 71, 73
Jehoshaphat 58, 71, 72, 73, 75, 77
Jehu 54, 67, 73, 74, 75, 76
Jephthah 43, 44, 45
Jeremiah 54, 67, 68, 77, 82, 88, 89, 92, 93, 94, 95, 97, 98, 99
Jeremiah's Confessions 92
Jeremiah's Scroll 92
Jericho 4, 30, 34, 36, 44, 136, 143
Jeroboam 22, 69, 70, 71, 76
Jeroboam I 54, 68, 69, 72
Jeroboam II 69, 73, 74, 76, 77, 78, 79
Jerome 147, 212
Jerusalem 21, 25, 26, 38, 39, 44, 47, 52, 54, 58, 60, 62, 64, 65, 67, 68, 69, 70, 83, 84, 88, 92, 93, 94, 95, 96, 98, 99, 100, 101, 102, 103, 106, 107, 108, 115, 116, 118, 119, 121, 122, 124, 125, 126, 127, 128, 129, 131, 132, 134, 138, 139, 141, 142, 149, 154, 165, 174, 178, 181, 182, 183, 184, 185, 186, 197, 200, 208
Jerusalem church 188
Jerusalem Council 185, 186, 188
Jerusalem temple 105, 109, 131, 136, 140, 197, 211
Jeshua 115, 116, 117, 118, 119, 120
Jesus 60, 109
Jesus' brothers and sisters 147
Jesus Christ, introductions to 145
Jesus of Nazareth 143
Jesus' Passion Week in Jerusalem 173
Jesus son of Sirach 157
Jesus, ascension 177
Jesus, at the Feast of Dedication 167
Jesus, attending the Feast of Tabernacles 163
Jesus, baptism of 153
Jesus, before Pilate the governor 174
Jesus, birth of 148
Jesus, burial 176
Jesus, childhood 150
Jesus, cleansing the leper 158
Jesus, crucifixion 175
Jesus, discourse while on the Mount of Olives 170
Jesus, early life 147
Jesus, early ministry in Galilee 157
Jesus, final journey to Jerusalem 164
Jesus, final ministry in Judea 166
Jesus, final week in Jerusalem 168
Jesus, first visit to Jerusalem 156
Jesus, from Galilee to Jerusalem 163
Jesus, last supper 172
Jesus, ministry in Galilee 154, 163
Jesus, mission of the 70 disciples 165
Jesus, plot, anointing, and betrayal 171
Jesus, prayer and arrest in Gethsemane 172
Jesus, preparation for the Last Supper 171
Jesus, rejection of 160
Jesus, resurrection 176, 183
Jesus, return of 190
Jesus, second visit to Jerusalem 161
Jesus, seven miracles of 156
Jesus, temple visit as young man 151
Jesus, temptation of 154
Jesus, transfiguration 162
Jethro 17
Jezebel 71, 72
Joab 51
Joash 73, 75, 76
Job 110, 112, 113, 114
Joel 103, 131
John 140, 146, 157, 181, 212, 213, 214, 215
John Hyrancus I 136, 141
John Mark 152, 189
John Rylands papyrus 52 146
John the Baptist 143, 144, 146, 147, 148, 151, 152, 153, 154, 156, 161, 163, 174
Jonah 67, 77, 85
Jonathan 50, 141
Jonathan Maccabeus 141
Jordan 17, 30
Jordan River 27, 30, 47, 135
Joseph (OT) 8, 9, 14
Joseph (NT) 143, 147, 149, 150
Joseph of Arimathea 176
Josephus 61, 64, 78, 127, 136, 144, 148, 170, 173, 188, 199, 200, 201, 211
Joshua 17, 26, 30, 34, 36, 37, 39, 43, 45, 119
Josiah 30, 32, 54, 69, 71, 75, 85, 86, 87, 88, 89, 90, 97
Jotham 74, 78, 79, 82
Journeys of Abraham 10
Judah 14, 102
Judaizers 186
Judas 141, 185
Judas Iscariot 171
Judas Maccabeus 136, 139, 141, 142, 167
Judas the Galilean 181
Judea 142, 178, 180, 184
judges 33, 41
Julius 136
Julius Caesar 141, 150, 179
Juvenal 201
Kaddish 160
Kadesh 22
Kadesh Barnea 27, 30
Kamose 19
Karnak 71
Kedar 127
Kedesh 36
Kenizzite 14
Khafre 10
Khufu 10
Kidron Valley 170
King Hadadezer 40
King Kamose 8
King Mesha 66
king of Salem 211
King of the Jews 175
king of the North 141
Kings as Vice-Regents 60
Kir 78
Knossos 9
Kohath 7
Kothar-and-Hasis 43
Laban 13
Lachish 67, 85
Lachish Letters 67, 95
Lagash 47
Laodicea 202, 203
Larsa 8, 11
Last Supper 171, 173
Late Bronze Age 7, 16, 17, 24, 41

Law Codes 33
Laws of Eshnunna 33
lawyers 166
Lazarus 156
Leah 8
Legend of Keret 28
Lemuel 61, 111
letter of James 188
letters of commendation 195
Levi 7, 14
Leviathan 114
levirate marriage 46
Levite 185
Levitical singers 129
Leviticus 17
Libyans 35, 37
Lion of the tribe of Judah 215
little horn 138
Livy 150
Logos 146
Lothan 114
Lower Egypt 2, 8, 19
Lucian 72
Lucifer 107
Lucius 185
Luke 147, 148, 181, 197, 202, 206, 207, 210
Lu-Nanna 111
Lycaonia 186
Lycia 139
Lycus River 203
Lycus Valley 202
Lydia 105, 179
Lystra 186, 187
Maccabean revolt 135, 141, 142
Maccabees 136
Macedon 137, 139
Macedonia 135, 189, 191, 202
magic 179, 191
magic amulets or charms 28
magic and magicians in Egypt 19
magic books 179
Magnesia 141
Magog 105
Malachi 102, 103, 124, 131, 134
Malta 200, 201
Manaen 185
Manasseh 14, 74, 75, 86, 90, 98
Manetho 19
Marcus Julius Agrippa 201
Marduk 35, 45, 85, 100, 103, 104, 109, 117, 123
Marduk temple 6
Marduka 123
Mari 7, 8, 11, 12, 26
Mari letters 7
Mari tablets 11, 12, 47, 82
Marisa 135
Mark 152, 202
Mark Antony 136, 150
Marriage 60
Mary 143, 147, 148, 149, 150
Mary, the sister of Lazarus 171
Masada 206, 211
Massa 111
Mattathias 141, 200
Matthew 148, 149
Medes 67, 90, 97, 104, 123
Media 104, 120, 121, 138
Median Empire 107
Megiddo 40, 62, 66, 71, 97, 98
Melchizedek 211
Memphis 32
Menahem 74, 75, 81
Menander of Ephesus 61
Menes 1, 2
Mephibosheth 52
Merenptah 16, 35, 37
Merodach-Baladan II 91
Meroe 183
Merom 36
Mesha 71
Mesolithic period 1
Mesopotamia 1, 2, 3, 4, 6, 7, 8, 9, 10, 11, 21, 24, 31, 37, 40, 41, 43, 47, 49, 55, 60, 75, 76, 89, 91, 93, 108, 110, 113, 114, 132, 137
Messiah 21, 109, 119, 143, 145, 148, 149, 152, 153, 154, 157, 164, 167, 181, 183, 197
messiah 60
Micah 67, 82, 131
Micaiah 73, 82
Michael 190
Middle Assyrian Empire 90
Middle Assyrian laws 33
Middle Bronze Age 7, 8, 9
Middle Kingdom 8
Middle Stone Age 1
Midian 18, 41
Midianite(s) 14, 17, 18, 39, 40
Miltiades 115
Minoan civilization 19
Mishnah 193
Mitanni Empire 16
Mittanni 31
Mizpah 39, 100
Moab 22, 26, 27, 28, 29, 30, 35, 44, 45, 47, 56, 66, 90
Moabite Stone 66, 71
Moabites 39, 58
Molech 83, 98
Monumentum Ancyranum 178
Mordecai 123
morning stars 114
Moses 3, 7, 14, 16, 17, 18, 21, 22, 24, 26, 28, 30, 31, 32, 34, 35, 51, 53, 122, 125, 159, 161, 162
Moses' father-in-law 14, 18
Most Holy Place 24
Mot 32, 114
Mount Carmel 72
Mount Ebal 38
Mount Ephraim 98
Mount Gerizim 21, 38, 136, 141, 157
Mount Hor 22
Mount of Olives 144, 170
Mount Seir 105
Mount Sinai 16, 18, 21, 23, 26, 28, 29, 30, 159, 161
Mount Zaphon 21
Mount Zion 21, 129
Mursilis 19
Music 56
Music in the Temple 54
Musical notation 11
Nabatean Arabs 136, 161
Nabateans 144
Nabonidus 85, 103, 104, 107, 120, 138
Nabopolassar 90, 92
Naboth 72
Nadab 69, 70, 72
Nag Hammadi 211
Nahor 7, 12
Nahum 68, 85, 89, 90, 91
Naomi 45, 46
Naram-Sin 6
Narmer, 1
Nash Papyrus 135
Nazareth 143, 147
Nazirite 44
Nebuchadnezzar 6, 67, 92, 94, 95, 96, 97, 101, 102, 104, 106, 107, 116, 138
Nebuchadnezzar II 90, 91, 100
Nebuchadrezzar 92
Nebuzaradan 95, 96, 97, 101
Necho 91, 92, 97
Necho II 97
necromancy 114
Negev 40, 42
Nehemiah 102, 103, 116, 122, 124, 126, 127, 130, 131, 132, 134
Nehushtan 28, 42
Neo-Assyrian Empire 13, 66, 67, 76, 78, 80, 84, 89
Neo-Assyrian period 64, 91
Neo-Babylonian Empire 66, 67, 87, 90, 96, 104, 108, 117
Neolithic period 1
Nergal 33, 114
Nergal-Sharezer 104
Neriah 67, 92, 93
Neriglissar 104
Nero 138, 179, 197, 202, 206, 208, 214, 216
netherworld 114
new earth 217
new heaven 217
new Jerusalem 133, 217
New Moon 30
New Stone Age 1, 90
Nicanor 141
Nicodemus 156
Niger 185
Nile 2, 4, 93
Nile River 10, 89, 183
Nimrod 6
Nineveh 77, 89, 90, 104, 121, 134
Ningirsu 47
Ninlil 73
Ninurta 33
Nippur 97
Niqmaddu II 54
Noah 5
Noah's family 2
Numbers 17, 27
Nuzi 7, 8, 11, 12
Nuzi tablets 11, 12
Nuzi texts 7, 8
Obadiah 68, 101
Octavian 142
Old Kingdom of Egypt 2
Old Stone Age 1
Olivet Discourse 213
Olympia 64
Olympias 139
Omri 71, 72, 74, 75, 98
Onesimus 202
Ophel synagogue 178
Ordeals 26
Origen 146, 147, 212
Orontes River 187
Orosius 191
Osorkon I 75
Ovid 150
Padan Aram 13
paganism 191
palace guard 199
Paleolithic period 1
Palestine 2, 4, 9, 13, 16, 17, 18, 27, 34, 37, 38, 40, 42, 45, 47, 54, 55, 66, 71, 75, 89114, 122, 133, 134, 135, 136, 137, 139, 140, 150, 198
Papias 152
parable 160
Parthenon 134, 194
Parthians 13
Passion Week 154, 168
Passover 28, 29, 36, 86, 120, 154, 156, 161, 163, 169, 171, 172, 181
Passover lamb 175
Passover Meal 21
Passover Papyrus 103

Pastoral Epistles 179, 205, 207
pastors 205
Patmos 146, 215
patriarch(s) 7, 11, 16, 69
patronage system 192
Paul 147, 178, 179, 181, 184, 185, 186, 187, 189, 197, 210, 211
Paul, arrested and sent to Rome 197
Paul, arrested in the temple 198
Paul, before Gallio 191
Paul, before the Areopagus 189
Paul, before the governor at Caesarea 199
Paul, beginning of a missionary 185
Paul, first missionary journey 187
Paul, imprisonment in Rome 202
Paul, second missionary journey 189
Paul, the end of his life 206
Paul, the Pharisee 200
Paul, third missionary journey 191
Paul, trip to Rome 200, 201
Paul, versus the goddess Diana 194
Paul's authority and Epistle 193
Paul's martyrdom 202
Peace of Callias 115
Pekah 74, 79, 81
Pekahiah 74, 79
Pella 178
Peloponnesian War 134, 137
Pentecost 154, 161, 180, 183, 192
Peor 29
Perea 161, 165
Persepolis 133, 139
Persia 117, 120, 121, 123, 137, 138, 140
Persian Empire 13, 58, 94, 103, 104, 115, 121, 123, 129, 131, 133, 134, 137, 139
Peter 146, 152, 179, 181, 188, 206, 208, 210
Peter's confession 162
Peter's mother-in-law 157
Pethuel 131
Petra 136
Pharaoh 18, 22, 32, 108
Pharaoh Akhenaten 27
Pharaoh Ramesses III 40
Pharaoh Shishak I 66
Pharisee(s) 142, 144, 164, 166, 167, 185, 200
Phasael 144
Philadelphia 144
Philemon 179, 206
Philip 150, 179, 183
Philip II 137, 139
Philippi 179, 189, 199
Philippian church 200
Philippians 179, 199
Philistia 37, 43
Philistines 37, 41, 45, 47, 48, 49, 54, 56, 58, 78
Philo 150
Philo of Byblos 47, 81, 206
Phinehas 125
Phoebe 196, 200
Phoenicia 47, 54, 55, 71
Phoenicians 11, 21, 64, 69, 98, 134
Phrygia 186, 191
Pilate 144, 175, 176
Pishon 4
Pisidia 186
Pisidian 187
Pithom 20
plains of Shinar 3
Plataea 123
Plato 134, 137
Pliny 77, 211, 212
Pliny the Elder 201
Pliny the Younger 184, 208
Plutarch 191, 194
Polybius 141
Polycarp 212
Pompeii 206
Pompey 136, 141, 142, 187
Pontius Pilate 143, 154, 163, 174, 183, 199
Pontus 184, 186, 208
Pool of Bethesda 144
Pool of Siloam 84
Poppaea 202
Porcius Festus 206
postal system 9
postmillennialism 217
Potiphar 14
Praetorium 175
Preacher 62
prehistory 1
premillennialism 217
Preterists 214
Priests 75
prince of Tyre 101
Priscilla 191, 200, 207, 210
Promised Land 15, 26, 27, 30, 34, 35, 36, 44, 49, 55
Prophets 59
prophets 9, 73, 82
prophets at Antioch 185
prostitution 79
Proverbs 110
Psalms 56
Psammetichus II 89
Psusennes II 71
Ptah 3
Ptolemies 135, 136, 139, 140
Ptolemy 139
Ptolemy I 139
Ptolemy II 140
public building projects 114
Pyramid Texts 19
pyramids 2, 4, 10
Pythagorean Theorem 11
Qarqar 66, 73, 75
Qatna 7
Qaynu 127
queen of Sheba 65
Quirinius 148, 150, 151
Qumran 136, 211
Rabshakeh 85
Rachel 8
Ramah 100
Ramesses 37, 48
Ramesses II 16, 17, 20, 29, 31, 76
Ramesses III 19, 37, 42, 45
Ramses 20
Re 3, 19, 32
Rebekah 8, 15
rebuilding of the temple 118
rebuilding the walls 127
Red Sea 20
Rehoboam 53, 54, 64, 65, 66, 68, 69, 70, 72
resurrection 176
return from captivity 125
Reuben 41, 49
Rezin 81
Rezon 54
ritual purity 166
ritual uncleanness 24
River Chebar 97
Rizpah 52
Roman citizenship 198
Roman Empire 142, 150, 178, 179, 188, 214
Roman family values 203
Roman period, 143
Roman Senate 150
Roman society 196
Romans 64, 136, 179, 196, 197
Rome 134, 138, 139, 141, 142, 152, 163, 178, 188, 197, 198, 199, 200, 201, 202, 203, 206, 208, 211, 216
Romulus 142
Ruth 45, 46
Saba 65
Sabbath 25, 30, 131
Sabbath Year 25, 30
Sabeans 65
sacred mountains 21
sacred oracles 24
Sadducees 142, 144, 164, 169
Salome Alexandra 142
Salonika 189
Samaria 74, 75, 79, 80, 82, 83, 84, 98, 103, 115, 135, 165, 178, 180, 184
Samaritan Pentateuch 5
Samaritans 21, 103, 115, 136, 144, 157, 183, 206
Samson 41, 44
Samuel 44, 46, 49, 50, 52
Sanballat 103, 127
Sanballat the Horonite 127
Sanhedrin 182
Sarah 8, 9, 11, 12, 13
Sarai 10, 11, 12, 13
Sardis 123
Sarduri II 81
Sargon 2, 6, 47, 82
Sargon II 65, 80, 82, 84, 98
Satan 58, 119, 154, 214, 217
Saul 43, 45, 46, 47, 48, 49, 50, 52, 53, 56, 68, 121
Saul of Tarsus 180, 182
scarlet beast 216
school of Tyrannus 191
Scourging 175
scribal wisdom 128
scribes 125, 166
Scythians 105
Sea of Reeds 20
Sea People(s) 16, 19, 35, 37, 40, 41, 45, 48, 54
sea serpents 114
Second Coming 177, 214, 217
Second Coming of Christ 190
Second Temple 117
seer 59
Seleucid dynasty 141
Seleucids 135, 136, 139, 140
Seleucus 139
Seleucus I 187
Seleucus IV 140
Semitic 13, 14
Seneca 196
Sennacherib 67, 80, 83, 84, 85, 89, 90
Septuagint 5, 44, 50, 139
Seraiah 92
seraphim 81
Sermon on the Mount or Plain 159
Servant of the Lord 109
Servant Songs 109
Sesostris III 8
Seth 5, 211
Seti I 19
seven churches of revelation 215
seven seals 215
Seven Wonders of the ancient world 194
sevenfold plagues 215
sexual immorality 167, 195
Shahar 107
Shalim 107
Shallum 74, 75, 79
Shalmaneser 67, 75, 84
Shalmaneser I 16
Shalmaneser III 121
Shalmaneser III 66, 74, 75, 76, 80

Shalmaneser V 79, 80, 82
Shamaneser I 31
Shamash 3, 25, 33, 85
Shammai 167
Shamshi-Adad I 8
Shapshu 43
Shar-kali-sharri 6
Shatiqatu 28
Sheba 65
Shechem 10, 38, 43, 44, 45, 136
Shemesh 3, 124
Sheol 59, 107, 114
Sheshbazzar 115, 117
Sheshonk 32, 71
Shihor 89
Shiloh 39, 41, 47
Shishak 42, 64, 69, 70, 71
Shoshenq 71
Shoshenq I 32
Shulamite 63
Shulgi 111
Siamun 60
Sidon 36, 43, 45, 71, 72
Sihor 89
Silas 185, 189, 205, 210
Simeon 185
Simeon, a cousin of Jesus 178
Simon "the Zealot" 145
Simon Maccabeus 142
Simon Peter 157
Simon the Pharisee 171
Sinai Peninsula 18
Sippar 25
Sisera 43, 45
slave masters 209
slaves 202
Smerdis 129
Socrates 137
Solomon 14, 20, 39, 40, 47, 51, 53, 56, 57, 59, 60, 61, 62, 63, 64, 66, 68, 70, 88, 110
Solomon's temple 40, 55, 61, 65, 129
Son of God 145
Songs of Ascents 129
sons of God 113, 114
soothsaying 24
Sophocles 137
"South Galatian" theory 186
Spain 69, 77, 202
Sparta 134, 137
Spirit of God 153
star of Bethlehem 148
stele 71
Step Pyramid 10
Stephen 178, 179, 187
Stephen 18
Stephen, the First Martyr 182
Stone Age 1
Strabo 77
Strato 199
Suetonius 184, 191
suffering 188
Sumer 1, 2, 4, 6, 11
Sumerian civilization 8
Sumerians 1
Sun of Righteousness 124
Susa 103
suzerain 10
Sylvanus 208
symbols 216
synagogue 182
Synagogue of the Freedmen 178, 182
Synoptic Gospels 145, 151, 153, 154, 158, 159, 163, 165, 174
Syntyche 200
Syria 7, 11, 13, 16, 17, 30, 37, 39, 40, 43, 47, 54, 73, 139, 140, 142, 187
Syrians 78
Syria-Palestine 114
Syro-Ephraimite War 79, 81, 98
Tabernacles 154
tabernacle 18
Tabernacle 28, 29
Tacitus 184
Tahpanhes 100
Tarquinius Superbus 142
Tarshish 77
Tarsisi 77
Tartessus 77
Tattenai 120
Tefnut 3
Tekoa 78
Tell Deir ëAlla 29
Tell el-Amarna 38, 44, 60, 111
temple 59, 206
Temple Mount 143, 144, 170
temple of Karnak 42
Temples 100
Ten Commandments 18, 30, 33, 135
tenth 127
Terqa 47
Tertullian 147, 202
The Jewish War 211
The Twelve Tribes of Israel 14
The Wars of the Jews 201
The Wisdom of Jesus Son of Sirach 128
Thebes 8, 14, 19, 90
Theodotus Inscription 178
theophany 21
Theophilus 181
Theophilus of Antioch 146
Thermopylae 123
Thessalonica 189
throne 215
Thummim 24
Thutmose I 24, 27
Thutmose II 24
Thutmose III 17, 20, 24, 28, 32
Tiamat 35
Tiberius 152, 154, 163
Tibni 72
Tiglath-Pileser I 54
Tiglath-Pileser III 65, 67, 76, 79, 80, 81, 98
Tigris 2, 13
Tigris River 4, 67, 80
Timothy 189, 195, 205, 207, 210
Tirhakah 83
Tirzah 70
tithe 127
tithing 166
Titus 170, 179, 206, 211, 216
Tobiah 103, 130
Tomb of Mary 144
Tophet 83, 98
Topheth 83
Torah 61, 104, 128, 194, 200
Tower of David 143
tradition of the elders 161
Trajan 184, 208, 211, 212
tribulation 217
Triumphal Entry 171, 173, 174
Troy 40, 42
trumpet of God 190
Turkey 194
Tutankhamun 64
Tychicus 202
Tyre 36, 47, 64, 71, 77, 133, 134, 139, 197
Ugarit 7, 21, 28, 32, 37, 40, 42, 51, 54, 55, 71, 72, 114, 127
Ugaritic ritual 32
Ugaritic texts 22
United Israel 54
United Kingdom 14
unknown God 189
Upper Egypt 2
Ur 2, 6, 8, 9, 10, 111
uraeus 81
Urartu 76, 80
Urim 24
Ur-Nammu 8
Uruk 4, 5, 6
Utnapishtim 5
Uz 112
Uzziah 76, 79
Valley of Aijalon 37
Valley of Hinnom 98
Valley of the Son of Hinnom 83
Vashti 122
vassal 10
Vassal Treaties of Esarhaddon 33
Venus 107
Vespasian 211, 216
Vesuvius 206
Virgil 150
visons 216
voice of an archangel 190
Wailing Wall 143
Where Was Eden? 4
widows 182, 205
wilderness 16, 18, 24
Wilderness 26, 27
Wisdom 61, 110
Wisdom of Agur and Lemuel 111
Wisdom of Jesus ben Sirach 61
Wisdom of Jesus Son of Sirach 136
Wisdom of Solomon 61
Wisdom Psalms 128
wisdom teachings 110
wisdom tradition 60
wives 209
Wives submitting to husbands 204
Women leaders 200
wooden images 22
Xerxes I 103, 115, 122, 123, 129, 137
Xerxes II 129, 137
Yahweh 44, 83, 89, 100, 102, 105, 108, 109, 111, 113, 117, 124, 132, 133
Yam 114
Yamhad 54
Yarim-Lim 54
Year of Jubilee 25, 30
Zagros Mountains 5, 8
zeal 200
Zealots 144, 145
Zebedee 212
Zebul 44
Zechariah 74, 79, 102, 103, 118, 133, 134, 135, 213
Zedekiah 75, 88, 92, 95, 96, 97, 100
Zephaniah 67, 86
Zerubbabel 103, 115, 116, 117, 118, 119, 120, 121, 128
Zeruiah 51
Zeus 138, 139, 141, 194
ziggurat(s) 2, 3, 6, 7, 21
Zimri 72
Zobah 40, 58
zodiac 93
Zophar 112
Zoroaster 58
Zoroastrianism 58
Zuph 49

IMAGE CREDITS

ii 2008 Jupiterimages Corporation • **iii** David Roberts • **ix** imam121 (Flickr) • **x** 2008 Jupiterimages Corporation • **1** Arranged with permission by Bill Noller International Publishing, San Dimas, CA 91773, © Lion Hudson plc., Oxford, England • **3** 2008 Jupiterimages Corporation • **4** 2008 Jupiterimages Corporation, Koechel Peterson & Associates • **5** © Marie-Lan Nguyen (Wikimedia Commons), 2008 Jupiterimages Corporation • **6** © Marie-Lan Nguyen (Wikimedia Commons) Sumerophile (Wikimedia Commons) Gustave Doré • **7** Gustave Doré • **10** 2008 Jupiterimages Corporation • **12** Francesco Hayez (Wikimedia Commons) • **15** 2008 Jupiterimages Corporation • **16** 2008 Jupiterimages Corporation • **21** Graye (Flickr) • **22** © Marie-Lan Nguyen (Wikimedia Commons), 2008 Jupiterimages Corporation • **23** Arranged with permission by Bill Noller International Publishing, San Dimas, CA 91773, © Lion Hudson plc., Oxford, England • **28** Gustave Doré • **32** Jon Bodsworth • **37** Koechel Peterson & Associates, BrokenSphere (Wikimedia Commons) • **39** Arranged with permission by Bill Noller International Publishing, San Dimas, CA 91773, © Lion Hudson plc., Oxford, England • **44** Gustave Doré • **45** Nigel Silcock (iStockphoto) • **50** Julius Kronberg • **55** Carl Lindström (Wikimedia Commons) • **57** 2008 Jupiterimages Corporation • **62** Golf Bravo (Wikimedia Commons) • **64** Arranged with permission by Bill Noller International Publishing, San Dimas, CA 91773, © Lion Hudson plc., Oxford, England • **65** Sir Edward John Poynter • **66** David Roberts • **69** Stuart Yeates • **70** The American Bible Society • **71** Sir Edward John Poynter • **74** Jamie Barras • **77** vassil (Wikimedia Commons) • **84** Jerry Culbertson • **85** 2008 Jupiterimages Corporation • **93** Mikalojus Konstantinas Ciurlionis • **99** Rembrandt • **102** David Roberts • **114** Koechel Peterson & Associates • **129** 2008 Jupiterimages Corporation • **135** David Roberts • **139** Gunnar Bach Pedersen (Wikimedia Commons) • **142** William R. Shepherd. Historical Atlas. Henry Holt and Company. 1923. • **143** David Roberts • **153** Wojciech Gerson • **157** CrniBombarder!!! (Wikimedia Commons) • **159** Gustave Doré • **162** Raphael • **169** El Greco • **172** Leonardo da Vinci • **174** Nikolai Ge • **176** Jacopo Tintoretto (Robusti) • **177** Il Garofalo • **178** David Roberts • **182** Raimond Spekking (Wikimedia Commons) • **187** William Miller • **194** MM (Wikimedia Commons) • **201** Bukvoed (Wikimedia Commons) • **216** Bamberger Apokalypse Folio • **217** Pieter Paul Rubens

NOTES